LEVERAGED FINANCIAL MARKETS

A COMPREHENSIVE GUIDE TO HIGH-YIELD BONDS, LOANS, AND OTHER INSTRUMENTS

WILLIAM F. MAXWELL
MARK R. SHENKMAN

McGraw Hill

New York Chicago San Francisco Lisbon
London Madrid Mexico City Milan New Delhi
San Juan Seoul Singapore Sydney Toronto

The McGraw·Hill Companies

1 2 3 4 5 6 7 8 9 0 WFR/WFR 1 9 8 7 6 5 4 3 2 1 0

ISBN: 978-0-07-174668-7
MHID: 0-07-174668-4

This book is printed on acid-free paper.

CONTENTS

1

AN OVERVIEW OF LEVERAGED FINANCE

William F. Maxwell

Rauscher Chair in Financial Investments,
Cox School of Business at SMU

Broadly defined, *leveraged finance* deals with the riskiest forms of debt financing. These encompass original issue debt from investment-bank-issued debt, high-yield bonds, or bank-issued debt (leveraged loans), and debt that has fallen from investment grade to high-yield status ("fallen angels"). Credit default swaps also play an important role in these markets because they are derivative contracts deriving their value from the risk of default on specific firm debt or aggregate default risk. As such, they provide an alternative mechanism for investors to take short or long positions on the underlying assets.

The modern high-yield bond market began in the early to mid-1980s when Drexel Burnham started issuing bonds, which were rated high yield at issuance. Before this time, high-yield bonds consisted of "fallen angels." Since the mid-1980s, the high-yield market has gone through significant changes and upheavals, and the market has evolved from being solely based on high-yield bonds to being a broader and more diverse market. Leveraged loans (the equivalent of high-yield bonds issued by banks) and credit default swaps (default-triggered derivative instruments) became prevalent in the market in the middle to late 1990s.

The leveraged finance market has always been a volatile market, with the market experiencing significant boom and bust periods. It is not surprising then that the leveraged finance market as well as all aspects of the financial market experienced dramatic upheaval during 2008. In 2008, the high-yield bond, leveraged loan, and credit default swap (CDS) indexes were down by 27%, 29%, and 13%, respectively. However, the high-yield bond and leveraged loan markets recovered with historically high returns of 50% in 2009. In addition, 2009 was a record year for high-yield bond issuance, but it also evolved back closer to its roots with the virtual disappearance of leveraged loans. Even after the financial market meltdown in 2008, it is clear that leveraged finance remains one of the cornerstones of financial markets.

Leveraged finance is a large and significant component of the fixed-income market. It has grown dramatically since its inception, and there were $864 billion and $1.64 trillion in high-yield bonds and leveraged loans outstanding in 2007. In total this represents 8% of all fixed-income assets (see Figure 1.1).

Debt is the primary source of external capital for public companies. Within the broader category of debt financing, leveraged finance is the predominant source (Table 1.1 provides issuance volume by security class). It is clear that leveraged finance (high-yield and leveraged loans) is the primary source of capital. However, there is significant variation in the proportion of new financing associated with leveraged finance over time. During down economic periods, access to these markets is limited. This is apparent as issuance volume in the leveraged finance market can drop significantly in down periods.

What also is apparent from Tables 1.1 and 1.2 is that there has been dramatic growth in the use of leveraged loans. (Some of the leveraged loans issuance volume can be misleading because it includes "revolvers." These are a commitment by the banks to issue short-term debt, less than a year to maturity, but rarely do firms fully draw on these

FIGURE 1.1 Fixed-Income Asset Classes, 2007

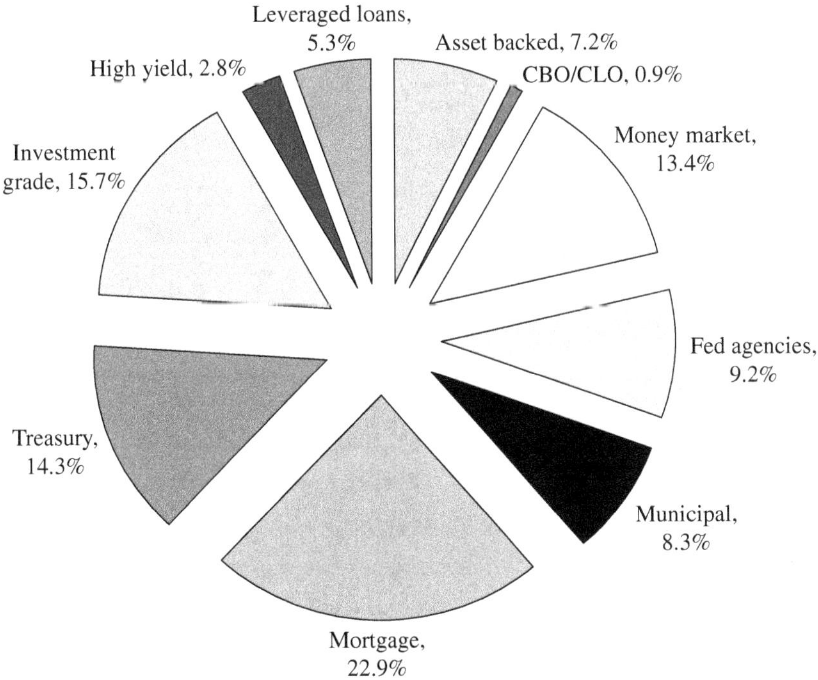

Source: Bond Market Association/Credit Suisse

TABLE 1.1 Issuance Volume by Security Class as Percent

	Equity Markets		Corporate Debt		
Year	**Initial Public Offerings**	**Seasoned Equity Offerings**	**Investment Grade**	**High Yield**	**Leveraged Loans**
1998	6.5%	8.0%	35.4%	16.8%	33.4%
2000	11.3%	14.5%	36.6%	5.0%	32.6%
2002	4.7%	8.3%	49.4%	6.8%	30.7%
2004	6.6%	8.0%	30.8%	12.3%	42.4%
2006	4.6%	8.1%	35.8%	3.2%	48.3%

Source: Lehman Brothers

TABLE 1.2 Issuance Volume by Security Class

Year	High Yield	Leveraged Loans
2004	158	154
2005	106	184
2006	149	306
2007	148	387
2008	53	71
2009	164	38

Source: J.P. Morgan

"revolvers.") The growth of leveraged loans is the result of the introduction of the institutional leveraged loan market, loans that are syndicated to nonbank institutions. Until the late 1990s, leveraged loans were issued by banks with the loans typically being syndicated to other banks. In the late 1990s, loan documentation was standardized, which permitted the development of a secondary market in bank loans. This was necessary before nonbank institutional investors would purchase the securities in either the primary or the secondary market. In addition, the late 1990s and early 2000s led to an increased demand for securitized products. Given the matched payout structures and variable rates of leveraged loans and securitized products, there was a strong demand for leveraged loans, which were then packaged into collateralized loan obligations (CLOs). With these developments, the leveraged loan market exploded (see Tables 1.1 and 1.2).

The sizes of the leveraged loan and high-yield bond market were roughly equivalent in 2004 (Table 1.2). But by 2007, the leveraged loan market was 2.5 times larger than the high-yield market in terms of new issuance. However, the financial meltdown in 2008 brought about a fundamental shift back to the issuance of high-yield bonds away from leveraged loans for corporations. While new issuance volume dropped dramatically for both high-yield bonds and leveraged loans in 2008, this shift was more pronounced in the leveraged loan markets as bank capital was seriously constrained. This trend continued into 2009 as the high-yield bond market experienced a historical peak of new issuance volume while the leveraged loan market was next to nonexistent.

The Increasing Use of High-Yield Debt as a Financing Source

As we note above, until the mid-1980s firms had very limited ability to issue high-yield bonds. Since this constraint has been relaxed, there has been a huge growth in the market as more firms restructured, were acquired, or gradually added leverage to their financial structures. In doing so, firms and acquirers relied more on debt financing, and thus we see on average more debt in the capital structure and lower bond ratings. One way to demonstrate this change is to look at the percentage of U.S. industrial publicly traded firms by rating class over time. We track this information over time from the early stage of the modern high yield market, 1986, through 2008 (Table 1.3). In viewing Table 1.3, what is readily apparent is the structural shift in credit ratings over time. Across the board, bond ratings have declined. For example, the highest level of credit rating (AAA–A) represented over 30% of U.S. industrial firms in 1986. This had fallen to only a little over 11% by

TABLE 1.3 U.S. Publicly Traded Companies by Rating Class (Industrials Only)

Bond Ratings	1986	1991	1996	2001	2006	2008
AAA	3.2%	4.0%	2.6%	1.0%	0.9%	0.6%
AA	7.5%	5.7%	3.6%	1.5%	1.5%	3.0%
A	20.7%	21.2%	16.4%	11.5%	9.0%	13.3%
BBB	15.8%	21.4%	22.1%	23.4%	21.8%	24.2%
Investment grade	47.3%	52.2%	44.8%	37.4%	33.2%	41.2%
BB	13.0%	16.3%	20.2%	22.7%	25.4%	29.1%
B	32.1%	25.6%	30.9%	32.1%	34.2%	26.7%
CCC/C	7.7%	5.8%	4.1%	7.8%	7.3%	3.1%
High yield	52.7%	47.8%	55.2%	62.6%	66.8%	58.8%

Source: Compustat

TABLE 1.4 High-Yield New Issues by Rating

High-Yield Bond Rating	1986	1991	1996	2001	2006
BB	29.9%	76.9%	34.5%	55.0%	38.9%
B	63.3%	12.8%	59.5%	43.1%	53.2%
CCC	1.8%	0.0%	0.8%	1.1%	7.7%
NR	5.0%	10.3%	5.2%	0.8%	0.2%

Source: Credit Suisse

2006. Accordingly, the total level of investment-grade firms fell from 47% in 1986 to 33% in 2006. This trend reversed slightly by the end of 2008 because firms had significant concerns about accessing the capital markets during what is expected to be a protracted period of economic uncertainty.

Looking at the overall percentage of firms by rating class can mask some of the variation that we see over time in the new issuance market, which reflects the demand for a particular level of rating quality at that time. In Table 1.4, we show how the variation in rating class within the high-yield market can vary over time. For example, in 1991 77% of high-yield bonds issued were rated BB, and only 13% were rated B. In contrast, in 2006 only 39% were BB and the majority, 53%, were rated B. Part of the trend reflects differences in acquisition activity. During periods of increased leveraged buyouts (LBOs) and mergers and acquisitions (M&A) activity, firms are being financed at the lower end of the rating spectrum. Other differences reflect demand-driven considerations from the capital markets. During periods of higher defaults, it can be difficult for firms to issue debt in the lowest rating classes (B and below).

The Demand for Leveraged Finance

The increased use of leveraged finance is a function of investor demand. Leveraged finance provides investors with a correlation structure that is favorable to other asset classes, an attractive risk/return profile, and a constant income stream.

TABLE 1.5 Correlation Structure—10 Years (2000 to 2009)

Indexes	Treasury 10 Year	J.P. Morgan High Grade	J.P. Morgan Leveraged Loans	J.P. Morgan High Yield	S&P 500
J.P. Morgan high grade	0.61				
J.P. Morgan leveraged loans	−0.37	0.28			
J.P. Morgan high yield	−0.20	0.49	0.83		
S&P 500	−0.25	0.21	0.45	0.63	
Russell 2000	−0.25	0.18	0.46	0.64	0.64

Source: J.P. Morgan

Table 1.5 presents the correlation structure of various asset classes over the last 10 years and includes two significant downturns in the high-yield markets. It is apparent that both leveraged loans and high-yield bonds have a low correlation with traditional fixed income and, in fact, have higher correlations to stock indexes. Overall, the leveraged financial markets fit somewhere between traditional fixed income and stocks as an asset class and thus provide investors with an attractive asset class in which they can diversify risk.

Even more important, the leveraged finance market has provided an excellent risk/return profile for investors. Table 1.6 provides

TABLE 1.6 Risk Versus Return—15 Years (1996 to 2009)

Category	Mean	Volatility	Sharpe Ratio
J.P. Morgan global high yield	7.8%	9.1%	0.85
Leveraged loan	5.2%	6.4%	0.82
Investment-grade bonds	7.5%	5.7%	1.33
S&P 500	8.0%	15.8%	0.51
Russell 2000	7.3%	20.3%	0.36

Source: J.P. Morgan

information regarding the long-run risk versus return trade-off of the leveraged loan and high-yield bond markets. When examining a risk versus return measure, the Sharpe ratio, the leveraged loan, and the high-yield market have produced a significantly higher Sharpe ratio than either a large-cap (S&P 500) or small-cap stock index (Russell 2000).

Finally, most leveraged finance products provide significant yearly cash flows to investors. This is attractive to investors seeking current income from their portfolios. Overall, given the low correlation and impressive risk and return trade-off, it is not surprising that investors continue to demand leveraged finance products. Hence, while the issuance of leveraged finance products may vary over the economic cycle, it is apparent that it is an ever growing presence in the financial markets.

Resilience of Leveraged Finance

Even after the most significant financial crisis since the Great Depression, it remains clear that leveraged finance is an integral part of the world's financial markets. The leveraged financial markets not only survived their most tumultuous period, but they have in fact recorded a record year of issuance in the high-yield market in 2009. High yield remains the predominant rating for U.S. industrial firms issuing bonds. It offers an impressive risk/return metric for investors. Hence, while leveraged finance will continue to evolve over time, it will remain one of the predominant asset classes for investors and companies.

2

THE COMPONENTS OF THE LEVERAGED FINANCE MARKET

William F. Maxwell

Rauscher Chair in Financial Investments,
Cox School of Business at SMU

In this chapter, we examine the growth of the main components of the leveraged finance market and how they have evolved over time. We begin by discussing the high-yield bond market. Second, we examine the leveraged loans market, and finally, we examine credit default swaps.

High-Yield Bonds

As a viable new issuance market, the high-yield market began in the mid-1980s with the rise of Drexel Burnham Lambert. The market has gone through a number of peaks and valleys as periods of easy financing have been followed by higher default rates. For example, new issuance volume from 1986 to 1989 was consistently around $30 billion with much of the proceeds used to funds the leveraged buyouts (LBOs) market during that time (see Table 2.1). But the economy slowed in the late 1980s and into the early 1990s, which led to a significant peak in

TABLE 2.1 High-Yield Bond Market

Year	Amount Outstanding	New Issuance Volume	Moody's Speculative Grade Default Rate
1986	136	33	5.6%
1987	181	30	4.2%
1988	206	32	3.6%
1989	242	28	5.8%
1990	214	2	9.9%
1991	205	15	9.2%
1992	205	47	5.1%
1993	247	77	3.0%
1994	283	43	2.1%
1995	308	45	2.9%
1996	363	72	1.6%
1997	467	133	1.9%
1998	580	151	3.1%
1999	652	101	5.4%
2000	668	45	6.3%
2001	737	89	10.0%
2002	853	67	8.0%
2003	881	136	5.1%
2004	848	135	2.4%
2005	878	82	1.7%
2006	876	116	1.7%
2007	888	113	0.9%
2008	928	40	4.1%
2009	1,012	138	9.4%

Source: Credit Suisse

default rates, over 9% in both 1990 and 1991. During this period of time there was very little new issuance volume, and the total market value of high-yield bonds outstanding actually decreased from 1990 to 1991. A similar pattern emerged around the economic downturn in the early 2000s. On a compressed scale, we see a similar bust and boom period in 2008 and 2009. What is of interest to note is the lagged relation between default rates and high-yield markets. Default rates lag according to the economic condition of the high-yield bond market.

New issuance patterns are also related to the overall cost of debt capital, which is driven by macroeconomic factors, the government cost of debt, and the risk of a particular asset class defined by the spread relative to Treasuries (the spread is measured as the additional yield for an asset class above and beyond the government yield of a similar maturity). The correlation among spreads, new issuance patterns, and default rates is easy to see when one examines Tables 2.1 and 2.2.

Spreads can vary significantly over time as demonstrated in Table 2.2. For the BB category the spread varied from a low of 206 basis points in 2006 to 591 in 2002 to a high of 1,182 at the end of 2008. There has been even greater variation in the B category as the spreads

TABLE 2.2 Spread (Basis Points) by Rating Category at Year End

Year	BB	B	CCC/C
1994	270	450	1,051
1995	306	562	1,013
1996	214	382	1,123
1997	229	367	926
1998	375	615	1,503
1999	300	483	1,452
2000	451	900	2,484
2001	471	733	2,351
2002	591	858	2,368
2003	292	462	1,033
2004	210	328	718
2005	256	356	822
2006	206	313	606
2007	444	565	969
2008	1,182	1,698	3,139
2009	459	629	1,082

Source: J.P. Morgan

were as low as 313 in 2006 and as high as 1,698 in 2008. These spreads can also change very quickly. The 2006 to 2009 time period demonstrates this phenomenon. It is also interesting to note that the spreads in the BB and B categories don't move in lockstep, thus demonstrating the segmented nature of the markets.

As shown in Table 2.3, the characteristics of the new issue high-yield bonds also vary over time. The percentage of senior debt has ranged from 67% in 1997 up to 99% in 2009. The market for deferred interest types of securities varies across credit cycles because these are typically some of the riskiest types of issuances. As seen in Table 2.3, deferred securities are at their lowest when defaults are at their highest (2001–2002 and 2009). Acquisition issuance volume follows a similar cyclical pattern. Finally, foreign issuance in the U.S. market had been decreasing after 2003, which does not reflect decreased demand

TABLE 2.3 Breakdown of New Issues by Type

Year	Senior Debt	Deferred/ Pay-in-Kind (PIK) Toggle	Refinancing Related	Acquisition Related	Foreign Issuance
1997	67%	9%	52%	20%	13%
1998	73%	11%	52%	21%	12%
1999	70%	7%	49%	27%	10%
2000	79%	7%	32%	26%	19%
2001	74%	1%	76%	13%	2%
2002	68%	1%	73%	15%	5%
2003	81%	2%	75%	13%	12%
2004	78%	2%	57%	26%	6%
2005	78%	4%	50%	38%	7%
2006	89%	8%	38%	44%	8%
2007	90%	12%	35%	51%	4%
2008	89%	11%	41%	46%	2%
2009	99%	1%	76%	5%	12%

Source: J.P. Morgan

for the product but instead reflects the rise of high-yield financing in Western Europe and even more recently Asia. This trend reversed in 2009 as foreign firms once again found the U.S. market the easiest to access.

Voluntary debt retirement by issuing firms either through tendering or calling bonds is related to the cost of debt, and thus voluntary retirement is also related to new issuance volume as the firms retire one debt and replace it with cheaper debt. Table 2.4 provides historical measures of voluntary debt retirement. It is apparent that debt retirement can be a significant issue as it can range up to almost 12% of the market. Second, while there is significant variation across time, there has been a general upward trend since 2002. This changed dramatically in 2008 and 2009 during the financial crisis.

TABLE 2.4 Nonmaturing Debt Retirement—High-Yield Bonds

Year	% Tendered	% Called	% Total Nonmaturing Retired
1995	1.2%	1.8%	3.0%
1996	1.7%	1.4%	3.1%
1997	2.9%	1.2%	4.1%
1998	3.9%	2.6%	6.5%
1999	2.4%	1.6%	4.0%
2000	1.9%	1.7%	3.6%
2001	1.3%	1.6%	2.9%
2002	1.0%	2.0%	3.0%
2003	2.1%	4.3%	6.4%
2004	4.7%	7.2%	11.9%
2005	4.4%	4.4%	8.8%
2006	5.6%	3.1%	8.7%
2007	6.0%	4.7%	10.7%
2008	2.8%	1.6%	4.4%
2009	3.9%	1.3%	5.2%

Source: J.P. Morgan

A natural question is, who owns high-yield bonds? The largest investor groups are insurance companies, pension funds, and high-yield mutual funds, which in aggregate represent approximately 60% of the market. Other significant groups of investors are investment, equity, and income mutual funds; collateralized bond obligations (CBOs); and hedge funds.

Leveraged Loan Market

Leveraged loans have expanded dramatically since the early 1990s. Until that time, leveraged loans were the exclusive domain of banks. Banks would issue loans and syndicate the majority of the loan to other banks, but the risk of this pool of securities could be shared only by other banks, which have a limited demand for speculative-grade debt. Therefore, the overall market was limited by the demand for such debt by banks.

The market for nonbank leveraged loans began to develop in the mid-1990s because of three factors. First, loan documentation and terms were standardized. Before this time, any sale of bank loans in the secondary market required the use of attorneys to draw up sale documents for every transaction. This was both costly and time consuming. The standardization of the contracts permitted the development of a secondary market in bank loans. This was necessary before nonbank institutional investors would purchase the securities in either the primary or the secondary market. Second, banks were aggressively pursuing lucrative fee-based services, and leveraged loans along with high-yield bonds produce significant fee income. Third, the growth of securitization allowed leveraged loans to be repackaged into collateralized loan obligations (CLOs) with multiple tranches and risk characteristics. These changes led to the development of the institutional leveraged loan market in which banks set up the financing and syndicated the loan to nonbank institutional investors. With this development, the leveraged loan market exploded (see Tables 2.5 and 2.6). In 1994, the total size of

TABLE 2.5 Size of the Leveraged Loan Market

Year	Institutional Leveraged Loans	Noninstitutional Leveraged Loans	Total Leveraged Loans
1994	16	161	177
1995	23	202	225
1996	34	250	284
1997	53	265	318
1998	88	464	552
1999	126	543	669
2000	145	663	808
2001	141	661	802
2002	141	558	734
2003	188	567	792
2004	307	588	922
2005	408	668	1,109
2006	617	647	1,313
2007	841	582	1,423
2008	885	725	1,610
2009	835	796	1,631

Source: Credit Suisse

TABLE 2.6 New Issuance Volume–Leveraged Loans

Year	Institutional Loans	Noninstitutional Loans	Total Leveraged Loans	Western European Leveraged Loans
2002	64	176	240	90
2003	118	211	329	124
2004	223	256	479	120
2005	241	260	501	200
2006	366	246	612	254
2007	426	263	689	289
2008	99	225	324	82
2009	56	183	239	n.a.

Source: Credit Suisse

the institutional leveraged loan market was $16 billion. This market grew and overtook the traditional noninstitutional leveraged loan (bank) segment of the market in 2006 and stood at over $1 trillion by 2007. The financial crisis in 2008 has led to a significant drop in the amount of capital that banks are willing to commit to the leveraged loan market. In addition, the demand for CLOs has disappeared. This has lead to a shift back toward the bond market by issuers.

Similar to the high-yield bond market, the Western European leveraged loan market has grown dramatically as well (Table 2.6). Because this is a newer market, the percentage of growth of new issuance volume has been even faster in Western Europe than in the United States since 2002.

As we noted previously, CLO growth is intertwined with the growth of leveraged loans as CLOs bought the majority of new issuance leveraged loans until 2007 (see Table 2.7). The securitized market for almost all products virtually shut down in 2008 and 2009. This, along with banks' decreased capital commitment, led to the significant drop in new issuance volume in 2008 and 2009. Prime rate funds were the second

TABLE 2.7 Owners of Institutional Leveraged Loans

Year	Collateralized Loan Obligations	Insurance Companies	Prime Rate Funds	Hedge and High-Yield Funds	Banks	Finance Companies
2000	64.0%	9.2%	26.7%	–	–	–
2001	74.4%	7.9%	16.9%	–	–	–
2002	66.7%	4.4%	20.2%	1.1%	–	7.6%
2003	61.9%	6.9%	11.5%	9.8%	–	6.1%
2004	61.8%	5.8%	17.7%	9.3%	–	5.5%
2005	63.0%	3.0%	17.0%	12.0%	–	5.0%
2006	61.2%	2.9%	12.9%	17.0%	–	6.9%
2007	56.3%	3.7%	8.3%	26.3%	1.9%	3.5%
2008	42%	2%	5%	25%	19%	7%

Source: J.P. Morgan

TABLE 2.8 Collateralized Loan Obligations and Leveraged Loans (in billions)

Year	CLO Market–Total Size (in $billions)	CLOs–New Issuance (in $billions)
1996	3.0	1.6
1997	7.0	4.5
1998	20.0	13.4
1999	30.0	19.1
2000	56.0	17.1
2001	69.0	13.7
2002	84.0	15.3
2003	101.0	20.5
2004	106.0	32.1
2005	147.0	58.4
2006	231.0	113.5
2007	333.0	120.5
2008	n.a.	13.5
2009	n.a.	0

Source: J.P. Morgan

largest buyer of leveraged loans until 2006. Hedge and high-yield funds were essentially nonexistent buyers in the market until 2002, but they became the second largest buyer, supplanting prime rate funds, by 2006.

One of the reasons for the explosive growth associated with CLOs was the spread difference between similarly rated CLO tranches and traditional high-yield bonds (Table 2.9). In some instances, the spread difference between CLOs and bonds was more than the spread on the BB bond itself (1999, 2003, 2004). This clearly indicates that institutional investors believed that similarly rated BB CLO tranches were significantly riskier than the rating agencies or that the CLOs were mispriced. Given the collapse in the value of CLOs in 2007 and 2008, it is clear that the rating agencies underestimated the risks.

TABLE 2.9 CLO Spreads Versus Corporate Spreads

Year	BB CLO Spread	BB High-Yield Bond Spread	Difference Spread
1999	628	300	328
2000	618	451	167
2001	631	471	160
2002	756	591	165
2003	781	292	489
2004	638	210	428
2005	482	256	226
2006	398	206	192
2007	435	412	23

Source: J.P. Morgan

Credit Default Swaps (CDSs)

The most recent development in the leveraged finance market is the advent of credit default swaps. As shown in Table 2.10, CDSs were essentially nonexistent until the early 2000s, but they grew into a market

TABLE 2.10 Credit Default Swaps

Year	CDSs Outstanding (Notational Amount in billions)	Change from Prior Year
2001	919	n.a.
2002	2,192	139%
2003	3,779	73%
2004	8,422	123%
2005	17,096	103%
2006	34,423	101%
2007	62,173	81%
2008	38,564	–38%
2009	31,223	–19%

Source: ISDA

with over $62 trillion of swaps outstanding (notational amount) by 2007. Given the concern about counterparty risk and the central role of CDSs in the financial market collapse in 2008, it is not surprising to see the significant decline in CDS usage in 2008 and 2009.

In the early stages of the CDS market, the primary type of CDSs was the single-name CDS, which pays on the default of a company (Table 2.11). As it relates specifically to high-yield bonds, Bank of America estimates in 2007 that 13% of high-yield issuers had actively traded CDSs. This represents 42% of the market value of high-yield because single-name CDSs are typically written on the largest, most actively traded high-yield firms. The market has evolved, and we now see a wider gamut of CDS contracts with the index or tranched index products now accounting for close to 40% of the market (index CDSs pay on defaults reaching a certain level for a particular industry or index).

Institutions can be either sellers and/or buyers of CDSs. These instruments allow investors to manage their risk more effectively, but they also allow for placing significant bets on individual credits. This dichotomy is reflected in the fact that the primary buyers and sellers of CDSs are banks/dealers and hedge funds. They represent approximately

TABLE 2.11 CDS Product Usage, 2003 and 2008

Market Share of CDS by Type	2008	2003
Single-name CDS	30%	51%
Index	29%	9%
Synthetic collateralized debt obligations (CDOs)	16%	16%
Tranched index	10%	2%
Other	8%	9%
Credit-linked notes	3%	6%
Options	3%	3%
Basket products	1%	4%

Source: Bank of America

TABLE 2.12 Sellers and Buyers–CDSs

Institution Type	Sellers	Buyers	Net: Buyer/Seller
Pension funds	5%	2%	3%
Mutual funds	3%	2%	1%
Hedge funds	31%	28%	3%
Insurers	18%	6%	12%
Loan portfolios	7%	20%	-13%
Banks and dealers	33%	39%	-6%
Corporations	2%	2%	0%
Other	1%	1%	0%

Source: Bank of America

60% and 70% of the sellers and buyers of CDSs (Table 2.12). The net effect of CDSs on the financial market in general and leveraged finance in particular is still uncertain. While they do provide the ability to mitigate risk, they also afford the possibility of a systematic shock to the financial system related to their counterparty risk. The near collapse of Bear Stearns and AIG brought home the risk that these products might present.

3

UNDERSTANDING THE ROLE OF CREDIT RATING AGENCIES

William F. Maxwell

Rauscher Chair in Financial Investments,
Cox School of Business at SMU

Philip Delbridge

Vice President Credit Risk Management,
Credit Suisse Securities (USA) LLC

The primary role of a credit rating agency (CRA) is to assess the credit risk of a counterparty or debt instrument. CRAs have existed since the beginning of the twentieth century and play a key role in the operation of capital markets.[1] Some studies have accounted for almost 150 different CRAs around the world. These CRAs use both qualitative and quantitative methods to measure credit risk. In the United States the CRA market is dominated by Standard & Poor's (S&P), Moody's Investor Services (Moody's), and Fitch Ratings (Fitch). This chapter outlines the role CRAs play in financial markets, how credit ratings are produced for corporate borrowers, and some key issues faced by CRAs, such as conflicts of interest and rating triggers.

The Role of Credit Rating Agencies

CRAs play two key roles in financial markets. First, CRAs disseminate information about the financial performance and repayment capacity of borrowers active in capital markets. Ratings are generally required for bond issues to attract investors, and the ratings can improve a borrower's visibility, as well as affect liquidity, pricing, and the cost of capital. Passive bondholders seek rated debt because the ratings are often derived from nonpublic information and thus can enhance the evaluation of credit risk.[2] CRAs are important even to active investors who do not rely on CRAs for any risk assessment of individual credit because many investment guidelines are related to CRAs ratings, and CRAs' ratings may be used for internal or external value-at-risk measures.

There is a wide range of users of credit ratings beyond the traditional fixed-income investor. Other users include banks, security firms, and regulators. For example banks often use ratings and research produced by CRAs to supplement their own due diligence. External credit ratings can provide an effective tool for banks in assessing counterparty risk and managing exposures to other financial institutions, given the large volume of transactions banks handle.

Second, the information produced by CRAs is used in private contracts between financial markets participants and by regulators.[3] Credit ratings can be incorporated into financial contracts to establish key terms between the contracting parties. For example, loan agreements can contain pricing grids based on one or more external rating from S&P, Moody's, or Fitch. Internal governance rules of fund managers may require bonds to be sold if a rating falls below a particular letter grade (typically subinvestment grade). Finally contracts can incorporate rating triggers, which can have adverse liquidity implications for borrowers (rating triggers are discussed in more detail later in this chapter).

Regulations and Credit Rating Agencies

Credit ratings also play an important role in the regulation of financial markets. Regulators use credit ratings in a variety of ways to set benchmarks and maintain standards. For example, companies are often required to have debt instruments rated for shelf registration pursuant to Form-3 rules of the Securities and Exchange Commission (SEC)[4] and to sell paper for investments by money market funds under Rule 2a-7 under the Investment Company Act.[5] Also members of the Federal Reserve System and the Federal Home Loan Bank System are only permitted to invest in securities that are rated AAA to AA–.[6]

One of the most significant regulatory effects of credit ratings relates to capital adequacy requirements of banks. The Bank of International Settlements has revised its international capital accord to include a more prominent role for CRAs.[7] Under Basel II, banks can choose between two broad methodologies for calculating their capital requirements for credit risk. The first method allows banks to use internal credit models approved by the relevant bank regulator. The second method allows banks to measure credit risk in a standardized manner by using external credit ratings.[8] The external credit ratings produced by CRAs are used to determine the risk weights applied to various assets, which in turn affects the level of regulatory capital set aside by banks.

CRAs are closely scrutinized by regulators given the important role of credit ratings in financial markets. In the United States the major CRAs are part of the "nationally recognized statistical rating organizations" or NRSROs. The first NRSRO was established in 1975 to certify agencies whose ratings could be used by broker-dealers to comply with SEC requirements.[9] The first three NRSROs in the United States were S&P, Moody's, and Fitch. In 2007 the SEC expanded the number of CRAs recognized as an NRSRO from three to seven. NRSROs now include A.M. Best Company, Inc., DBRS Limited, Japan Credit Rating Agency, Ltd., and Rating and Investment Information, Inc. This has been expanded to 10 CRAs. These CRAs are subject to the Credit Rating Agency Reform Act. This act was enacted in 2006 and gives the SEC authority to implement registration, record keeping, financial reporting, and oversight rules with respect to registered CRAs.[10]

Credit Ratings

The major CRAs assign credit ratings to both issuers (borrowers seeking to have their debt rated) and issues (the particular debt instruments to be sold in the market). Credit ratings represent a CRA's opinion of the creditworthiness of a specific issuer or debt issue. However S&P notes that its ratings are not a recommendation to buy, sell, or hold a particular security, nor does it advise whether a particular security is a suitable investment.[11] The CRAs provide ratings for a range of issuers. The categories of issuers rated by S&P, Moody's, and Fitch include corporate institutions, financial institutions, municipals, project financing, managed funds, sovereigns, and structured financing. This chapter focuses on the rating process for corporate borrowers.

Credit ratings for corporate issuers can be broken down into short-term and long-term ratings. Short-term ratings are a CRA's opinion of the capacity of an issuer to meet short-term financial obligations for instruments of maturities that are typically no more than one year.[12] The short-term ratings are assigned to firms that access the commercial paper market. Long-term credit ratings, on the other hand, are assigned to instruments with maturities of more than one year and reflect not only the likelihood of default over a longer-term horizon but also the expected level of recovery or loss given default (LGD) of a particular debt issue. Long-term ratings are assigned to firms that access the corporate bond market, and hence, firms may have a long-term rating and no short-term rating. But it is very rare to find a firm with a short-term rating and no long-term rating.

As noted earlier, the CRAs assign both issuer ratings and issue ratings. Issuer ratings focus entirely on the default risk of the entity. For investment-grade borrowers, S&P and Moody's will assign the issuer rating to a borrower's most senior long-term debt issue, which is typically senior unsecured debt. For example, if S&P assigned a BBB+ rating to a 19-year senior unsecured bond of XYZ Corporation, then XYZ Corporation will receive an issuer rating of BBB+. S&P refers to the issuer rating as the *corporate credit rating.* Moody's has replaced the issuer rating with a *corporate family rating* and *probability of default rating* for speculative-grade borrowers.

A critical point with issuer ratings is that they assume a common likelihood of default across all different types of debt instruments. In other words, the default risk is the same for the firm's subordinated debt as it is for the senior secured debt (most debt instruments have cross-default provisions so a default on one instrument triggers default on all others). In contrast, recovery ratings and hence the issues ratings between the two instruments can vary significantly.

Table 3.1 summarizes the long-term ratings of S&P, Moody's, and Fitch. Table 3.2 summarizes their short-term ratings.

S&P, Moody's, and Fitch add modifiers to each long-term rating between the AAA/Aaa and CC/Ca levels. The modifiers (denoted by +/– or 1, 2, 3) show the relative standing within the major rating categories. The rating agencies also provide rating outlooks and watch lists. A rating outlook, which can be stable, positive, or negative, provides an indication of a potential rating change over a long-term horizon.[13] A credit watch indicates that the rating is under review for possible change in the short term.

For example, an issuer could have its rating placed on negative outlook if the CRA believes that the issuer is faced with deteriorating industry conditions, which could lead to a rating downgrade over the longer term. A negative watch could be assigned if the issuer announced a debt-funded acquisition that would lead to an immediate increase in leverage and weaker credit measures. Empirical evidence suggests that the use of rating outlooks and watch lists enhances rating quality. Moody's has shown that simple adjustments to its ratings based on

TABLE 3.1 Long-term Corporate Obligation Ratings of S&P, Moody's, and Fitch

S&P	Moody's	Fitch	Description*
AAA	Aaa	AAA	Obligations rated AAA/Aaa are judged to be of the highest quality with minimal credit risk.
AA+ AA AA–	Aa1 Aa2 Aa3	AA+ AA AA–	Obligations rated AA/Aa are judged to be of high quality and are subject to very low credit risk.
A+ A A–	A1 A2 A3	A+ A A–	Obligations rated A are considered upper-medium grade and are subject to low credit risk.
BBB+ BBB BBB–	Baa1 Baa2 Baa3	BBB+ BBB BBB–	Obligations rated BBB/Baa are subject to moderate credit risk. They are considered medium grade and as such may possess certain speculative characteristics.
BB+ BB BB–	Ba1 Ba2 Ba3	BB+ BB BB–	Obligations rated BB/Ba are judged to have speculative elements and are subject to substantial credit risk.
B+ B B–	B1 B2 B3	B+ B B–	Obligations rated B are considered speculative and are subject to high credit risk.
CCC+ CCC CCC–	Caa1 Caa2 Caa3	CCC+ CCC CCC–	Obligations rated CCC/Caa are judged to be of poor standing and are subject to very high credit risk.
CC	Ca	CC	Obligations rated CC/Ca are highly speculative and are likely in, or very near, default, with some prospect of recovery of principal and interest.
C	C	C	Obligations rated C are the lowest-rated class of bonds and are typically in default, with little prospect for recovery of principal or interest.

* Rating descriptions provided by Moody's Investor Services, Inc. (2008), "Moody's Rating Symbols and Definitions," p. 8.

TABLE 3.2 Short-term Corporate Obligation Ratings of S&P, Moody's, and Fitch*

S&P	Moody's	Fitch	Description†
A-1	P-1	F-1	Issuers have a superior ability to repay short-term debt obligations.
A-2	P-2	F-2	Issuers have a strong ability to repay short-term debt obligations.
A-3	P-3	F-3	Issuers have an acceptable ability to repay short-term obligations.
B	NP	–	Issuers do not fall within the investment-grade rating categories.

* S&P and Fitch also have an A-1+ and F-1+ rating.
† Rating descriptions provided by Moody's Investor Services, Inc. (2008), "Moody's Rating Symbols and Definitions," p. 10.

outlooks and watch lists substantially increase rating accuracy in predicting three-year default risk.[14]

For the most part, the different CRAs' definitions for long-term debt are similar, but as ratings fall into the CCC to C category, the different rating agencies' definitions diverge. A firm is considered to have a split rating if two CRAs have different major ratings. A split rating is not that significant unless the split spans the investment versus high-yield designation (S&P rates the firm BBB and Moody rates the firm Ba). However, for the most part, Moody's and S&P usually rate firms into similar categories. We find that when looking at year-end ratings for industrial firms between 1982 and 2004, 86% of the time the difference between the ratings is plus or minus one modifier.

Origins of High-Yield Ratings

Credit ratings at BB+/Ba1 and lower are commonly referred to as high-yield speculative-grade, or subinvestment-grade debt. BBB–/Baa3 ratings or higher are known as investment grade. The true source of the split between investment and subinvestment grade at the BBB and BB rating level is unknown. Moody's points out that the split was not derived by the ratings agencies, but rather by the private sector and regulating conventions in the early part of the 1900s. The split at this level was supported by default data which showed that the average default rates for a BB (2.52%) credit was 3.5 times higher than a BBB (0.72%) credit between 1920 and 1935.[15] Historically, the most significant jump in default rates has been between the BBB and BB levels; however, with today's rating scale, where modifiers are added to each rating, there is a more modest difference in credit quality when moving from a BBB– to a BB+ rating.

However, a high-yield/investment-grade rating can affect debt issues. Currently, most investment-grade bonds are issued without financial covenants. In contrast, almost all bonds and bank loans that are rated high yield at the time of issuance include financial covenants. In addition, most bank loans that are rated high yield (leveraged loans) are secured by assets of the borrower, whereas security is not required for investment-grade debt. In addition, many life insurance companies and mutual and pension funds place restrictions on the percentage of securities in the portfolio which may be rated below the investment-grade level. In fact, some funds require that a manager divest a security once its rating falls below investment grade.

Issue Ratings and Notching

Lenders and investors are concerned not only with the likelihood of a borrower defaulting (or the probability of default) but also with the amount to be recovered following a default (or loss given default). Therefore CRAs not only provide an opinion of a borrower's creditworthiness but also give an indication of prospective recovery of particular debt issues.

Incorporating loss indicators into credit ratings is referred to as *notching*. Notching involves assigning a higher or lower rating to individual debt issues. As noted earlier, the issuer rating is generally set equal to the senior unsecured rating for investment-grade borrowers. Issue ratings can be notched up if the debt instrument has a higher expected recovery than senior unsecured debt and notched down if the debt instrument has a lower expected recovery than senior unsecured debt. The number of notches between the ratings depends on the magnitude of the difference in expected recovery.

For example, S&P applies a threshold approach to determine the degree of notching on investment-grade issues. S&P looks at the proportion of priority claims for available assets. If the proportion of priority claims reaches a certain threshold (20% for investment grade),[16] the next more junior debt is notched down because recovery is expected to be materially less than the senior claim.

Differences in recovery rates between debt instruments are driven by a number of factors, including legal, contractual, and structural subordination. For example, a senior secured debt issue can be notched up because of the priority of claims over unsecured debt, or a subordinated debt issue can be notched down because of intercreditor agreements that restrict payments of principal and interest. Finally, holding company debt can be notched down if lenders to downstream subsidiaries have priority claims over subsidiary assets. Different legal jurisdictions will affect the degree of notching as bankruptcy regimes around the world can influence the degree of recovery across different levels of debt.

Senior and Subordinated Issues, Debt Ratings, and Impact on Price

Notching is not the only way that S&P, Moody's, and Fitch assess recovery prospects. The three agencies also produce recovery ratings on specific debt instruments. These recovery rates provide lenders and investors with a forward-looking assessment of the prospects of recovery of principal (and sometimes interest) of certain debt issues.[17] Recovery ratings use a scale that is different from traditional ratings. For example, S&P presents its recovery ratings on a scale of 1+ to 6, with 1+ representing full recovery and 6 representing little recovery prospects. Moody's uses a similar approach to recovery ratings based on expected loss given default rates.

S&P and Moody's use recovery ratings as a basis for notching different high-yield issues, whereby the issue rating is notched up or down from the issuer rating based on the expected level of recovery. The recovery ratings were initially produced for secured bank loans, but they have expanded to cover other types of secured and unsecured debt. Table 3.3 contains S&P's expected recovery rates and the corresponding level of notching for high-yield issues.

CRAs have been able to observe recovery rates for different types of debt issues given the variation in the level of losses across borrowers' capital structure. Moody's has calculated recovery rates by debt class of corporate issuers from 1982 to 2007 with results summarized in Table 3.4.[18] The general trend for average recovery rates between 1982 and 2007 shows that senior debt issues have higher recovery rates than do more junior debt issues.

Numerous studies have examined trends in recovery rates over time and have found that recovery rates can vary significantly across asset types and industry classes. Borrowers in industries with high-quality liquid assets coupled with stable cash flows tend to have higher

TABLE 3.3 S&P Recovery Rates

Recovery Rating	Recovery Description	Recovery Expectations	Issue Rating Notches
1+	Highest expectation, full recovery	100%	+3
1	Very high recovery	90%–100%	+2
2	Substantial recovery	70%–90%	+1
3	Meaningful recovery	50–70%	0
4	Average recovery	30%–50%	0
5	Modest recovery	10%–30%	–1
6	Negligible recovery	0%–10%	–2

Source: Standard & Poor's (2007), "Recovery Analytics Update: Enhanced Recovery Scale and Issue Ratings Framework," p. 2.

TABLE 3.4 Moody's Average Corporate Debt Recovery Rates, Measured by Postdefault Trading Prices (1982–2007)

Issuer-Weighted Recovery Rates	Years	Value-Weighted Recovery Rates	Years
Lien position	1982–2007	Lien position	1982–2007
Bank Loans	**Rates (%)**	**Bank Loans**	**Rates (%)**
Senior secured	70.47	Senior secured	65.52
Senior unsecured	54.02	Senior unsecured	46.00
Bonds	**Rates (%)**	**Bonds**	**Rates (%)**
Senior secured	51.89	Senior secured	54.21
Senior unsecured	36.69	Senior unsecured	34.85
Senior subordinated	32.42	Senior subordinated	29.80
Subordinated	31.19	Subordinated	27.58
Junior subordinated	23.95	Junior subordinated	16.79
Preferred Stock	**Rates (%)**	**Preferred Stock**	**Rates (%)**
Trust preferred	11.66	Trust preferred	12.97
Nontrust preferred	23.22	Nontrust preferred	19.92

Source: Moody's Investors Service, Inc. (2008), "Corporate Default and Recovery Rates, 1920–2007," p. 9. Report.

recovery rates.[19] Furthermore, studies have shown that there is an inverse relationship between default rates and recovery rates.[20] Recovery rates on speculative-grade bonds tend to have a stronger inverse relationship compared to loans resulting from the tighter controls lenders have as the borrower approaches default.

The relationship between default rates and recovery rates affects the pricing of risk and capital management. For example, banks establish lending margins based on expected loss, which is the probability of default (default rate) multiplied by the loss given default (one minus the recovery rate). Therefore, deterioration in the credit quality of a borrower could result in an increase in the probability of default and a decrease in the expected recovery rate. A bank's pricing of risk will need to be adjusted to reflect both changes.

The Rating Process

The quality of credit ratings underpins the demand for the information provided by CRAs. Therefore, it is important to understand how credit ratings are derived. In this section we look at how and why ratings are initiated, the costs involved in obtaining a rating, potential conflicts of interest, and the general methodology used by S&P, Moody's, and Fitch to arrive at a rating.

Fees

CRAs were founded as a subscription-based service with investors paying subscription fees to access rating information and analysis. Over time CRAs started charging issuers for ratings as pure subscription-based services became less profitable. It is now common practice for issuers to request a rating prior to the sale or registration of a debt issue. Most new ratings are initiated at the request of the issuers.

The fee structure is a function of the nature of the issue and the size of the debt being rated. For example, S&P charges up to 4.25 basis points (bps) for new debt issues of corporate and financial institutions.[21] Issuers are also charged an ongoing maintenance fee. CRAs still charge subscription fees and receive fees for ancillary business.

One of the criticisms of CRAs is that the issuer-based fee structure creates a potential conflict of interest. A potential conflict arises because issuer-based fees have become the major source of income for CRAs, and the fees are a function of the size of the transaction. Therefore, it is argued that CRAs could be tempted to produce softer ratings to retain the business of larger clients. However, there are several factors that mitigate this potential conflict of interest. First, the CRAs note that damage to their reputation from poor rating opinions is far greater than the benefit of large issuer fees. Second, the CRAs argue that the large number of issuers means that no single issuer can have material economic influence. Finally, the CRAs have detailed policies and procedures (discussed later in this chapter) to prevent such conflicts from arising. There are a number of reforms being proposed by the SEC and Congress to further mitigate CRAs' agency conflicts.

The two largest CRAs, S&P and Moody's, rate all public bond issues in the United States.[22] This leads to what is known as an *unsolicited rating.* Unsolicited ratings are controversial because these ratings are not based on complete information. S&P and Moody's often rely solely on public information and have no direct access to management when determining unsolicited ratings. Therefore, the quality of the ratings may be inferior to that of solicited ratings.

The Credit Committee

Following the completion of primary due diligence for new issues (discussed in more detail in the following section), the rating process moves to a rating committee. The primary functions of a rating committee include deciding on a rating, considering rating changes, and assessing events that could affect a rating. The size and composition of a credit committee vary among the three largest agencies. The size may range from four to eight members depending on the nature and complexity of the transaction under consideration.

The composition of a committee will include the lead and secondary analyst covering the issuers, industry head, and other senior analysts to provide diverse experience and input into the process. Voting during the committee process is typically in the sequence of least senior to most senior member. An issuer is usually given the opportunity to appeal a rating before it is released to the public, and the committee can reconvene to assess any additional information provided by the issuer to support the appeal.

The CRAs have identified a number of benefits of the credit committee process, which include encouraging differences of opinion, challenging ideas and assumptions of key facts, and providing a consistent and impartial approach to rating methodologies.[23] Furthermore a credit committee mitigates any potential conflict of interest arising from the actions of individual analysts.

Rating Methodology

CRAs have developed a wide range of methodologies to assign credit ratings to issuers and specific debt issues. The variation among the methodologies is primarily a function of the type of issuer or issue. As noted earlier, the larger CRAs cover a wide range of categories, including corporate and financial institutions, managed funds, structured finance, on so on. A different approach to derive a rating has been developed for each category. For example, financial institution ratings will consider key variables such as credit risk concentration, capital adequacy ratios, asset and liability management, and economic stability. A rating for infrastructure assets such as a port would focus on trade activity, quality of the facilities and location, shipping alliances, and fixed charge cover ratios. The major rating agencies have significantly improved the transparency of the rating process in recent years, and they all now provide documentation on their Web sites explaining the rating process and the factors they consider.

This section focuses on rating methodologies for corporate issuers. While there is a common foundation for all corporate ratings, methodologies do vary among industries. Therefore CRAs typically divide analysts along industry and geographic lines. According to Moody's.com, examples of the major industry categories include:

- Auto and manufacturing
- Basic industries and home building
- Business and consumer services
- Consumer products, retail, and food
- Energy and utilities
- Health care and pharmaceuticals
- Technology, media, and telecommunications
- Transportation, aerospace, and defense

Industry analysts for the major CRAs use fundamental analysis as the basis for deriving credit ratings. Fundamental analysis employs a systematic approach to capture all risks associated with a business. S&P, Moody's, and Fitch typically divide risks into two broad categories, (1) business risk and (2) financial risk. For S&P, business risk captures:

1. Country risk
2. Industry factors
3. Company position
4. Profitability/peer group comparisons

On the other hand, financial risk captures:

1. Accounting
2. Governance/risk tolerance/financial policies
3. Cash flow adequacy
4. Capital structure/asset protection
5. Liquidity/short-term factors[24]

The business risk analysis focuses on more qualitative aspects of an issuer's credit quality. Factors that are considered when assessing business risk include:

1. Location of operations and impact of local economic conditions and government regulation
2. Industry conditions for growth, maturity, or decline
3. Exposure to business cycles and level of cyclicality
4. Market share and position relative to competitors
5. Size, diversification, and economies of scale of a firm's operations
6. Management's ability to implement the stated objectives of the firm

The ultimate goal of any credit analysis is to assess the repayment capacity of a borrower. Financial risk analysis is the primary tool used to assess repayment capacity in the context of a firm's business risk.

Financial risk is assessed using primarily quantitative measures. Some of the key ratios used to assess financial risk for corporate borrowers include:

1. Debt/EBITDA
2. Debt/capitalization
3. Funds from operations/debt
4. Free cash flow/debt
5. EBIT (or EBITDA)/interest expense
6. Fixed charge cover ratio

However, CRAs do not capture all financial risk through ratio analysis. For example, CRAs consider liquidity as a key measure of financial risk. The strength of a firm's liquidity is assessed by looking at factors such as size and tenure of standby facilities, debt maturity profiles, access to capital markets, level of off-balance-sheet contingent claims, and impact of rating triggers.

CRAs also undertake extensive accounting analysis as part of their financial risk assessment. Accounting analysis is used to adjust the financial statements of a borrower to ensure a consistent comparison across all firms being benchmarked. Typical accounting adjustments include conversion of operating leases to capital leases, liability adjustments for unfunded pensions, capitalized interest, and LIFO to FIFO conversion.

CRAs also use financial projections as part of the rating process. S&P notes that its internal projections do not attempt to forecast performance precisely; rather, the projections are used to consider the variability of cash flow and potential impact on repayment capacity under a range of different scenarios.[25] These projections play an important role in the rating decision but are not disclosed to the public.

CRAs also focus on event risks and off-balance-sheet commitments, particularly given the events surrounding high-profile defaults such as Enron and WorldCom. The CRAs will consider an issuer's exposure to an event that could have an adverse impact on repayment capacity. Event risk could include market turbulence, acquisition, litigation, regulatory changes, and fraud. Moody's notes that off-balance-sheet exposure can be in three primary forms, (1) unsolicited legal entities, (2) executory contracts, and (3) contingent claims.[26] A CRA will try to assess and quantify the risks associated with off-balance sheet exposures and adjust its financial analysis accordingly.

Following the completion of the business and financial risk analysis, S&P and Moody's will use a ratings matrix to rank the key business and financial risk factors to determine a final rating. The form of the rating matrix varies between the CRAs. S&P uses a matrix that ranks business risk from "excellent" to "vulnerable" and combines the rating with a ranking of financial risk based on a variety of quantitative measures.[27] Moody's publishes a rating matrix for most corporate issuers based on key industry factors and benchmarks. Table 3.5 provides a hypothetical ratings table for a mining company, XYZ Corporation, which is similar to the one used by Moody's. The matrix captures both quantitative and

TABLE 3.5 Rating Matrix Example for XYZ Corporation

Category	**Rating in Comparison to Industry**					
Mining industry	AA	A	BBB	BB	B	CCC
Reserves years		52				
Product diversity			X			
Size			$4.8b			
Market share		X				
EBITDA margin			9.1%			
Return on assets			4.7%			
Earnings volatility				X		
Liquidity		X				
Debt to capitalization				56%		
Debt to EBITDA				4.2×		
Interest coverage				2.3×		
Funds from operations to debt					30%	
Rating from methodology				BB		
Actual assigned rating				BB+		

qualitative rating factors. Each of these factors may be assigned different weights to establish a rating. The final rating can be adjusted for other subjective factors not captured in the traditional methodology. For example, CRAs may take into account the possibility of event risk (restructuring, acquisition-related activities, lawsuits, etc.).

The matrix for XYZ Corporation highlights the importance of both quantitative and qualitative risk measures in the rating process. Many users of credit ratings often underestimate the importance of the business risk analysis and other qualitative performance measures and place too much emphasis on quantitative measures and ratios.

New Focus on High-Yield Ratings

The increase in the volume of high-yield debt, recent volatility in credit markets, and rising corporate default rates in 2008 have led to greater scrutiny of speculative-grade borrowers. In May 2008 S&P announced changes to its rating approach for speculative-grade corporate borrowers to provide more timely ratings. S&P will place greater emphasis on near-term risk factors and assign ratings over a two-year time horizon for speculative-grade issuers, whereas investment-grade issuers will continue to be assessed over a three- to five-year horizon based on the "rating-through-the-cycle" approach.[28]

Rating Triggers

Credit ratings are used in private contracts between financial markets participants. These contracts can include terms and conditions based on changes in the credit ratings of one or more of the contracting parties. An adverse consequence of the use of credit ratings in contracts has been the emergence of rating triggers. Moody's defines a rating trigger as "a provision in a financial contract, which is subject to the credit rating of a party to the agreement and, if activated, has monetary implications."[29] Rating triggers exist in debt instruments across the rating spectrum; however, triggers are more common in contracts of investment-grade issuers.

Moody's has identified some common effects of rating triggers, which include the following:

1. Collateral calls
2. Pricing amendments
3. Self-insurance elimination
4. Termination provisions
5. Change of control
6. Default/debt acceleration
7. Dilution reserves[30]

The impact of rating triggers varies. At one end of the scale, rating triggers may not have a material impact on the repayment capacity of a borrower. This is often the case with pricing grids contained in credit agreements. Investment-grade borrowers can easily absorb a 10–basis point increase in interest following a one-notch downgrade of a rating without experiencing any further deterioration in credit quality.

At the other end of the spectrum, rating triggers can create what S&P refers to as a "credit cliff," or a trigger that could turn an otherwise nominal change in credit quality into a major liquidity crisis or default event. For example, many rating triggers are contained in ISDAs between well-rated financial institutions. The ISDA can be terminated if the rating of one of the counterparties falls below a rating threshold such as A– or BBB–. A termination event can require the counterparty with the out-of-the-money position to satisfy its obligations under the ISDA. While one contract in isolation might not create a liquidity crisis for the financial institution, triggers contained in multiple ISDAs could give rise to a "rating cliff" event. The higher the rating that triggers the termination event, the greater the risk.

There have been several well-published events concerning the impact of rating triggers, including WorldCom, Tyco, and Enron. In the case of Enron, rating triggers existed in a wide range of contracts from energy trading agreements to structured finance arrangements. These triggers resulted in payments and collateralization in excess of $4 billion and contributed to Enron's demise.[31]

CRAs will factor the nature and potential impact of rating triggers into an issuer's credit rating and will not hold back from downgrading a rating if the borrowers would experience further credit deterioration from such triggers. Therefore, CRAs have called for greater disclosure of rating triggers to investors and regulators to avoid such situations.

Summary

Credit ratings provide an opinion of the creditworthiness of issuers and issues, in terms of the of default and recovery expectations. The ratings produced by the major credit rating agencies enhance an issuer's access to capital markets and are often required for new debt to be issued to capital markets. Credit ratings are also used by a wide range of investors, lenders, and regulators and can provide an efficient means of disseminating information about the credit quality of issuers. Furthermore numerous studies have been conducted by S&P, Moody's, and Fitch to examine the relationship between credit ratings and historical default rates. The evidence shows that higher letter ratings correspond to lower default rates and vice versa. This relationship validates the methodologies used by S&P Moody's, and Fitch. However, users of credit ratings should understand the methodologies behind ratings, and the variations in ratings between investment-grade, high-yield, and potential issues when incorporating ratings into financial contracts.

4

LEVERAGED LOANS AS AN ASSET CLASS

Daniel D. Toscano

Global Co-Head of Leveraged Finance,
Morgan Stanley & Company, Inc.

A syndicated loan is one that is provided by a group of lenders and is structured, arranged, and administered by one or several commercial or investment banks known as arrangers.

Starting with the large leveraged buyout (LBO) loans of the mid-1980s (see Table 4.1), the syndicated loan market has become the dominant way for issuers to tap banks and other institutional capital providers for loans. The reason is simple: Syndicated loans are less expensive and more efficient to administer than traditional bilateral, or individual, credit lines, while allowing issuers to access a growing institutional investor base that provides floating-rate debt on attractive terms.

The most profitable loans are those to leveraged borrowers—issuers whose credit ratings are speculative grade and who are paying spreads (premiums above LIBOR, London Inter-Bank Offered Rate, or another base rate) sufficient to attract the interest of nonbank term loan investors, typically LIBOR + 200 or higher, though this threshold moves up and down depending on market conditions.

TABLE 4.1 Size of the Leveraged Loan Market

Year	Institutional Leveraged Loans	Noninstitutional Leveraged Loans	Total Leveraged Loans
1994	16	161	177
1995	23	202	225
1996	34	250	284
1997	53	265	318
1998	88	464	552
1999	126	543	669
2000	145	663	808
2001	141	661	802
2002	176	558	734
2003	225	567	792
2004	332	588	920
2005	472	668	1,140
2006	746	647	1,393
2007	1,061	528	1,589
2008	885	725	1,610
2009	835	796	1,631

Source: Credit Suisse

The "retail" market for a syndicated loan consists of banks and, in the case of leveraged transactions, finance companies and institutional investors. Before formally launching or selling a loan to these retail accounts, arrangers will often get a market read by informally polling select investors to gauge their appetite for the credit. Based on these discussions, the arranger will launch the credit at a spread and fee it believes will clear the market. Until 1998, this would have been the end of it. Once the pricing was set, it was set, except in the most extreme cases. If the loan was undersubscribed, the arrangers could very well be left above their desired hold level. Since the Russian debt crisis roiled the market in 1998, however, arrangers have adopted market-flex language, which allows them to change the pricing of the loan based on investor demand—in some cases within a predetermined range—as well as shift amounts between various tranches of a loan, as a standard feature of loan commitment letters. Market-flex language, in a single stroke, pushed the loan market, at least the leveraged segment of it, across the Rubicon, to a full-fledged capital market.

Initially, arrangers invoked flex language to make loans more attractive to investors by hiking the spread or lowering the price. This was logical after the volatility introduced by the Russian debt debacle. Over time, however, market-flex became a tool either to increase or decrease pricing of a loan, based on investor reaction.

As a result of market-flex, a loan syndication today functions as a "book-building" exercise, in bond-market parlance. A loan is originally launched to market at a target spread or, as was increasingly common by 2008, with a range of spreads referred to as price talk (i.e., a target spread of, say, LIBOR + 250 to LIBOR + 275). Investors then will make commitments that in many cases are tiered by the spread. For example, an account may put in for $25 million at LIBOR + 275 or $15 million at LIBOR + 250. At the end of the process, the arranger will total up the commitments and then make a call on where to price the paper. Following the example above, if the loan is vastly oversubscribed at LIBOR + 250, the arranger may reduce the spread further. Conversely, if it is undersubscribed even at LIBOR + 275, then the arranger will be forced to raise the spread to bring more money to the table.

The Syndication Process: The Information Memo, or "Bank Book"

Once the mandate is awarded, the syndication process starts. The lead arranger will prepare an information memo (IM) describing the terms of the transactions. The IM typically will include an executive summary, investment considerations, a list of terms and conditions, an industry overview, and a financial model. Because loans are not securities, this will be a confidential offering made only to qualified banks and accredited investors. If the issuer is speculative grade and seeking capital from nonbank investors, the arranger will often prepare a "public" version of the IM. This version will be stripped of all confidential material, such as management financial projections, so that it can be viewed by accounts that operate on the public side of the "wall" or that want to preserve their ability to buy bonds or stock or other public securities of the particular issuer (see the Public versus Private section below). Naturally, investors that view materially nonpublic information of a company are disqualified from buying the company's public securities for some period of time.

As the IM (or "bank book," in traditional market lingo) is being prepared, the syndicate desk will solicit informal feedback from potential investors on what their appetite for the deal will be and at what price they are willing to invest. Once this intelligence has been gathered, the agent will formally market the deal to potential investors.

The executive summary will include a description of the issuer, an overview of the transaction and rationale, sources and uses, and key statistics on the financials. *Investment considerations* will be, basically, management's sales pitch for the deal. The *list of terms and conditions* will be a preliminary term sheet describing the pricing, structure, collateral, covenants, and other terms of the credit (covenants are usually negotiated in detail after the arranger receives investor feedback). *The industry overview* will be a description of the company's industry and competitive position relative to its industry peers. The *financial model* will be a detailed model of the issuer's historical, pro forma, and projected financials, including management's high, low, and base case for the issuer.

Most new acquisition-related loans are kicked off at a bank meeting at which potential lenders hear management and the sponsor group (if there is one) describe what the terms of the loan are and what transaction it backs. Management will provide its vision for the transaction and, most important, tell why and how the lenders will be repaid on or ahead of schedule. In addition, investors will be briefed regarding the multiple "exit strategies," such as an asset sale, which would create an inflow of cash to pay back the loan. (If it is a small deal or a refinancing instead of a formal meeting, there may be a series of calls or one-on-one meetings with potential investors.)

Once the loan is closed, the final terms are then documented in detailed credit and security agreements. Subsequently, liens are perfected, and collateral is attached.

Loans, by their nature, are flexible documents that can be revised and amended from time to time. Amendments require different levels of approval (see Voting Rights section below). Amendments can range from something as simple as a covenant waiver to something as complex as a change in the collateral package or allowing the issuer to stretch out its payments or make an acquisition.

Public versus Private

In the old days, the line between public and private information in the loan market was a simple one. Loans were strictly on the private side of the wall, and any information transmitted between the issuer and the lender group remained confidential.

In the late 1980s, that line began to blur as a result of two market innovations. The first was more active secondary trading that sprung up to (1) support the entry of nonbank investors in the market, such as insurance companies and loan mutual funds, and (2) help banks sell rapidly expanding portfolios of distressed and highly leveraged loans that they no longer wanted to hold. This meant that parties that were insiders on loans might now exchange confidential information with traders and potential investors who were not (or not yet) a party to the loan. The second innovation that weakened the public-private divide was trade journalism that focuses on the loan market.

Despite these two factors, the public versus private line was well understood and rarely controversial for at least a decade. This changed in the early 2000s as a result of:

1. The explosive growth of nonbank investors groups, which included a growing number of institutions that operated on the public side of the wall, including a growing number of mutual funds, hedge funds, and even CLO boutiques.
2. The growth of the credit default swaps market, in which insiders like banks often sold or bought protection from institutions that were not privy to inside information.
3. A more aggressive effort by the press to report on the loan market.

Some background is in order. The vast majority of loans are unambiguously private financing arrangements between issuers and their lenders. Even for issuers with public equity or debt that file with the SEC, the credit agreement becomes public only when it is filed, often long after closing, as an exhibit to an annual report (10-K), a quarterly report (10-Q), a current report (8-K), or some other document (proxy statement, securities registration, etc.).

Beyond the credit agreement, there is a raft of ongoing correspondence between issuers and lenders that is made under confidentiality agreements, including quarterly or monthly financial disclosures, covenant compliance information, amendment and waiver requests, and financial projections, as well as plans for acquisitions or dispositions. Much of this information may be material to the financial health of the issuer and may be out of the public domain until the issuer formally puts out a press release or files an 8-K or some other document with the SEC.

In recent years, this information has leaked into the public domain either via off-line conversations or in the press. It has also come to light through mark-to-market pricing services, which often report significant movement in a loan price without any corresponding news. This is usually an indication that the banks have received negative or positive information that is not yet public.

Recently, there has been growing concern among issuers, lenders, and regulators that this migration of once-private information into public hands might breach confidentiality agreements between lenders and issuers and, more important, could lead to illegal trading. How has the market contended with these issues?

1. *Traders.* To insulate themselves from violating regulations, some dealers and buy-side firms have set up their trading desks on the public side of the wall. Consequently, traders, salespeople, and analysts do not receive private information even if it is available somewhere else in the institution. This is the same technique that investment banks have used from time immemorial to separate their private investment banking activities from their public trading and sales activities.
2. *Underwriters.* As mentioned above, in most primary syndications, arrangers will prepare a public version of information in the form of a memorandum that is scrubbed of private information like projections. These IMs will be distributed to accounts that are on the public side of the wall. In addition, underwriters will ask public accounts to attend a public version of the bank meeting and distribute to these accounts only scrubbed financial information.
3. *Buy-side accounts.* On the buy side there are firms that operate on either side of the public-private fence. Accounts that operate on the private side receive all confidential materials and agree to not trade in public securities of the issuers for which they get private information. These groups are often part of wider investment complexes that do have public funds and portfolios but, via "Chinese Walls," are sealed from these parts of the firms. There are also accounts that are public. These firms take only public IMs and public

materials and, therefore, retain the option to trade in the public securities markets even when an issuer for which they own a loan is involved. This can be tricky to pull off in practice because in the case of an amendment the lender could be called on to approve or decline in the absence of any real information. To contend with this issue, the account could either designate one person who is on the private side of the wall to sign off on amendments or empower its trustee or assign the loan arranger to do so. But it's a complex proposition.

4. *Vendors.* Vendors of loan data, news, and prices also face many challenges in managing the flow of public and private information. In general, the vendors operate under the freedom of the press provision of the U.S. Constitution's First Amendment and report on information in a way that anyone can simultaneously receive it—for a price, of course. Therefore, the information is essentially made public in a way that doesn't deliberately disadvantage any party, whether it's a news story discussing the progress of an amendment or an acquisition or it's a price change reported by a mark-to-market service. This, of course, doesn't deal with the underlying issue that someone who is a party to confidential information is making it available via the press or it is reflected in the price to a broader audience.

Another way in which participants deal with the public versus private issue is to ask counterparties to sign "big-boy" letters acknowledging that there may be information they are not privy to and they are agreeing to make the trade in any case. They are, effectively, big boys and will accept the risks.

The introduction of loan credit default swaps into the fray (see below) adds another wrinkle to this topic because a whole new group of public investors could come into play if that market catches fire.

Second-Lien Loans

Although they are really just another type of syndicated loan facility, second-lien loans are sufficiently complex to warrant a separate description. After a brief rise in the mid-1990s, second-lien loans fell out of favor after the Russian debt crisis caused investors to adopt a more cautious tone. But after default rates fell precipitously in 2003, arrangers rolled out second-lien facilities to help finance issuers struggling with liquidity problems. By 2007, the market had accepted second-lien loans to finance a wide array of transactions, including acquisitions and recapitalizations. Arrangers reach out to nontraditional accounts—hedge funds, distress investors, and high-yield accounts—as well as traditional CLO and prime fund accounts to finance second-lien loans.

As their name implies, the claims on collateral of second-lien loans are behind those of first-lien loans. Second-lien loans also typically have less restrictive covenant packages in which maintenance covenant levels are set wide of the first-lien loans if there are any at all. As a result, second-lien loans are priced at a premium compared to first-lien loans. This premium typically starts at 200 bps when the collateral coverage goes far beyond the claims of both the first- and second-lien loans to more than 1,000 bps for less generous collateral.

There are, lawyers explain, two main ways in which the collateral of second-lien loans can be documented. Either the second-lien loan can be part of a single security agreement with first-lien loans, or it can be part of an altogether separate agreement. In the case of a single agreement, the agreement would apportion the collateral, with value going first, obviously, to the first-lien claims and next to the second-lien claims. Alternatively, there can be two entirely separate agreements. Here's a brief summary:

1. In a single security agreement, the second-lien lenders are in the same creditor class as the first-lien lenders from the standpoint of a bankruptcy, according to lawyers who

specialize in these loans. As a result, for adequate protection to be paid, the collateral must cover the claims of both the first- and second-lien lenders. If it does not, the judge may choose not to pay adequate protection or to divide it pro rata among the first- and second-lien creditors. In addition, the second-lien lenders may have a vote as secured lenders equal to those of the first-lien lenders. One downside for second-lien lenders is that second-lien loans are often smaller than the first-lien loans, and therefore, when a vote comes up, first-lien lenders can outvote second-lien lenders to promote their own interests.

2. In the case of two separate security agreements, divided by a standstill agreement, the first- and second-lien lenders are likely to be divided into two separate creditor classes. As a result, second-lien lenders do not have a voice in the first-lien creditor committees. Also, first-lien lenders can receive adequate protection payments even if collateral covers their claims but does not cover the claims of the second-lien lenders. This may not be the case if the loans are documented together and the first- and second-lien lenders are deemed a unified class by the bankruptcy court.

Covenant-Lite Loans

Like second-lien loans, covenant-lite loans are really just another type of syndicated loan facility. But they also are sufficiently different to warrant their own mention.

At the most basic level, covenant-lite loans are loans that have bondlike financial incurrence covenants rather than traditional maintenance covenants that are normally part and parcel of a loan agreement. What's the difference?

Incurrence covenants generally require that if an issuer takes an action (paying a dividend, making an acquisition, issuing more debt), it would need to still be in compliance. So, for instance, an issuer that has an incurrence test that limits its debt to 5× cash flow would be able to take on more debt only if, on a pro forma basis, it was still within this constraint. If it is not, then it would have breeched the covenant and be in technical default on the loan. If, on the other hand, an issuer found itself above this 5× threshold simply because its earnings had deteriorated, it would not be in violation of the covenant.

Maintenance covenants are far more restrictive. This is because they require an issuer to meet certain financial tests every quarter whether or not the issuer takes an action. So, in the case above, had the 5× leverage maximum been a maintenance rather than incurrence test, the issuer would need to pass it each quarter and would be in violation if either its earnings eroded or its debt level increased. For lenders, clearly, maintenance tests are preferable because it allows them to take action earlier if an issuer experiences financial distress. What's more, the lenders may be able to wrest some concessions from an issuer that is in violation of covenants (a fee, incremental spread, or additional collateral) in exchange for a waiver.

Conversely, issuers prefer incurrence covenants precisely because they are less stringent. Covenant-lite loans, therefore, thrive only in the hottest markets when the supply/demand equation is tilted persuasively in favor of issuers.

Pricing Terms

In this section, we provide details on what is reflected in the pricing terms of a deal.

Rates

Bank loans usually offer borrowers different interest-rate options. Several of these options allow borrowers to lock in a given rate for one month to one year. Pricing on many loans is tied to performance grids, which adjust pricing by one or more financial criteria. Pricing is typically tied to ratings in investment-grade loans and to financial ratios in leveraged loans. Communications loans are invariably tied to the borrower's debt-to-cash-flow ratio.

Syndication pricing options include prime, LIBOR, CD, and other fixed-rate options:

1. The *prime* is a floating-rate option. Borrowed funds are priced at a spread over the reference bank's prime lending rate. The rate is reset daily, and borrowers may be repaid at any time without penalty. This is typically an overnight option, because the prime option is more costly to the borrower than is LIBOR or CDs.
2. The *LIBOR* (or Eurodollar) option is so called because, with this option, the interest on borrowings is set at a spread over LIBOR for a period of one month to one year. The corresponding LIBOR rate is used to set pricing. Borrowings cannot be prepaid without penalty.
3. The *CD* option works precisely like the LIBOR option, except that the base rate is certificates of deposit, sold by a bank to institutional investors.
4. *Other fixed-rate options* are less common but work like the LIBOR and CD options. These include federal funds (the overnight rate charged by the Federal Reserve to member banks) and cost of funds (the bank's own funding rate).

LIBOR floors put a floor under the base rate for loans. If a loan has a 3% LIBOR floor and 3-month LIBOR falls below this level, the base rate for any resets defaults to 3%. For obvious reasons, LIBOR floors are generally seen during periods when the market conditions are difficult and rates are falling as an incentive for lenders.

Fees

The fees associated with syndicated loans are the up-front fee, the commitment fee, the facility fee, the administrative agent fee, the letter of credit (LOC) fee, and the cancellation or prepayment fee:

1. An *up-front fee*, which is the same as an original-issue discount in the bond market, is a fee paid by the issuer. It is often tiered, with the lead arranger receiving a larger amount in consideration of its structuring and/or underwriting the loan. Co-underwriters will receive a lower fee, and then the general syndicate will likely have fees tied to its commitment. Most often, fees are paid on a lender's final allocation. For example, a loan has two fee tiers: 100 bps (or 1%) for $25 million commitments and 50 bps for $15 million commitments. A lender committing to the $25 million tier will be paid on its final allocation rather than on its initial commitment, which means that, in this example, the loan is oversubscribed and lenders committing $25 million would be allocated $20 million and the lenders would receive a fee of $200,000 (or 1% of $20 million). Sometimes up-front fees will be structured as a percentage of final allocation plus a flat fee. This happens most often for larger fee tiers, to encourage potential lenders to step up for larger commitments. The flat fee is paid regardless of the lender's final allocation. Fees are usually paid to banks, mutual funds, and other nonoffshore investors as an up-front payment. CLOs and other offshore vehicles are typically brought in after the loan closes as a "primary" assignment, and they simply buy the loan at a discount equal to the fee offered in the primary assignment, for tax purposes.
2. A *commitment fee* is a fee paid to lenders on undrawn amounts under a revolving credit or a term loan prior to drawdown. On term loans, this fee is usually referred to as a "ticking" fee.
3. A *facility fee*, which is paid on a facility's entire committed amount regardless of usage, is often charged instead of a commitment fee on revolving credits to investment-grade borrowers, because these facilities typically have Competitive

Bid Options (CBOs) which allow a borrower to solicit the best bid from its syndicate group for a given borrowing. The lenders that do not lend under the CBO are still paid for their commitment.

4. A *usage fee* is a fee paid when the utilization of a revolving credit falls below a certain minimum. These fees are applied mainly to investment-grade loans and generally call for fees based on the utilization under revolving credit. In some cases, the fees are for high use and, in some cases, for low use. Often, either the facility fee or the spread will be adjusted higher or lower based on a preset usage level.
5. A *prepayment fee* is a feature generally associated with institutional term loans. This fee is seen mainly in weak markets as an inducement to institutional investors. Typical prepayment fees will be set on a sliding scale, for instance, 2% in year one and 1% in year two. The fee may be applied to all repayments under a loan or "soft" repayments, those made from a refinancing or at the discretion of the issuer (as opposed to hard repayments made from excess cash flow or asset sales).
6. An *administrative agent fee* is the annual fee typically paid to administer the loan (including distribution of interest payments to the syndication group, to update lender lists, and to manage borrowings). For secured loans (particularly those backed by receivables and inventory), the agent often collects a collateral monitoring fee to ensure that the promised collateral is in place.

Original Issue Discounts (OIDs)

An original issue discount is another term imported from the bond market. The OID from par at the time of the loan is offered in the new issue market as a spread enhancement. A loan may be issued at 99 to pay par. The OID in this case is said to be 100 bps, or 1 point.

OID versus Up-Front Fees

At this point, the careful reader may be wondering just what the difference is between an OID and an up-front fee. After all, in both cases the lender effectively pays less than par for a loan.

From the perspective of the lender, actually, there isn't much of a difference. But for the issuer and arrangers, the distinction is far more than semantics. Up-front fees are generally paid from the arranger's underwriting fee as an incentive to bring lenders into the deal. An issuer may pay the arranger 2% of the deal, and the arranger, to rally investors, may then pay a quarter of this amount, or 0.50%, to lender groups.

An OID, however, is generally borne by the issuer, above and beyond the arrangement fee, so that the arranger would receive its 2% fee, and the issuer would receive only 99 cents for every dollar of the loan sold.

For instance, take a $100 million loan offered at a 1% OID. The issuer would receive $99 million, of which it would pay the arrangers 2%. The issuer then would be obligated to pay back the whole $100 million, even though it received $97 million after fees. Now take the same $100 million loan offered at par with an up-front fee of 1%. In this case, the issuer gets the full $100 million. The lenders would buy the loan not at par, but at 99 cents on the dollar. The issuer would receive $100 million, of which it would pay 2% to the arranger, which would then pay half that amount to the lending group. The issuer gets, after fees, $98 million.

Clearly, OID is a better deal for the arranger and, therefore, is generally seen in more challenging markets. Up-front fees, conversely, are more issuer-friendly and therefore are staples of better market conditions. Of course, during the most muscular bull markets, new issue paper is generally sold at par and therefore requires neither up-front fees nor OIDs.

Voting Rights

Amendments or changes to a loan agreement must be approved by a certain percentage of lenders. Most loan agreements have three levels of approval: required-lender level, full vote, and supermajority:

1. The "*required-lenders*" level, usually just a simple majority, is used for approval of nonmaterial amendments and waivers or changes affecting one facility within a deal.
2. A *full vote* of all lenders, including participants, is required to approve material changes such as RATS (rate, amortization, term, and security, or collateral) rights, but, as described below, there are occasions when changes in amortization and collateral may be approved by a lower percentage of lenders (a supermajority).
3. A *supermajority* is typically 67% to 80% of lenders and is sometimes required for certain material changes such as changes in amortization (in-term repayments) and release of collateral. Used periodically in the mid-1990s, these provisions fell out of favor by the late 1990s.

Covenants

Loan agreements have a series of restrictions that dictate, to varying degrees, how borrowers can operate and carry themselves financially. For instance, one covenant may require the borrower to maintain its existing fiscal-year end. Another may prohibit it from taking on new debt. Most agreements also have financial compliance covenants, for example, that a borrower must maintain a prescribed level of equity, which, if not maintained, gives banks the right to terminate the agreement or push the borrower into default. The size of the covenant package increases in proportion to a borrower's financial risk. Agreements to investment-grade companies are usually thin and simple. Agreements to leveraged borrowers are often much more onerous.

The three primary types of loan covenants are affirmative, negative, and financial:

1. *Affirmative covenants* state what action the borrower must take to be in compliance with the loan, such as that it must maintain insurance. These covenants are usually boilerplate and require a borrower to pay the bank interest and fees, maintain insurance, pay taxes, and so forth.
2. *Negative covenants* limit the borrower's activities in some way, such as regarding new investments. Negative covenants, which are highly structured and customized to a borrower's specific condition, can limit the type and amount of investments, new debt, liens, asset sales, acquisitions, and guarantees.
3. *Financial covenants* enforce minimum financial performance measures against the borrower, such as that it must maintain a higher level of current assets than of current liabilities. The presence of these maintenance covenants—so called because the issuer must maintain quarterly compliance or suffer a technical default on the loan agreement—is a critical difference between loans and bonds. Bonds and covenant-lite loans (see above), by contrast, usually contain incurrence covenants that restrict the borrower's ability to issue new debt, make acquisitions, or take other action that would breach the covenant. For instance, a bond indenture may require the issuer to not incur any new debt if that new debt would push it over a specified ratio of debt to EBITDA. But, if the company's cash flow deteriorates to the point where its ratio of debt to

EBITDA exceeds the same limit, a covenant violation would not be triggered. This is because the ratio would have climbed organically rather than through some action by the issuer.

As a borrower's risk increases, financial covenants in the loan agreement become more tightly wound and extensive. In general, there are five types of financial covenants—coverage, leverage, current ratio, tangible net worth, and maximum capital expenditures:

1. A *coverage covenant* requires the borrower to maintain a minimum level of cash flow or earnings relative to specified expenses, most often interest, debt service (interest and repayments), and/or fixed charges (debt service, capital expenditures, and/or rent).
2. A *leverage covenant* sets a maximum level of debt relative to either equity or cash flow, with the debt-to-cash-flow level being far more common.
3. A *current-ratio covenant* requires that the borrower maintain a minimum ratio of current assets (cash, marketable securities, accounts receivable, and inventories) to current liabilities (accounts payable, short-term debt of less than one year), but sometimes a "quick ratio," in which inventories are excluded from the numerate, is substituted.
4. A *tangible-net-worth (TNW)* covenant requires that the borrower have a minimum level of TNW (net worth less intangible assets, such as goodwill, intellectual assets, excess value paid for acquired companies), often with a buildsup provision, which increases the minimum by a percentage of net income or equity issuance.
5. A *maximum-capital-expenditures covenant* requires that the borrower limit capital expenditures (purchases of property, plant, and equipment) to a certain amount, which may be increased by some percentage of cash flow or equity

issuance, but often allowing the borrower to carry forward unused amounts from one year to the next.

Mandatory Prepayments

Leveraged loans usually require a borrower to prepay with proceeds of excess cash flow, asset sales, debt issuance, or equity issuance:

1. *Excess cash flow* is typically defined as cash flow after all cash expenses, required dividends, debt repayments, capital expenditures, and changes in working capital have been deducted. The typical percentage required is 50% to 75%.
2. *Asset sales* are defined as net proceeds from an asset sales, normally excluding receivables or inventories. The typical percentage required is 100%.
3. *Debt issuance* is defined as net proceeds from any debt issuance. The typical percentage required is 100%.
4. *Equity issuance* is defined as the net proceeds of any equity issuance. The typical percentage required is 25% to 50%.

Often, repayments from excess cash flow and equity issuance are waived if the issuer meets a preset financial hurdle, most often structured as a debt/EBITDA test.

Collateral

In the leveraged market, collateral usually includes all the tangible and intangible assets of the borrower and, in some cases, specific assets that back a loan.

Virtually all leveraged loans and some of the riskier investment-grade credits are backed by pledges of collateral. In the asset-based market, for instance, that typically takes the form of inventories and receivables, with the amount of the loan tied to a formula based on these assets. The common rule is that an issuer can borrow against 50% of inventory and 80% of receivables. Naturally, there are loans backed by certain equipment, real estate, and other property.

In the leveraged market, there are some loans—since the early 1990s, very few—that are backed by capital stock of operating units. In this structure, the assets of the issuer tend to be at the operating company level and are unencumbered by liens, but the holding company pledges the stock of the operating companies to the lenders. This effectively gives lenders control of these units if the company defaults. The risk to lenders in this situation, simply put, is that a bankruptcy court collapses the holding company with the operating companies and effectively renders the stock worthless. In these cases, which happened on a few occasions to lenders to retail companies in the early 1990s, loan holders become unsecured lenders of the company and are put back on the same level with other senior unsecured creditors.

Change of Control

Invariably, one of the events of default in a credit agreement is a change of issuer control.

For both investment-grade and leveraged issuers, an event of default in a credit agreement will be triggered by a merger, an acquisition of the issuer, some substantial purchase of the issuer's equity by a third party, or a change in the majority of the board of directors. For sponsor-backed leveraged issuers, the sponsor's lowering its stake below a preset amount can also trip this clause.

Equity Cures

Equity cures allow issuers to fix a covenant violation—exceeding the maximum debt to EBITDA test for instance—by making an equity contribution. These provisions are generally found in private equity–backed deals. The equity cure is a right, not an obligation. Therefore, a private equity firm will want these provisions, which, if the firm thinks it's worth it, allow it to cure a violation without going through an amendment process, through which lenders will often ask for wider spreads and/or fees in exchange for waiving the violation even with an infusion of new equity. Some agreements don't limit the number of equity cures, while others cap the number to, say, one a year or two over the life of the loan. It's a negotiating point, however, so there is no rule of thumb. Some agreements offer none; others, an unlimited number. Bull markets tend to inspire more generous equity cures for obvious reasons, while in bear markets lenders are more parsimonious.

Summary

The goal of this chapter is to provide an overview of the leveraged loan market. Firms will often issue both high-yield bonds and leveraged loans. However, while high-yield bonds and leveraged loans are similar at first blush, leveraged loans have many unique features that any institutional investor must understand. When compared to high-yield bonds, leveraged loans differ in pricing, maturity, fees, covenants, and priority.

5

COLLATERALIZED LOAN OBLIGATIONS

Frederic R. Bernhard, CFA

Vice President, Business Development,
Shenkman Capital Management, Inc.

John E. Kim

Former Director Structured Products,
Deutsche Bank Securities

Jonathan A. Savas

Vice President, Portfolio Manager,
Shenkman Capital Management, Inc.

A collateralized loan obligation (CLO) is a special-purpose vehicle designed to act on the arbitrage principles of a bank, such that the CLO borrows money at a lower rate than it lends it out. Similar to a bank, a CLO will issue "equity" (in the form of subordinated notes) that will be entitled to excess cash flow on the CLO's portfolio (after its senior obligations have been satisfied) and take a first loss on assets, much like a bank's reserve account. The money the CLO lends out is invested in high-yield leveraged bank loans (leveraged loans), also referred to as collateral obligations. The money the CLO borrows is in the form of subordinated notes and senior notes that it issues to investors in exchange for money.

The corporate capital structure of a CLO can be thought of in the same way as the three main components on a corporate balance sheet:

assets, liabilities, and equity. The assets are high-yielding leveraged loans (below investment grade); the liabilities are prioritized senior notes and subordinated notes, which provide excess capital to protect the more senior notes from loss. This subordination enables the more senior classes of notes to receive investment-grade ratings even though the cash flow on the notes is generated by noninvestment-grade collateral. Unlike the senior notes, which receive a predetermined coupon, the subordinated notes receive any excess cash flow after paying the interest on the notes and expenses. These excess cash flow amounts compared to the subordinated notes can equal an internal rate of return (IRR) in the mid to high teens.

There are three types of CLOs: cash flow, market value, and synthetic, with the majority of CLOs being cash flow. Cash flow CLOs are intended to be buy-and-hold vehicles with a fixed capital structure, which allows the underlying arbitrage principle to work. Money is borrowed in the form of notes and used to buy leveraged loans.

Synthetic CLOs use loan credit default swaps (LCDSs)—a derivative—to create a synthetic portfolio instead of investing in the actual leveraged loans. The synthetic CLO sells credit protection and receives an income stream to pay interest on the money it has borrowed. The value of the LCDS the CLO has written, which is the expected future payments less expected probable default, is held as collateral, or protection, against losses. Both cash flow and synthetic CLOs are generally non-mark-to-market, long-only portfolios.

A market value CLO is a dynamic vehicle that marks its portfolio daily and allows the fund to realize gains to maximize profits and, unlike the static CLOs, distribute those profits to its subordinated note holders so long as the senior notes are supported by the proper amount of overcollateralization. Market value CLOs carry more volatility but are tested more often, making them less risky in part because the monitoring is more transparent and allows the manager to address problems more quickly as compared to a cash flow deal in which the manager is not required to pay attention to price data. Also, since market value CLOs generally have more liquid deals in their portfolios and are encouraged to trade quickly to avoid problems, there is a selection bias toward larger, more liquid names, which suggests that market value CLOs could carry more market risk than cash flow deals, which in turn could carry more volatility risk.

CLOs are part of the broader class of instruments known as collateral debt obligations (CDOs). CDOs are special-purpose vehicles that issue notes; the proceeds are then used to invest in some form of interest-paying debt, such as student loans, prime mortgages, subprime mortgages, auto loans, and credit cards.

There are CLOs worth $248 billion in cash flow in existence today. The market started in 1997 and saw its highest period of growth between 2006 and 2007. Table 5.1 traces this growth. CLOs provide two important functions on Wall Street. First, from an investor's perspective, the cash flow CLO provides the possibility of investment-grade exposure to a diversified portfolio of below-investment-grade assets and often a higher yield than other single-name, undiversified investments (e.g., bonds) with comparable ratings. Second, from the underwriter's perspective, CLOs increase demand and liquidity for leveraged loans; at the peak more than 60% of all newly issued leveraged loans went into CLOs, so the growth of CLOs has helped to establish the leveraged loan market from $5 billion in 1993 to just short of $1 trillion today. This leveraged loan growth in turn has helped provide more financing for companies seeking to recapitalize.

Why CLOs Are Attractive

Cash flow CLOs are attractive structured finance investments that provide institutional investors with three investment features that collectively are not easily found elsewhere in the market: (1) an arbitrage trade similar to a currency carry trade, (2) excess returns over like-rated securities and with better diversification, and (3) low volatility in a non-mark-to-market structure. The counterbalance to these benefits is a lack of liquidity that inhibits the note and subordinated note holders' ability to "exit" or sell their investment.

TABLE 5.1 CLO: 535 Deals; $248,862,768,933 Current Balance

Vintage	Deal Count	WARF*	Curr. Bal. ($ mm)	% Issuers Mapped	% Rated Assets	% Assets Defaulted
1997	1	4,846	62	80.4%	98.6%	
1998	7	3,509	224	80.8%	87.3%	20.8%
1999	5	3,215	574	76.4%	94.4%	14.6%
2000	8	2,435	890	86.0%	86.7%	4.4%
2001	9	2,507	3,070	87.0%	96.2%	1.9%
2002	17	2,455	5,174	90.1%	94.6%	2.1%
2003	31	2,464	10,890	90.5%	89.7%	1.2%
2004	59	2,421	24,514	92.6%	94.2%	1.3%
2005	92	2,413	45,164	87.1%	92.8%	1.2%
2006	151	2,401	74,340	87.2%	94.3%	1.1%
2007	160	2,457	81,960	86.9%	92.5%	0.7%
2008	5	2,340	2,001	89.6%	88.7%	
Total	535	2,432	248,863	87.8%	93.2%	1.1%

Vintage	% Assets Rated Caa1–Ca*	Deals with IC Failures	Deals with OC Failures	% Exposure to Issuers in LCDX†	% Exposure of Cov-Lite Loans†	% Exposure with First-Lien Loans under 80†
1997	69.3%	1	0	0.0%		6.5%
1998	9.0%	5	5	8.7%	5.3%	8.8%
1999	6.8%	2	2	16.8%	6.9%	13.2%
2000	5.7%	2	0	27.4%	4.4%	10.9%
2001	4.2%	0	0	32.7%	13.8%	11.1%
2002	5.1%	1	0	31.3%	15.4%	14.4%
2003	4.1%	0	0	33.5%	18.4%	12.4%
2004	4.1%	0	2	33.0%	18.1%	14.1%
2005	4.6%	1	2	30.7%	19.0%	13.1%
2006	4.5%	0	0	29.6%	19.0%	13.5%
2007	4.7%	0	0	28.8%	22.1%	14.0%
2008	3.3%	0	0	35.6%	20.5%	11.2%
Total	4.6%	12	11	30.1%	19.7%	13.6%

*These calculations only include Moody's rated assets.
†These calculations only include mapped issuers.
Source: Wachovia Capital Markets, LLC, Intex, LoanX, Moody's

The Arbitrage

A CLO's success is dependent on the spread created by the fact that it borrows at a cheaper rate than it lends. For example, borrowing $370 million at LIBOR (London interbank offered rate) plus a spread of 50 basis points (weighted average rate of the notes issued) and then lending that same money out at LIBOR plus 250 basis points (weighted average rate for assets purchased) offers a 200 basis point difference—or spread—on $370 million, which is $7.4 million annually (200 basis points = 2%, and 2% × $370 million = $7.4 million). The CLO should be relatively indifferent to changes in interest rates since it receives LIBOR on its assets and pays LIBOR only on its senior notes. It is important for the manager to maintain the arbitrage since many of the collateral obligations that comprise the portfolio are amortized before the CLO's liabilities mature. Part of the manager's role is to find new leveraged loans that maintain or improve that initial spread between monies borrowed. Maximizing this arbitrage for the longest time period possible is most important for holders of the subordinated notes (equity).

The history of CLO arbitrage since 2000 is well maintained because as risk on the market declined and returns on leveraged loans dropped, the coupons on CLO senior notes shrunk to historic lows. However, in the later half of 2007 and in 2008, the perceived risk in the leveraged loan and structured finance marketplace required a greater premium on the borrowed monies of the CLO. Since the spreads on leveraged loans did not immediately increase to the same degree, the arbitrage between monies borrowed and lent by the CLO became too narrow to justify investment in subordinated notes, which provided the all-important excess capital to the CLO. Consequently, CLO issuance severely dropped in volume.

Low Volatility

A cash flow CLO is not marked-to-market, which means the value of the CLO's collateral obligations is not adjusted to reflect current market prices. As a result, for the purposes of monitoring the transaction and testing compliance with the rules that protect the CLO's rated debt, the underlying portfolio of leveraged loans is generally assumed to be worth par during the life of the CLO unless there is a default in the underlying collateral or an excess of CCC-rated assets. The premise behind this principle is simple: the CLO is meant to be a static arbitrage or a buy-and-hold strategy on a portfolio of leveraged loans that are not intended to be traded for gains but held for their interest-paying cash flow. As long as the leveraged loan pays its interest, the market price of the loan does not affect the vehicle. An asset sold at a loss, however, does degrade the overall par value of the portfolio.

Structure

A CLO is a securitization of bank loans into a special-purpose corporation with three parts: assets purchased, liabilities borrowed to buy the assets, and excess interest, which is sometimes used to buy more assets and provide additional subordination to the liabilities. A CLO corporate entity often has two parts: a tax-free offshore vehicle and a Delaware corporation. The offshore vehicle is often registered in the Cayman Islands and titled "CLO Ltd." Its sole purpose is to acquire the collateral obligations in a tax-free manner. The U.S.-registered entity is often registered in the state of Delaware as a special-purpose company and is given the title "CLO Corp." It exists to issue CLO liabilities to certain investors that require their securities to be issues from U.S. corporations for tax and/or investment reasons. Together the Ltd. and Corp. are called the coissuers and effectively act as one for the purpose of this chapter. The coissuers are set up to have a corporate life typically ranging from 8 to 15 years.

A CLO's liabilities, or notes, are *tranched* (French word for "sliced") into a series of four or five separate notes, each having a different priority of payment. This tranching and prioritizing allow the notes to have different ratings from those provided by the rating agencies.

Following the principles of the capital asset pricing model and risk and return, the higher the rating, the lower the return or "spread" over a floating benchmark called LIBOR.

Figure 5.1 depicts the assets of the CLO on the left, which sends cash flow to pay for the interest on the money borrowed.

FIGURE 5.1 CLO Assets Produce Varying Cash Flows According to the Rating of the Assets.

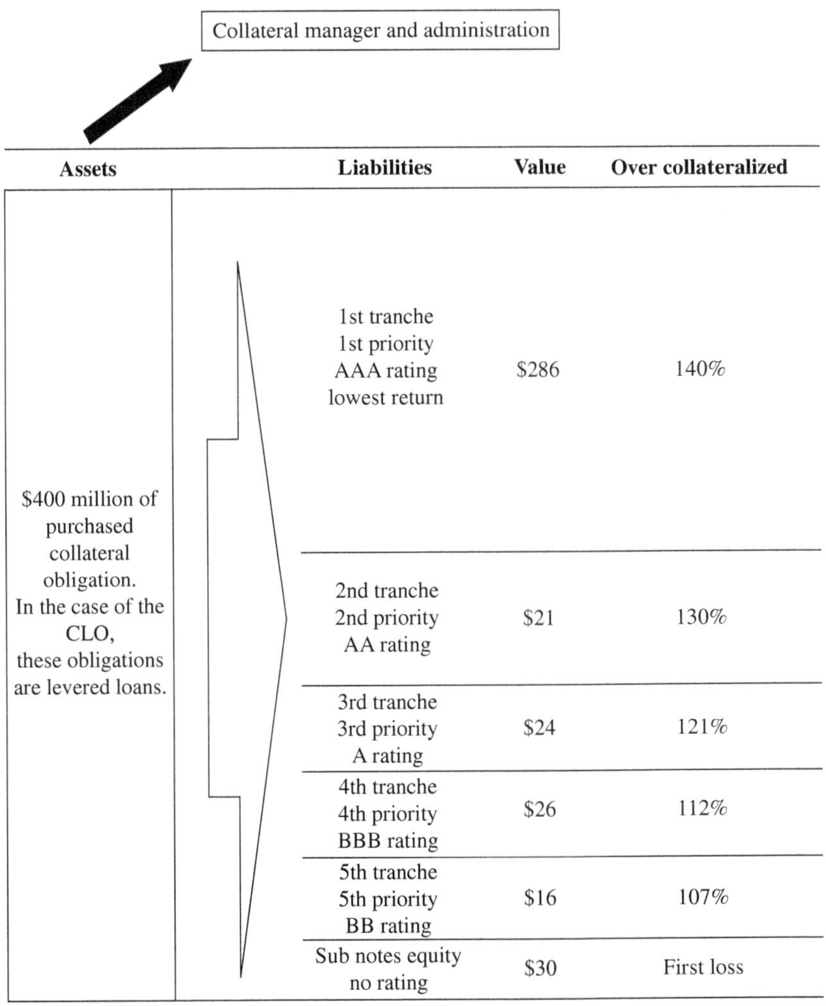

Match Funding and Arbitrage

CLOs are attractive because of their "match funding" structure, which means that the cost of liabilities and the return on assets move in the same direction and magnitude. Both notes and collateral obligations are priced in terms of a spread—or excess return—over LIBOR, which, when brought together in the CLO, offset or "match" each other.

The long-term matched funding element allows for an arbitrage to be set up, and it is the subnote capital provided that creates a "cushion" of portfolio losses that are away from the notes. The large cushion—also referred to as overcollateralization—protecting the most senior notes allows them to be rated AAA and therefore to be priced at a very low spread. AAA notes make up approximately 70% of the CLO's capital structure, so their low spread price is a large driver for the weighted average cost of debt, which should be lower than the spreads on the collateral obligations to maintain the transaction's arbitrage. The economic payoff of the three main parts of the CLO is detailed in Table 5.2.

TABLE 5.2 Economic Payoff of the Three Main Parts of the CLO

	Description	Amount	Economic Interest
Uses of cash	Assets (Collateral obligations = leveraged bank loans)	$400*	Receives L† + 300 bps‡
Sources of cash	Liability: Notes	$370	CLO pays out weighted average cost of debt of L + 100 bps
	Liability: Subordinated notes	$30	CLO pays out what is left over + [$400 * (L + 300 bps)] – ($370 * L + 100 bps) – fees ÷ [$370 * 200 bps + ($30 * L + 300 bps) – fees]
	Total	$400	

* All dollar amounts in millions.
† L = LIBOR.
‡ bps = basis points.

The Assets (Collateral Obligation = Leveraged Loans)

The CLO assets are high-yield, below-investment-grade leveraged bank loans. Leveraged loans are floating rate first- and second-priority corporate bank loans arranged by banks, and they typically earn a spread over LIBOR of between 175 and 400 basis points and are syndicated to institutional investors. Because these leveraged loans are privately arranged by banks, they are not public securities, so they are not traded over an exchange the way stocks are. Rather they are quoted by brokers to qualified institutional buyers (QIBs), investors with $100 million in assets under their management.

Leveraged loans are the "sweet spot" for CDO collateral obligations because they possess three elements: (1) enough yield for the arbitrage, (2) senior claim on company assets, which helps minimize losses and volatility, and (3) the floating rate interest, which helps to reduce broader interest-rate volatility.

First, the high-yielding floating rate on leveraged loans makes them ideal for CLOs because other, less risky securities do not offer enough yield to make the arbitrage spread possible. For example, the lower-risk investment-grade bank loans come much cheaper, at L + 50 and would not make the arbitrage possible, which typically requires a difference between assets and liabilities of 200 basis points to support the subordinated notes return hurdle of 14% to –20%.

Second, the senior claim provided in leveraged loans helps to reduce potential future losses incurred by the CLO if an underlying issuer defaults. When a company issues leveraged loans, it is typically the most senior obligation the company has and means that the leveraged loan receives first claim at the assets of a company if it defaults.

The institutional nature of the leveraged loan market helps to limit the number of active investors in the market, which reduces the trading volatility. Leveraged loans cannot be directly shorted like a bond or stock, which further reduces the trading volatility. Note that an LCDS could be sold to mirror a sale. While volatility is not a day-to-day concern for the CLO, it does reduce the ability to trade out of positions or improve the portfolio.

The Assets (Collateral Obligation = Other Assets)

While the pool of leveraged loans is the majority of the CLO collateral, other assets may be purchased such as second-lien leveraged loans and high-yield bonds. Most CLOs have a minimum threshold requiring that 90% of the collateral must be first-lien leveraged loans, leaving the other 10% up to the discretion of the manager. Purchasing high-yield bonds and second-lien loans provides more diversity, more yield, and in some cases a fixed coupon against a shrinking LIBOR. However, these non-first-lien securities also possess more risk for higher default and lower recovery, so their use must be tempered within the broader portfolio context.

Maturity/Average Life

CLOs typically have a long maturity of "life," between 12 and 16 years, and have three phases. The first phase is the ramp-up period, which is the first four to ten months, when collateral is purchased on the underwriter's balance sheet and the deal is marketed to potential investors. The second phase takes place after the deal closes or is sold to investors and is off the underwriter's balance sheet. This is called the reinvestment period. During this phase, proceeds from leveraged loans that repay (or mature) are reinvested in new loans. This phase is about half the stated life of the CLO. The third phase is the wind-down period, when proceeds from repaid leverage loans are used to deleverage, or buy back debt the CLO has issued, starting with the AAA tranche. The length of this phase is hard to predict because of the uncertainty of when loans may be repaid (loans have the ability to be repaid before maturity without penalty, and many are).

The Liabilities (Notes)

The CLO liabilities, or notes, are issued by the CLO issuer or coissuer, and the proceeds are used to purchase leveraged loans. The CLO notes are similar to a general corporate obligation in that they have rights through covenants, receive periodic interest, take first priority over the equity owners, and have a stated maturity. In addition, CLO notes generally receive at least one (and often two) ratings from nationally recognized rating agencies that apply specialized CLO stress criteria to the notes in evaluating their probability of repayment. Most CLOs will have a stated maturity of 12 to 14 years (less often up to 16 years), but the notes begin to get paid down (starting with the most senior class first) after 6 or 7 years and may retire all notes by the eighth year. The length of time is important to the most junior part of the capital structure, the subordinated notes, because time helps the subordinated notes recoup monies used to start the deal and offset any early losses. This is covered in greater detail in the pages that follow, where we discuss subordinated notes.

While investors in the CLO notes will look at a variety of issues, most focus on two key items: the relative value and the covenants. Relative value is dictated by two components: other similarly rated securities' yields in the marketplace and a junior or senior tranche. For example, if a new AAA CLO tranche was recently issued at LIBOR + 25 basis points and a new AAA tranche was being sold a week later, then the L + 25 of the previous issue would be the starting point. Basis points would be added or subtracted to the previous L + 25 based on (1) changes in the market, (2) structural differences, and (3) the collateral manager. Over several years the pricing can move quite a bit based on changes in the economy and market. Table 5.3 shows a representative sample.

It is sometimes possible to insure the most senior tranche against a loss of principal and interest; this is referred to as "wrapping" the AAA tranche. When the AAA tranche is wrapped, a bond insurance

TABLE 5.3 Pricing Quality Differential

Hypothetical Pricing Scenario		
Economy CLO Demand	**Good CLO Strong**	**Poor CLO Weak**
AAA L+	23 bps	150 bps
AA L+	45 bps	425 bps
A L+	70 bps	550 bps
BBB L+	170 bps	600 bps
BB L+	370 bps	800 bps

company like Assured Guaranty, MBIA, FSA, and others will charge the purchaser a fee, perhaps 25% of the spread, for protection.

The covenants are the other key aspect of the notes and are important because they both govern the portfolio actions composition of the portfolio and provide rights to the note holders, such as the right to remove the collateral manager. The covenants can be broken into three types of tests: (1) portfolio profile tests, (2) collateral quality tests, and (3) coverage tests. These test groups are tiered such that each group's respective tests analyze more severe parameters of the portfolio, as summarized by Table 5.4.

The portfolio profile tests focus on the broader market characteristics of the portfolio, requires little or no calculation, and entails simply putting the portfolio into different market "buckets." The goal is to assess the risk of the portfolio a year out, such as exposure to a certain economic region or type of security. These tests can be considered "soft tests" because a test "failure" does not require immediate action to pass the violation. It does restrict future trades in that any future trades must improve the failed test.

Portfolio profile tests measure:

1. Domicile of collateral
2. Delayed drawdown collateral obligations
3. Revolving collateral obligations

TABLE 5.4 Covenant Summary

Test Descriptions	Tests Type	Purpose	Action
Portfolio profile tests	Maximum exposure of the portfolio's composition, expressed as a percentage of the portfolio's value, which may differ for non-U.S. issuing countries or different asset classes, or different types of coupons, or a percentage of CCC-rated securities.	Gauge the broader risk parameters related to macro issues	Trading must bring test levels back into compliance
Collateral quality tests	Calculate quality and return metrics such as weighted average rating and spread over LIBOR	Gauge the rating quality and return capability of the portfolio	Trading must maintain or improve test levels
Coverage tests	Calculate the amount of excess capital in the portfolio	Gauge the amount of asset protection the portfolio has	Interest to sub note holders may be diverted to purchase more collateral obligations or to pay down the CLO liabilities. This can significantly alter the IRR of the sub notes

4. Moody's counterpart criteria
5. Senior/junior loan amounts
6. Fixed-rate test
7. Participation interest
8. Deferrable securities
9. Obligor test
10. CCC or Caa1 test

The collateral quality tests seek to calculate and measure deeper risk metrics such as average rating or spread over LIBOR. These tests are important for the note holders because they ascertain if the portfolio is on track to make payments in the coming year. Of these the weighted average rating factor (WARF), weighted average spread (WAS), and Moody's diversity tests are of particular note because collectively they create a key constraint of quality and return that the CLO must operate within.

WARF is calculated using a point system for each leveraged loan in the collateral obligation pool; the lower the rating, the higher the point. The goal is to have as low a WARF as possible. The WARF is not a simple averaging; there are some adjustments made based on an issuer's capital structure (e.g., small amount of bank debt relative to cap structure). The WAS is a weighted averaging of the spread over LIBOR of the loans in the portfolio, and the goal is to achieve as high a WAS as possible. The diversity test is calculated with a point system which gives the issuer within each industry a point based on its historical default performance and rewards the manager on how well the portfolio is spread over the industries; here the goal is the higher, the better.

Collateral quality tests measure:

1. Minimum coupon test
2. Weighted average spread (WAS)
3. Weighted average rating factor (WARF)
4. Moody's diversity test
5. S&P CDO monitor test

The coverage tests are the strictest because they measure two critical near-term elements: the portfolio's ability to pay its obligations currently and in the near future and the amount of excess cushion in the capital structure to protect the notes.

The collateral quality and coverage tests require that action be taken to rectify the failure, and as a result these are considered "hard tests." Some CLOs may have provisions that divert cash flow from the equity holders to buy more assets to offset losses should a cushion threshold be breached.

Coverage tests measure:

1. Overcollateralization ration
    - CCC/Caa basket
        - Haircut above 7.5% at market value
    - Discount obligations
    - Default and deferred obligation at recovery rate and "0" after three years
2. Interest coverage ratio

Liabilities (Subordinated Notes or Equity)

- Income
    - Performance assets
        - (LIBOR + spread of portfolio) × collateral obligations
    - Nonperforming assets
        - Cash × Fed funds rate
- Expenses
    - Liabilities
        - Average cost of debt × liabilities
    - Management fees
    - Administrative fees: trustee, rating agencies, and board
    - Loss of assets
        - Defaulted securities
- Realized loss on securities sold at loss

The most junior part of the capital structure is the subordinated notes, and it is commonly known as the "equity" in a CLO because, like a true equity investor in a company, it is the last to get paid earnings, first to realize losses, and last to get repaid its initial capital. Since the equity investor has the most risk and expects the most return, it will therefore do a lot of analysis on an array of factors, which include: (1) modeling the deal, (2) assessing the manager, and (3) analyzing the market.

Modeling the deal involves modeling potential returns to the subordinated notes over the projected life of the deal. Some of the things that need to be considered are projected LIBOR, initial and projected average spread of collateral obligations over LIBOR, and management and administrative fees as well as any realized losses (from defaults or trades) to the collateral obligations that support the liabilities.

The excess income over expenses is distributed to the subordinated note holders on a quarterly basis, which creates an internal rate of return. Typical IRRs for CLOs can range from 12% in strong markets to 23% in weak markets.

An important part of modeling CLO returns is what will be the assumed loss of PAR. This is because as the first loss tranche, the returns of the subordinated notes are most sensitive to losses of collateral obligation which are caused by either realizing a trading loss (selling a loan for less than it was bought) or incurring a default which causes the CLO to realize a loss on the defaulted security. The annual loss, either from realized losses or defaults is measured by the constant default rate (CDR), which assumes a percentage default rate and a recovery. For example, a 2% CDR means that 2% of a $400 million collateral obligation pool will default each year, or lose $8 million. The model will further assume that there will be a recovery on those defaulted assets when the bankruptcy process is completed—this recovery assumption can be set, for example, at 80%. This results in 20% of the $8 million being lost each year, and this amount will not be recovered. In the case above, the amount would be $1.6 million.

FIGURE 5.2 Effect of High and Low LIBOR on the Assets and Liabilities of CLOs

High LIBOR				Low LIBOR			
Assets		Liabilities		Assets		Liabilities	
Amount	$400	Amount	$370	Amount	$400	Amount	$370
Spread (bps)	250	Spread (bps)	50	Spread (bps)	250	Spread (bps)	50
LIBOR	5.00%	LIBOR	5.00%	LIBOR	2.00%	LIBOR	2.00%
Total	7.50%	Total	5.50%	Total	4.50%	Total	2.50%
		Expense	**($20.35)**			Expense	**($9.25)**
		Fees	**($2.16)**			Fees	**($2.16)**
Income	$30.00	Total	**($22.51)**	Income	$18.00	Total	**($11.41)**

Return to equity $7.49 ⟷ Return to equity $6.59

Another thing to consider when modeling is the movement in LIBOR over the life of the CLO, as illustrated by Figure 5.2. CLO subordinated notes are sensitive to moves in LIBOR because the overcollateralization or subordinated notes, which do not receive fixed payments, earn a return on LIBOR.

The last major component to consider when modeling a CLO is the movement in the spread over LIBOR of the collateral obligation, or WAS. See Figure 5.3. The WAS moves over time as the underlying loans of the collateral obligations pay off or get sold and new loans are

FIGURE 5.3 Effect of Low and High Spreads over LIBOR on Assets and Liabilities of CLOs

Low SPREAD				High SPREAD			
Assets		Liabilities		Assets		Liabilities	
Amount	$400	Amount	$370	Amount	$400	Amount	$370
Spread (bps)	250	Spread (bps)	50	Spread (bps)	500	Spread (bps)	50
LIBOR	5.00%	LIBOR	5.00%	LIBOR	5.00%	LIBOR	5.00%
Total	7.50%	Total	5.50%	Total	10.00%	Total	5.50%
		Expense	**($20.35)**			Expense	**($20.35)**
		Fees	**($2.16)**			Fees	**($2.16)**
Income	$30.00	Total	**($22.51)**	Income	$40.00	Total	**($22.51)**

Return to equity $7.49 ⟷ Return to equity $17.49

purchased at different spreads. Increasing spread over time can have a dramatic effect on the subordinated notes' IRR. For example a doubling of the spread over LIBOR of the collateral obligations can have a 2.4 times impact on the subordinated notes proceeds distribution.

What truly differentiates one CLO from another is the collateral manager, whose role is to manage the assets day to day within the covenants, minimize the losses, maintain quality, and possibly increase spread over LIBOR on the assets. The collateral manager also provides input during the structuring process, providing input on covenants that protect the notes and subordinated notes but also providing enough trading flexibility. When assessing the manager, there are four main criteria the subordinated note holders focus on: (1) stability and reputation of the manager, (2) the manager's ability to assess individual credits, (3) the experience of the manager in a downturn, and (4) infrastructure and history in managing structured products.

The quality of the collateral manager's broader investment company is important to the long-term stability and viability of the CLO. It is important to look at how long the investment firm has been in business, if it is growing, or if it has been shrinking in the number of people working for it or in assets. It is important to know if the investment manager is part of a larger broker-dealer or a private equity firm which may cause a conflict of interest, whereas an independent investment company is free to play all origins of deals. Another very important area of consideration is the back office or trade processing and corporate actions group and whether the investment manager has the ability to promptly and accurately process trades and capitalize on consents and tenders.

The ability to assess credits is important for safeguarding the quality of the portfolio, and managers provide alpha if they can. Alpha can be gained by rooting out credit problems before they are reflected in the price or rating. This can be achieved by having a collateral manager who has a deep and experienced team of analysts that focuses on leveraged companies. These analysts should have in-depth knowledge of each company they cover, a relationship with the management of those companies, and a detailed financial model of the companies' profits and losses specifically focused on the cash flow generation and debt repayment ability of an investment.

Another important category to assess is the collateral manager's experience in a credit downturn. Specifically, does the collateral manager focus on execution during times of illiquidity, and does the manager have relationships with top-tier trading desks on Wall Street?

A manager's ability to operate within the constraints of a structured product is a helpful predictor of how a manager will do in tough times. Many managers' historical strength may come from their ability to trade with great flexibility. But when they are put into a constrained situation requiring hypothetical modeling, they seize up with analysis paralysis. As discussed in the covenant section, CLO constraints range from limits on buckets to requiring average rating or spread, and a manager must take all these into consideration before a trade is executed. Managers should have a computer modeling system that provides them with the tools to hypothetically see how and why the portfolio compares to its test threshold after a potential trade takes place.

The last major category to consider when assessing the collateral manager is the health of the economy, financial market, CLO market, and leveraged loan market. The strength of the economy drives the overall credit market, which in turn drives the CLO and loan markets. In addition, individual idiosyncrasies within CLOs or loans, such as trade processing rules, can cause a market to trade off.

Primary and Secondary Markets

The CLO market has grown from its infancy in 1997 to become a critical part of the fixed-income market. Structured finance vehicles took flight in the early 1990s with the collateral bond obligations or CBOs that were developed by now defunct Drexel Burnham Lambert as a way to create more demand for high-yield bonds in the 1980s. The CLO was an offshoot that offered a less risky, lower-return vehicle. But as the CBOs began to mature, two flaws became evident that CLOs overcame: low-default recovery values and fixed-rate debt. CBOs had trouble matching their floating-rate liabilities with the fixed-rate coupon of the bonds, and even though swaps were used, they could not effectively match the assets and liabilities as well as a CLO. Additionally, the CBOs had assumed a default rate that was lower than realized and a default recovery rate that was higher than realized. In 2001–2002 these structural deficiencies caused CBO notes and subordinated notes to be impaired far beyond previous cycles and effectively shut down the CBO market.

Even though CLOs offered long-term average IRRs in the mid-teens compared to the CBOs in the low twenties, the certainty of getting the CLO IRR was much greater and therefore helped to propel the CLOs to be used more.

Who Invests

Table 5.5 outlines and compares the different ways to buy loans.

The subordinated note holders are one of two types of institutional investors: the first type is large insurance companies and banks, and the second is hedge funds. The banks and insurance companies like the leveraged loan market because it has been a less volatile asset class with stable positive return. As they look to increase their exposure to the asset class through leverage, the CLO is a natural fit.

TABLE 5.5 Comparing Different Ways to Buy Loans

	Buy Leveraged Loan	Buy Leveraged Loan Portfolio	Buy Subnote in CLO
Historical return over 10 years after fees	5.0%	4.5%	18%
Leverage	0	0	13×
Diversified	No	Yes	Yes
Protective portfolio measures in place	No	No	Yes

The other subordinated note investor group is the hedge fund community, which enjoys the higher potential returns. Often hedge funds aggregate various subordinated note positions into one large fund of subordinated notes tranches which may also employ leverage. These hedge funds are typically the holders of some of the mezzanine—or BB, BBB—tranches. The more senior tranches are held by banks which are seeking to invest their reserves in slightly higher-yielding AAA, AA, and A tranches than can be found in the corporate market.

Organization or Primary Process

The process of creating a CLO is called the origination process, and the market it is sold into is called the primary market. The governing law for most CLOs is either in the United States or Europe. In the United States the CLO's notes are privately placed with qualified purchasers under exemptions to the Securities Act, the Investment Company Act of 1940. This means that the notes are issued by the CLO's U.S. corporation without being registered with a government agency, such as the Securities and Exchange Commission, and do not afford the notes with the protection typical of public securities. It further means that the qualified purchasers must rely on their own expertise and due diligence process to analyze the notes.

Privately placed securities are typically created and distributed through a registered broker-dealer. The investment banking division of the broker-dealer will have a dedicated team of investment bankers that is experienced in structuring and syndicating the CLO and that is in charge of managing the organization process.

The CLO's notes are syndicated, or sold, to selected qualified purchasers around the globe through the syndication process, called the "roadshow." The roadshow usually involves a private meeting of 4 to 10 people and includes representatives of the collateral manager and the investment bank, who make a sales pitch to representatives of the buyer of each tranche. (See Figure 5.4 and Table 5.6.)

FIGURE 5.4 Flowchart Illustrating the Steps in the Syndication Process, or "Roadshow"

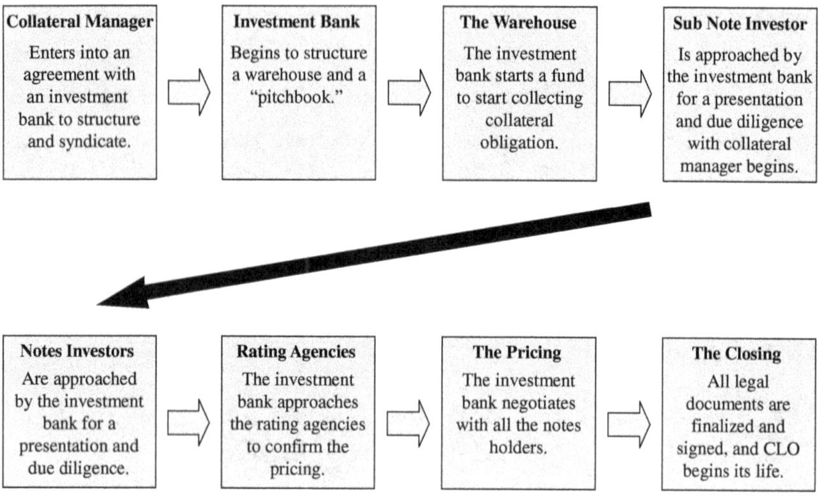

Warehousing and Hedging

Warehousing and hedging are a small but important part of the underwriting process. In bull issuance markets the underwriter will directly "warehouse," or collect, the leveraged loans, which means the broker-dealer will purchase leveraged loans at the direction of the collateral managers on behalf of the future CLO. Having a warehouse of collateral obligations

TABLE 5.6 Trough to Peak Issuance of All CLOs (Cash Flow, Market, and Synthetic)

	Early Year 2001	Peak Year 2007	Year to Date 6/30/08
New number of CLOs	32	171	33
Total number of CLOs	824	1,435	1,468
New money for CLOs	$14.42 BN*	$93.86 BN	$17.93 BN
Total dollar size of CLOs	$96.69 BN	$399.00 BN	$416.94 BN

*BN = billion.
Source: Intex, Bloomberg

(loans in the case of a CLO) already purchased before the notes or subordinated notes are sold allows the pricing and closing of the CLO to take place much faster. Potential investors can "see" how the portfolio is being constructed, and, in certain cases, a warehouse of settled collateral can start to provide income to investors as soon as the transaction closes, although most times the income is reserved for the senior lender's risk book.

In a bull market, the warehouse is purchased on the underwriter's balance sheet which means that the broader broker-dealer's treasury department lends the money to the CDO desk to purchase loans on behalf of the collateral manager. The CDO desk will earn a spread between what it borrows from its treasury department and what it receives for the loans. This profit can be kept on the desk or shared with potential note or subordinated notes investors.

If a CDO desk has numerous warehouses for several pending CLO deals, the CDO desk may want to hedge its risk. Before the spring of 2007, a CDO desk had limited options for hedging its warehouse risk, such as short a comparable asset class liquid index like high-yield bonds, or it could write protection through an LCDS on individual leveraged loans. Either choice was not optimal because either correlation was not ideal, as with bonds, or there were not enough securities, such as LCDSs. When the LCDX index (a broad array of LCDSs mirroring the leveraged loan market) was created on May 22, 2007, it allowed CDO desks to short the leveraged loan market and offset its long risk in the warehouse and thus reduce the broker-dealer's exposure to the capital markets and focus on making a profit on services.

Secondary Process and Investors

CLO notes and subordinated notes can trade from one party to another in a way similar to traditional bond and equity securities. The difference with CLO notes is that they must be sold to qualified purchasers, which means that the notes trade privately and indicate that there is no organized exchange, only the market (or quotes) made by secondary trading desks, usually affiliated with broker-dealers' CDO desks. Quotes on CLO tranches are transmitted directly to qualified buyers known to the secondary desk over Bloomberg or by telephone calls and are only indications of where trades may take place. There is no official public record for historical CLO trades available. In the past few years, the secondary market has played an increasingly important role in the CLO origination process because a new purchaser of a tranche will assess a broker-dealer's ability to "make a market" in a tranche and thus allow the initial buyer the "liquidity" or possibility of selling the debt should it want to in the future.

Management and Analysis

At the heart of any successful CLO is a strong and capable collateral manager who is hired by the CLO investment corporation to manage the portfolio day to day.

The Role of the Collateral Manager

The portfolio manager's responsibilities have two main components: managing the portfolio and managing the structure because unlike a separate account long-only fund, the CLO has a series of constraints that must be taken into consideration every day. These constraints, or covenants, must be managed for the near term and the long term, which can create an added unintended consequence.

In theory, a CLO is "lightly managed." For example, if a manager were to purchase 75–100 credits that never defaulted, been prepaid, or had a rating change, then there would be little for the manager to do except manage the quarterly distribution. In reality, loan ratings change, which forces action, and companies default, which results in action. These realities cause the CLO to be managed around these potential future obstacles.

Managing the Portfolio

The first phase of constructing the initial portfolio is important because it is difficult to trade out of a bad portfolio, especially a CLO. When choosing the initial leveraged loans, collateral managers must put fundamental credit analysis at the heart of the their investment process, which is achieved by having a culture of bottom-up credit analysis married to a deep team of research professionals trained to carry out the analysis. Bottom-up credit analysis goes beyond reading the underwriter-provided "bank book" to include a thorough vetting of the business model in the context of the economic outlook, a stress test of cash-flow generation in various scenarios, a detailed accounting of the cash flow, and a legal review of the leveraged loan covenants. Perhaps the most important bottom-up component in the process is a credit committee which is a peer review of completed research work that debates the pros and cons in an effort to tease out details and scenarios to make sure the credit is a strong survivor.

The second phase, managing the ongoing CLO portfolio, requires credit discipline to sell credit problems early before a loss could be incurred. For example, spotting potential credit impairments ahead of the market and selling at or near PAR is a collateral manager skill that will lead to better-than-average performance of the CLO. Early detection is possible with a deep and experienced investment team that monitors investments and anticipates events by continually speaking with managers. It should also have insightful industry knowledge.

Managing the Structure

CLOs have long-term constraints in the form of covenants that the portfolio of collateral obligations must adhere to; this is addressed above in the covenant section. The impact these covenants have on the decision made in a portfolio is present every day. Although the daily decision may not trigger a test violation, each trade has the potential to move the portfolio toward a violation six months, nine months, or a year out. With two dozen tests, the collateral manager must perform hypothetical portfolio analysis, often called a "hypo trade," to determine what might happen to the portfolio in the future. Therefore a handful of trades, each causing its own ripple effect in the portfolio, require a computer program to oversee the outcomes. There is a variety of software tools that help manage CLO portfolios, and many will perform the analytical outcome from hypo trades.

One of the key sets of tests the collateral manager will watch is the WARF, WAS, and diversity test, which together make up a matrix (see the discussion in the covenant section). The collateral manager will seek to balance a particular trade so that it best moves the portfolio within these three tests. For example, a portfolio manager may decide to make a trade that improves the WARF by 5%, but the trade hurts the WAS by 1%. The next trade hurts the WARF by 1% but helps the WAS by 6%. In isolation each trade is not ideal because it moves the portfolio closer toward a violation, but together they improve the portfolio. This is but a small example of the types of input collateral managers must consider in their decisions because there are over two dozen tests and hundreds of impacts to consider.

Strategies

Given the two portfolio management components, portfolio and structure, there is a series of strategies collateral managers have historically considered:

1. *First, build in a principal cushion of realized gains on collateral obligation to offset potential future losses.* Should no future losses be incurred, then the excess realized gain would go to the equity after all the debt has been retired.
2. *Second, avoid losses before they get worse but hold if the portfolio will recover back to PAR.* Selling out of a leveraged loan before it defaults can save the CLO. However, realizing a loss on a name that eventually recovers hurts the portfolio

when it should not have (assuming its rating stayed the same). Therefore, the manager must have excellent credit skills to differentiate between a technical price decline that will recover and a fundamental price decline that will get and stay worse.

3. *Third, build in other test cushions to provide more flexibility to a portfolio in lean years.* For example, if two leveraged loans trade at the same price, have the same spread over LIBOR and maturity, and are in the same industry but one is rated higher than the other, then swapping from the lower- to the higher-rated leveraged loan will improve the WARF while keeping all else constant. Seeking these types of CLO-improving trades requires daily flows on the market.

Analysis of a CLO

Analysis of a CLO is done by two distinct groups: the rated note holders and the unrated subordinated note holders. The subordinated note holders, also called the equity, receive the first loss, the most risk, and the most return through excess monies received from the underlying collateral obligations after all debt and expenses are paid. The subordinated note holders are incentivized if the CLO takes more risk, up to the point that it incurs too many losses, so their focus is on return characteristics of the portfolio and flexibility of the structure. Contrasted are the note holders, who focus on preservation of the capital of the collateral obligation, so their focus is on the quality of the portfolio and the restrictions of the structure.

Note Holders

The note holders, which are the rated liabilities and typically represent the top 92% of the liabilities, want the underlying loans of the collateral obligations to be of the highest quality, and they want those assets to stay that way. The note holders will drill down to three key areas of analysis when considering purchasing a CLO liability: portfolio quality, manager quality, and structure strength.

From the note holders' perspective, the ideal portfolio will be well diversified, investing in as many different industries as possible, and have a WARF that is low. A low-yielding, well-diversified conservative portfolio of only first-lien loans would be ideal for note holders because it minimizes volatility as well as the chance for losses in a credit downturn. The note holders may look at the warehouse portfolio and stress test it based on certain loss assumptions. Their goal is to make sure that the portfolio survives their worst-case scenario with a cushion. The note holders also analyze the collateral manager to determine if they have a history of style drift which is a change in the way they manage money. They will also analyze the collateral manager's resources to make sure that the manager has the right people and systems to anticipate, strategize, and take action when there are changes in the market.

The last CLO specific issue the note holders will look at is the deal structure and covenants to make sure that the covenants are restrictive enough to prevent the collateral manager from taking risks that could jeopardize the quality of the portfolio. For example, note holders would want WARF tests set low and diversity tests set high to encourage the manager to stay in higher-quality loans and be diverse. They may also want to limit the non-first-lien basket to be small in order to minimize losses from riskier assets.

The note holders also analyze two other issues that are not part of a specific CLO: outlook on the CLO and leveraged loan markets and broader market volatility. It is important that the outlook for leveraged loans be strong because the portfolio of collateral obligations will require replenishment with new leveraged loans as initial ones get paid off. If the outlook for leveraged loans is for lower-quality deals to come at higher spreads, then there is a risk that the underlying portfolio will slip in quality and incur more default. Similarly if the outlook for the CLO is poor, then there is a risk that the market value of the note holders' tranche will erode as the CLO market sells off. Another broader risk is market volatility. Although a CLO is not marked-to-market, it cannot be blind to market movements which can change the relative value of the CLO. For example, when the leveraged loan market saw an 11% decline in quoted prices, the liquidity for CLO secondary trades withered as many investors shied away from a market they perceived to be in turmoil.

Subordinated Note Holders

The subordinated note holders have a different set of objectives from the note holders. Like the note holders, the subordinated note holders want the underlying capital to be preserved so that the value of their notes, which are first in line to realize a loss in value from realized portfolio losses, is preserved. However, because the subordinated note holders earn a return on the residual excess value after funding the liabilities, they want more return on the underlying collateral, and with this comes more risk. Therefore, the subordinated note holders seek to optimize the portfolio to meet all the risk tests with a cushion while also maximizing return, or spread, over LIBOR.

When analyzing an investment into the subordinated notes, investors will look at four things. First, they want to know that the collateral managers' interest is aligned with theirs, perhaps through a partial ownership of the subordinated notes. This assures investors that the manager's economic interest is focused on a shared incentive to maximize income while preserving credit quality, rather than simply seeking safe but low-yielding investments in order to preserve their management fee stream. Second, an investor wants to see that the portfolio has the right balance of return and risk because, while investing in a manager that is extremely conservative might mean that your return is more certain, the level of that return might be very low. Subordinated note holders typically look for an internal rate of return in the mid to high teens over the average seven-year life of the portfolio, and to get this the portfolio must seek spreads over LIBOR that are 200–250 basis points more than the cost of funding. Ideally the collateral manager should have a history of optimizing trading strategies to increase the IRR (either to avoid losses and/or to increase the WAS).

Third, similar to the note holders, the subordinated note investor will want to see that collateral managers have the ability to provide alpha as witnessed through (1) their track record during tough credit environments, (2) their loss avoidance record, which is the collateral manager's ability to spot credit problems before they are reflected in the prices of collateral obligations, and the (3) collateral managers' dedicated resources to the CLO. Fourth, subordinated note investors want to see that the CLO structure has enough flexibility for the collateral manager to reach for some higher-yielding leveraged loans that could improve the IRR.

Service Providers

All investors in the CLO will want to analyze the service parties involved, such as the trustee who settles the trades, monitors the portfolio, and sends the reports out, and the auditing firm to make sure it has experience with CLOs. Poor reporting or auditing can lead to misinformation and inability to fix any early and minor portfolio problems before they become large.

Future of CLOs

The CLO as a product category has grown from an afterthought of the CBO market to become an anchor component of the CDO universe, growing from $62 million in its first year of existence in 1997 to $248 billion in 2008. The dramatic growth of CLOs has been the result of regulatory changes in the Basel II/IRB accords, which effectively encouraged banks to offload risk in the form of securitization rather than hold it on their books. Simultaneously, investors found the highly rated, higher-spread notes an attractive way to boost capital returns. The effect of strong CLO growth has been to spur the growth of leveraged loans. As CLOs pulled more leveraged loans out of the system, spreads tightened and LBO sponsors found the financing vehicle very attractive for takeovers. As the LBO sponsor brought more deals, more CLOs could be created, which in turn brought more managers to the CLO space which created a CLO platform business model.

So after the creation of first loan credit default swaps (LCDSs), a form of purchasing insurance against a default, the index of LCDSs called the LCDX was formed and allowed market participants a vehicle to short or bet against leveraged loans for the first time. As banks used the LCDX to hedge warehouses and hedge funds used them to make bets on the market, the LCDX began to drop almost as soon as it was created. The drop in the LCDX caused the underlying LCDSs to drop, and in turn the leveraged loans decreased in value. As the prices on the leveraged loans fell, the value of the warehouses, which were owned by the broker-dealers on behalf of CLOs not yet sold, began to fall. This put pressure on their overall balance sheet. To solve this balance sheet problem the broker-dealers (some of which were banks) acted to avoid further losses and sold the underlying leveraged loan collateral in the warehouses at a loss.

This put further negative pressure on the prices of leveraged loans, since there were many more sellers than buyers. It also discouraged the new issuance of leveraged loans, since the cost to finance with a leveraged loan was so high that it did not become attractive to LBOs, the main creator of leveraged loans. Additional selling pressure came from market value CLOs and other leveraged vehicles that invested in loans as price drops triggered margin calls. These pricing and market pressures caused the prices of existing CLO notes to fall because their underlying assets were leveraged loans and caused CLO new issuance prices to be so high that the arbitrage was no longer attractive to the risk part of the CLO capital structure.

The extreme economic volatility of 2007 and 2008 was unexpected and unprecedented, and this has caused many investors in CLOs to question the viability of the asset class. What drives a CLO's (cash flow) success is not price movement; it is defaults. If price movements are reflective of future expected defaults, then a decline in the price of the CLO notes is justified. But if the price decline is caused by technicals in the broader market, then there are buying opportunities.

The future of the CLO market will rest on two factors over the coming few years: the magnitude of defaults and the extent of recovery from defaults. Should defaults for leveraged loans materialize as expected—at only about 2%—and should the recovery be as expected—about 80%—then the CLO market will effectively be battle-tested during a credit crisis and proven to withstand it, as initially expected.

Post–Financial Crisis Update:

Despite widespread fears of massive defaults of CLOs and secondary prices well below their underlying collateral values, the actual performance of the asset class held up fairly well during the 2008–2009 financial and economic crisis. In fact, as of January 31, 2010, according to Wells Fargo Securities, LLC, there have been no defaults in the conventional senses. Several nonstandard vehicles, such as CLOs whose collateral was other CLO notes (called CLO-squared) and synthetic CLOs (collateral was CDS-based with Lehman Brothers being the counterparty), and a couple of "procedural" (as opposed to C-based) defaults also occurred.

During the period, however, the CLO asset class did not escape unscathed. With CLO indentures written during a period when the historical evidence indicated the underlying asset (leveraged loans) had little volatility, CLO managers had few tools to deal with plummeting prices, a surge in loan defaults, and a rapid level of ratings downgrades. While cash flow CLOs are generally insulated from market prices, this does not typically apply to defaulted loans or an excessive level of CCC-rated loans (typically 7.5% of the portfolio). Additionally, the purchase of loans below $80 or $85 typically requires the loan to be carried at a discount to par. This latter restriction made purchasing loans extremely difficult when the average loan price tumbled to the $60s in late 2008.

As a result, many CLOs began to fail OC tests, and the "soft" test (OC/Interest Diversion), whereby 50% of interest proceeds after the interest in debt classes are paid are to be used to purchase additional collateral as opposed to going to the subordinated noteholders (equity). Additionally, subordinated management fees are suspended when interest is being diverted. According to Wells Fargo, by mid-2009 approximately 57% of all post-2002 CLOs were failing an OC test, with 70% failing either an OC test or diverting interest. These levels have declined with the recent surge in valuations; however, on February 1, 2010, Wells Fargo reported that 30% of deals are still failing an OC test and 50% either are failing an OC test or are diverting interest. With fees being cut to managers of these deals, managers focused solely only on managing CLOs ("CLO shops") have seen talent leave their firms and investors seeking collateral management replacement.

In addition to breached tests during this period, ratings agencies downgraded CLO debt tranches as collateral quality and coverage metrics deteriorated. With the exception of most Aaa debt tranches, virtually every tranche of a traditional cash flow CLO ever issued had been downgraded, pressuring certain investors and therefore secondary valuations of CLO debt.

As the loan market has largely healed, there has been a lot of talk about the emergence of newly issued CLOs. As it currently stands, however, the arbitrage for subordinated note investors is currently not there. While structures with 8–12 times leverage were the norm during the 2005–2007 period, tarnished ratings agencies are looking for structures levered in the 4–6 times area. Unless Aaa CLO spreads decline from current levels of 110–130 bp, the arbitrage simply is not there for adequate equity returns.

6

DIFFERENCES BETWEEN CLOs AND STRUCTURED FINANCE CDOs

Jonathan S. Blau

Managing Director,
Credit Suisse Securities (USA) LLC

Given the spotlight on mortgage, securitization, and credit markets in 2007, this chapter compares and contrasts these markets. We discuss the main differences between bank loan syndication and mortgage origination. We also highlight the differences in the origination and ongoing monitoring of the two asset classes, with key differences in the number of lenders involved, monitoring transparency, compliance triggers, and subordination of collateral. Then we address many of the headline topics regarding corporate bank loans, subprime home equity bonds (HEQs), structured finance collateralized debt obligations (SF CDOs), and collateralized loan obligations (CLOs). We discuss differences between CLOs and SF CDOs, in terms of diversity of the underlying collateral, structural subordination, and recent collateral downgrades/defaults. (See Table 6.1.)

A collateralized debt obligation is a type of fund structure. The collateral underlying a CDO varies greatly, ranging from residential

TABLE 6.1 Leveraged Loan versus Subprime Loan Characteristics and Monitoring Process

Factor	Leveraged Loans	Subprime RMBS
Underlying collateral	Corporate loans to noninvestment-grade companies	Residential mortgages to lower-credit borrowers
Industry exposure	Broad exposure to all 22 industries of the U.S. economy	U.S. residential housing
Issuance history	Since 1992	Since 1997
Size of universe	Over $1 trillion	Over $900 billion
Collateral training	Yes; active secondary loan market	Yes; active secondary HEQ bond market
Historical default or 60 day +	2.3% (1992–2007)	9.51% (1998–11/2007)*
Delinquency rate: LTM 12/2007 def. or 60-day + del. rate	0.20%	16.81%
Historical recovery rate	75% (1992–2007)	60% (based on rating agency assumptions)
Factors	**Corporate Bank Loan Organization and Monitoring Process**	**Subprime Loan Origination and Monitoring Process**
Parties involved	A group of investment banks will syndicate the corporate loans to a universe of several hundred investors. The due diligence performed by these banks verifies the credit quality of the borrower.	Bilateral agreement between a bank and a borrower. The credit quality of the borrower can be verified to a limited extent (i.e., self-employed, little or no credit history).
Transparency	Initial financial report and ongoing monthly/quarterly reporting	Only initial financial report

(Continued)

TABLE 6.1 *(Continued)*

Factors	Corporate Bank Loan Organization and Monitoring Process	Subprime Loan Origination and Monitoring Process
Triggers	Ongoing maintenance and incurrence tests	Once borrower becomes delinquent, the mortgage servicer can attempt to work out new payment terms or ultimately foreclose on home, which may take months.
Subordination	30% to 40% junior debt and equity	As little as 0% to 10%; based on 90% to 100% loan-to-value ratio
Collateral	Loans typically secured by a diverse pool of tangible assets depending on the corporation	Loans only secured by real estate

* Delinquencies are a total of 60-day and 90-day delinquencies and pending foreclosures.
Sources: Credit Suisse and Mortgage Bankers Association Survey

mortgage-backed securities and credit card debt to corporate bank loans. CDOs backed by mortgage securities and other types of asset-backed securities (ABSs) are called structured finance CDOs or ABS CDOs, while CDOs backed by corporate bank loans are called collateralized loan obligations (CLOs). The key driver of investment performance in a CDO is the underlying pool of assets, which in the case of CLOs are bank loans of corporations. The primary risk of a cash flow CLO is the deal's default rate, which determines the likelihood that the expected stream of cash flows will be collected.

Table 6.2 highlights key differences between corporate banks loans and subprime HEQ bonds.

SF CDOs/ABS CDOs and CLOs both utilize the same legal structure; they are investment vehicles that capture the spread differential between debt securities and the liabilities issued to finance them. However, an examination of the assets in these structures and their associated

TABLE 6.2 CLOs versus Mezzanine ABS CDOs

Factors	CLOs	Mezzanine ABS CDOs
Collateral pool	Corporate loans to non-investment-grade issuers	Residential home equity bonds
Representative collateral pool	90% corporate loans, 10% high-yield bonds, **0% subprime HEQ**	**80% subprime HEQ, 10% ABS CDOs, 10% other ABS**
Issuance history	Since 1994	Since 2003
Size of universe	Over $300 billion	Over $200 billion

Source: Credit Suisse

issuance history reveals stark differences. Mezzanine ABS CDOs are a significant fraction of recent SF CDO issuance, and 80 percent of the collateral of these CDOs consist of mezzanine (AA, A, and BBB) home equity bonds (HEQs), the so-called subprime mortgage loans. In contrast, CLOs have 0 percent exposure to subprime. Furthermore, CLOs have experienced a full economic cycle, whereas ABS CDOs have yet to be cycle-tested.

Differences between Leveraged Loans and Subprime Mortgages

With liquidity deteriorating in all credit markets, from residential mortgaged-backed securities (RMBSs) and CDOs to high-yield bonds and leveraged loans, new issue velocity and secondary levels have decelerated, and technical factors in high-yield bonds and leveraged loans have moved prices lower without a corresponding increase in fundamental risk. The repricing of illiquid assets such as mezzanine ABS CDOs, subprime RMBS bonds, and other securitized credit instruments helped to create forced selling in the credit markets, as fund managers met margin calls, incurred fund redemptions, and repositioned their portfolios.

However, if we move away from technical drivers and examine the fundamental risks involved in leveraged loans versus subprime

FIGURE 6.1 Corporate Leveraged Loan Subordination versus Mortgage Borrower's Subordination

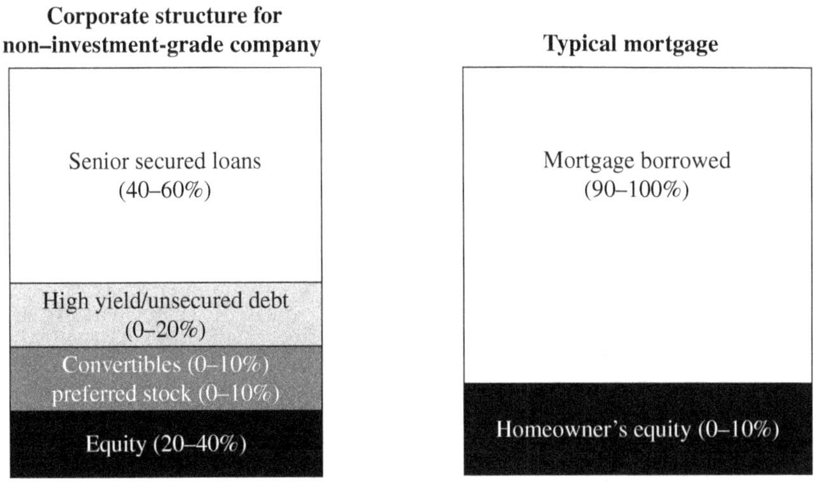

Source: Credit Suisse

mortgages from origination to ongoing monitoring, there are numerous differences. First, leveraged loans are secured by all assets of a company and rank ahead of 40–60 percent of subordinated debt and equity holders in the event of bankruptcy. In contrast, subprime mortgages are secured only by real estate and are senior to just 0–10 percent of the equity, depending on the down payment a borrower makes on a home. In the ongoing supervision of bank loan lending, corporate management provides financial projections with monthly or quarterly consistency.

However, for subprime mortgages, there is a one-time application and credit check and no additional monitoring. In Figure 6.1 we take an in-depth look at the origination processes.

Leveraged Loan Origination

When noninvestment-grade companies look for debt financing, they consider issuing bank debt or high-yield bonds. Leveraged loan transactions have a formal and established institutional process and typically take six to eight weeks from marketing to execution depending on the complexity of the deal. There are two main stages to the overall process: the preparatory stage and the execution stage.

The preparatory stage begins with due diligence. The investment bank's industry coverage team and capital markets team recommend a specific deal structure to the company. The investment bank's credit committee also reviews the proposed transaction and provides feedback on the structure/terms of the agreement. After the terms are negotiated with the company, a bank book, a management presentation, credit documents, and other legal documents are prepared. A term sheet, a bank book, and consolidated financial statements for the deal are all posted on a proprietary Web site for review by potential investors and participants in the market.

Members of the bank will also meet with rating agencies (Moody's, S&P, Fitch, etc.) in order to determine the potential ratings of newly issued loans. The rating process is extremely thorough. Rating agencies carefully scrutinize the issuer's financials. Also, the debt maintenance covenants are negotiated toward the end of the preparatory stage.

After terms are finalized in the bank book and management has made its presentation to interested investors at the bank meeting, the deal is ready to be executed. The execution stage consists of finalizing covenants, obtaining a rating from the rating agencies, and arranging the syndication. All documentation is completed, and the syndicate begins to establish commitments from investors. Additional feedback from investors is received, and deal pricing may be adjusted. Once the syndicate has established commitments for the total loan offering, the deal is allocated accordingly. After the allocation is completed, the process closes and funding begins. (See Figure 6.2.)

What rattled loan market investors in the first half of 2007 was the rapid issuance of loans without stringent covenants—the so-called covenant-lite loans. Leveraged loan borrowers had typically been required to include incurrence and maintenance tests. But covenant-lite loans stripped investors of the right to monitor and restrict corporate borrowers' behavior via maintenance tests. The shift in market

FIGURE 6.2 Leveraged Loan Origination Process and Timeline*

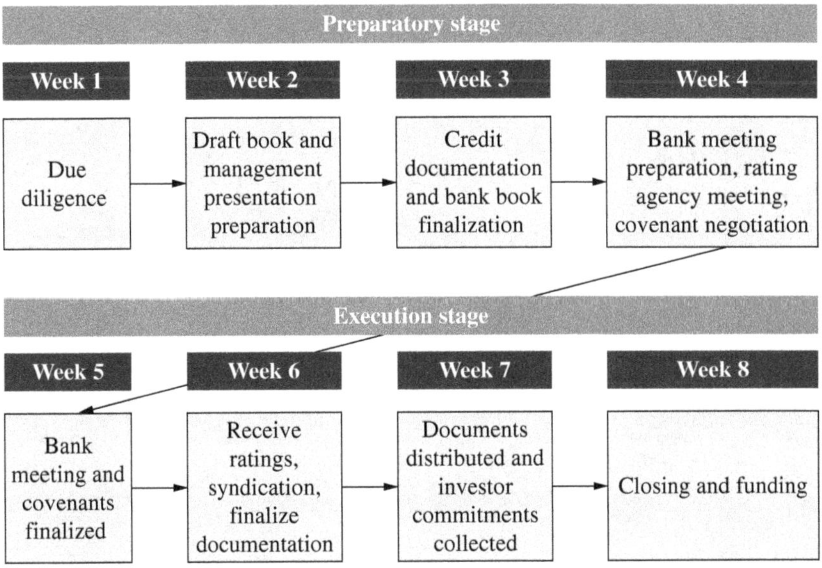

*A loan syndication transaction typically takes six to eight weeks to complete.
Source: Credit Suisse

sentiment since the dislocation in the second half of 2007 will limit covenant-lite issuance going forward.

While covenant-lite loan issuance was historically high in the first half of 2007, leveraged loan default rates did not increase and are, in fact, at historic lows. Furthermore, because CLO managers have discretion in selecting assets for their portfolios, above-average CLO managers have historically experienced below-market default rates.

Subprime Mortgage Origination

There are three major participants in the modern subprime mortgage origination process: (1) mortgage broker, (2) mortgage lender or conduit, and (3) mortgage servicer. (See Figure 6.3.) Today, two-thirds of subprime mortgages are originated by mortgager brokers who market and evaluate the creditworthiness of potential borrowers. They submit

FIGURE 6.3 Mortgage Origination Process

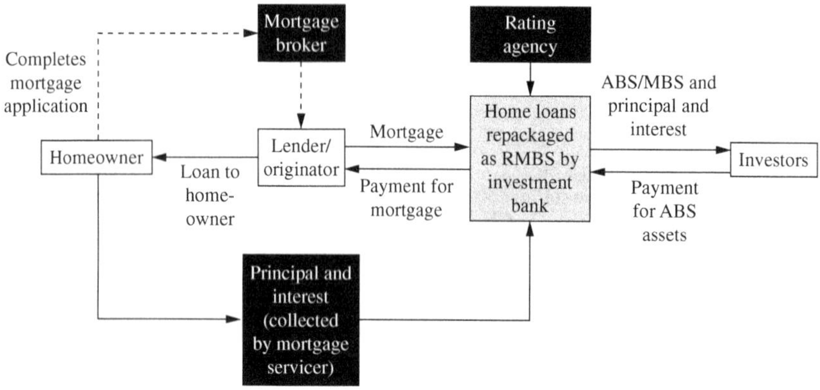

Source: Credit Suisse

applications to mortgage lenders or originators who finance the approved loans. The lenders/originators of loans usually sell the pool of mortgages to a trust. The trust now owns the pool of loans. Finally, the loans are securitized by the trust into home equity (HEQ) bonds; they are underwritten and syndicated by investment banks to institutional investors such as pension funds, insurance companies, and mutual funds.

The mortgage servicer is responsible for (1) loan administration and client servicing, (2) payment collection and processing, and (3) delinquent loan collections. Importantly, the servicer also manages delinquencies, loss mitigation, and foreclosures. In early-stage delinquency, the servicer advances delinquent payments to the trust, sends out a notice of default, makes collection calls, and may suggest an alternative payment plan. In late-stage delinquency, loss mitigation strategies such as modifying the loan by reducing the rate and extending the term of the loan are employed. Borrowers are encouraged to sell the property without going through the foreclosure process, since this usually results in lower losses than foreclosure. If the loan is not cured (paid in full, current, and made up for missed payments), then the servicer resorts to foreclosure, a costly and time-consuming process.

Creditworthiness evaluations of subprime borrowers faltered in recent years because mortgage lenders/originators relaxed lending standards and trusts/underwriters turned a blind eye. The vast majority of subprime loans in recent years were originated through independent mortgage brokers and lenders that operate separately from the trust that is responsible for securitizing the HEQ bonds. In order to acquire funding from the trust, the mortgage lenders/originators must make certain representations and warranties concerning the condition of the property and the accuracy of the loan and borrower information. The low-interest-rate environment, coupled with rising home prices, encouraged lenders to overestimate the borrower's income, thus assuming that the borrowers would be able to service the loan. Therefore, the lenders underestimated the initial perceived risk associated with subprime HEQ bonds and the subprime mortgages backing these structured bonds. However, many of these loans were adjustable rate mortgages (ARMs), and as interest rates increased in the 2005–2007 period, the borrowers' ability to consistently service their debt was hindered, resulting in higher delinquency rates than was historically experienced.

Loan applications can be processed manually. However, mortgage brokers and lenders began streamlining the loan application process with automated loan origination systems (LOSs), which do not go through independent verification and are only as accurate as the information entered. A push to increase volume with commission structures and quotas led to the issuance of low documentation loans (low-docs). These are loans that have documented fields in the borrower's profile that are not verified by the lender (such as the primary income). An example of these low-doc loans was the stated income loan, which gave the broker discretion in determining an "estimated," unverified income to be stated on the loan application.

Also increasing sharply in the subprime residential mortgage market in 2005–2006 were so-called "piggyback 1st" loans, or first-lien

FIGURE 6.4 Risky Subprime Mortgage Loan Attributes on the Rise

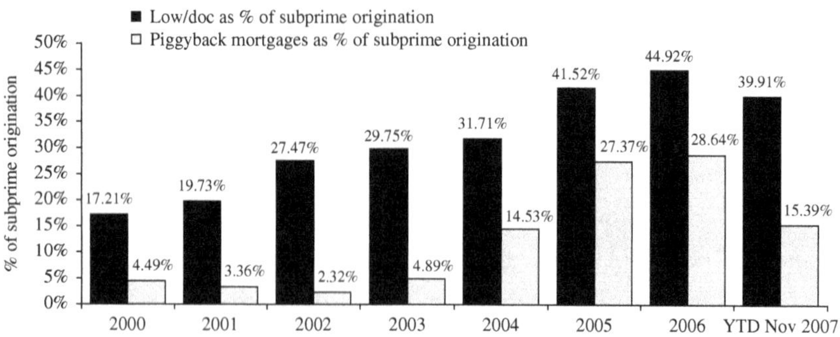

Source: Credit Suisse

mortgages on properties where a second-lien mortgage was also incurred to facilitate the closing of the first-lien loan. Thus the home loan borrower incurred additional debt with a second-lien claim to the home in order to secure the first-lien loan, often without disclosing the second mortgage, or piggyback loan, to the first-lien lender. Going forward, our ABS analysts expect a sharp decline in low-doc and piggyback loans. (See Figure 6.4.)

Historically, overall payment delinquencies for home equity loans have been much higher than those in the corporate leveraged loan market. Subprime delinquencies have experienced a historical average delinquency rate of 12.6 percent compared to the long-term average default rate for leveraged loans of only 2.3 percent. (See Figure 6.5.)

Since mortgage lending was driven by expectations of home price appreciation, the recent decline in year-over-year home prices is alarming. Based on historical experience, we believe that inventory levels need to be worked down before home prices will see an increase. During the previous housing decline, 1990–1993, negative home price appreciation lasted for four quarters, and home prices were flat for an ensuing six quarters. (See Figure 6.6.)

FIGURE 6.5 Historical Home Equity Loan Delinquencies

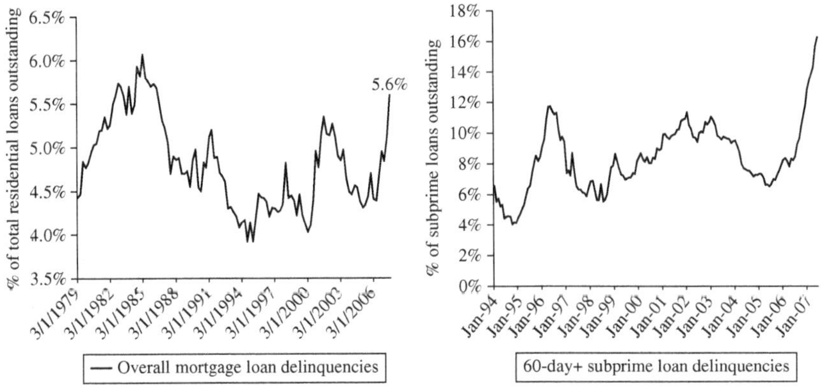

Sources: Mortgage Bankers Association and Credit Suisse

FIGURE 6.6 Yield-on-Year (YOY) Change in Home Prices versus Number of Months' Supply of Existing Homes

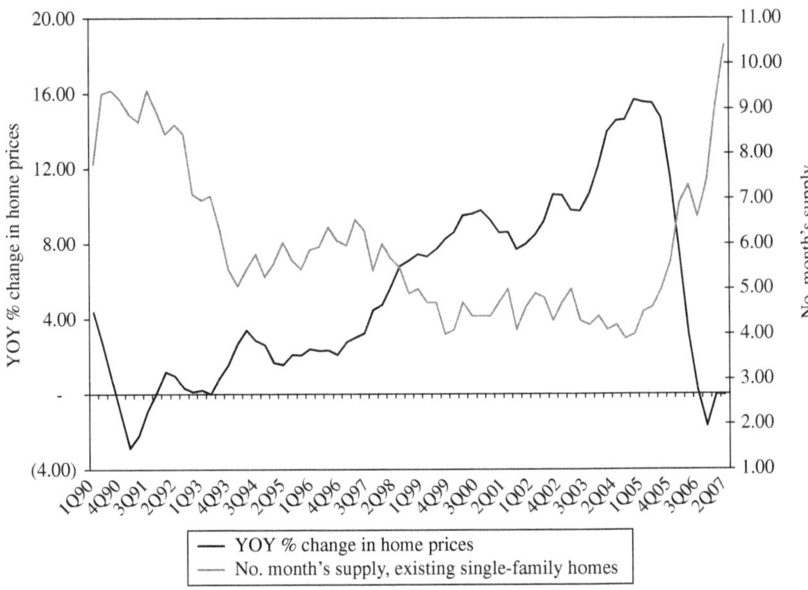

Sources: National Association of Realtors, Number of Months Supply of Existing Single-Family Home Sales. Case-Shiller, S&P Shiller Home Price Index

Differences between ABS CDOs and CLOs

ABS CDOs have experienced a significant deterioration in the diversity and quality of underlying collateral, while CLOs have remained consistently diversified across multiple industries.

Diversity of Underlying Collateral

Figure 6.7 compares a representative ABS CDO issued in 2006 with CLOs issued in 2007.

Differences in CDO Structural Subordination and Overcollateralization

In the pooling and tranching of CDOs, different tranches, or slices of risk, will have different ratings based on their subordination and overcollateralization. The AAA tranche of a typical mezzanine ABS CDO has 20 percent subordination, since 20 percent of the remaining debt issued by the CDO ranks junior to the AAA's, whereas the AAA tranche of a CLO has 25 percent subordination. Because HEQ bonds were perceived to be less risky than leveraged loans by rating agencies, CLOs have more subordination, and debt tranches have greater overcollateralization or cushioning from losses. (See Figure 6.8.)

Downgrades of Underlying Collateral

HEQ bonds have seen increasing numbers of downgrades, while corporate issuers have maintained their rating levels and low default levels. In a recent six-month period, HEQ bonds have experienced one upgrade for every 16 downgrades, a ratio of 0.06. In contrast, the ratio of upgrades to downgrades for high-yield corporate issuers has held steady at 0.79. (See Figures 6.9 and 6.10.)

FIGURE 6.7 Representative CDO Underlying Collateral Breakdown

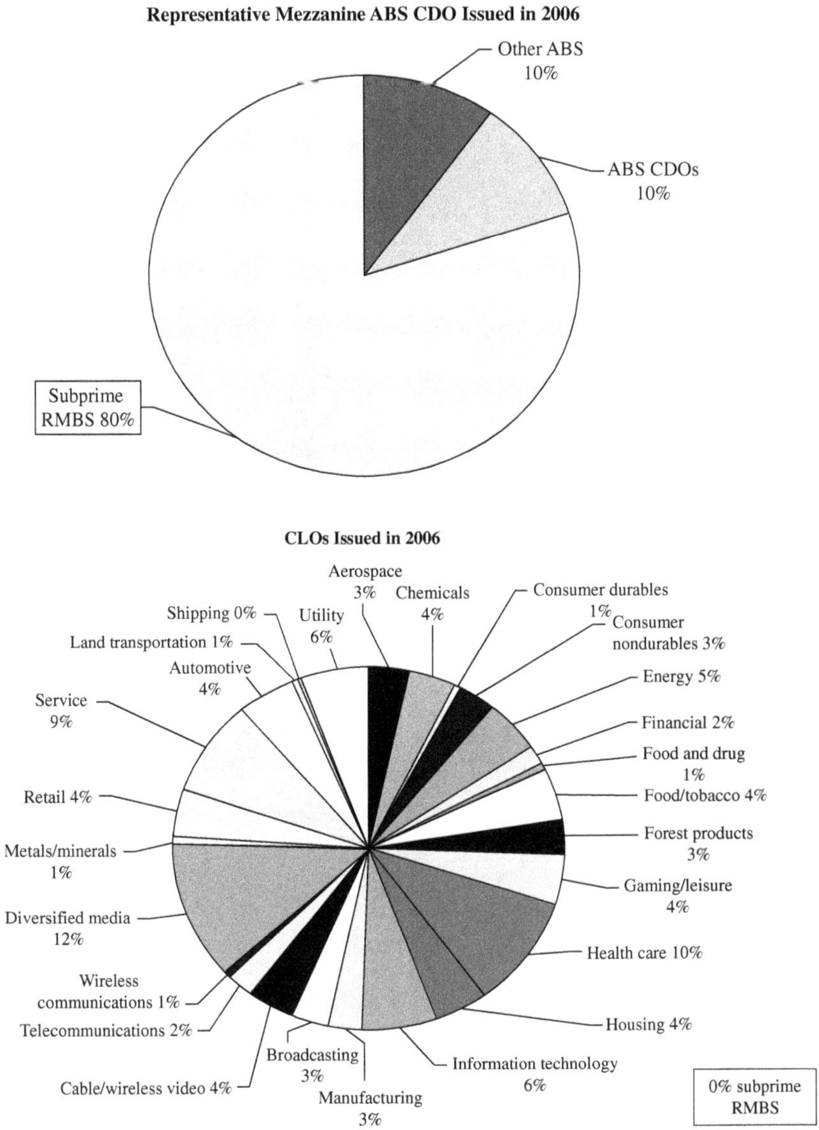

Source: Credit Suisse

FIGURE 6.8 Representative CLO versus Mezzanine ABS CDO Liability Structure

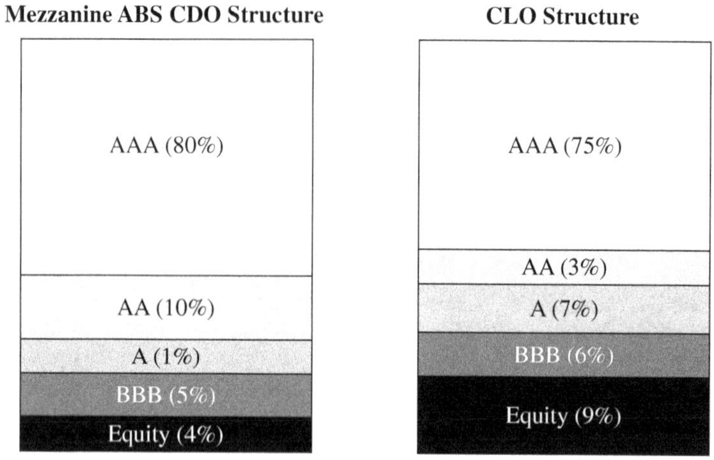

Source: Credit Suisse

FIGURE 6.9 Ratio of Upgrades to Downgrades for HEQ Bonds

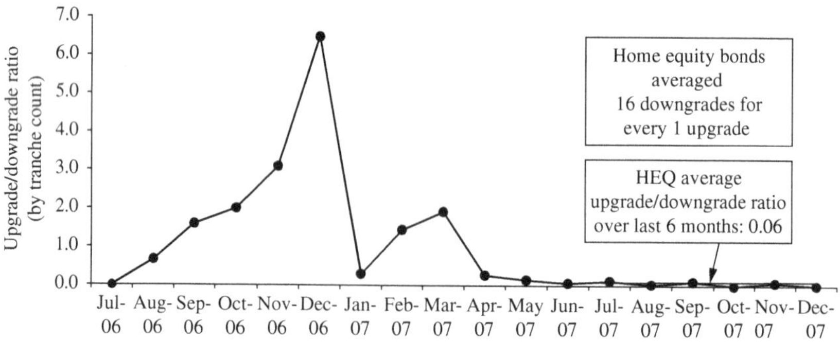

Sources: Credit Suisse and Moody's

FIGURE 6.10 Ratio of Corporate Upgrades to Downgrades

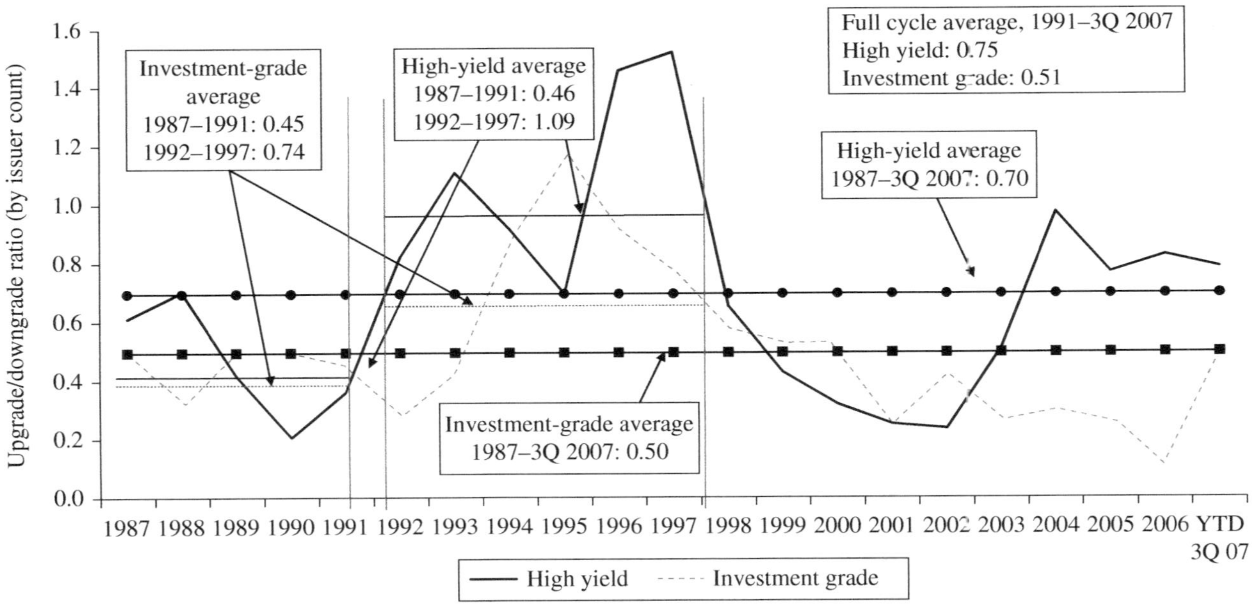

Sources: Credit Suisse and Moody's

TABLE 6.3 Average One-Year Downgrade Risk, 1996–2006

Rating	CLO*	SF CDO†	Corporate Bonds‡
Aaa	0.10%	1.80%	3.50%
Aa2	1.50%	4.40%	7.10%
A2	0.00%	3.40%	6.60%
A3	1.30%	6.10%	10.50%
Baa2	1.20%	7.70%	12.00%
Ba2	2.40%	10.00%	18.10%
Ba3	5.60%	12.50%	18.90%

*Probability of downgrade is adjusted for withdrawn ratings.
†For the period 2000–2006.
‡Figures are from "theoretical" corporate transition matrix.
Sources: Credit Suisse and Moody's

Historically, CLO liabilities have had the lowest probability of ratings downgrade relative to both corporate bonds and structured finance CDOs. (See Table 6.3.)

7

CREDIT ANALYSIS AND ANALYZING A HIGH-YIELD ISSUANCE

Amy Levine, CFA

Vice President, Assistant Director of Research
Shenkman Capital Management, Inc.

Nicholas Sarchese, CFA

Senior Vice President, Director of Research
Shenkman Capital Management, Inc.

Credit analysis can be simply defined as determining the ability and willingness of a borrower to meet its interest and principal obligations when due. It is often identified with financial ratio analysis. However, true credit analysis is much more comprehensive and encompasses much more than an analysis of the financials and ratios. Two credits with identical financial ratios will not have the same credit risk. Credit analysis can be broken down into four key focus areas: business risk, financial risk, management/ownership risk, and covenants. (See Figure 7.1.)

A thorough credit analysis is not complete without a thorough examination of all four key focus areas. Weakness in any one of the four

FIGURE 7.1 Credit Analysis

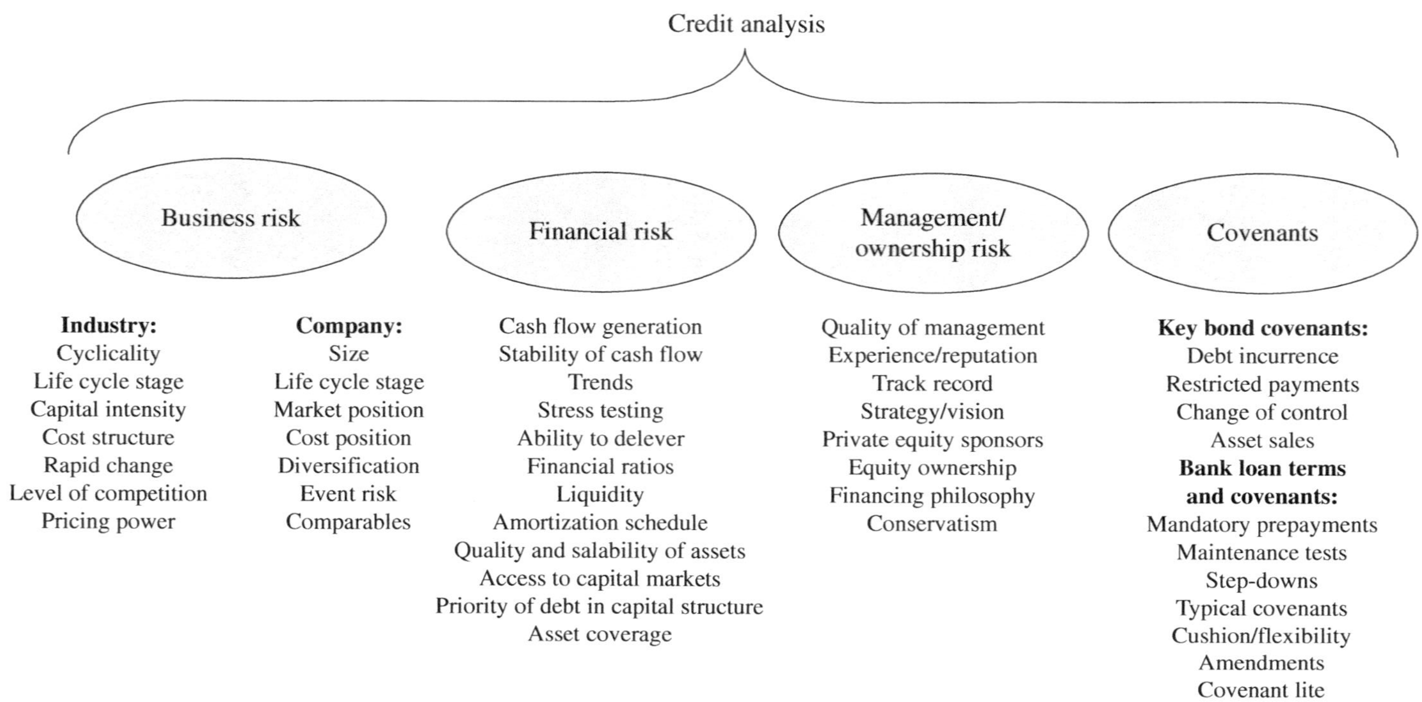

focus areas can ultimately offset strength in the remaining three and result in high credit risk for a particular issue.

Examples include:

1. *Strong ratios with low leverage + strong management + strong covenant protection:* May not be able to offset a high business risk where the industry structure is unfavorable and the company is weakly positioned.
2. *Strong business/industry fundamentals + strong financial profile + reasonable covenant package:* May not be able to offset the negative impact of a weak management team with aggressive financial policy—or—bondholder unfriendly private equity sponsor.
3. *Strong business/industry fundamentals + strong financial profile + strong management team:* May not be able to offset the negative impact of a weak covenant package.
4. *Strong business/industry fundamentals + strong management team + strong covenant protection:* May not be able to offset the financial risk of a company that is overleveraged.

Analysts must focus their analysis on taking a "forward-looking" view of all four key risk areas in their credit assessment. While historical results are important for perspective, it is ultimately the future credit trend that will dictate the performance of a given issue.

While credit analysis is arguably the most important component of the security analysis process, trading liquidity factors and relative value ultimately round off the investment equation to determine if a "good credit" will make for a good investment. Poor relative value and overpaying for a good credit could ultimately lead to underperformance. Weak trading liquidity factors can magnify the downside and disrupt the value equation in a downside surprise scenario. Figure 7.2 shows the six steps in credit analysis and analyzing a high-yield issuance that this chapter covers.

FIGURE 7.2 Security Analysis

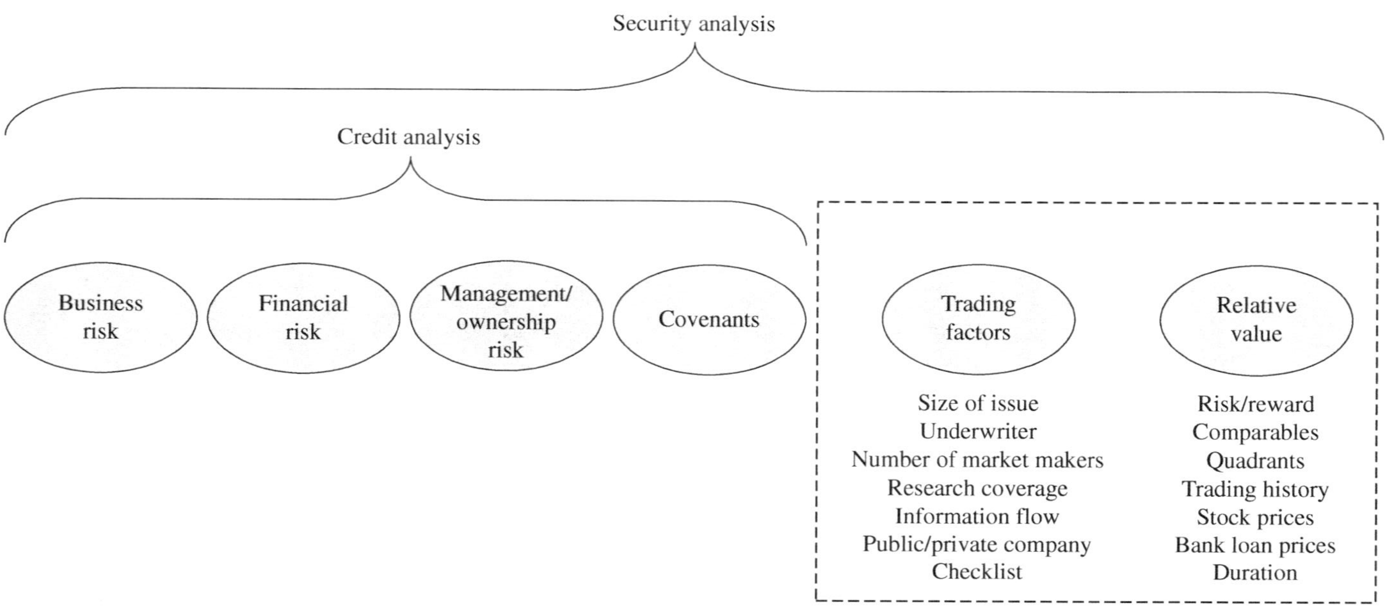

Step 1: Business Risk Part 1, Industry Analysis

Analyzing the business risk of a particular credit involves an assessment of both the industry risk and company-specific risk from a strategic perspective. The analysis will involve not only determining whether the industry structure and fundamentals are favorable but what the company's strategic positioning is within the industry.

The first step in analyzing a high-yield bond is examining the industry risks. High levels of debt can be manageable and appropriate for certain industries but not for others. Some industries are more conducive to leverage because their high operating margins, solid growth rates, and consistency of earnings enable companies within these industries to service a higher degree of indebtedness. However, for other industries that have low operating margins and growth rates, a heavy debt burden may weaken a company's ability to service debt in an economic downturn or a prolonged period of sluggish product demand.

For industries that have more predictable and stable cash flows, higher leverage can be appropriate. For example, companies in an industry such as biotech generally do not have high-yield bonds because the success of the business could involve the high-risk proposition of a new drug and the need for FDA approval. The success of such a venture is highly unpredictable, and such risk is better suited to an equity investor, where the upside reward is more appropriate given the risk. Factors used to assess an industry include stability of cash flows, stage in industry life cycle, capital intensity, cost structure/operating leverage, level of rapid change, level of competition, and pricing power.

Cyclicality/Stability of Cash Flows

It may not be appropriate for industries with volatile cash flows to have a high level of debt. Some industries, such as waste management, have very consistent and recurring cash flows and are favored by analysts. On the other hand, other industries, such as those that may rely on large government or industry contracts, can have quite lumpy revenue streams. The more stability, the more comfort the analyst can have that the company can meet its obligations. For cyclical companies, such as construction companies or industrials, a high debt burden may not be manageable during a period of weak economic growth. During a recession the company may not generate enough cash flows to service its debt and may find itself out of compliance with financial covenants. As such, a less leveraged capital structure would be appropriate because it would give these companies more flexibility to access capital and survive during these downturns. For example, chemical companies earn high profits and generate significant cash during peak years but have significantly lower earnings in trough years. To ensure liquidity during those trough years, it is not prudent for a cyclical company to have an elevated level of debt and a high interest burden heading into a recession.

Similarly, highly seasonal companies may find it difficult to operate with a lot of debt. In seasonal businesses, such as ski resorts and outdoor theme parks, much of the free cash flow is generated during a short period of time, and, if the weather or other factors do not cooperate, the company could find itself having to wait a whole year before getting the opportunity to improve its results. However, if a cyclical or seasonal business is also diversified geographically or by end market, it could help cushion the impact of any particular event.

Stage in Industry Life Cycle

Industries go through a natural life cycle, from infancy to growth to maturity, and perhaps to decline. Industries with positive growth characteristics likely have high operating margins and can make good high-yield investments. If a company is experiencing growth, it can afford to have higher leverage because it can "grow into its capital structure." Over time, as the company's earnings and cash flow grow, its leverage will be reduced and its debt can be paid down. However, the analyst should have a high level of confidence in the growth rate before accepting the higher risk and higher level of leverage. Certain healthcare sectors would be a good example of growth areas. Companies in mature industries can have a moderate amount of debt, particularly if cash flow is abundant and reasonably stable. As such, these companies can improve their financial metrics by using their free cash flow to pay down debt. Industries with secular demand declines should have less leverage and should be viewed more skeptically by analysts. A decline in operating performance will make meeting interest obligations and refinancing debt maturities more difficult.

Capital Intensity

Different industries have different amounts of capital that need to be consistently reinvested in the business to maintain performance. For example, cable companies have high levels of capital spending as a percentage of sales in order to maintain the assets of the business or risk losing customers to competing technologies. On the other hand, service companies generally have very low levels of capital required because the company's assets are generally its people. Industries with lower capital needs can afford higher leverage since more cash will be available to pay interest and debt. It's also important for the analyst to understand if an industry is going through a change that will require large capital spending in the future even if spending has been historically low. For example, an industry with old and underinvested equipment could require higher capital spending which would make future deleveraging more difficult.

Cost Structure/Operating Leverage

A business with high operating leverage has a high percentage of fixed costs in its cost structure. In a period of increasing sales, this is a positive as more of the incremental sales drop to the bottom line. However, on the flip side, in a declining sales environment, a large percentage of the sales decline detracts from the bottom line. For example, an airline has high operating leverage. An individual flight has a certain cost structure, including the staff and fuel, independent of the number of passengers (revenues) on the plane. A high percentage of the revenues from an incremental passenger on a given plane drops to the bottom line. Of particular concern would be industries that have high operating leverage and inherently low margins, since these businesses leave little room for error. For example, distributors or grocery stores typically have very low margins, and small changes in volumes can have a devastating effect on the bottom line. Given the more volatile nature of earnings in industries with high operating leverage, they tend to warrant less financial leverage.

Rapid Change

Industries that are undergoing rapid change should avoid excessive leverage. An industry that is going through technological change, including a shift in the business or distribution model, may need to have higher spending in order to maintain its competitive edge. A highly levered balance sheet may limit the cash available for that spending. Lack of investment might leave the company open to threats from new competitors that may not be burdened by an incumbent business model. For example the U.S. auto companies are seeing a shift in demand away from heavier trucks and SUVs toward smaller cars or hybrid vehicles. Additional capital will be needed in order for these companies to stay competitive.

Level of Competition

Industries that are characterized by intense competition may present an unfavorable level of risk since such an environment could lead to lower profitability. High levels of competitive behavior can be seen in industries with low barriers to entry, plentiful substitutes, disruptive players, and foreign competition. An industry such as gaming or television broadcasting may have high barriers to entry as the competitors are limited by government licenses. Similarly, an industry such as energy exploration has high barriers to entry because of the high cost of entering the business.

The availability of substitutes is also an important concept. An industry might not have many players, but the competitive dynamic might be intense if customers have alternative options. An otherwise solidly profitable industry could also be disrupted from irrational competitors that are more focused on gaining market share than on maximizing profitability. A company that has many different business lines may be able to sacrifice profitability in one division in the short term for long-term volume gains and market share. In the meantime, competitors with a more limited business profile could be driven out of business.

Capital-intensive industries with high fixed costs can also have high levels of competition if asset utilization is low. If a company has already spent money for its assets, the cost to serve the additional customer could be very low and could lead to competitive behavior. Threat of foreign competition is also a factor if the industry is more domestically focused. The severity of foreign competition can be influenced by relative labor and input costs, shipping ability, costs for the product, and foreign exchange rates.

Pricing Power

Industries with good pricing power are more able to control their own destiny and are more conducive to leverage. Companies that operate in industries with favorable competitive dynamics, in niche markets, or in an oligopolistic environment can be saddled with greater indebtedness because competitive conditions allow companies with pricing flexibility to maintain their bottom line during periods of declining demand or rising costs. Industries that have diverse customers, diverse end-user segments, and favorable contract terms are favored because

TABLE 7.1 Sample Industry Analysis

Industry	Airlines	Waste Management
Stability of cash flows	Cyclical	Stable
Stage in life cycle	Mature	Mature
Capital intensity	High	Moderate
Operating leverage	High	Moderate
Rapid change	Neutral	Neutral
Level of competition	High	Low
Pricing power	Mixed	Yes

the ability to raise prices is likely greater. Companies in industries with the most price power should have greater earnings stability and therefore should be able to accommodate more financial leverage in their capital structure. For example, companies in the waste services industry have good pricing power because there are barriers to entry, limited substitutes, no threat of imports, and a diverse customer base. On the other hand, pure commodity companies, such as precious metals, have little control over their own destiny because pricing is primarily driven by overall industry supply and demand.

Table 7.1 highlights a bad industry (airline) and a good industry (waste management) based on the metrics discussed above.

Step 1: Business Risk Part 2, Company Analysis

In addition to assessing the industry, it is important to understand company-specific factors as well as how an individual company fits into a particular industry. A company can be in a great industry but have obsolete technology, or conversely a company can be in a declining industry but have a leading market position and generate significant cash flow. The size of the company, stage in company life cycle, market position, diversification, and potential for event risk can all affect the creditworthiness of the borrower.

Size

Two companies can have very similar profiles; they are in similar industries and have solid management and similar financial metrics. However, an analyst is likely to prefer the larger of the two companies. There are various metrics to measure the size of a company, including revenues, cash flow, earnings, and assets. Regardless, a larger company usually has greater diversification and/or market share and can better withstand troubles in an industry versus a smaller player. Additionally, in times of difficulties, a larger player may have more options in terms of selling assets or accessing bank financing in order to meet debt maturities.

While larger companies are generally preferable, there are some cases in which bigger isn't necessarily better. For example, there may be smaller companies that may have a strong exposure to a higher growth and a less competitive niche segment. The bottom line is that the analyst must consider both the positive and negative attributes of a company's size.

Stage in Company's Life Cycle

Just as industries as a whole transition through life cycles (as previously described), so too do individual companies within a given industry. An individual company within an industry can be in its infancy, growth, maturity, or perhaps decline phase. While an industry as a whole may be mature, individual companies with different product niches, technologies, or processes could be in different stages of maturity. For example, the beverage industry as a whole is mature, although enhanced water products are still in the growth phase, while cola beverages are in decline. The risks associated with each phase as described in the industry section are equally applicable for individual companies.

Market/Cost Position

How an individual company fits into an industry is an important factor to consider when a high-yield issue is being analyzed. A company that has proprietary technology, patents, or niche products will likely outperform its peers, particularly in times of stress. A company with commanding market share can better withstand difficulties in an industry compared to a smaller player. Additionally, a company's cost structure relative to its peers is crucial. If a company has higher-cost assets and a higher cost of production, it is less likely to succeed in a demand downturn as selling prices will move downward to reflect the marginal cost of production.

As shown in Figure 7.3, if cumulative industry demand moves downward from point A to point B, operators that have costs per ton higher than point B on the cost-per-ton axis will no longer be able to operate profitably. If a company has a weak market position and a highly levered balance sheet, it may not be able to survive an overall decline in industry conditions.

FIGURE 7.3 Cumulative Industry Capacity

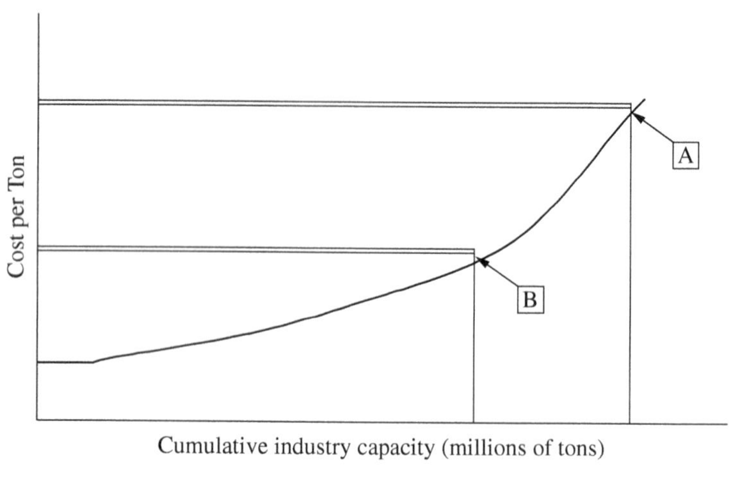

Diversification

Diversification plays a key role in assessing a particular company. If a company has a concentration of customers or suppliers, it could be at a higher risk of default if it loses just one customer or supplier. Conversely, with many customers or suppliers, it is less likely that an unexpected loss of a large part of the business would occur. For example, a major ladder producer had two customers, Home Depot and Lowe's, that represented over 50% of its sales. When Home Depot decided to use a different supplier, the company's financial performance deteriorated, and ultimately the company was no longer able to service its debt load.

Revenue diversification by end market, geography, and product are also of great help. This diversification limits the company's risk should weakness develop in certain areas. A company may not have specific customer concentrations; however, if a majority of the customers are in the same end market, this concentration will still pose a significant risk in an industrywide slowdown. For example, if a company produces automotive tires, it may serve numerous automotive customers, but it will perform badly if the entire automotive industry is in a slump.

Geographic diversity, however, can offset this negative as the company can benefit from global diversification if not all regions are experiencing a slowdown. Product concentrations can also pose a risk. For example, a telephone company may be providing only wire-line phone services, which is a declining business. This company would have a higher risk profile than a company that provided both wire-line and wireless services because overall customer loss in the more diverse business, all things being equal, would be lower.

Event Risk

Event risk is also an important concept. Certain dramatic and sometimes unforeseen events can interfere with a company's obligation to pay interest and repay principal. Examples include outcomes of litigation, environmental rulings and other governmental laws, labor strikes, technological obsolescence, and major acquisitions. Analysts should consider these potential events to determine the probability of such events causing a significant deterioration in cash flow. Analysts should weigh the probability of such event risks occurring prior to the maturity of the debt. While some industries as a whole are susceptible to event risk, some companies can be more susceptible than others in a particular industry.

Comparables

Last, company comparables must be incorporated into the analysis to show the relative financial condition of companies within the same industry sector (see the Relative Value section later in this chapter for more detail). All relevant companies within the same industry should be examined. The financially weaker issuers should have a higher yield, reflecting their ranking within the industry. Many times the market may not differentiate the credit quality between one or more companies within the same industry. Any discrepancies identified in the comparative analysis may offer an opportunity for investors to exploit these market inefficiencies.

Step 2: Financial Risk

After assessing the overall industry and company profile, the analyst will begin his or her financial analysis. The financial performance of a company is a key variable that will determine high-yield bond performance, and an analyst will want to study past financial performance to understand the drivers of the business. The analysis will focus on the credit quality of the overall company as well as the relative merits of a particular security. There are numerous financial metrics and ratios that can be used to compare the relative merits of an issuer. However, given the highly leveraged nature of a high-yield issuer, we tend to focus on specific ratios and liquidity metrics.

The key analytical tools for a high-yield issuer are EBITDA (earnings before interest, taxes, depreciation, and amortization) and cash flow; the stability of cash flows; recent and near-term projected performance trends; stress testing; analysis of free cash flow and the ability to deleverage; leverage and cover statistics; liquidity; amortization/maturity schedule; quality and salability of assets; access to capital markets; priority of debt in the capital structure; and asset coverage. After understanding historical performance, an analyst will make projections and perform scenario analysis to best estimate the future financial profile of the company. While historical results are important for perspective, it is ultimately the future credit trend and outlook that will dictate the performance of a given issue. We use the examples in Figure 7.4 and Table 7-2 to discuss financial and liquidity analysis, respectively.

Definitions: EBITDA/Cash Flow/ Free Cash Flow

As a bond analyst, our key focus is cash flow. Bond investors are looking to receive their interest and principal, and thus they focus on the available resources for such purposes. The most commonly used metric is EBITDA (line G in Figure 7.4). The purpose of EBITDA is to understand the earning power of the company after adjusting for noncash items. For example, depreciation is added back to operating income since it is an expense on the income statement, although it is a not a cash payment a company makes.

Another metric is cash flow (line K in Figure 7.4). With cash flow we adjust EBITDA for other cash disbursements (i.e., interest payments, capital expenditures, taxes) to assess what cash is available to pay down debt and deleverage the company. Finally, we use free cash flow (line O in Figure 7.4). Free cash flow is the cash that the company generates in a given period after *all* items are deducted including items that are at

FIGURE 7.4 Sample Financial Analysis (All Amounts in Millions of Dollars)

	Company A—Good company	2007	2008	2009	2010E	2011E
A	Revenues	900	945	1,087	1,141	1,198
B	Cost of goods sold	720	747	848	890	935
C	Gross margin (A-B)	180	198	239	251	264
D	Selling, general & administrative costs	45	47	54	57	60
E	Operating income or EBIT (C-D)	135	151	185	194	204
F	Depreciation and amortization	100	100	100	100	100
G	Earnings before interest, depreciation, and amortization (EBITDA) (E+F)	235	251	285	294	304
H	Cash interest	70	66	62	58	53
I	Cash taxes	23	30	43	48	53
J	Capital expenditures	90	95	109	114	120
K	Cash flow (G-H-I-J)	52	61	71	74	78
L	Dividends/stock buybacks/stock issuance	—	100	—	—	—
M	Working capital		—	(20)	(10)	(10)
N	Acquisitions	—	(100)	—	—	—
O	Free cash flow (K-L-M-N)	52	61	51	64	68
P	Total debt	1,000	939	889	824	756
Q	Equity market capitalization			1,750		
R	Total enterprise value (P+Q)			2,639		
	Financial analysis					
S	Revenue growth		5%	15%	5%	5%
T	Gross margin	20%	21%	22%	22%	22%
U	EBITDA margin	26%	27%	26%	26%	25%
V	Leverage (debt/EBITDA) (P/G)	4.26	3.74	3.12	2.80	2.49
W	Interest coverage (EBITDA/interest) (G/H)	3.36	3.82	4.58	5.10	5.74
X	Enterprise value/EBITDA (R/G)			9.27		

	Company B–Bad company	2007	2008	2009	2010E	2011E
A	Revenues	900	810	867	858	738
B	Cost of goods sold	720	680	711	704	612
C	Gross margin (A-B)	180	130	156	154	125
D	Selling, general & administrative costs	45	41	43	47	52
E	Operating income or EBIT (C-D)	135	89	113	107	74
F	Depreciation and amortization	100	100	100	100	100
G	Earnings before interest, depreciation, and amortization (EBITDA) (E+F)	235	189	213	207	174
H	Cash interest	105	113	116	117	124
I	Cash taxes	11	—	—	—	—
J	Capital expenditures	90	90	90	100	150
K	Cash flow (G-H-I-J)	30	(14)	6	(10)	(100)
L	Dividends/stock buybacks/stock issuance	—		(50)	—	—
M	Working capital		—	—	—	—
N	Acquisitions	—	(100)	—	—	—
O	Free cash flow (K-L-M-N)	30	(114)	(44)	(10)	(100)
P	Total debt	1,500	1,615	1,660	1,670	1,770
Q	Equity market capitalization			200		
R	Total enterprise value (P+Q)			1,860		
	Financial analysis					
S	Revenue growth		10%	7%	–1%	–14%
T	Gross margin	20%	16%	18%	18%	17%
U	EBITDA margin	26%	23%	25%	24%	24%
V	Leverage (debt/EBITDA) (P/G)	6.38	8.54	7.81	8.06	10.18
W	Interest coverage (EBITDA/interest) (G/H)	2.24	1.67	1.83	1.77	1.40
X	Enterprise value/EBITDA (R/G)			8.75		

TABLE 7.2 Sample Liquidity Analysis (All Amounts in Millions of Dollars)

Company A, as of December 30, 2009–Good Company

Capital Structure:		**Amortization Schedule:**	
$300 million Revolver due 2016	–	2010	2
Term Loan due 2017	189	2011	2
8.5% Sr. Nts due 2019	500	2012	2
9.5% Sr. Sub. Nts due 2020	200	2013	2
Total Debt	**889**	2014	2
Preferreds	–	2015+	879
Total Debt + Preferred	**889**	**Liquidity:**	
Shares Outstanding	88	Cash	500
Stock Price	20	Availability	300
Equity Market Cap	**1,750**		
Total Enterprise Valve	**2,639**		

Company B, as of December 30, 2009–Bad Company

Capital Structure:		**Amortization Schedule:**	
$300 million Revolver due 2014	250	2010	7
Term Loan due 2015	650	2011	207
8.5% Sr. Nts due 2011	200	2012	7
9.5% Sr. Sub. Nts due 2020	560	2013	7
Total Debt	**1,660**	2014	257
Preferreds	–	2015+	1,175
Total Debt + Preferred	**1,660**	**Liquidity:**	
Shares Outstanding	50	Cash	10
Stock Price	4	Availability	50
Equity Market Cap	**200**		
Total Enterprise Value	**1,860**		

the discretion of management. From cash flow we subtract items such as stock buybacks, dividend payments, acquisition payments, and divestiture proceeds to arrive at free cash flow.

While we include working capital below the cash flow line, we recognize that it is a necessary cost of doing business for the company.

However, given the significant variability of working capital for certain companies, as well as management's significant influence on managing working capital, we include it as discretionary. We suggest noting the importance and less discretionary nature of this line in one's analysis to the extent that it is a meaningful factor. By studying the historical and future cash flow, we can assess an issuer's viability and strength.

Stability of Cash Flows

Cash flow stability and predictability are of utmost importance in high-yield analysis. Given the limited amount of cash flow to pay interest, a relatively small swing in cash flow can leave the company unable to meet its obligations. Reviewing an issuer's EBITDA trend over the last couple of years and expected trends is essential in determining a company's viability. Company A is viewed more favorably because it has consistently grown EBITDA and cash flow, while in 2008 Company B saw EBITDA decline by 20% and cash flow turn negative. Borrowers with erratic or declining cash flow are inherently riskier credits.

Recent and Near-Term Credit Trends

In addition to overall stability of cash flows, it is important to look at recent trends in financial performance. Has EBITDA increased or decreased in the last year and last couple of quarters? What is EBITDA forecast to do over the next quarter and year? What are the risks to achieving that forecast? In Figure 7.4 we see that Company A is preferable to Company B because Company A's EBITDA is increasing while Company B's is decreasing on an organic basis. The only growth in 2009 is attributed to an acquisition. If management of Company B is providing guidance that EBITDA will grow dramatically, the analyst may be skeptical given the historic performance.

Other metrics besides EBITDA can also be used to assess performance. For example, industries such as cable and telecom provide subscriber metrics. Some industries, such as energy and paper, have industry pricing or margin data. Weakness in near term trends can affect the price of the bond while not necessarily permanently impairing the credit. Forecasting is crucial, but because of uncertainty in overall economic conditions, forecasting beyond two years tends to be less reliable and to provide less insight than forecasting for the nearer term.

Stress Testing

As part of building the financial model, including historical and projected results, an analyst should perform stress case scenarios. The purpose is to understand under different assumptions whether the company will be able to meet its interest and debt obligations. For example, for a cyclical company, the analyst would want to understand how much EBITDA the company generated in the last downturn or the last recession while taking into account the factors or conditions that may be different within the current environment.

The analyst would ask questions such as, has the company's cost structure or product mix improved? Are the economic conditions more severe? Are there incremental cost pressures that did not exist in prior periods of weakness? Is there enough to meet the company's cash obligations? How leveraged would the company be under this scenario? Alternatively, the analyst would want to know what level of EBITDA the company would have to produce in order to violate its debt covenants. How much cushion is there compared to the most recent results? A stress case can also be used to review alternative outcomes. For example, if the company has a large customer, what would EBITDA, interest coverage, and leverage look like if it lost this customer? Solid financial metrics even under a stress case indicate a higher-quality credit.

Analysis of Free Cash Flow/Ability to Deleverage

While it is important to understand the earnings of the company and particularly the trends in EBITDA, as debt holders we also need to assess the free cash flow trends. If the company has large capital expenditures that are not discretionary, it may not generate much free cash flow despite good operating performance. The company also might be undergoing an expansion and thus may be incurring additional debt to fund a large capital spending budget. Alternatively, the company may be issuing or repurchasing equity. Bond investors generally prefer companies that generate excess free cash flow and use their excess cash to pay down existing bank debt or purchase their high-yield bonds in the open market. A look at the historical data can reveal management's priorities for its cash. What have managers done with their cash? Have they consistently returned money to shareholders or used it to pay down debt?

Company B (in Figure 7.4) has several red flags for the analyst. Capital expenditures are expected to go up dramatically in 2011, leading to negative free cash flow; the company made a debt-financed acquisition in 2008 (thereby increasing leverage); and in 2009 the company bought back $50 million of stock. While Company A also made an acquisition in 2008, it issued equity to finance it. It is also useful for the analyst to understand the historical record to see if it is consistent with management's strategy. A serious concern would be if Company B had publicly stated in 2007 that its intentions were to reduce leverage and then proceeded to do just the opposite.

Leverage and Coverage Statistics

Two key ratios in financial analysis are leverage, or debt divided by EBITDA (line V in Figure 7.4), and coverage, or EBITDA divided by interest expense (line W in Figure 7.4). By reviewing these statistics we can get a sense of the trends in financial performance and the ability of the company to meet its obligations. Is the company improving its credit profile or is it worsening? What is the outlook for the future? These metrics can be used to assess the relative value between different issuers. As of the end of 2009, Company B had higher leverage than Company A, and Company B was forecast to have higher leverage in 2010 than it did in 2009. As a result we expect Company B's bonds to have higher yields.

Additionally, the analyst wants to review how leverage compares to overall enterprise valuations. For example, Company B trades at a lower multiple than Company A (likely because of its more volatile earnings), and since Company B has higher leverage, the equity cushion is lower for Company B than for Company A. A lower equity cushion implies less room for error. Similarly, we would want to compare leverage to average multiples that companies in a similar industry have been purchased at. Regarding the coverage ratio, we would be extremely concerned if coverage dropped below 1×, implying that the company does not have enough EBITDA (and most likely also does not have enough cash flow) to pay its interest expense. For high-yield issuers we like to see interest coverage of at least 2×, to leave ample room for error. The greater the coverage and lower the leverage, the more confident we are in a company's ability to meet its interest obligation.

Liquidity

In addition to assessing the quality and trends in earnings, it is also important, as fixed-income analysts, to assess the balance sheet for liquidity. Ultimately a company ends up in bankruptcy when it cannot meet its financial obligations, either interest or principal. The liquidity of a high-yield company is a paramount consideration in the serviceability of a company's debt obligations in the event of unforeseen business reversals, and, as such, bondholders prefer companies with ample liquidity and limited near-term maturities. The best liquidity source is cash on the balance sheet, which typically is easily available to make payments. (See Table 7.2 for a sample liquidity analysis.)

Liquidity can also be in the form of availability on revolving credit facilities. However, covenants on these facilities can make them unavailable at just the time a company needs this extra liquidity. The amount of liquidity that is appropriate depends on both the operating needs of the company and the variability in cash flows and ultimately the amortization schedule. For example, Company A has a lower risk profile than Company B because it has much greater liquidity, in the form of both cash on the balance sheet and revolver availability. If the company is expected to have significant capital requirements resulting from ambitious business plans, prearranging appropriate financing is important because market conditions may not always be conducive to accessing the capital markets.

Amortization/Maturity Schedule

Companies with aggressive debt repayment schedules to either banks or bondholders run a higher risk that a shortfall in their cash positions could imperil their ability to remain financially sound. Bondholders typically prefer several years of cushion before a company's debt begins to amortize, thereby allowing needed flexibility to arrange refinancing, build cash balances through free cash flow, or generate returns on new capital expenditure projects.

For example, as Table 7.2 shows, Company A has very little debt maturing in the near term (low amortization), plenty of cash on the balance sheet, and ample availability on the revolver. Company B, on the other hand, could be facing a crisis in 2011. Given its bond maturity in 2011, limited liquidity on the balance sheet, and expected negative free cash flow, the company will have to rely on other sources, such as asset sales or raising money in the capital markets, to meet its obligation. With a $200 million bond maturity in 2011 we would be highly concerned about Company B's ability to access the capital markets to refinance its bond maturity. Company B's combination of erratic cash flow, dim prospects for future free cash flow, and early debt payment schedule must be carefully monitored and evaluated.

Quality and Salability of Assets

One potential strategy to meet a pending debt amortization payment is the sale of assets. Hence, analysts should examine the various corporate assets that can be divested on a quick timetable in order to generate cash for required debt prepayments. Some companies may have easily separable facilities that frequently trade in the marketplace and an easily assessable value. These types of companies can benefit from the availability of this additional avenue for capital. Of course, depending on the asset and the number of potential buyers, a seller may not get the best price if the buyer perceives that the seller is in financial distress.

The quality of the asset is also important. When valuing a plant or facility, not all assets are created equal, and a low-quality asset may not find any buyers. Assets that are well invested, have low cost structures, have high replacement costs, and are in strategic geographies are likely to be more successful in finding buyers. Additionally, assets that have scarcity value can present good value. For example, broadcast stations are valuable because of the limited number of licenses granted by the government. Nuclear plants can have value because of the difficult regulatory process involved in building a new one. While the book value of the asset may indicate a certain value, the factors described above could indicate a very different market value.

Ability to Access Capital Markets

In addition to internal liquidity and the ability to sell assets, the company can meet its obligations by accessing the capital markets. The equity, bank, or bond markets may be inclined to buy the company's securities. A public company with a large equity float would likely find it easier to raise equity capital than would a small privately held business. Similarly, a company that has already tapped the high-yield market, that is known to the participants, and whose bonds trade in line with the overall market would likely be able to access the market to refinance any debt maturities. Companies that operate in industries that are in favor have an advantage because they will likely have more access to capital markets during difficult market periods. Even if companies in out-of-favor industries can complete a financing transaction, it will likely be at a much higher cost.

Priority of Debt

While avoiding bankruptcy is paramount, we also want to understand, if the company should enter bankruptcy, what our likely recovery is. Unlike equity holders, the recovery rate for debt holders in bankruptcy can vary greatly. Key to this analysis is the priority of the debt in the capital structure. In the most simple capital structure, the priority of claims will be in the following order: secured claims, senior unsecured claims, senior subordinated claims, and then equity. However, this can be complicated by several factors, including structural subordination and guarantees. With structural subordination you could have two debt tranches that are both senior unsecured; however, one could be at the operating company, while the other is at a holding company. The debt that is structurally closer to the assets would have a priority claim.

It is also important to note whether the debt has guarantees. Two debt tranches can both be senior unsecured, although one could have guarantees from an operating subsidiary and one could not. In this case, the debt with the guarantees would have a senior claim to the assets at the operating subsidiary, whereas nonguaranteed debt would likely be included in the general claims pool along with other unsecured creditors. Overall, the general complexity of the capital structure should be taken into account as the more complex it is the more room there is for negotiation among creditors in a bankruptcy court. Table 7.3 gives the analyst a four-question checklist to help determine whether a bond is well located in a company's capital structure. The best scenario, in Sample 1, shows the bonds at the operating company, while the worst

TABLE 7.3 Corporate Structure

	Issue				
Sample	**Is the Bond Issue at the Operating Company?**	**Are Bonds Guaranteed?**	**Are Banks at the Same Level?**	**Do Banks Have a Guarantee?**	**Outcome**
1	Yes				Best
2	No	Yes	Yes		Good
3	No	Yes	No		Okay
4	No	No	Yes	No	Weak
5	No	No	No	Yes	Bad
6	No	No	Yes	Yes	Bad

scenarios (Samples 5 and 6) show the bonds at a holding company with no guarantees and with other debt (banks) structurally senior to the bonds.

Asset Coverage

An important tool for analysts is the concept of asset coverage. Is the debt secured, and by what assets? Ideally the security would consist of all the assets of the company, although inventories and accounts receivable are good collateral because they can usually be liquidated in a reasonable amount of time and at a reasonable approximation of their full value. Coverage by the company's property, plant, and equipment is also important, although the value of these may not be as clear-cut. To the extent that the assets are not sufficient to cover the secured obligations, the secured creditor may not get full recovery in a bankruptcy process.

Another method to determine asset coverage is to use the total enterprise value of the company and compare that to the debt. The implication is that in a bankruptcy, the company would not liquidate but would exit as an ongoing concern. An analyst will look at the total enterprise value of the company using public multiples of total enterprise value to EBITDA or private transaction multiples for comparables. The priority of the debt will need to be factored in to establish asset coverage. For example, service companies have few hard assets and could be valued using the enterprise valuation method.

Step 3: Management/Ownership Risk

While the factors discussed in other areas of this chapter are crucial in credit analysis, it is up to the owners and the management of the company to devise effective strategies as circumstances change in order to effectively implement those strategies and run the day-to-day operations of the business. At the end of the day, good management can make all the difference in how a company performs.

Quality of Management

The quality of the management team is highly critical in making a good investment. While successful companies must pursue effective strategies, the development and execution of those strategies hinge on the management team. Companies often rely on synergies from a prior acquisition or cost savings programs in order to grow cash flow. The difference between success and failure in these areas can be up to the quality of the integration plan and the management team that implements it. If the company is highly leveraged, a good management team will understand the risks involved in operating under that capital structure and work to mitigate it. Direct contact with management (i.e., road show, one-on-one or conference call) is the best way to understand and evaluate management and can provide insight into the risk and return parameters for a specific high-yield issuer.

It is also important that analysts be able to maintain an ongoing dialogue with management as the opportunities, risks, and priorities of the company change over time. If, during times of stress, management does not remain accessible, investors will have limited understanding of and confidence in the company, and the bonds may not perform well. While management assessment is a judgment call and improves with experience, good qualities to look for in a management team include low turnover, tenure, reputation within the industry, strong track record, timeliness in filing financial statements, forthrightness in answering questions, strategic vision, a deep bench, and following through with stated goals.

The absence of frequent strategic shifts or persistent "restructurings" are favored as well. Good managers will be able to effectively communicate the company's strategy and vision, articulate the opportunities and risks facing the company, and act early and proactively in times of change.

Private Equity Sponsors/Ownership

In addition to the quality of the management, the quality of the owners is important as well. Often a highly leveraged company is owned by a private equity "sponsor" as a result of a leveraged buyout. In these cases, the equity sponsor may ultimately drive the strategic direction and financial policy of the company, with the operating senior management of the company (CEO, COO, CFO) potentially having much less influence in the overall direction and financial risk tolerance of the company. The interests of the sponsor might not necessarily align with those of bondholders, although the owners ultimately dictate the fate of a company. Owners may be more interested in taking dividends out of the company as quickly as possible, which would enhance equity returns yet lead to the deterioration of the company's credit quality.

If the owners have little capital at risk in the company, they could try for a "swing for the fences" type strategy, since they have little downside (having taken their money out) but a lot of upside if the strategy pays off. This strategy is not a good one for bond investors because they have little upside but a lot of downside. An example of a strategy like this could be making a large investment or spending a lot of money on new or unproven technologies to launch new businesses. The sponsor's investment track record, default history, and acquisition record in paying down debt quickly should be taken into consideration. Another factor for the analyst to consider is the equity ownership by the management team. If equity ownership is spread throughout managers, they are likely to be more engaged in the success of the overall enterprise, and turnover could be reduced.

Financing Philosophy

An analyst should understand both the owners' and the management team's intentions regarding the balance sheet of the company. Is the company comfortable operating with high levels of debt and leverage, or is it more conservative and does it prefer to have more financial flexibility and lower leverage? Is it comfortable with the current amount of debt, or is debt pay-down a key priority? How committed is the company to paying down debt? Is it opportunistic in that it would consider making an attractive acquisition even if it involved increasing the financial risk profile of the company? If the management team is comfortable at the current level of debt, the team might focus on using cash flow toward paying dividends, share buybacks, or acquisitions. If debt pay-down is a key priority and the company generates a large amount of free cash flow, the company's credit metrics are likely to improve.

Understanding these intentions is of vital importance for analysts in order for them to improve their forecasts for the credit profile of the company since it will guide them toward the application of free cash flow. It is also important for analysts to understand management's philosophy in order to judge whether they will follow through with stated goals and to judge their credibility. For example, if the management team has stated its intention to deleverage and then initiates a large stock buyback, the bonds likely will not perform well because the credit profile has not met expectations and investors will have less confidence in management.

Step 4: Covenants

While the previously outlined credit analysis steps are focused on the business, financial, and management risk factors of overall credit, an analysis of a company's debt covenants is specific to each individual debt instrument within a company's capital structure. Although each debt instrument may contain its own specific debt covenants, the instruments collectively affect a company's overall credit risk profile and financial flexibility and are therefore critical to the overall credit analysis process.

Bond Covenants

Contained within the indenture of all high-yield bond offerings are certain covenants (or agreements) between the issuing company and bondholders. *Indenture* is the formal word describing the written agreement or contract between the issuer of a bond and its bondholders, the bulk of which is included in the description of notes within the final and preliminary prospectus. Covenants are essentially restrictions on the borrower/issuer imposed by the lender/bondholder that require the company to do, or refrain from doing, certain things. The covenants are primarily designed to protect bondholders from credit deterioration that would hinder the company's ability to service the interest and repay its obligations in a timely manner.

While bond covenants can certainly be restrictive, it is important to note that an issuer cannot violate a high-yield covenant by inaction alone. With the exception of payment defaults and filing of financial reports, a company must take some action in order to default under the bond indenture. Weak financial performance in and of itself will not cause a default under the typical high-yield indenture. To that end, most bond indentures contain "incurrence" covenants which are measured only when the issuer undertakes an action such as incurring additional debt or making a restricted payment.

While covenants are described in greater detail in Chapter 8, "Bond Indentures and Bond Characteristics," the focus in this chapter is on some of the key covenants and how they are incorporated into analyzing a high-yield issue on a more applied level. We caution that covenants are very complex legal statements that have very carefully crafted and deliberate language that is not in "plain English." Given the precise language, we note that it is critical for analysts to pay close attention to the defined terms that are included as part of every indenture and prospectus. For example, upon closer examination, EBITDA may be defined to include a significant part of prospective cost savings as part of the calculation, thereby weakening the overall test by inflating the EBITDA metric in ratio calculations.

Covenants are often referred to as tight/strong or loose/weak, depending on the specific terms and ultimate financial flexibility they provide the issuer. A weak covenant package can significantly increase the risk of a high-yield bond investment, even though the credit's business and financial risk profiles can be very strong. This is because the covenant package may not protect the bondholders by prohibiting enough actions by the issuer that could be detrimental to its ability to repay the bonds and service the interest.

The four key covenants we discuss in the pages that follow are limitation on indebtedness, restricted payments, change of control, and asset sales.

Limitation on Indebtedness

The limitation on indebtedness covenant is important because it restricts additional indebtedness that an issuer can incur. Additional indebtedness can ultimately dilute the claims of the existing debt and weaken the credit profile of the company because of the increased debt service requirements, unless they are kept in proportion to operating cash flow and assets. The covenant restricts the incurrence of debt unless (1) the ratio test is met or (2) the debt is allowed under the "permitted debt" basket, otherwise known as carve-outs.

There are two kinds of ratio tests: (1) fixed-charge coverage ratio tests (EBITDA/interest expense + dividends), which are usually 2.0×, and (2) leverage ratio tests (debt/EBITDA), which are usually 5.0× to 7.0×. Covenants will have one or the other ratio test, with fixed-charge coverage being the more prevalent. Additionally, the key components of the permitted debt basket are (1) credit facility (fixed amount or based on secured leverage ratio) and (2) general debt basket (generally a fixed amount). It is very important to review the issuer's carve-outs in concert with the ratio tests. (See Table 7.4.)

TABLE 7.4 Limitation on Indebtedness Example
Ratio Test: 5.0 × Leverage Ratio
Carveout: $400 Million Credit Facility

($ millions)	Scenario A	Scenario B	Scenario C
EBITDA	$100	$150	$100
Credit Facility	400	400	300
Sr Subordinated Notes	200	200	200
Total Debt	$600	$600	$500
Total Debt/EBITDA	6.0×	4.0×	5.0×
Additional Debt Permitted	$0	$150	$100

Scenario commentary for Table 7.4 follows:

1. *Scenario A:* The debt incurrence test prevents the company from incurring additional indebtedness as neither of the covenant's components (ratio test and carve-out) allows additional debt in this scenario. Current leverage is already in excess of the incurrence test, and the credit facility carve-out has already been fully utilized. It is important to note

that the company would not necessarily be in violation of the covenant unless it were to need to incur at least $1 of additional indebtedness. If the company had sufficient liquidity and did not need to incur additional debt, it would avoid violating this covenant.

2. *Scenario B:* The company has already utilized the full amount of its $400 million credit facility carve-out. However, since its leverage ratio is within the 5.0× leverage ratio incurrence test, the company is able to borrow an additional $150 million (5.0 × $150 million EBITDA = $750 million permitted total debt – $600 million current total debt = $150 million additional debt permitted).
3. *Scenario C:* Although the company is already at its 5.0 leverage ratio test, it has additional borrowing capacity given that it has only used up $300 million of its $400 million credit facility carve-out.

While the preceding examples are meant to illustrate the basics of the covenant, it is important to note that the scenarios above did not assume that any proceeds from the incremental debt issuances were used to make an acquisition with an incremental EBITDA contribution. In an acquisition scenario, a company that may appear to have little room for additional debt incurrence may still be able to incur a significant amount of additional debt to finance an acquisition, provided that the pro forma leverage ratio is in compliance with the ratio test. The covenant still serves its purpose in protecting bondholders because it permits additional debt so long as it is in proportion to additional assets and cash flow measured via that ratio test.

There is also another important point to keep in mind. Although Scenarios B and C above both show incremental debt capacity, senior managers of those companies will likely look to leave some cushion to those maximum additional debt permitted amounts so that they are not putting the credit at significant risk of default.

Restricted Payments

The restricted payments covenant protects bondholders' interest in the assets of the company by restricting the flow of money outside the company and thereby preserving the company's ability to repay its indebtedness. Undesirable distributions and asset transfers that are limited by this covenant include dividends, repurchases of equity, investments in unrestricted third parties, and retiring debt that is subordinate to the bonds before retiring the bonds. It is important to note that the restricted payments covenant does not limit acquisitions and capital expenditures, both of which should ultimately result in incremental cash flow. The test is ultimately backward looking in that it determines whether the company has earned the right to make a payment to benefit the equity of the company as opposed to the debt.

The basic restricted payments covenant prohibits all restricted payments unless

1. No default has occurred or will occur as a result of the restricted payment.
2. Total restricted payments are less than the sum of (a) a growing calculated "basket" for restricted payments and (b) identified carve-outs or "permitted restricted payments."
3. The company could incur at least $1 of additional debt versus the debt incurrence ratio (exclusive of limitation on indebtedness test carve-outs).

The key carve-outs of the permitted restricted payment basket are (1) permitted investments (as defined) and (2) general restricted payment basket (usually a specified dollar amount). Restricted payments under the carve-outs can be made even if the issuer is unable to incur additional indebtedness under the debt incurrence test. Additionally, there are two types of basket calculations: (1) 50% of cumulative net income (most common) and (2) excess of 1.5× cumulative interest

FIGURE 7.5 Restricted Payments Example

($ millions)	**Year 1**	**Year 2**	**Year 3**	**Cumulative**
EBITDA	$250	$250	$250	**$750** (a)
Interest expense	100	100	100	**300** (b)
Net income	100	100	100	**300** (c)

Restricted payment basket calculation

50% net income = (c) $300 mm × 50% = **$150 mm**

Excess 1.5x cov = (a) $750 mm – [1.5 × (b) $300 mm] = **$300 mm**

$750 mm – $450 mm = **$300 mm**

coverage. Both are calculated as one accounting period from a specified start date (usually the security's issuance date) until the measurement date which is ultimately the last financial reporting date prior to the contemplated restricted payment. The calculation also allows add-backs for events, such as contributed equity, which ultimately increase the basket size.

Figure 7.5 demonstrates an example of the restricted payment basket calculation under both types of tests. The net income basket calculation is the more favorable method for bondholders because it takes into consideration other expenses beyond interest expenses, such as taxes and depreciation, as well as a more balanced 50% ratio, whereas the excess interest coverage calculation provides more flexibility to the company as the basket grows significantly faster using an excess hurdle rate of only 1.5× coverage of interest.

Table 7.5 summarizes five scenarios involving restricted payments. The scenarios are described in more detail following the table.

Following is the scenario commentary for Table 7.5:

1. *Scenario A:* The restricted payments test prevents the company from making a restricted payment even though the basket

TABLE 7.5 Restricted Payments Scenarios
Basket Calculation: 50% Net Income
Carveout: $50mm General

Debt Incurrence Ratio Test: 5× leverage

($ millions)	**Scenario A**	**Scenario B**	**Scenario C**	**Scenario D**	**Scenario E**
EBITDA	$100	$160	$100	$200	$125
Total Debt	$600	$600	$500	$500	$600
Total Debt/EBITDA	6.0×	3.8×	5.0×	2.5×	4.8×
General Carve-out Used:	$50	$0	$0	$50	$50
Rest. Pmt. Basket Calculation:	$150	$150	$150	$0	$150
Permitted Restricted Payment:	**$0**	**$200**	**$50**	**$0**	**$25**

This table assumes the restricted payment is funded wth additional indebtedness

calculation is $150 million. The limiting factor is that the company is not able to incur $1 of additional indebtedness under its 5.0× leverage test as its current leverage is 6.0×. Also, the company's general carve-out has already been utilized.

2. *Scenario B:* The company is able to utilize its entire $150 million basket calculation as well as the $50 million general carve-out because its leverage is below the 5.0× debt test.
3. *Scenario C:* Although the company has a basket calculation of $150 million, the company is not able to incur $1 of additional indebtedness under the 5.0× leverage test because the company is already leveraged at 5.0× currently. However, the company is able to utilize the $50 million general carve-out which has not yet been used.
4. *Scenario D:* Although the company has relatively low leverage of 2.5× which is ample room under its debt incurrence test of 5.0×, the company is not able to make any restricted payment because its basket calculation is $0 and the $50 million general carve-out has already been utilized.

5. *Scenario E:* Although the company has a basket calculation of $150 million, the company's restricted payment is limited by the 5.0× incurrence test given that current leverage is 4.8×. If the company distributed more than $25 million, it would not be able to incur $1 of additional indebtedness under its 5.0× leverage test.

Change of Control

The change of control covenant requires the issuer to make an offer to purchase the notes at 101% of principal if a change of control occurs. It is the bondholder's option to accept or decline the offer. The rationale behind the change of control covenant is that it protects bondholders from a change in controlling interest by an owner who may have a different financial strategy for the issuer that could ultimately lead to the deterioration of the company's credit quality.

The basic change of control triggering events are as follows:

1. Any person other than permitted holders become owners of more than 50% of the voting stock.
2. The majority of the members of the board of directors ceases to be continuing directors.
3. Merger or consolidation with another entity unless preexisting equity holders own at least a majority of the new entity.
4. Adoption of plan related to the liquidation or dissolution of the company.

The covenant is particularly important in cases in which companies with ample flexibility under their debt incurrence or restricted payment covenants could see a significant increase in leverage and financial risk resulting from a leveraged buyout of the company. See Figure 7.6.

In the figure, the pre-LBO company is subject to significant risk in a change of control scenario resulting from the ample flexibility

FIGURE 7.6 Change of Control Example

		Without Change of control	With Change of control
($ millions)	**Pre-LBO**	**Post-LBO**	**Post-LBO**
EBITDA	$300	$300	$300
Total debt	$600	$1,500	$1,500
Total debt/EBITDA	2.0×	5.0×	5.0×
Debt incurrence test: *(leverage based)*	5.0×	5.0×	5.0×
Additional debt permitted:	$900	$0	New bonds
Restricted payment basket:	$1,000	$100	New bonds
Bond price upside/(downside)	98	88 –10	101 +3
Spread to treasuries	+500 bp	+750 bp	Retired

provided by its debt incurrence and restricted payment covenants. In this particular LBO scenario without a change of control, the new owner was able to increase total debt by 150% and take cash out of the company without improving its business profile. This led to a 10-point decline in bond price given that the bond's pricing needed to reflect the significant increase in financial risk as a result of the new owner and aggressive leverage.

Conversely, if the bonds were to contain a change-of-control covenant, bondholders would have received an offer from the company to purchase the bonds at 101 for a 3-point gain as opposed to a 10-point loss. The example highlights how credit analysis is incomplete without a thorough grasp and understanding of the bond covenants and how they could affect an investment's ultimate risk and return.

Limitation on Asset Sales

In contrast to its title, the asset sale covenant doesn't necessarily limit the ability of the issuer to sell assets. Its true purpose is to define the acceptable use of the proceeds from asset sales. The proceeds must be used to permanently repay debt or to reinvest in replacement assets. The rationale is that the assets sold were generating earnings and cash flow to service debt, thus providing ultimate credit support and asset coverage.

The key terms in this covenant outline that the issuer may sell assets but must receive fair market value and cash consideration (generally for at least 70% to 90% of the sale price). The company must then use the proceeds (typically within 365 days) to repay senior debt, reinvest in the business, or make an offer to repurchase the bonds at par (if it hasn't already applied proceeds toward the previous two uses).

Following is the scenario commentary for Figure 7.7.

1. *Scenario A:* Issuer sells assets and distributes the proceeds to shareholders. Total debt remains the same, while EBITDA and underlying asset value are meaningfully reduced. The resulting impact on the bonds is clearly negative as the

FIGURE 7.7 Asset Sale Example

	Pre-asset sale	Scenario A without asset sale covenant	Scenario B with asset sale covenant	Scenario C with asset sale covenant
EBITDA	$200	$150	$200	$150
Total debt	$1,000	$1,000	$1,000	$675
Total debt/EBITDA	5.0×	6.7×	5.0×	4.5×
Estimated asset value	$1,300	$975	$1,300	$975
Asset value/total debt	130%	98%	130%	144%
Impact to bonds		**Negative**	**Neutral**	**Modestly positive**

company's asset value coverage has been dramatically reduced, while the leverage ratio has increased meaningfully. The bondholders now have fewer assets and less cash flow to support the issuer's obligations. (It is assumed that other covenants, such as the limitation on indebtedness and restricted payments test, permit the distribution to shareholders.)

2. *Scenario B:* Issuer sells assets and reinvests the proceeds in other assets of similar value that generate similar EBITDA. While there may be some timing difference impact on EBITDA, the end result on the credit is essentially neutral as asset coverage and leverage remain unchanged.
3. *Scenario C:* Issuer sells assets and repays senior debt with the proceeds. Although the EBITDA generated from the assets is not replaced, debt is reduced, thus modestly improving the leverage ratio of and the asset value coverage for the remaining debt. While assets were sold and the asset base was reduced, bondholders were protected from the impact of the sale as proceeds were used to reduce debt and ultimately maintain an appropriate balance between assets and obligations.

Bank Loan Covenants

Although the focus of this chapter is on credit analysis as it pertains to high-yield bonds, a thorough analysis of the issuer's bank loan terms and covenant package contained within its credit agreement is very important in order to assess a company's overall financial flexibility and liquidity. For public companies or issuers that have registered securities outstanding and are required to file financials with the SEC, credit agreements must be posted and can often be found in 8-K filings or as exhibits to other filings such as financial reports or registration statements.

A credit agreement is similar to a high-yield bond indenture because it is ultimately a written contract between the issuer and its lenders. The credit agreement contains:

1. Terms of the credit facility (interest rate, amounts, mandatory repayments, optional repayments, maturity).
2. Affirmative covenants (actions that the company must take, such as submit financials).
3. Negative covenants (actions that the company may not take such as incurring additional debt beyond the covenant limitation) and financial covenants (ratios that must be maintained in order for the company to remain in compliance).

While there are many similarities between credit agreements and bond indentures, there are some very significant differences. First, the covenants are in most cases significantly more restrictive as compared to those found in bond indentures, both in terms of the absolute number of financial covenants and the overall level of flexibility provided in each. The tighter covenants are meant to drive credit improvement by improving financial ratio targets over time. The covenants ultimately provide lenders with significant influence in forcing issuers to take corrective action if an issuer violates the covenant terms because the lender is entitled to accelerate repayment of the loan. At the very least, lenders can demand additional yield in order to be compensated for the additional risk resulting from the violation.

Second, the overall formal process for amending covenant terms is generally easier as compared to bonds, given the meaningful presence and involvement of lead or agent banks. Similar to bond covenant analysis, we note that it is critical for analysts to pay close attention to the defined terms that are included as part of every credit agreement. For example, one should not assume that the EBITDA metric used in ratio calculations will be defined identically in every credit agreement or ratio.

The six bank loan covenants or features that we will discuss in the pages that follow are mandatory prepayments, maintenance covenants, covenant step-downs, typical covenants, amendment process, and covenant lite.

Mandatory Prepayments

Mandatory prepayments are important to both bank and bond investors because they require the company to pay down debt. Without these provisions the company might use cash for purposes that do not benefit bondholders, such as dividends (if allowed under other provisions) or other investments that may not produce cash flow. The types of mandatory prepayments typically required in a credit agreement are described here:

1. *Amortizations:* These are the required principal repayments that are calculated and scheduled from the outset of the loan. See the example in Table 7.6.

   A meaningful amortization schedule is to the bondholders' advantage because it forces the company to deleverage and thus reduces the amount of secured debt that has a priority claim in the event of bankruptcy ahead of it. The offsetting risk may be that it is too onerous a repayment schedule for a company to manage if operations were to unexpectedly weaken.
2. *Excess cash flow sweeps:* Principal repayments that are calculated based on the degree of leverage and "excess" free cash flow in the business. This helps ensure that a company focuses some portion of its remaining free cash flow after required expenditures on debt reduction. A typical version of this feature may state that if a company's leverage ratio is

TABLE 7.6 Sample Term-Loan Amortization Schedule for an Amount of $2,000 Million

Amortization	Year 1	Year 2	Year 3	Year 4	Year 5
Percentage	5%	10%	15%	25%	45%
$ Amount (in millions)	$100	$200	$300	$500	$900

above 4.0×, the company must utilize 50% of excess free cash flow to repay term debt.

Excess cash flow is typically defined as EBITDA less interest expense, taxes, change in working capital, scheduled principal repayments, and capital expenditures. Typically, the percentage that must be used to pay down debt is based on a leverage grid such that the required repayment percentage will decrease as leverage improves and the company earns more flexibility. These provisions are very beneficial to bondholders because they help mandate and incentivize debt repayment and ultimate credit improvement.

3. *Asset sales:* Borrowers are typically required to repay senior debt with 100% of net proceeds from asset sales.

Maintenance Covenants

Credit agreements generally contain a mixture of both maintenance covenants and incurrence covenants. A maintenance covenant requires the issuer to maintain or achieve a certain level of financial performance in order to avoid default. For example, the credit agreement may contain a covenant requiring the issuer to maintain a leverage ratio (total debt/EBITDA) of below 5.0×. See the example in Figure 7.8.

In general, maintenance covenants are based on a 20% haircut to the issuer's projections provided to the bank group at the time of the financing so as to provide a reasonable cushion within which to operate. Tight covenants are favorable to bondholders because they limit the company's ability to increase leverage and financial risk. Analysts must pay close attention to the degree of cushion relative to maintenance covenants. A covenant violation will ultimately cause a default unless the issuer receives amendments or waivers from a majority of its lenders.

A potential violation for a weak company in a difficult financing environment could be a trigger for restructuring if senior lenders are concerned about the credit risk profile and may want to accelerate

FIGURE 7.8 Maintenance Test Example

	Q1	Q2	Q3
LTM EBITDA	$100	$82	$75
Total debt	$400	$400	$400
Total debt/EBITDA	4.0×	4.9×	5.3×
Covenant:			
Maximum leverage ratio	5.0×	5.0×	5.0×
Maintenance covenant violation?	**No**	**No**	**Yes**
Analysis calculations:			
Minimum LTM EBITDA	$80	$80	$80
(Formula: Total debt/max leverage ratio)			
$ EBITDA cushion	$20	$2	Violation
(Formula: current LTM EBITDA – minimum LTM EBITDA)			
$ incremental debt cushion	$100	$10	Violation
(Formula: [current LTM EBITDA × max leverage ratio] – current total debt			

default to ensure the highest potential recovery and repayment of their loan. Loose covenants provide a window into how aggressive a company can be and still remain within its covenant requirements. Sponsor deals typically have very loose covenants with maximum flexibility.

Covenant Step-Downs

Most financial covenants in typical credit agreements contain "step-downs." Step-downs are essentially covenant measures that are scheduled to tighten over the life of the agreement. See the example in Table 7.7.

In the table, a company may have a current leverage ratio of 5.0x, in which case the analyst has a window into the pace of credit improvement the company and its senior lenders expect. Step-downs are very beneficial to bondholders because they necessitate credit improvement for the issuer. Analysts must be careful to project the company's

TABLE 7.7 Maximum Leverage Ratio

For Period Ending	Leverage Ratio
6/30/10–3/31/11	5.50×
6/30/11–3/31/12	5.00×
6/30/12–3/31/13	4.50×
6/30/13–3/31/14	4.00×
6/30/14 and thereafter	3.75×

cushion with respect to covenant step-downs in order to anticipate any potential negative liquidity events.

Typical Covenants

The most typical financial-related covenants found in credit agreements are as follows:

1. *Maximum total leverage:* Typically calculated as total debt divided by last 12 months' EBITDA. The issuer is not permitted to allow the ratio calculation to exceed the specified covenant level. The covenant is intended to limit the amount of total indebtedness relative to the cash flow of the company.
2. *Maximum senior secured leverage:* Typically calculated as senior secured debt divided by last 12 months' EBITDA. The issuer is not permitted to allow the ratio calculation to exceed the specified covenant level. The covenant is intended to limit the amount of senior secured indebtedness relative to the cash flow of the company.
3. *Minimum interest coverage:* Typically calculated as last 12 months' EBITDA divided by last 12 months' total interest expense. The issuer is not permitted to allow the ratio calculation to be less than the specified covenant level. The covenant is intended to ensure an appropriate level of cash flow relative to the interest obligations of the issuer.

4. *Limitation on restricted payments:* Typically calculated as an absolute specified dollar amount or a basket based on a certain percentage of free cash flow over a specified measurement period. The issuer is not permitted to distribute cash flow in excess of the specified amount or basket. The covenant is intended to limit the amount of cash flow that is distributed outside the company that is not used for the benefit of the company.
5. *Maximum capital expenditure limitations:* Typically calculated as an absolute specified maximum dollar amount that an issuer can spend on capital expenditures. The covenant is intended to limit the issuer's allocation of cash flow toward capital expenditures beyond a specified predetermined schedule or amount.

Amendment Process

Most credit agreement terms can be amended by a simple majority of lenders. Given the still meaningful presence and influence of the lead arrangers in the bank group, in many cases the process can be completed rather quickly provided that appropriate pricing or consent fee incentives have been provided to lenders. Changes in scheduled principal payments and collateral typically require a higher threshold for approval.

Analysts must be cautious in being too comforted by the credit protection implied by the credit agreement's financial covenants. In strong financing market conditions, issuers can easily refinance their credit facility for better and more flexible terms as bank debt is often prepayable at any time with little to no premium. For example, a 5.0× leverage maintenance covenant with step-downs to 3.0× over a three-year period could be replaced with a 6.0× leverage maintenance test with no step-downs. In this example, covenants necessitating an improving credit profile have been replaced with much more lenient covenants whereby an issuer could increase its credit risk immediately and not have to improve its credit profile over the life of the loan.

Covenant Lite

An unfortunate development of the easy credit markets of 2006 and 2007 was the advent of "covenant-lite" bank loans. Covenant lite typically signifies that the credit agreement lacks a traditional leverage or coverage maintenance test. Instead, the traditional maintenance-based test is replaced with an incurrence test that is similar to bonds but is ultimately a materially weaker protection measure for senior lenders because the likelihood of violation is much lower, providing lenders with little ability to force corrective action or demand increased consideration. Without maintenance covenants, a company will have greater flexibility to further delay potential bankruptcy triggers that could ultimately lead to lower recoveries. This is the result of the fact that operations will have additional time to weaken further before the covenants are violated and necessitate action being taken.

Step 5: Trading Liquidity Factors

While credit analysis is focused on assessing the credit risk of a particular bond issue, an analysis of a particular bond's trading liquidity factors is a critical component of the overall risk of the investment. While trading liquidity factors can certainly hamper the performance of a particular bond issue that may possess a very favorable credit risk profile, the far more significant risk is that a poor trading liquidity profile will dramatically magnify the downside risk of a weak credit profile. It is already difficult to garner investment interest and new buyers in a weak or deteriorating credit that may have disappointed, but it is considerably more challenging to garner investment interest in a weak credit that also possesses a weak trading liquidity profile.

For example, a disappointing earnings announcement could result in a two-point drop in bond price if the issue possesses favorable trading liquidity factors, whereas the same announcement could easily result in a five-point (or greater) drop in bond price if it possesses very weak trading liquidity factors. Any negative credit developments are ultimately magnified, resulting in significant downside risk. An analyst must have an extremely high confidence level in the credit profile to be willing to take on significant trading liquidity risk.

The following is a checklist of key trading liquidity factors. The more checks an analyst makes on the list, the greater his or her level of trading liquidity risk.

Trading Liquidity Checklist

- ____ Is the issue size less than $200 million?
- ____ Is there only one tranche of bonds in the capital structure or less than $750 million in total bond issues outstanding?
- ____ Is there only one market maker for the bonds as opposed to multiple market makers?
- ____ Is there only one underwriter for the issue as opposed to multiple underwriters, including at least one top-tier firm?
- ____ Is the issue listed on a credit default swap index (CDX)?
- ____ Is there little volume of trading on the trade reporting and compliance engine (TRACE)?
- ____ Is the issuer a private company with no publicly traded stock?
- ____ Is the issuer *not* an SEC registrant or filer?
- ____ Is the issuer a small company and/or in a one-off industry?
- ____ Is there only limited sell-side analyst coverage as opposed to multiple sell-side analysts that publish research on the firm, including an analyst from at least one top-tier firm?
- ____ Is the issuer's management team *not* accessible to investors?
- ____ Is the issue rated triple-C on one or both sides?

Some of these factors are discussed in greater detail in Chapter 11.

Step 6: Relative Value

Relative value is the final focus in the security analysis process. Once all the credit and trading liquidity risks of the security have been determined and evaluated, the overall expected risk premium for the security can be appropriately established. Spread analysis is typically the most appropriate metric in determining whether the security's return is commensurate with its overall credit and investment risk.

Risk/Reward

Determining relative value in high yield is more art than science. All risk is not created equal. For example, it is much easier to compare and value the risk of financial leverage across two credits than it is to determine how much incremental return or yield is required to compensate for the potential risk presented by significant covenant flexibility that can be utilized to the detriment of bondholders. Many investors may use credit ratings to determine their credit risk and then evaluate the spreads on that basis. For example, a single-B rated issue yielding 500 basis points over riskless Treasuries may be considered attractive relative to another single-B rated issue yielding 350 basis points or versus the current high-yield single-B average spread of 400 basis points.

In order to make this assessment, however, one must assume that the credit ratings themselves are accurate and that they are a "leading" indicator of credit risk. More important, investors must realize that credit ratings do not contemplate many of the investment risks discussed above, such as bond covenants, size of issue, quality of underwriter(s), number of market makers, Wall Street sponsorship, and information flow. Relying on the credit rating alone to determine risk will not give a complete picture and is a perilous exercise in our opinion.

Comparables

The basic formula for assessing relative value is to compare the spread of the security being evaluated to the bond spreads of industry peers and other credits of similar risk. The chart shown in Figure 7.9 is a

FIGURE 7.9 Sample Credit Comp Sheet

LTM period	Company A 12/31/09	Company B 12/31/09	Company C 12/31/09
Revenue	**6,000**	**800**	**3,500**
EBITDA	**1,000**	**140**	**430**
Margin	**16.7%**	**17.5%**	**12.3%**
Capital expenditures (capex)	350	11	180
Interest	250	80	288
Tax	50	0	30
Cash flow	**350**	**49**	**(68)**
Working capital changes	50	(10)	0
Other (including acquistions/dividends)	(1,000)	0	0
Free cash flow (FCF)	**(600)**	**39**	**(68)**
Financial statistics			
EBITDA/interest	4.0	1.8	1.5
(EBITDA-capex)/interest	2.6	1.6	0.9
Bank debt/EBITDA	**2.8×**	**3.8×**	**2.6×**
Sr. notes/EBITDA	**3.0×**	**3.8×**	**6.0×**
Sub. notes/EBITDA	**3.0×**	**6.3×**	**7.2×**
Total debt/EBITDA	**3.6×**	**6.3×**	**7.3×**
Net debt/EBITDA	**2.9×**	**5.9×**	**6.7×**
Free cash flow/total debt	–17%	4%	–2%
% Total debt/TEV	46%	—	99%
TEV/EBITDA	**7.9×**	**—**	**7.3×**
Liquidity			
Cash	750	60	250
Availability	650	50	275
Total liquidity	**1,400**	**110**	**525**
10 Amortization	270	12	15
11 Amortization	70	11	500
12 Amortization	70	11	15
13 Amortization	70	11	400
14 Amortization	70	11	15
15+ Amortization	3,050	824	2,185
Capitalization			
Bank debt	2,800	530	1,120
Sr. notes	200	0	1,460
Sub notes	0	350	500
Other debt	600	0	50
Total debt	**3,600**	**880**	**3,130**
Preferred	250		
Number of shares	150	—	75
Stock price	$37.00	—	$7.00
Equity market cap	5,550	—	525
Total enterprise value (TEV)	8,650	—	3,405
LESS: Cash	(750)	(60)	(250)
LESS: Other value		—	
Adjusted TEV	7,900	—	3,155
Bond pricing			
Coupon	7.500%	9.500%	11.500%
Maturity	11/15/14	4/15/17	12/1/16
Moody's/S & P ratings	B1/BB-	B3/B-	Caa1/B-
Price	**98.00**	**91.50**	**77.75**
Yield to worst (YTW)	**7.91%**	**11.04%**	**16.65%**
Spread to worst (STW)	458	730	1289
Spread per unit of net leverage	161	125	192

typical "comp sheet" an analyst could prepare to help assess the relative value of one bond versus another.

Analyzing the credit comparables in Figure 7.9, it is apparent that Company C is a weaker credit. Compared to the other two companies, Company C has higher leverage, weak interest coverage, negative cash flow, and significant near-term amortization for which it does not appear to have ample liquidity to address. Given the higher-risk credit profile, the spread on Company C's sub notes is meaningfully wider than its comparables, as one would expect.

In contrast, Company A's stronger credit profile has resulted in a meaningfully tighter spread than its comparables. Although it also has a meaningful debt amortization in the current year, it appears to have ample liquidity (as measured by its cash and availability) to absorb the amortization. Ideally, the credit comparable would include a snapshot of the trailing 12-month operating results as well as a forward look at the next 12 months credit profile.

Quadrants

As discussed previously in this chapter, many investors use credit ratings to determine risk and evaluate comparable spreads. Given the market prevalence of ratings, we would recommend that investors be at least cognizant of the findings of this method; however, we recommend a more comprehensive risk assessment approach as the primary method.

Constructing a risk/return matrix can be helpful in determining a framework. Credits can be divided into quadrants, as show in Figure 7.10.

Following is the quadrant commentary for Figure 7.10:

1. *Quadrant 1:* Very solid credits with strong credit statistics, moderate leverage, and strong free cash flow. Typical characteristics would include companies with predictable and improving cash flows, deleveraging companies, and companies that have substantial assets well in excess of debt. Objective: capital preservation.

FIGURE 7.10 Quadrant Matrix

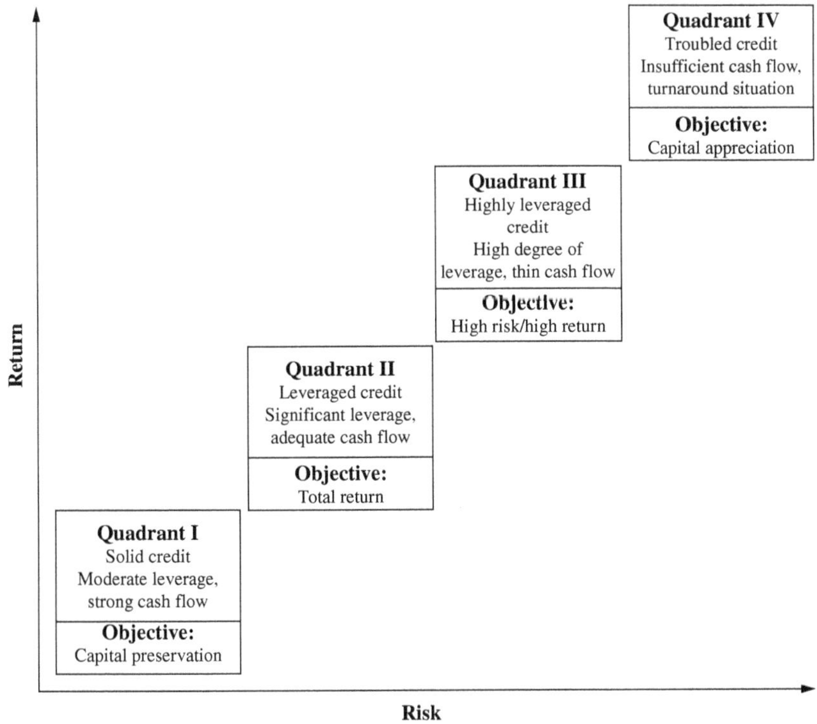

2. *Quadrant 2:* Good credits with significant leverage that must show stability and/or improvement in the credit profile via improved results and lower leverage. Quadrant 2 companies can appreciate or depreciate depending upon their ability to execute their business plan and ultimate credit trend. These credits are typically good companies/businesses with weak balance sheets and relatively weak asset value coverage of their total debt. Credits in Quadrant 2 essentially fall in the middle between Quadrants 1 and 3. Objective: capital preservation/total return.
3. *Quadrant 3:* Weak credits with extremely high leverage and deteriorating or at-risk credit trends. These credits have very little margin for error and therefore require higher yields to compensate bondholders for these risks. Typical characteristics

would include little to negative free cash flow (best measured relative to total debt) and deteriorating credit statistics. They may also include start-up companies, companies with large capital requirements, and aggressive capital structures that utilize zero coupon notes, payment in kind (PIK), or PIK toggle notes. Asset value coverage of total debt is typically extremely weak. Objective: high risk/high return.

4. *Quadrant 4:* Troubled credits that are distressed and may be in actual or technical violation of covenants. Bonds are likely to be impaired and therefore require much higher equitylike returns. Objective: capital appreciation.

When assigning quadrants to specific credits, they should be assigned with an emphasis on the prospective forward-looking view of the credit. The reason for this is that the credit markets are more focused on where a credit is going than on where it has been. Those investors that are best able to correctly forecast the credit trend will have the greater advantage. Placing too much emphasis on past results and a trailing credit risk profile could ultimately provide a misleading risk assessment and thereby corrupt the risk/reward equation and relative value analysis.

Within the quadrant framework, spreads can be analyzed relative to credits within the same quadrant. Given the potentially wide range of credit quality that may fall within a specific quadrant, each quadrant may be further subdivided into lower and upper quadrants for more defined segmentation. Once quadrants have been assigned, investors should compare spreads of companies within the same quadrant that are most similar. When possible, comparisons should be made to companies within the same industry and quadrant.

Other relative considerations include trading history, analyzing stock and bank loan prices, and duration.

Scenario Analysis

Scenario analysis is another tool that can be utilized to better frame relative value and determine an appropriate investment recommendation.

TABLE 7.8 Scenario Analysis Example

Trading Level	Probability	Bond Price	Yield-to-Worst	Spread-to-Worst	Leverage Ratio
Current		$98	8.3%	487 bp	5.0×
Scenario A*	75%	$92	9.4%	596 bp	6.3×
Scenario B†	25%	$99	8.2%	470 bp	4.7×

*Scenario A assumes 100% debt-financed acquisition.
†Scenario B assumes acquisition is financed with 60% equity and 40% debt.

This method is particularly useful in circumstances with possible multiple outcomes or potential event risk evaluation. (See Table 7.8.)

In the table, the subject company has just announced a significant acquisition, although financing has not yet been determined. After having assessed the amount of flexibility provided by the company's existing covenants as well as taking into account current capital market conditions for debt and equity, the analyst can utilize a scenario analysis to determine a potential trading recommendation. Given management's prior comments and long-standing financial policy, the analyst has assigned a 75% probability to a debt-financed acquisition as opposed to a more balanced combination of debt and equity financing. Likely potential trading levels after the events are then assigned to each of the scenarios based on relative value for the pro forma risk profile. The scenario analysis example indicates that there is six points of potential downside on the higher-probability outcome as opposed to one point of upside on the less likely outcome. Based on this analysis, the recommendation would likely be to sell or reduce the position if possible, or at the very least proceed with caution.

Trading History

To the extent that an issuer has had other bonds outstanding for a longer period of time, investors may also want to examine the bond trading history in a variety of different ways to provide a better overall perspective. The following is a list of key trading history questions:

1. What is the issuer's bond price history? Has the bond been very volatile, in which case a higher risk premium may be more appropriate?
2. What is the issuer's bond spread history relative to the current spread? Is it at the tight end or wide end of its historical range? Should it be there?
3. What is the issuer's bond spread relative to its industry or the high-yield index? How has this relationship trended over time? Is it at the tight or wide end of its historical range? Where is it relative to where you feel it should be?
4. What is the current spread level relative to the spread at issuance? Has it widened or tightened dramatically? Were the moves associated with a change in credit profile as opposed to more technical factors?

Stock Prices

Because high-yield companies are highly leveraged, their bond performance may sometimes be highly correlated to stock prices. In some cases equity prices may be a leading indicator, and in other cases bond prices may reflect the risk sooner. In any event, equity (if it is public) prices of the specific credit or its public peers and competitors may have a significant impact on bond prices. As equity prices rise and fall, the equity valuation of the company changes. This essentially measures the degree of "equity cushion" on a specific credit. For example, a stock price that has declined by 20% will signal that the implied asset value cushion relative to the bonds has also been dramatically reduced, thereby increasing the overall risk of the credit. If an investor is looking at two similar credits in the same industry with the same leverage, the investor would rather own the one with the higher enterprise value-to-EBITDA valuation multiple because it ultimately

FIGURE 7.11 Enterprise Value-to-EBITDA versus Leverage

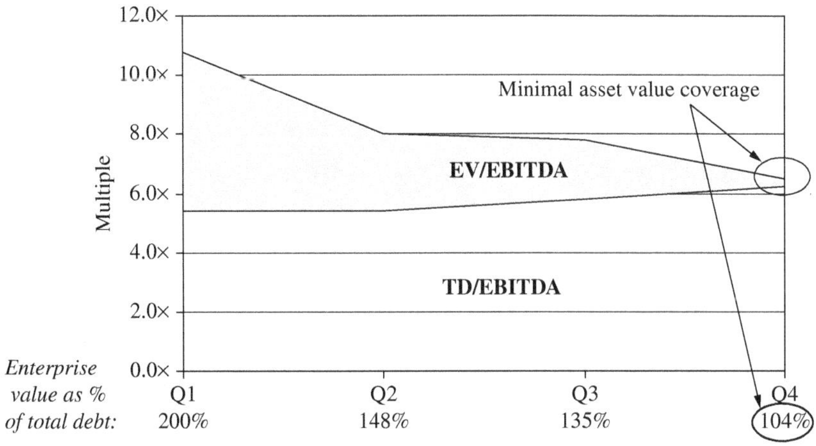

implies greater asset value coverage and thereby less risk, all other things being equal.

In Figure 7.11, a company's leverage has not changed dramatically over the four quarters, but because of a severe decline in the stock price, the enterprise valuation of the company has fallen. As a result, the enterprise value coverage of total debt has declined dramatically, and the credit risk has increased. The equity cushion is represented by the shaded area in Figure 7.11.

Examples like those depicted in Figure 7.11 are an important reason why analysts should not take too much comfort in high implied levels of asset coverage based on the stock price and enterprise value. For example, if equity investors no longer have a favorable view concerning the company's growth prospects, multiples may contract. It is important for the credit analysis to include alternate independent methods of asset and enterprise valuation while monitoring and taking into consideration movements in the current public equity value.

Although credit metrics may not change dramatically in the near term, a forward-looking view of the equity valuation may be important in determining perceived enterprise value coverage and trading outlook. In Figure 7.11, the 104% enterprise value-to-total debt coverage in Q4 strongly suggests that the bonds will now require equitylike returns because the implied asset coverage is now extremely weak.

Bank Loan Prices

It is also important to monitor how more senior instruments in the capital structure are trading. As the lines between high-yield bonds and bank loans are increasingly blurring as the two markets and investor bases converge, the relationship between the two becomes increasingly important. For example, if the yield on a company's term loan is too close to the yield on its bonds, this may signify that one or both instruments are mispriced. In order to make an appropriate comparison, the analyst must first attempt to evaluate both yields on an equivalent basis given that the bank loan yield is LIBOR-based and floating rate whereas the bonds are fixed rate and based on Treasury.

In the example of Company A in Table 7.9, the risk/reward profile for the bond is unfavorable because there is meaningful

TABLE 7.9 Comparable Bank and Bond Trading Levels

	Company A		
	Yield	**Spread**	**Leverage***
Term loan B	7.8%	430 bp	3.25×
Sr. sub bond	8.0%	450 bp	5.00×
Difference	*0.2%*	*20 bp*	*1.75×*
Relative value: TOO TIGHT			

	Company B		
	Yield	**Spread**	**Leverage***
Term loan B	7.8%	430 bp	3.25×
Sr. sub bond	12.0%	850 bp	3.75×
Difference	*4.2%*	*420 bp*	*0.50×*
Relative value: TOO WIDE			

*Debt/EBITDA through that security.

incremental financial risk given the significant incremental financial leverage at the bond investment level as well as the bonds' typical subordination in the capital structure with lack of security. An incremental 20 basis points would not be sufficient compensation for the incremental risk.

On the other hand, in the example of Company B in the table, the risk/reward profile for the bond would be much more favorable. While there still exists the lack of seniority in the capital structure inherent in nearly all bond-versus-bank debt investments, the incremental financial leverage at the bond investment level is fairly modest, while the incremental yield is very meaningful.

While this example was meant to isolate the relative value perspective between bank debt and bonds, it is important to note that there may be other justifications for the trading relationships because they take a forward-looking perspective in their analysis. For example, weak bond covenants and an extremely high event risk profile might indicate that the financial leverage for Company B is expected to increase dramatically, thereby justifying the incremental yield required by investors to compensate for the risk.

Duration

Duration is the calculation of the relationship of time value to a bond's interest and principal payments. Duration takes into account interest payments as well as the final principal payment at maturity. The longer the duration, the more sensitive the price will be to interest-rate fluctuations. Overall, bonds with high yields will have shorter durations than will lower-yielding issues.

Analysts must calculate a bond's duration and factor in the duration based on the investment strategy of the portfolio. While duration risk is ultimately more relevant from a portfolio manager's perspective, it is important for the analyst to consider duration when assessing relative value in order to account for the impact of a bond's structure on pricing.

Conclusion

Having covered the key steps of the entire security analysis process, it is essential to emphasize the critical importance of credit analysis in particular. Thorough credit analysis is ultimately the foundation for a successful high-yield investment because its primary focus is on avoiding defaults. While relative value is an important final step of the security analysis process, we would emphasize that the far greater investment risk is getting the credit analysis wrong as opposed to potentially overpaying for a good credit. It is important to keep in perspective that the high-yield asset class involves highly leveraged companies that have disproportionately less room for error and an inherently greater risk profile.

The asymmetrical upside/downside return profile of bonds also highlights the importance of avoiding meaningful downside credit risk. In practice, the underperformance related to overpaying for a good credit will pale in comparison to the ultimate downside in holding the bonds of a credit that will default. Remember that a bond's upside is limited to par (plus perhaps an early takeout premium), while the downside is theoretically zero. Finally, the other key theme to emphasize is that all of the security analysis steps are significant in their own right. A favorable assessment on many of the steps may not necessarily outweigh an individual risk component.

8

BOND INDENTURES AND BOND CHARACTERISTICS

William J. Whelan, III

Partner,
Cravath, Swaine & Moore LLP

High-yield bonds are issued pursuant to a document called a trust indenture. The indenture is a contract between the issuer of the bonds and a banking institution that acts as trustee for the benefit of the holders of the bonds from time to time. High-yield bonds are most commonly sold to investors by the issuer through investment banks, or underwriters, in an offering that is registered under the Securities Act of 1933 or in a private placement (often referred to as a Rule 144A offering) that is exempt from the registration requirements of the Securities Act.

In the indenture, the issuer subjects itself to restrictions on its future ability to carry on certain activities, such as issuing additional indebtedness and paying dividends. These restrictions are called covenants, and although they reside in a contract signed by the trustee, they are there for the benefit of the bondholders. Since the terms of these covenants have to be included in the offering document that is distributed to investors to solicit their interest, they must be established in advance and are therefore typically negotiated between the issuer and its counsel on the one hand and the underwriters and their counsel on the other. In this chapter we describe some of the common characteristics of high-yield bonds in the U.S. market and also focus on some of the more standard covenants and related terms of U.S. high-yield indentures.

Common Characteristics

Almost all high-yield bonds are issued with a "bullet" maturity, which means that they have a single maturity date for the entire principal amount of the bonds. It is uncommon for bonds to have any early mandatory redemption terms (with the exception of some "put" provisions related to the occurrence of specified events, discussed below) or any sinking fund feature. Although high-yield bonds increasingly are issued with floating rates of interest, it is still more common for the bonds to be issued with a fixed coupon.

The decision concerning which type is appropriate in a particular situation will depend in part on the needs of the particular issuer but also on the judgment of the underwriter as to which will lead to the most successful offering. This in part depends on which type of institutional investors is most likely to participate in a transaction. If the bonds have a fixed coupon, interest is paid semiannually. Floating-rate bonds usually have quarterly interest payment dates. In either case, interest payment dates are typically the first or fifteenth of a month by market convention.

In addition to "cash-pay" high-yield bonds, some issuers will issue "zero coupon" bonds, where no cash interest payments are made for a period of time (not longer than five years, for U.S. tax reasons), but instead the original principal amount of the bonds accretes semiannually at the implied interest rate, such that at maturity the repayment obligation of the issuer is substantially in excess of the initial gross proceeds received by the issuer. Related to zero coupon bonds are "pay-in-kind" securities, where the semiannual payments of interest are made not in cash but in additional securities of the same class having a principal amount equal to the accumulated six months of interest.

During the initial term that the high-yield bonds are outstanding, typically approximating the halfway point of the scheduled term of the bonds, the issuer is precluded from redeeming the bonds at its option. From a bondholder's perspective, this is an important provision. Often referred to as the "no call" period, the prohibition on optional redemptions during this period means that the bondholder can "lock in" the yield for this period and is not at risk that it will have to reinvest redemption proceeds too soon after making the initial investment decision. Beginning at the end of the no-call period, the bonds can be redeemed (or "called") at a premium that thereafter declines on each anniversary date until there is no premium in the last year or two of the life of the bonds.

One significant exception to the no-call period, which is typically effective for the initial three years of the term of the bonds, was created to allow an issuer to redeem a portion (typically 35%) of the outstanding bonds, but only to the extent that it has raised cash proceeds from the issuance of common equity. From the bondholders' perspective, they are willing to give up some of their yield protection so long as the issuer's stockholders' equity is increased. The redemption price is usually par plus the coupon (e.g., 110% for a 10% bond). This provision is often referred to as the "equity clawback." This provision was originally limited to the issuance of equity in the public markets by a private company, since bondholders not only wanted an increase in equity but also a public company valuation (which would improve the valuation methodology on the bonds). However, that limitation has all but disappeared, particularly with the substantial involvement of private equity firms in the high-yield market to finance acquisitions.

High-yield bonds are typically denominated as senior notes or senior subordinated notes. Occasionally you will see a more junior subordinated security, which is often either a discount security or convertible into common stock of the issuer. It is important in any high-yield offering to understand the relative contractual and structural priorities of the potential claimants against the issuer and its subsidiaries. When bonds are "senior subordinated," this means that the bonds are contractually subordinated by their terms to other specified classes of indebtedness.

The other type of subordination, called "structural subordination," cannot generally be discerned from the title of the bonds, but rather only by an understanding of the corporate structure of the issuer and its affiliates and subsidiaries. Structural subordination refers to the fact that the liabilities of subsidiaries of the issuer, which often include claims in addition to those of debt holders (e.g., trade creditors and preferred stock of subsidiaries), are superior to the claims of the bondholders to the extent of the value of the assets of such subsidiaries, even if the bonds are senior notes. This is because in any bankruptcy or liquidation involving the issuer and its subsidiaries, bondholders who do not have any direct claims against the subsidiaries (e.g., through a subsidiary guarantee) are entirely dependent on the recovery by (or on behalf of) the issuer of any value of the issuer's common equity claim against the subsidiaries.

Of course, that common equity claim is junior to those of the debt, trade, and preferred stakeholders of the subsidiary. Thus the bondholders' claim against the issuer is said to be structurally subordinated to those against the subsidiaries. This can be particularly meaningful if the issuer is a shell holding company and most of the consolidated assets are held in the subsidiaries.

If the bonds are contractually subordinated, then pursuant to the subordination provisions of the indenture, the issuer will be contractually prohibited from making payments of principal or interest to bondholders under specified circumstances. In short, if there is a payment default with respect to senior indebtedness, the issuer is automatically prohibited from making payments on the bonds for as long as the default continues. If there are other defaults under senior indebtedness that entitle the holders to accelerate their debt, then the senior debt holders have the right to instruct the issuer not to make any payments with respect to the subordinated bonds. Such instructions are typically valid for no more than 179 days, at which point the issuer is entitled to resume making payments on the bonds unless the holders of the senior indebtedness have accelerated their indebtedness.

Notwithstanding this contractual arrangement, the nonpayment on the bonds by the issuer during the 179-day period constitutes a default under the indenture, and depending on the specific provisions of the indenture, the bondholders may have certain rights to accelerate payment of the bonds as a result of such nonpayment. However, the bondholders' right to actually receive payment from the issuer will continue to be restricted by these very same contractual subordination provisions.

Nearly all Rule 144A high-yield offerings contain contractual obligations on the part of the issuer to ensure that the bonds are freely tradable under the securities laws within specified time periods following the closing of the Rule 144A offering. This can be achieved with the passage of time under Rule 144, which generally provides that after six or twelve months, nonaffiliates of the issuer can freely trade securities issued by the issuer in a private placement. Other methods to achieve this liquidity are to require the issuer to subsequently offer to the bondholders in an SEC-registered offering bonds that are identical to the restricted bonds acquired in the initial 144A distribution or to require the issuer to file with the SEC a "resale" registration statement that allows the investors to freely resell their bonds into the public markets.

The concept here is that in exchange for their willingness to buy the bonds without the benefit of a registration statement so that the issuer can obtain its financing on an expedited basis, the bondholders insist that the issuer agree to these obligations. The sole remedy available to the bondholders for the issuer's noncompliance with these obligations is an increase in the interest rate on the bonds for so long as the default continues. The failure to comply with these covenants does not constitute a default under the indenture.

Covenants

High-yield covenants are crafted to proscribe specified actions by the issuer on a case-by-case basis. As a result, they are often referred to as "incurrence-based" provisions, as opposed to provisions that require the issuer to maintain compliance with specified terms on an ongoing basis, which are referred to as "maintenance" covenants. Maintenance covenants are intended to measure the ongoing health of the issuer and to give "early warning signals" to the lenders if the business of the issuer is deteriorating. In such an event, the lead, or agent, bank may spearhead negotiations with the borrower to amend the applicable covenant to avoid an imminent default and possibly to provide new or incremental economic or contractual benefits to the bank group in order to obtain the requisite consent to the amendment. In many cases this process can be completed quickly and efficiently.

By contrast, an issuer's series of high-yield bonds might be held by 50 or more institutional investors, none of which has the predesignated role of lead or agent. If the high-yield indenture contained maintenance covenants, an issuer would be hard-pressed to get the holders organized on short notice to consider and agree to a revised maintenance covenant based on the issuer's then present financial condition. As a result, a covenant default would be hard to avoid, and the consequences of public disclosure and possible cross-defaults could be disastrous.

With incurrence-based covenants, an issuer need not worry about falling out of compliance based on events beyond its control. Rather, it need only test compliance with the covenant if it proactively intends to take an action, such as to borrow more money, to pay a dividend, or to sell assets. And if it finds itself in a situation in which it desires to solicit consents to amendments to the terms of the covenants in order to take an action, it can do so in an orderly process where the result, even if unfortunate, is not disastrous if it fails to obtain the requisite consent of bondholders.

The three primary objectives of the covenants from the bondholders' perspective are to (1) prevent the issuer from undertaking new obligations that could divert the issuer's cash flows toward competing claimants, rather than being available to meet its preexisting cash obligations, including debt service on the bonds themselves, (2) prevent the issuer from favoring another class of creditors over the bondholders by preserving the relative priorities of claimants, and (3) prevent the issuer from disposing of assets for less than equivalent value such that the remaining assets are not sufficient to discharge its remaining obligations, including debt service on the bonds. In crafting these covenants, a balance must be struck between achieving these objectives and giving the issuer the flexibility to grow and execute its business plan (which is presumably in the bondholders' interest) during the term of the bonds, which might be as long as 10 years.

Most bond indentures will contain the same list of covenants that will all start with the same basic proscription and then include a list of exceptions, some of which will be customary from deal to deal and the rest of which will be specifically negotiated for each deal. Many regular participants in the market will agree that some terms are "absolutely market" and then disagree about the rest. In fact, the concept of "market" evolves over time and depends on the type of issuer, the then strength of the high-yield market, the prospective rating on the bonds, and other factors. Certainly the active participation of private equity funds in the high-yield market over the past decade has had a substantial impact on the form of the covenants, particularly the emergence of significant exceptions and carve-outs from the basic covenants.

The marketing spin on the issuer's business strategy will also justify certain departures from market: for example, a start-up company may need to borrow substantial amounts after the bonds are issued, so the concept of leveraging new equity (permitting the incurrence of new amounts of debt based on the amounts of the equity raised after the bonds are issued) was created; similarly, a company with the stated strategy of pursuing joint ventures needs plenty of room to make investments.

One last general observation: the definitions matter. Much of the substance in understanding the covenants is actually in the definitions. They are often complex, and all the participants, but particularly the issuer's internal finance staff, must familiarize themselves with their nuances.

Restricted Subsidiaries versus Unrestricted Subsidiaries

It goes without saying that the issuer itself will be governed by the covenants. The other entities that will also be governed by the covenants will be certain of the issuer's subsidiaries, which are referred to as restricted subsidiaries. Generally, a subsidiary is any entity (corporate, partnership, etc.) in which a majority of the voting power is held by the issuer. Thus, the borrowing and other activities of a 50%-owned joint venture are not governed by the covenants. Because the activities of restricted subsidiaries are governed by the terms of the covenants to the same extent as those of the issuer, generally an issuer is free to conduct any business transactions (e.g., intercompany borrowings and investments) with subsidiaries that are restricted subsidiaries.

The activities of unrestricted subsidiaries are not governed by the covenants. In fact, the covenants treat unrestricted subsidiaries as if they were unrelated third parties, and accordingly the issuer has to evaluate every transaction with an unrestricted subsidiary for its compliance with the covenants. Thus, while cash generally is permitted to flow freely among the issuer and its restricted subsidiaries, this is not the case with unrestricted subsidiaries.

Whether a subsidiary is restricted or unrestricted is ultimately up to the issuer, although for the reason stated at the end of the preceding paragraph, most subsidiaries are restricted, even though this requires that they must abide by the indenture covenants. So why would an issuer elect to treat a subsidiary as unrestricted? An issuer might conclude that a start-up subsidiary, especially one that is engaged in a business line that represents a new venture for the issuer and is incurring net losses in its early start-up phase, might adversely affect the calculation of the issuer's covenant net income if it is part of the restricted group; at the same time, if it were not governed by the covenants and could incur substantial amounts of debt to finance its growth, it might thrive. Whatever the reason, a bondholder would generally be willing to allow an issuer to designate a subsidiary as unrestricted (which would leave it exempt from the covenants and therefore potentially of no residual value to the bondholders), if this designation is made at the time of the issuance of the bonds. Bondholders are also usually willing to permit issuers to designate a subsidiary as unrestricted after a bond has been issued, so long as at the time of designation the subsidiary has only nominal assets or the issuer is forced at the time of the designation to tap into one of its covenant baskets that it might have otherwise used for some other purpose, such as paying out a dividend to equity holders.

If the issuer chooses to bring a previously unrestricted subsidiary back into the restricted group (it may elect to do this because the subsidiary is now generating positive net income and it wants to be allowed by the covenants to freely transfer cash or other assets to and from such subsidiary), it may do so under the covenants only if, after giving pro forma effect on a consolidated basis to that subsidiary's then outstanding levels of indebtedness and cash flow, the issuer would have the capacity to incur additional indebtedness according to the indebtedness covenant. In this way the bondholders can have some assurance that the issuer is not bringing into the restricted group an entity with too much debt that may need to be serviced by cash flow from the issuer or other restricted subsidiaries.

Change of Control

The change of control provisions of the indenture are designed to allow the bondholder, upon the occurrence of certain events, to reevaluate the investment in the issuer represented by the bonds. If in light of the occurrence of such an event, the bondholder for any reason elects to exit the investment (and does not want to sell on the open market because the then current market price of the bonds is depressed), the issuer is required to buy the bonds at a purchase price of 101% of the principal amount of the bonds. This is commonly referred to as a change of control "put." Also common, especially in private equity deals, the indenture also includes a change of control redemption right on the part of the issuer. The market will accept this concept, even if it infringes on the no-call period, because the redemption premium is typically quite expensive for the issuer.

If the issuer is not at the time of bond issuance a public company, a change of control is often deemed to occur if a designated group of controlling shareholders (the so-called "permitted holders") fails to continue to own at any time a majority of the outstanding voting stock of the issuer. The permitted holders will usually include the majority shareholder, if there is such a single shareholder at the time issuance, or a group of shareholders that at the time of the issuance of the bonds collectively owns a majority of the voting stock of the issuer. The theory is that the bondholders have made an investment decision based upon an evaluation of the merits of shareholder control at the time of the investment, and if such controlling shareholders fail to continue to hold that controlling position (which in a private company context is assumed to be a majority), then the bondholders should be entitled to reevaluate their investment in the bonds.

Another event that is considered a change of control is somewhat similar to the first, but it applies in a public company context (whether the issuer was public at the time of issuance or becomes so thereafter). Here the permitted holders are entitled to fall below 50% and in fact could fall all the way to zero in terms of voting percentage ownership, without triggering a change of control. A change of control under this prong occurs only if persons other than the permitted holders acquire (typically) 35% or more of the voting power of the issuer and the permitted holders own a smaller percentage and the permitted holders do not have the right, by contract or otherwise, to elect or designate a majority of the members of the board of directors. The 35% level is used as a proxy for a level of voting power in a public company that is considered to be *de facto* controlling, even if not in actuality. Many private equity deals are negotiated so that this event does not happen unless the voting power of third parties exceeds 50%.

Other events that can trigger a change of control would be a successful proxy fight for control of the board, without regard to who holds shareholder voting power, as well as a liquidation of the issuer. A final common event that would constitute a change of control is an acquisition of a publicly held high-yield issuer by merger with another publicly held company, such that the public shareholders of the acquirer are the majority shareholders of the survivor, even if after the merger the voting stock of surviving entity in the merger is widely held. Many bondholders believe that a transaction of such magnitude is a significant enough event in the life of a high-yield issuer to allow the bondholders to reevaluate the investment, even if no single shareholder is technically in "control."

Restricted Payments

The restricted payment covenant is focused on limiting what the issuer is allowed to do with cash or other assets that it may have generated from operations or otherwise. The general principle is that the bondholders want to trap the cash and other assets of the issuer and its restricted subsidiaries and allow them to exit the credit group only under limited circumstances. Restricted payments include dividends on capital stock, the purchase of capital stock, the early purchase or redemption of debt that is subordinated to the bonds, and the making of investments.

With respect to dividends, the payment of a dividend in an issuer's own stock (other than certain types of stock), is freely permitted. The type of stock that would not be permitted (so-called "disqualified stock") is stock that has terms that are debtlike—they may have mandatory redemption provisions or otherwise be subject to maturity prior to the maturity of the bonds.

With respect to the purchase of capital stock, restricted payments include not only the purchase of the issuer's own capital stock but also, typically, the purchase of capital stock of a restricted subsidiary to the extent it is held by an affiliate of the issuer. Investing in or purchasing capital stock of restricted subsidiaries is generally viewed as a permitted investment (that is, not subject to this covenant). However, if such capital stock is held by an affiliate, the benefits for creditors such as bondholders obtained by the issuer's acquisition of a greater percentage of the restricted subsidiary may be offset to the extent that a controlling person is perceived to be cashing out of at least a part of his or her investment.

The term *investment* has a broad definition to include any debt or equity investment in another person. Guarantees of another person's debt are also typically considered to be investments in that person. Capital expenditures, or acquisitions of assets, are not investments and are not restricted by this covenant.

Certain types of investments are excluded from the definition of restricted payments. These permitted investments are generally ordinary course types of investments, such as accounts receivable (which are in effect investments in the customer), and advances to employees (which are investments in the workers). However, permitted investments also include any investment that the issuer makes in a restricted subsidiary or in a person that as a result of the investment will become a restricted subsidiary. These are important provisions that permit the free flow of cash and assets between an issuer and its restricted subsidiaries and are the quid pro quo for subjecting the restricted subsidiaries to the terms of the indenture.

This is perhaps the most significant consequence of having distinctions between restricted subsidiaries and unrestricted subsidiaries (cash is not permitted to flow freely from the issuer to an unrestricted subsidiary). Occasionally one will also see significant exceptions to the restricted payments covenant buried in the definition of permitted investments. For instance the definition might include joint venture investments up to a specified dollar amount.

Once an issuer has determined that the action it proposes to take involves a restricted payment, it must test it against the covenant itself. In the first instance, before an issuer can make a restricted payment, it must be in a position to incur indebtedness under its general debt incurrence test that is discussed below. The theory of this requirement is that if the issuer is not healthy enough to meet the minimum threshold for incurring debt (i.e., it doesn't have sufficient cash flow vis-à-vis interest expense), then it should not be permitted to make any restricted payments for the benefit of junior security holders.

The amount that can be paid out by the issuer as a restricted payment at any time is often referred to as the "dividend basket" or the "restricted payment basket." This basket will be increased, or built up, by the factors described below and will be reduced, or depleted, by the amount of restricted payments actually made over time.

The general test for building up the restricted payment basket is based on the cumulative consolidated net income of the issuer and restricted subsidiaries subsequent to the issue date of the bonds. To the extent that the issuer has recognized, over the entire time period since the issuance of the bonds, positive net income, it is allowed to take 50% of that amount and pay it out as dividends or make other restricted payments. Net income is essentially based upon generally accepted accounting principles (GAAP) and is not a cash calculation. On the other hand, if the issuer has, since the original issuance date of the bonds, recognized a cumulative net loss, then 100% of the loss counts against the issuer in determining dividend-paying capacity. This negative amount will become relevant if the issuer has otherwise developed some dividend-paying capacity pursuant to other methods of increasing the dividend basket.

In calculating consolidated net income, the net income of an unrestricted subsidiary (even if wholly owned by the issuer) or of any "investee" company (i.e., less than majority-controlled) can be included by the issuer only to the extent that cash is actually received by the issuer or one of its restricted subsidiaries from such unrestricted subsidiary or investee company. This limitation recognizes that the issuer probably does not, typically because of limitations in other contracts, have full access to the net income of these entities, and therefore it should not be entitled to a full credit for the net income—only for the cash it receives. Similarly, to the extent that a restricted subsidiary is subject to restrictions (contractual or otherwise) on its ability to pay dividends to the issuer, the issuer does not get credit for the net income of that restricted subsidiary, except to the extent that the issuer receives (or could have received) cash from that restricted subsidiary.

The second important way that an issuer can develop or increase its dividend basket is through the issuance of equity. If the issuer raises equity proceeds after the issuance of the bonds, other than proceeds from the issuance of disqualified stock, then it is entitled to receive a dollar-for-dollar credit to its dividend-paying capacity. Bondholders are willing to give credit to an issuer for this purpose to the extent that the issuer has raised the corresponding amount of cash through the issuance of junior securities. The issuer can also develop or increase its dividend basket through the conversion of its outstanding debt into equity or through the realization of proceeds from the divestment or repayments of certain investments it has made since the issuance of the bonds.

Many indentures include some common exceptions to the restricted payments covenant that entitle the issuer to make specified types of payments even if it is unable to incur additional indebtedness under the debt incurrence test or it has been unable to generate sufficient dividend-paying capacity through net income and equity proceeds to make these payments. The first exception allows the issuer to make a restricted payment with the proceeds of the issuance of capital stock (so long as it is not an issuance of disqualified stock), provided that the making of the restricted payment must occur substantially concurrently with the issuance of the new stock. Note, as discussed above, that while ordinarily the issuance of capital stock would increase an issuer's dividend-paying capacity, the issuer may not be able to access that capacity if it is unable to pass the debt incurrence test (the first condition described above under the covenant). In that event, this exception allows the issuer to use equity proceeds to effect a restricted payment when it is not otherwise allowed to make a restricted payment, although of course it is not entitled to double-count the dollar amount of the proceeds of this equity offering by adding it to the dividend basket.

The second common exception allows the issuer to acquire subordinated debt with the proceeds of other subordinated debt. Generally the bondholder is indifferent to the exchange of one subordinated security for another, and allowing the issuer to do this may help the issuer to avoid defaults or other financial crises under the debt to be replaced.

There are usually several customized exceptions for each issuer based upon its particular capital structure (e.g., if there is an existing class of preferred stock, you may see an exception to allow the issuer to pay dividends on the preferred stock). You may also see exceptions designed to permit the issuer to effect its ongoing business strategy (e.g., if it is the stated intent of the issuer to make certain investments, then this covenant should allow the issuer to make these investments, usually up to certain specified dollar levels).

Indebtedness

The limitation on the incurrence of indebtedness is designed to protect the bondholders from the issuance by the issuer of additional debt unless the issuer has the demonstrated capacity (usually tested based upon a comparison of cash flow to interest expense) to service all its debt, including the proposed new debt. This test is generally known as the "coverage" or "debt incurrence" test, and the debt permitted to be incurred is generally referred to as "coverage debt." If the issuer does not have the demonstrated capacity, then it may not incur any additional debt except to the extent that it can take advantage of certain specified exceptions to the debt incurrence test that are available to the issuer without regard to its debt-servicing capacity. This kind of debt is often referred to as "permitted debt."

This is a limitation on the incurrence of indebtedness; once incurred, the issuer is permitted to leave that debt outstanding notwithstanding any subsequent deterioration in debt-servicing capacity.

Indebtedness as defined in most high-yield indentures generally includes indebtedness for money borrowed, lease obligations that would appear on the balance sheet of the issuer, reimbursement obligations with respect to standby letters of credit (i.e., excluding trade letters of credit that are obtained in the ordinary course of the issuer's business), obligations with respect to disqualified stock, preferred stock of subsidiaries, guarantees issued by the issuer that are in respect of indebtedness of other persons, and security arrangements undertaken by the issuer to secure indebtedness of other persons. Indebtedness does not include obligations to pay interest or dividends. Note that guarantees are indebtedness (they are also investments in the person whose obligation is guaranteed).

The basic debt incurrence test allows the issuer to incur "coverage debt" if the issuer—on a trailing 12-month basis and on a pro forma basis assuming the proposed indebtedness had been incurred at the beginning of such 12-month period—has enough cash flow (typically based on earnings before interest expense, taxes, depreciation and amortization, or EBITDA) in relation to its cash and noncash interest expense (typically a minimum ratio of 2 to 1). An occasional alternative to the interest coverage test is a leverage test, which evaluates the relationship of the issuer's consolidated debt to its trailing 12-month EBITDA on a pro forma basis for the incurrence of the indebtedness.

Regardless of whether a proposed borrowing would be considered coverage debt or permitted debt, it is important to the issuer and bondholders alike whether the covenant allows restricted subsidiaries, as well as or instead of, the issuer to incur the debt. For instance, if the bonds are senior notes, the bondholders would prefer that most, if not all, incremental debt be issued by the issuer itself and not by subsidiaries. If subsidiaries were allowed to issue the incremental debt, substantial amounts of indebtedness could potentially be issued at a structurally superior level, and thus the notes, which were marketed as senior notes, might become structurally subordinated to substantial amounts of debt. The same considerations may not exist in a senior subordinated note offering, where the bondholders have already agreed to contractual subordination and may therefore care somewhat less about the potential amounts of structurally superior debt.

In calculating an issuer's interest coverage ratio to determine eligibility at any time to issue coverage debt, the indenture definitions look back over the preceding four fiscal quarters and include on a pro forma basis the incurrence of the proposed indebtedness and any other incurrences or repayments of indebtedness as if these incurrences and repayments had occurred at the beginning of the period. Similarly the definitions give the issuer pro forma credit for investments that have had the effect of adding EBITDA during the course of the preceding four fiscal quarters and require the issuer to subtract EBITDA that may have been attributable to a restricted subsidiary or line of business that may have been disposed of during the course of the year.

If an issuer does not qualify at the time to issue coverage debt, it would then review the various categories of permitted debt to determine whether the proposed borrowing can fit in one of those exceptions. Almost every high-yield debt covenant contains an exception for the issuer to incur bank debt. The exception may be constructed around the issuer's borrowing base (inventory and accounts receivables), or it may be limited to a specified dollar amount. Another important category of permitted debt is intercompany debt between the issuer and its restricted subsidiaries, so long as it is issued to the issuer or a restricted subsidiary and also remains with that person (or with another member of the same group). If the debt is transferred outside the group to a third party, it no longer qualifies for this exception and is deemed to be incurred again at the time of transfer. In that event, the issuer would need to identify another provision of the covenant that would allow it to incur this debt.

Every indenture needs to permit the issuer to refinance any of its indebtedness, whether it was outstanding at the time of the indenture or was issued after the debt was incurred, in order to limit the possibility of a default at the maturity of the other indebtedness. In issuing any refinancing debt, the issuer may not increase the principal amount (except to the extent needed to pay related costs, e.g., accrued interest, premium, and other retirement costs), the issuer may not shorten the average life of the debt that is being refinanced, and the issuer may not refinance subordinated debt with senior debt.

Almost every high-yield debt covenant contains a general basket—generally referred to as the "debt basket"—that permits the issuer, and sometimes its restricted subsidiaries, to issue a specified dollar amount of indebtedness, again without regard to whether the issuer has the necessary interest coverage ratio that would permit it to issue coverage debt. This catchall basket is intended to protect the issuer in the case of an "emergency," where it may need to incur debt and cannot satisfy the debt incurrence test and cannot identify any other specific exception.

In addition to these customary categories of permitted debt, most indentures will include additional exceptions that would apply to a specific issuer. For instance, an issuer that historically has acquired capital assets with purchase money indebtedness or through capital lease transactions would typically negotiate for an additional exception that would permit such transactions in the future.

In connection with any individual incurrence of indebtedness, the issuer does not need to identify a single provision that will permit the entire amount of this indebtedness. For instance, the issuer could incur a portion of the indebtedness based upon the credit agreement exception and could also incur a portion of the indebtedness with respect to its general basket.

In senior subordinated note indentures, the issuer is not allowed to incur any debt that is contractually subordinated to any indebtedness unless the debt to be incurred is also senior subordinated (i.e., equal to the high-yield bonds) or is subordinated to the bonds. In other words, the issuer cannot have any subordinated debt that is senior to these senior subordinated bonds.

Restrictions on Distributions from Restricted Subsidiaries

The general thrust of the covenant that places restriction on distributions from restricted subsidiaries, which is not heavily negotiated, is to prevent the issuer and its restricted subsidiaries from agreeing to any contractual limitations on the ability of the subsidiaries to send cash and other assets, whether in the form of dividends or loans or other property transfers, to the issuer. Obviously, to the extent that such contractual limitations were in place, the issuer would have substantially less ability to service its own debt, including the bonds. Generally the exceptions to this proscription include those that are in effect on the date the bonds are issued (and presumably are disclosed to prospective investors) and encumbrances that are contained in refinancing agreements and which are not more restrictive than those in the debt agreement to be refinanced. Given the adverse consequences of these limitations to the issuer's cash flow and therefore to the issuer's creditors, to the extent that a subsidiary is allowed by this covenant to contractually restrict itself from paying dividends to the issuer, the definition of consolidated net income typically excludes some or all of the income of a subsidiary from the issuer's calculation of consolidated net income.

Sales of Assets

The limitation on the sales of assets covenant does not prohibit an issuer from effecting asset sales. Although the covenant requires sales of assets to be made at fair value and that a large percentage (between 70% and 90%) of the consideration be received in cash, the main purpose of the covenant is to limit the uses of proceeds in the event that the issuer does sell assets. From the bondholders' perspective, when an issuer sells an asset, it has removed potential income-producing assets from the consolidated group. As a result the bondholder expects the issuer within some reasonable period of time to either pay off debt (thereby reducing the debt service burden on the assets that remain) or else invest in new assets (typically only assets that are related to the issuer's core business) that in theory will also be producing income.

This covenant is one of the easiest for an issuer to comply with because the issuer has substantial discretion over a period that often extends for a year whether to retire other indebtedness or to make capital expenditures (or even certain investments) with the proceeds of the asset sale. To the extent that the issuer does neither within this period, the covenant requires the issuer to make an offer to the bondholders to purchase their bonds at par to the extent of the proceeds. To the extent that any proceeds remain after all bonds tendered in such an offer are in fact purchased, they are usually available to the issuer to use however it sees fit, including, if the issuer has built up any dividend-paying capacity, making restricted payments.

This covenant is designed to capture proceeds only from asset dispositions that are outside the ordinary course of business, and then only to the extent that they exceed some negotiated floor amount that is deemed immaterial. Issuers may request special treatment or other exceptions from the application of this covenant for dispositions that are reasonably foreseeable by the issuer at the time the bonds are issued. Since most issuers usually intend to or are required by their bank lenders to repay debt with the proceeds of asset sales anyway, issuers often decide not to spend much time negotiating significant carve-outs to this covenant.

Transactions with Affiliates

The covenant relating to transactions with affiliates is designed to prevent the issuer from circumventing the restricted payment covenant by disguising a dividend-like transaction in the form of a business transaction. Accordingly, the covenant requires the issuer to ensure that any transaction with an affiliate is conducted on terms that are similar to those that would be obtained with unrelated third parties and, depending upon the dollar amount involved in the transaction, that such terms are approved by the majority of disinterested directors and/or that such terms are determined to be fair to the issuer in the opinion of an independent valuation firm.

This covenant takes on added significance when the issuer is a private company that is controlled by one shareholder or a small group of shareholders. An issuer that is publicly held is likely to be concerned about the fairness of affiliate transactions for reasons of corporate law and usually does not object to any significant degree to the terms of this covenant. A private company issuer is likely to request carve-outs for fees paid to financial sponsors, for example, and for other transactions that are reasonably foreseeable. These exceptions are typically kept to a minimum, since the effect of creating an exception is to permit a transaction that may have terms that are not fair to the issuer.

A common exception recognizes that if an issuer is permitted by the restricted payments covenant to pay a dividend that depletes its dividend basket, thereby sending assets completely out of the consolidated group, the investor should be relatively indifferent if, rather than electing to pay the dividend, the issuer elects to enter into some other kind of transaction (e.g., an investment) with an affiliate. Another common exception permits transactions between the issuer and its restricted subsidiaries. Also permitted are transactions with entities that are technically affiliates of the issuer because they are controlled by the issuer (e.g., 45% voting stake), but otherwise should be viewed as a third party (e.g., the remaining 55% voting stake is held broadly by persons that are not affiliates of the issuer). The covenant does not typically restrict the issuer from issuing capital stock to affiliates (other than disqualified stock). Among other common carve-outs are provisions that permit transactions relating to contracts in effect at the time of the issuance of the bonds (and which should probably be described in the offering document), as well as relating to renewals or extensions of the contracts that have terms not less favorable to the issuer than those in the original contract.

Liens/Sale-Leasebacks

The lien covenant has primary importance in an indenture for senior notes. In a senior subordinated note offering, the holders typically insist only on the "antilayering protection" arising from the issuer's agreement not to grant any liens to secure other subordinated debt. Conversely, the holders of senior notes, in an effort to remain as senior as possible with respect to the assets of the issuer, restrict the issuer from incurring liens (which includes security interests, mortgages, and similar contractual or legal encumbrances) on its assets except for limited permitted exceptions, or unless the issuer is willing to simultaneously grant an equal lien for the benefit of the bondholders.

These exceptions usually appear in a definition of permitted liens, which usually includes a long laundry list of ordinary course liens (e.g., warehousemen's liens). In addition to those, however, and the ones that are typically the most important to the issuer, are those that deal with purchase money financings, financings under one or more of the categories of permitted debt, preexisting or acquired liens, and refinancings of debt that is already secured. An important but subtle point is to determine whether the assets that are permitted to be subject to the liens should be limited (e.g., for purchase money debt, only the asset acquired should be permitted to secure purchase money debt, but for permitted bank debt, any assets of the issuer or its restricted subsidiaries are typically permitted collateral).

Another covenant that would typically be found only in a senior note offering and is considered a corollary to the limitation on liens covenant is a covenant limiting the issuer's ability to enter into sale-leaseback transactions. A sale-leaseback transaction, in which the issuer sells an asset and immediately leases it back, is economically very similar to a secured financing, since the issuer will receive sale proceeds (similar to loan proceeds) and will make rental payments over the life of the lease (similar to loan repayments). Thus, this covenant generally permits an issuer to enter into sale-leaseback transactions as long as the issuer has the ability to incur the related indebtedness represented by the lease obligation and would be able to incur the lien on the property securing the lease. However, since the asset has been sold and is therefore not part of the issuer's consolidated assets subsequent to the sale (unlike a secured financing), this covenant contains the added requirement that the issuer treat the sale proceeds as it would in connection with any other asset sale.

Mergers and Consolidations

The merger covenant is designed to ensure that the successor or survivor in any major transaction involving the issuer, including the transferee of substantially all the assets of the issuer, assumes the obligations with respect to the bonds. As for substantive requirements in connection with such transactions, the covenant requires that the issuer on a pro forma basis be able to incur indebtedness under the debt incurrence test. This substantive requirement is often the subject of some negotiation because it is not readily clear to many issuers why this particular measurement is relevant in determining whether a merger is one that makes financial and business sense from the perspective of the bondholders.

Nonetheless, the high-yield market has historically insisted that the issuer be financially healthy (as measured by the debt incurrence test) before it is entitled to engage in any significant merger transactions. As a general rule, bondholders reasonably expect some improvement in the issuer's creditworthiness over the life of the bonds, as measured by interest coverage, and it could substantially and adversely affect the secondary trading value of bonds if the indenture permitted a reasonably healthy and deleveraged issuer to releverage itself as part of a merger transaction.

SEC Reporting

In the infancy of the high-yield market, many issuers were able to avoid regular reporting to bondholders and certainly often were able to avoid regular SEC reporting. Since most high-yield note deals are ultimately held by fewer than 300 holders, issuers would automatically be relieved, pursuant to the Securities Exchange Act of 1934, of any SEC reporting requirements beginning with respect to the fiscal year following the year in which the registration statement for the bonds became effective. It is now almost universally true in high-yield indentures that the issuer is required to make regular SEC reports (and to post such information on the issuer's own Web site) to ensure the steady flow of readily accessible information for current holders and prospective holders. (Note that this is one of the few affirmative covenants in a high-yield indenture and one that does require some maintenance efforts on the part of the issuer.)

It is important in transactions involving foreign issuers to review the indenture language to understand whether they are bound to report on a basis similar to U.S. domestic issuers or whether they are entitled to follow the more relaxed SEC rules for foreign private issuers. This is usually a matter of some negotiation prior to the issuance of the bonds. Because of the uptick in the number of financial restatements by SEC-reporting companies in the past few years, which causes delays in the filing of regular reports with the SEC and therefore defaults under this covenant in high-yield indentures, issuers are likely to obtain some relief in the language of this covenant (or in the language in the related default provision) to avoid a hair-trigger event of default and acceleration of the bonds as a result of a tardy SEC filing.

Defaults

High-yield indentures contain standard default provisions for the nonpayment of principal or interest. While there is no grace, or cure, period for principal payment defaults, the grace period for nonpayment of interest is typically 30 days. It is also common that issuers have a 30-day grace period after notice to the issuer to comply with the substantive covenants of the indenture before an event of default is deemed to have occurred (which would allow for the exercise of contractual remedies against the issuer). As for more administrative obligations of the issuer under the indenture (e.g., maintaining a registrar for the registration of the bonds), the grace period is typically 60 days following notice to the issuer. High-yield indentures also contain a default provision related to the noncompliance by the issuer with its obligations under other debt instruments (e.g., bank credit agreements), but the default is triggered upon the actual acceleration of indebtedness (a "cross-acceleration" provision) by the other lender, not simply the right of the other lender to accelerate (known as a "cross-default" provision, which is the standard in bank credit agreements).

Amendments/Waivers

The general rule for amendments in high-yield transactions is that the issuer needs to obtain the consent of a majority in principal amount of the outstanding bonds in order to effect amendments or waivers to the indenture. To the extent that the issuer does seek the consent of holders and offers to pay them for their consent, many indentures require the issuer to offer to pay a consent fee to every holder that is willing to provide its consent in the prescribed time period. The indenture usually includes a list of those items in the indenture, generally related to the "money terms," such as principal, interest rate, and maturity, that may not be amended except with the unanimous consent of the holders. There usually are also included a list of amendments that can be made without the consent of any holder on the theory that amendments are harmless to the bondholders (e.g., clarifying ambiguities, adding covenants on the part of the issuer, adding guarantees).

Defeasance

Keeping in mind that the issuer is typically subject to some period during which it is not entitled to redeem the bonds, the indenture does allow the issuer at any time to escape the restrictions in the covenants through the mechanism of defeasance. Essentially the issuer is required to deposit in trust with the bond trustee enough cash or government securities with a present value based on calculations confirmed by an independent accounting firm so that there will be sufficient cash available, after taking into account the earnings on the deposited funds, to pay all the interest and principal of the bonds when they are due. Once the issuer has made the deposit of cash or government securities into the defeasance trust, it is entitled to ignore the substantive covenants discussed in this chapter. Similarly the related events of default are rendered inoperative.

Defeasance is expensive for an issuer because the earnings growth rate the issuer must use in calculating the minimum cash deposit is low—the U.S. Treasury rate then in effect. As a result, defeasance is not an attractive option to most issuers. A common alternative is for issuers to offer to buy the bonds from holders in a tender offer that is usually accompanied by a solicitation by the issuer for consent of the tendering holders to amendments to the indenture. As long as a majority of the holders give their consent, then the issuer can usually achieve its goal of obtaining relief from the covenants, and the price that it needs to pay to clear the market is usually less expensive than the defeasance option.

Conclusion

In this chapter we attempt to describe the common characteristics of high-yield bonds as well as the most common covenants that can be found in high-yield indentures. Every bond indenture is different, however, and in practice significant variations will be found both in the types of covenants and in the types of exceptions to the covenants based on the issuer's industry, the proposed ratings on the bonds, general economic and market conditions, and the sophistication and experience of the issuer and its counsel. In reviewing actual covenant language, it bears repeating that the language of the accompanying definitions is critical. Well-crafted high-yield covenants will usually strike a balance between the bondholders' reasonable and legitimate expectations for the protection of their investment and the legitimate needs of an issuer to have the flexibility to grow its business in accordance with its stated business strategy.

9

CREDIT MODELS FOR ASSESSING FIRM RISK

William F. Maxwell

Rauscher Chair in Financial Investments,
Cox School of Business at SMU

Philip Delbridge

Vice President, Credit Risk Management,
Credit Suisse Securities (USA) LLC

Fundamental analysis is the traditional approach to credit risk analysis. Fundamental analysis involves a detailed review of a borrower's industry, cost structure, financial flexibility, liquidity, and quality of management to derive a risk rating that reflects the likelihood of the borrower defaulting on its obligations. While fundamental analysis is the most comprehensive approach to credit risk analysis, it is often time-consuming and subjective. It also requires a subjective weighting of different metrics to make an overall conclusion. Over time, credit models have been developed to provide a more objective and timely approach to the evaluation of credit risk. This chapter contrasts fundamental analysis with common types of credit models, both historical accounting- based models and market data-driven models. For market-driven models, we focus on Moody's KMV EDF model, which is the most widely used quantitative credit model around the world.

Fundamental Analysis versus Credit Models

Lenders, institutional investors, and credit rating agencies (CRAs) adopt a similar approach to assess counterparty credit risk (we refer to lenders and institutional investors jointly as investors). For investors, the aim is to assess the repayment capacity of a borrower and derive a rating to reflect the borrower's credit risk. For example, at CRAs such as S&P, Moody's, and Fitch, fundamental analysis is used to assign ratings for both the counterparty and the underlying debt issue. No matter what the ultimate objective, investors and CRAs undertake careful due diligence when evaluating the credit risk of a borrower. This is especially true in the leveraged financial market as risk assessment is the primary goal in a successful investment strategy. This is in contrast to investment-grade investing because most credit rated A and above is usually considered to be homogeneous as it relates to credit risk.

Chapter 3 contains a detailed review of the rating process using fundamental analysis. Investors follow a similar approach to the CRAs when conducting fundamental analysis for large corporate borrowers. Investors and CRAs will use the information from fundamental analysis to construct a risk-weighted matrix for key rating criteria such as market position, seasonality, earnings stability, cash flow coverage, and liquidity sources. A risk matrix allows the analyst to derive an ordinal ranking of key risks and prescribe an overall risk rating.

The main drawback of fundamental analysis is that it requires analysts to have an in-depth understanding of the industry, undertake an in-depth review of financial statements and other relevant data of the borrower, and then compile the information to project the financial performance with sophisticated financial models. This process is subjective, and differing views of the risk profile of a borrower can affect lending and investing decisions.

For example, if two banks are competing for the business of a particular borrower, the bank with the lower risk rating will often win the business because of its cheaper pricing. Also, the bank with the fastest turnaround time will have a competitive advantage if the client is seeking a quick response. The credit due diligence phase is often considered the bottleneck in the investment process. In an ever-increasingly com petitive landscape, techniques have evolved to assist investors by providing a more timely and accurate analysis of credit risk. Quantitative credit risk models have gained widespread appeal and are now used to assess credit risk across a broad range of borrowers from large Fortune 500 companies to small businesses and consumers.

Measures of Credit Risk

A single risk rating such as a AA– or BB+ does not quantify the credit risk of a borrower. Rating scales such as the ones used by S&P, Moody's, and Fitch provide an ordinal measure of risk. In other words, the purpose of the rating is to rank counterparties from highest to lowest risk. However, investors and lenders often require a cardinal ranking of credit risk for both pricing and portfolio analysis. Cardinal rankings are measured by default probabilities. In order to convert ordinal rankings of credit risk into cardinal measures, investors and CRAs must rely on ex-post historical default rates. Credit models, on the other hand, provide an ex-ante direct measure of default risk.

Classifications of Credit Risk Models

The primary goal of most credit risk models is to generate a measure of default or probability of default. The quantitative models that have been developed to estimate default probabilities can be classified into two broad categories: (1) fundamentals-based models, which rely on accounting and economic information; and (2) market-based models, which rely on security prices.[1] Academic literature has also grouped credit models into three broad categories: credit scoring, structural, and reduced form.[2] This chapter focuses on credit scoring and structural models.

Fundamental-based models have been around for some time. The most common type of fundamental-based model is the credit scoring (or accounting-based) model. These types of models use accounting data to estimate the likelihood of default. The most well-known accounting-based model for estimating default probabilities is the Altman Z-score model (the "Z-score"). The Z-score is discussed in more detail in Chapter 10.

First, accounting-based models such as the Z-score have been subject to criticism by academics and practitioners. The main criticism is that accounting-based models are backward-looking and can only incorporate data that are several months old. Second, financial statements are based on historical cost accounting. In most cases, historical costs do not reflect current market values. Finally, accounting-based models typically exclude volatility as an explanatory factor of default, and we know that volatility is a key factor in determining financial distress and defaults.[3] A reliable volatility measure is difficult to obtain from quarterly or annual financial statements. The flaws with accounting-based models led to the development of market-based models. Market-based models, which rely on security prices, derive a forward-looking estimate of default.

Moody's KMV

The Moody's KMV model is the most well-known and widely used market-based credit model. KMV is a San Francisco-based borrower that sells credit-analysis-based models. The company was acquired by Moody's in 2002. According to its Web site, KMV products are used by more than 2,000 financial institutions and corporations around the world. The next few sections of this chapter cover the theory underlying the KMV model and how the model generates default probabilities, and contrast the performance of credit models with bond ratings. Fitch

Ratings has developed a similar model called "equity implied ratings" and probability of default (equity implied rating, or EIR), which is covered later in this chapter.

The KMV EDF Model

The leading example of market-based credit measure is the expected default frequency (EDF) model of KMV. The term "expected default frequency" is the same as a probability of default. An EDF represents the probability that the borrower will fail to service its obligations. For example, a borrower with a current EDF credit measure of 1% has a 1% probability of defaulting within the next 12 months. Or if we create a portfolio of 1,000 such borrowers, on average, 10 will default over the next year, and 990 will not. KMV defines default as the nonpayment of any scheduled payment, interest, or principal.[4]

The KMV model uses a combination of financial statement information and market data to produce a more powerful predictor of default. The foundation of the KMV model is based on Merton's general derivative pricing model. The Merton model is an example of a structural-based model, which estimates default probabilities through the relationship between asset values and financial leverage. The main idea of a structural model is that a borrower will default if the market value of its assets falls below the value of its debt obligations.

Option pricing theory is used to capture the relationship between financial statement information, market values, and default probabilities. Robert C. Merton developed his own option pricing model to predict default risk based on the work of the Black-Scholes model. A detailed explanation of the Merton model is beyond the scope of this book. However, the basic idea of the Merton model is that a borrower's equity has the same payoff as a call option, where the strike price of the option is equal to the face value of the borrower's debt. If the value of a borrower's assets is less than the face value of debt, the equity is worthless. Once the borrower's assets are worth more than the face value of debt, equity will be worth the difference between the value of the assets and debt. Using the Merton-based option approach, KMV derived three main drivers of default: (1) asset value, (2) asset volatility, and (3) leverage.

Asset value represents the market value of a borrower's assets. The asset value can be viewed as the total value of the firm. Traditionally, asset value is calculated as the present value of free cash flow available to all claim holders, including stockholders, preferred stockholders, and creditors.

Asset volatility represents the uncertainty or riskiness surrounding the value of a borrower's assets. Asset volatility can be viewed as the standard deviation of the annual percentage change in the market value of the borrower's assets. The higher the asset volatility, the more uncertainty there is around the borrower's future cash flows. The following section provides an overview of how KMV applies the option pricing models to obtain an asset value and asset volatility.

Leverage is the third driver of the EDF. The higher a borrower's financial leverage, the greater the likelihood of default. Thus the default risk of a borrower increases as the value of the assets approaches the value of the liabilities. The process does not simply involve calculating a point of insolvency where assets are less than liabilities. A borrower can have assets worth less than its liabilities but still remain liquid. A borrower funded with liquid assets and long-term liabilities can avoid default. Thus the maturity profile of a borrower's liabilities plays a crucial role in determining default. KMV has taken this into account with its EDF calculations.

KMV found that a borrower's asset value will need to fall to a point somewhere between total liabilities and current liabilities for default to occur. Therefore, KMV derived a specific measure to determine when a borrower will default. This measure is called the "default point" and is shown in the following equation:

$$\text{Default point} = \text{Short-term liabilities} + 50\% \text{ of long-term liabilities}$$

In summary, KMV implements a three-step approach to determine an EDF using the above foundations of the Merton model and default point. These steps are:

1. Estimate asset value and asset volatility.
2. Calculate the distance to default.
3. Calculate the default probability (EDF).[5]

Estimating Asset Value and Asset Volatility

As noted earlier, the market value of a borrower, or asset value, represents the present value of free cash flow available to all stakeholders. However the market value of a borrower's assets is not readily observable. Furthermore the volatility of the borrower's assets is also unobservable. Therefore, the option-based Merton model described above is used by KMV to calculate an asset value and asset volatility using observable equity prices and the book value of a borrower's liabilities. Table 9.1 contains a comparison between the traditional inputs of the Black-Scholes model and the Merton model used by KMV. It should be noted that KMV uses a proprietary model for these calculations and must solve for the asset value and asset volatility simultaneously.[6]

TABLE 9.1 Comparison of Inputs to the Black-Scholes and Merton Option Pricing Models

Typical Notation	Traditional Black-Scholes Model Inputs	Merton Model Equivalent
C	Value of the call	Underlying stock price
S	Underlying stock price	**Asset value (unknown)**
K	Strike price	Face value of debt
T	Time to maturity	Time to maturity (of debt)
r	Risk-free rate	Risk-free rate
σ	Volatility of stock price	**Asset volatility (unknown)**

Calculating the Distance to Default

The second step KMV uses to compute an EDF is the estimation of the distance to default. The *distance to default* incorporates a borrower's asset value, asset volatility, and default point into a single measure of risk. As noted earlier, the likelihood of a borrower defaulting increases as its financial leverage increases. In the context of KMV EDF, this is where the market value of a borrower's assets is equal to the default point. Furthermore, an increase in a borrower's asset volatility, or business risk, can magnify the level of uncertainty around the future cash flows of the borrower and thus increase the likelihood of default.[7] The distance to default is calculated using the following equation:

$$\text{Distance to Default} = \frac{(\text{Market Value of Assets}) - (\text{Default Point})}{(\text{Market Value of Assets}) \times (\text{Asset Volatility})}$$

As the distance to default decreases, the probability of default increases. In other words, as the market value of a borrower's assets moves closer to the default point, the EDF will increase. The distance to default itself is not a quantified measure of risk; it is an ordinal measure similar to that of a bond rating. Therefore, KMV must undertake a third step to obtain the EDF.

Calculating the Default Probability or EDF

KMV obtains its EDFs from the distance to default. KMV employs a similar process to the rating agencies when converting ordinal ratings into default probabilities. KMV has a database that includes data on more than 250,000 companies and over 4,700 incidents of default or bankruptcy. From this database KMV is able to map distance to default to EDFs, thus generating a cardinal measure of credit risk.

Historically, KMV mapped distance to default to EDFs on a scale of 0.02 to 20%. In 2007, KMV released EDF 8.0, which refines the mapping of the distance to default to the EDFs. The EDF estimates are now bound between 0.01% and 35% with a term structure of one to ten years (previously one to five years).[8]

Analyzing EDFs

When analyzing KMV EDFs, it is important to break down the data into three key variables: asset value, asset volatility, and leverage. Table 9.2 summarizes how a change in each of the three variables affects the EDF.[9]

Typically these changes do not happen in isolation, and the ultimate movement in EDF will depend on which factor has the largest impact. For example, a debt-funded share buyback can boost a borrower's share price and equity value. This could increase the asset value and lower EDF. However offsetting forces will come from the increase in leverage as the borrower takes on more debt to finance the buyback, leading to an increase in the EDF.[10]

EDFs can also move in the opposite direction to what an analyst would anticipate. This is often seen with the relationship between equity prices and credit default swap (CDS) spreads. Typically, the equity and CDS markets are inversely related. That is, when a borrower's stock is increasing, CDS spreads are usually narrowing. This is because a borrower's financial health improves via the generation of

TABLE 9.2 Impact of EDF Variables

Characteristic	If Factor:	Distance to Default:	EDF:
Asset value	Increases	Increases	**Decreases**
	Decreases	Decreases	**Increases**
Asset volatility	Increases	Decreases	**Increases**
	Decreases	Increases	**Decreases**
Leverage or default point	Increases	Decreases	**Increases**
	Decreases	Increases	**Decreases**

more cash, increasing the value of equity and reducing the likelihood of default, thus narrowing the credit spread.

There are exceptions to this rule, the most obvious example being a leveraged buyout (LBO). A typical LBO will see a private equity firm use the existing assets of the borrower to buy out incumbent shareholders and replace equity with more debt. Prior to the LBO, the borrowers' share price will rise on the announcement of the buyout (lowering the EDF); however, credit spreads will widen because of the increased financial leverage (or increase in the probability of default) following the LBO.

Changes in asset volatility figures also have a major impact on EDFs. Many analysts that use KMV find that small changes in asset volatility can result in large fluctuations in the EDF. The calculation of the asset volatility remains a "black box." This makes it difficult for analysts to reconcile changes in asset volatility with changes to the fundamentals of the borrower. Bharath and Shumway (2004)[11] examined some of the properties of the KMV model in relation to the unobservable values of asset value and asset volatility.

Bharath and Shumway found that alternative measures of asset volatility, including equity volatility from historical prices and implied volatility from traded options, explain almost all the volatility in the KMV model. This is an important finding for analysts trying to interpret the impact of asset volatility on EDFs. When equity markets are volatile, one would expect the market instability to affect the volatility of an individual's stocks, thus flowing through to the asset volatility of the borrower. This would make it difficult for analysts to separate idiosyncratic risk from systematic risk when analyzing changes in EDFs. For example, a borrower's EDF could increase sharply because of a change in asset volatility from equity market volatility, even if there is no material change in the underlying credit quality of the borrower. This issue is addressed with alternative models such as Moody's "Market Implied Ratings," which isolate idiosyncratic risk by tracking changes in credit spreads of individual borrowers relative to systematic changes in spreads of the broader market.[12]

Another issue to consider when analyzing EDFs is the time lag of up-to-date default point information. Unlike asset values and asset volatility figures which are observable on a daily basis, the default point is calculated using liabilities from the financial statements. There is often a time lag of several weeks between the balance date, the release of financial statements such as 10-Ks and 10-Qs, and the input into the KMV's EDF model. This problem is often evident with large debt-funded acquisitions. For example a borrower may elect to increase leverage by 50% to fund the purchase of another company. However, the 50% increase in leverage will not be reflected in the EDF until the updated financial statements are released following the close of the acquisition.[13] By this time the market has already factored the increase in leverage from the acquisition into credit spreads, and the CRAs have changed the rating or rating outlook of the borrower.

The Fitch Model

Fitch has developed a similar model to KMV EDF. Fitch's EIR model also provides probability of default estimates based on market data and financial information. Fitch uses its own proprietary default database, which contains more than 13,000 North American borrowers and over 14,000 non-North American borrowers from more than 70 countries, with over 7,900 defaults from 1960 to 2006.[14]

Fitch notes the following key attributes of its model[15]:

- Structural default probability model with hybrid adjustment of borrower's financial information and market information.
- Provides daily output of estimated default probability for both one-year and five-year horizons and the implied agency rating.
- Incorporates financial statement information and market information. Fitch selected a combination of financial ratios to be incorporated into the model. These ratios include cash leverage, cash flow to total liability, net income to total asset, equity to sales, and cash to total asset.

The Fitch EIR is known as an option-based barrier model with adjustment of a firm's financial information and market information. One of the underlying assumptions of the Merton option-based model is that default can occur only at maturity. Alternatively, barriers like financial covenants can be incorporated into the model, and default will occur when the value of the borrower's assets crosses the barrier. In other words, the model recognizes that the borrower has breached its financial covenants resulting in a timelier predictor of default. The accuracy of the KMV and Fitch models is discussed Chapter 10.

Relationship between EDFs and Credit Spreads

In recent years empirical work has been undertaken to examine the relationship between EDFs and credit spreads for bonds and CDSs. As part of this work, academics have tried to assess how much of the variation in EDFs can be explained in credit spreads and how these relationships can be applied by investors. The most promising application of these studies is the use of KMV EDFs to exploit mispricing in the bond and CDS market.

Studies by both KMV and independent researchers have found a close relationship between EDFs and credit spreads. The relationship arises because of the probability of default incorporated into credit spreads. For example CDS spreads are a function of the reference entities' credit risk, defined as the product of the probability of default (PD) and the recovery rate (R):

$$\text{Credit risk} = PD \times (1 - R) \times 100$$

Because recover rates tend to be sticky, it is possible to observe a relationship between the probability of default incorporated in CDS spreads and the KMV EDF. Studies have found that EDFs explain over 74% of the variation in CDS rates across issuers (Berndt et al., 2005)[16] and more than 70% variation in bond spreads (Agrawal et al., 2004.[17])

The strong relationship between EDFs and credit spreads has been tested in the context of trading strategies for investors. Tindlund (2006)[18] examined the relationship between EDFs and CDS spreads to evaluate whether the relationship could be exploited by investors. The central idea is that if EDFs have some predictive power, CDS spreads should move toward an implied market spread derived from EDFs. This was tested by dividing a portfolio of CDSs into two categories: an overpriced portfolio where CDS spreads were wider than the spreads implied by EDFs and an underpriced portfolio where CDS spreads were narrower than the spreads implied by EDFs. If EDFs have some predictive power, the CDS spreads of both the over- and underpriced portfolio should converge on the spread implied by the EDFs. The results showed that the both portfolios outperform the market at a statistically significant level, confirming some predictive power in EDFs. Agrawal et al. (2004) found similar results for bond spreads. If this holds, a possible investing strategy could be implemented. For example, if the five-year market CDS spread of Ford Motor Company was 100 bps and the implied spread from KMV was 90 bps, an investor could go long (sell protection) on Ford with the expectation that spreads will narrow based on the KMV EDF and then go short (buy protection) once spreads reverted to the predicted level of the EDF model.

Stickiness of Ratings Relative to EDFs

Enron is often cited as an example of how market-based models such as KMV EDF provide a more timely measure of default than do the rating agencies. In the case of Enron, the KMV EDF reached default eight days before the rating agencies downgraded the rating to subinvestment grade. KMV also showed a deteriorating trend in the EDF of WorldCom 12 months prior to bankruptcy. The EDF reached default when S&P's rating of WorldCom was still BB.[19]

However, KMV EDFs do not always estimate weaker default probabilities than the rating agencies. At any given point in time, there are numerous examples of borrowers with a bond rating much lower than the KMV EDF equivalent. Anecdotal evidence suggests that KMV EDFs can be much lower than bond ratings when equity market conditions are strong, resulting in many high-yield issuers having EDFs equating to equivalent ratings as high as AAA. Kealhofer et al. (1998) argue that this type of situation in which bonds have lower EDFs compared to their credit rating appears to be caused by lack of timeliness in upgrade decisions.[20]

Studies have shown that bond ratings tend to move in steps and often lag changes in EDFs (the performance of ratings relative to EDFs is discussed in Chapter 10). The stickiness of ratings relative to EDFs can be explained, in part, by the CRA approach to "rating through the cycle." One of the foundations of the rating process for S&P, Moody's, and Fitch is to ensure the stability of ratings through the business cycles. Key credit measures will typically deteriorate when industry conditions are weak during a cyclical downturn and improve during a cyclical upturn. The CRAs will select a band for credit measures to fluctuate during a cycle to avoid constant changes in a rating.[21]

Rating changes are only made based on long-term shifts in a borrower's financial policies, operating efficiency, competitive position within the industry, or structural decline of an industry in which the borrower is unable to adapt. Empirical studies have verified the "rating-through-the-cycle" approach and show that the rating agencies focus on long-term measures of default (as opposed to short term) and seek rating stability to maintain a prudent migration policy (see Altman and Rijken, 2004[22]).

The CRAs argue that the process of rating through the cycle to provide rating stability is a key requirement of investors. Moody's has conducted its own surveys, which show that investors seek rating stability because of the costs associated with unstable ratings.[23] These costs can take many forms. For example, International Swaps and Derivative Association (ISDA) agreements often include rating triggers that lead to the automatic close-out of positions if the rating falls below a certain threshold. Unstable ratings would lead to a liquidity squeeze for banks under these types of agreements. A bank could be required to settle out of the money positions with hundreds of counterparties following fluctuations of its rating around the threshold.

Studies have looked at the costs associated with unstable ratings in the context of governance rules for a bond portfolio. Governance rules require investment managers to sell bonds when a rating falls below a certain level, typically investment grade. The liquidation of the subinvestment-grade bonds includes irreversible costs. The studies have shown that stability of ratings leads to lower transaction costs compared to market-based models such as KMV. Lower costs can outweigh the benefits of more timely default measures of the market-based rating systems (see Löffler, 2004).[24]

Summary

The emergence of quantitative credit models over the last 20 years has provided lenders and investors with a more timely and direct way to measure credit risk. The KMV EDF model has established itself as the leader of market-based models. Cases such as Enron and WorldCom are clear examples of the power of market-based models to provide an early warning signal of default. However, investors and lenders should not view credit models as a substitute for fundamental analysis. Instead, these models along with market prices from credit spreads and ratings from Moody's, S&P, and Fitch should be used as complements to fundamental analysis. This way investors and lenders can equip themselves will a broad range of tools to arrive at informed decisions about credit risk.

10

PERFORMANCE OF CREDIT METRICS

William F. Maxwell
Rauscher Chair in Financial Investments,
Cox School of Business at SMU

Philip Delbridge
Vice President, Credit Risk Management,
Credit Suisse Securities (USA) LLC

In the previous chapters, we looked at the role of credit ratings and how credit rating agencies (CRAs) derive bond ratings. We also examined quantitative methods of measuring credit risk, including models such as Moody's KMV. In this chapter we measure the performance of different credit metrics as well as examine the ability of these metrics to explain variation in bond ratings across different industries. The first section of this chapter looks at default probabilities and rating performance measured by the CRAs, such as S&P, Moody's, and Fitch. The second section focuses on the performance of credit models and how well these models stack up against credit ratings. The final section of the chapter looks at correlations between different types of credit metrics.

Default Studies

CRAs use letter grades to rank issuers and issues of bonds from lowest to highest risk. However, investors and lenders often require quantitative measures of credit risk. Therefore, the major CRAs have tracked the performance of ratings with default studies that assign default probabilities to each letter rating. This section provides an overview of default studies.

The major CRAs use similar approaches to calculate default probabilities. For example, Moody's will calculate the one-year default rate as the number of rated issuers that defaulted over the previous one-year period divided by the number of Moody's-related issues that could have defaulted over that one-year period.[1] The issuer-weighted average of default rates represents an estimate of the risk of default within any one-year period. By tracking these groupings through the subsequent years, the agencies are able to determine cumulative default rates over multiple-year horizons.

Table 10.1 contains Moody's average default rates from 1994 to 2007 for corporate issuers. This is typical of the data produced by

TABLE 10.1 Moody's Average Volume-Weighted Corporate Bond Default Rates by Letter Rating, 1994–2007

Rating	Year 1	Year 2	Year 3	Year 4	Year 5
Aaa	0.00	0.00	0.00	0.00	0.00
Aa	0.00	0.00	0.00	0.00	0.00
A	0.26	0.58	0.84	1.02	1.25
Baa	0.51	1.19	1.73	2.42	3.02
Ba	1.48	3.30	5.32	7.29	8.87
B	4.62	11.10	16.59	20.78	23.71
Caa-C	20.62	31.12	37.92	41.83	43.87
Investment-grade	0.27	0.62	0.90	1.18	1.45
Speculative-grade	5.70	10.94	15.26	18.52	20.78
All rated	1.30	2.58	3.61	4.44	5.08

Source: Moody's Investors Service, Inc. (2008), "Corporate Default and Recovery Rates, 1920–2007," p. 29.

CRAs. The table shows default rates rising as you move down the rating spectrum. All three of the major U.S. CRAs release updated default studies on a periodic basis.

The numerous studies by S&P, Moody's, and Fitch show an inverse relationship between credit ratings and historical default rates. In other words a higher letter rating corresponds to lower default rates and vice versa. This can be considered a validation of the methodologies used by S&P, Moody's, and Fitch.

A number of studies have been conducted that examine trends in rating-based default data. Some key trends that have emerged include:

1. Higher credit ratings tend to be more stable, and lower ratings more volatile.
2. Default rates are cyclical in nature, with adverse business conditions corresponding to increased defaults.
3. High-yield bond ratings are more volatile and are more likely to default when economic conditions have deteriorated.
4. There is a seasoning effect with bond defaults. Default probabilities are low during the first three years following a new issue. Then defaults rise after three years as cash from the original bond issue has depleted.[2]

The likelihood of a credit rating moving up or down over a given time horizon is measured by transition or migration analysis. This analysis measures the change from one rating category to another and provides an insight into rating trends over time. Table 10.2 shows Moody's average one-year migration rates between 1970 and 2007. The vertical axis shows ratings at the beginning of a year, with the horizontal axis showing the ratings at the end of the year.[3] As an example, 7.74% of issuers rated Ba at the beginning of the year moved down to a B rating by the end of the year, 5.70% moved up to Baa, and 75.65% of Ba issuers remained unchanged.

TABLE 10.2 Moody's Average One-Year Letter Rating Migration Rates, 1970–2007

Rating	Aaa	Aa	A	Baa	Ba	B	Caa	Ca-C	Default
Aaa	88.65	7.45	0.64	0.00	0.02	0.00	0.00	0.00	0.00
Aa	1.08	87.19	6.88	0.25	0.06	0.02	0.00	0.00	0.01
A	0.06	2.72	87.56	4.93	0.49	0.09	0.02	0.00	0.02
Baa	0.05	0.19	4.89	84.35	4.31	0.77	0.21	0.02	0.17
Ba	0.01	0.06	0.38	**5.70**	**75.65**	**7.74**	0.53	0.05	1.10
B	0.01	0.04	0.16	0.35	5.57	73.44	4.95	0.64	4.48
Caa	0.00	0.03	0.03	0.19	0.66	10.73	57.24	3.62	14.67
Ca-C	0.00	0.00	0.00	0.00	0.40	2.59	9.44	38.27	29.78

Source: Moody's Investors Service, Inc. (2008), "Corporate Default and Recovery Rates, 1920–2007," p. 14.

Given the recent tightening in credit markets and the global economic downturn, it is anticipated that corporate default rates and migration rates will increase sharply when future studies are released which will include data for 2008–2010.

Performance of Credit Models

In the previous section we look at how CRAs quantify rating performance with studies of historical default trends. Studies have also been conducted on the performance of market-based credit models. There are two primary criteria for assessing the performance of market-based models: timeliness and accuracy. KMV conducted its own test on the timeliness and accuracy of its EDF and compared the results to other credit models such as the Altman's Z-score, as well as Moody's bond ratings.

A KMV study (Korablev and Dwyer, 2007)[4] tested the timeliness of EDFs' relative Moody's ratings and found in the United States that EDFs start rising 24 months before actual default, compared with 13 months for Moody's ratings. This timeliness test also produced similar results for non-U.S. borrowers. Furthermore, EDFs' movements are along a continuum, as compared to changes in Moody's ratings, which tend to move in steps. Chapter 9 notes that the "rating through the cycle" approach by CRAs might explain the apparent stickiness of ratings relative to EDFs and other quantitative models.

Accuracy of default is the second measure of model performance. The accuracy of default for structural or credit scoring models is typically tested by the ability to discriminate between good and bad credits. In other words, do not group defaulters with nondefaulters when testing for high-quality borrowers. Alternatively, do not group nondefaulters with defaulters when testing for low-quality borrowers. KMV found that EDF credit measures have more discriminatory power than do Moody's ratings at all time horizons. In other words, EDFs do a better job than bond ratings in distinguishing between defaulters and nondefaulters. The KMV study also demonstrated that EDF credit measures substantially outperform Z-scores in terms of their ability to discriminate between good borrowers and bad borrowers.

Academics have also conducted independent studies on the quality of the KMV EDF model. Some of these studies generated results similar to KMV's findings. For example, Dacorogna et al. (2003)[5] conducted a study to evaluate the performance of credit risk models using data from KMV and concluded that the KMV EDF model contains information that is not captured in traditional ratings and that the models predict defaults more than 10 months in advance of the other rating agencies.

Fitch also conducted a similar test with respect to its EIR model, which incorporates selected financial ratios. Fitch's results showed that the EIR model is consistently more effective than alternative models such as the Altman Z-score at predicting defaults.[6] We are not aware of any study that directly compares performance of KMV EDFs and Fitch EIR models.

Most empirical evidence would suggest that market-based models such as KMV's provide a more accurate and timely measure of default compared to bond ratings and accounting-based measures. However, as noted in previous chapters, market-based models should not be considered a substitute for fundamental analysis, and credit analysts should use all tools available to assess the creditworthiness of borrowers. Therefore, it is important to consider how different credit metrics relate to each other and how well they explain variation in bond ratings across industries.

Comparing Credit Metrics

In this section, we examine the relationship between commonly used measures of financial risk and bond ratings. (We focus solely on bonds that are rated BBB thru CCC/C.) Clearly more than one metric is necessary to assess a firm's bond rating. However, a single metric is helpful in quickly assessing credit quality.

While numerous metrics of default have been developed, we focus on five of the most prevalent measures of financial risk: book leverage, Z-score, O-score, idiosyncratic risk, and Merton-based KMV. After doing so, we then (1) examine the correlation between bond ratings and these measures, (2) examine how these measures can differ based on industry, and (3) provide median levels of these financial risk measures by rating each category within industry classifications.

Risk Metrics

Our analysis focuses on the following risk metrics:

1. Book leverage
2. The Z-score
3. The O-score
4. Idiosyncratic risk
5. Merton-based KMV model

Book Leverage

Book leverage is the simplest metric and is defined as the long-term debt of a firm relative to its total assets. The other commonly used financial metric, the coverage ratio (EBIT/cash interest expense), is highly correlated with the leverage metric and hence, not surprisingly, is found to be subsumed by the leverage ratio in determining financial risk. However, since the coverage ratio shows more time series variation and EBIT is cyclically related to the economy and can be influenced by one-time expenses or revenues, it might provide a better snapshot of the changing financial condition of a firm.

Z-Score

The Z-score was developed and published by Edward I Altman in 1968. Altman developed the Z-score by examining 22 different financial ratios and then used the 5 ratios that did the best overall job of predicting corporate bankruptcy.[7] The five key variables and the different weights used in the Z-score model are detailed in the list that follows. The Z-score model has been modified over time for private companies, nonmanufacturing borrowers, and emerging market companies.[8]

The Z-Score Model

$$Z = 1.2X1 + 1.4X2 + 3.3X3 + 0.6X4 + 1.0X5$$

X1 = working capital/total assets
X2 = retained earnings/total assets
X3 = earnings before interest and taxes/total assets
X4 = market value equity/book value of total liabilities
X5 = sales/total assets
Z = overall index or score[9]

The resulting Z-score is not a probability of default measure. Instead, the Z-score assigns each borrower a score between –5 and 10,

TABLE 10.3 Average Z-Score by S&P Bond Rating, 1995–1999

Rating	Average Annual Number of Firms	Average Z-Score Score
AAA	11	5.02
AA	46	4.30
A	131	3.60
BBB	107	2.78
BB	50	2.45
B	80	1.67
CCC	10	0.95

Source: Altman, E. (2002), "Corporate Distress Prediction Models in a Turbulent Economic and Basel II Environment," working paper, Stern School of Business, New York University.

with a high Z-score implying strong credit quality and a low Z-score indicating weak credit quality. Z-scores are not interpreted directly as default probabilities and therefore work as ordinal measures of credit risk. However the Z-score can be mapped to bond ratings and used to derive a probability of default using the same methodology discussed in the previous chapter. Table 10.3 details the average Z-score for S&P bond ratings between 1995 and 1999.

For the purposes of our study, we flip the sign of the Z-score to make the measure consistent with other metrics, increasing with respect to risk.

O-Score

The O-score was developed by James Ohlson in 1980. The O-score is similar in general design to the Z-score and is calculated as: O-score = −1.32 0.407 log (total assets) + 6.03 (total liabilities/total assets) – 1.43 (working capital/total assets) + 0.076 (current liabilities/current assets) – 1.72 (1 if total liabilities > total assets, or else 0) – 2.37 (net income/total assets) – 1.86 (funds from operations/total liabilities) + 0.285 (1 if net loss for last two years, or else 0) – 0.521 (net income_t – net income_{t-1})/ (|net income_t|) + (|net income_{t-1}|).

Idiosyncratic Risk

Campbell and Taksler (2003)[10] document that idiosyncratic risk explains a larger portion of the variations in bond yield spreads than do bond ratings. Campbell and Taksler noted that volatility can be good for shareholders when viewing equity as a call option[11] but that it hurts bondholders. Therefore, volatility can increase bond yields (depress prices) while having a positive impact on equity returns.

It was also noted that the idiosyncratic component of volatility had been trending upward since the 1970s, whereas the systematic risk component of volatility had remained stable. This was an important factor in explaining why their results show that idiosyncratic risk explains as much cross-sectional variation in yields as can credit ratings and that volatility matters as least as much as credit ratings when explaining bond yields. Idiosyncratic risk is the unexplained volatility (ε) associated with the following market model: $R_i = \alpha + \beta(R_{mkt}) + \varepsilon$.

Merton-Based KMV Metrics

Ideally our analysis should include a direct comparison between Moody's KMV EDFs and other credit metrics. However, KMV data are proprietary and cannot be obtained in the public domain. To overcome this problem, we calculated a proxy for the KMV EDF based on a recent empirical study. Bharath and Shumway (2008)[12] provide codes to estimate the Merton (1974) model implied default probability, which we used to estimate an EDF. Bharath and Shumway find that their estimates are highly correlated with the KMV default metric. We also note that basic intuition is similar to the idiosyncratic risk metric.

Correlations between Risk Measures

In this section, we examine the relation between the risk metrics. To do this, we calculate each of the metrics described above for all firms with bond ratings in 2006. To deal with the problem associated with extreme outliers when calculating any financial ratio, we Winsorized the data at the 5% level (2.5% of each tail). We then determined the correlation coefficient between the different metrics, which are reported in Table 10.4.

First, we notice that risk measures are all correlated with a firm's bond rating. However, the correlations differ significantly. We find that the financial statement–based measures (leverage, Z-score, and O-score) have the lowest correlation with bond rating, between 27% and 37%. On the other hand, the measures that incorporate volatility into them, idiosyncratic risk and the KMV proxy, have a much higher correlation. The correlation with KMV proxy is 52% and 70% for idiosyncratic risk. The financial statement metrics are highly correlated. The correlation between idiosyncratic risk and leverage is negative and follows from the fundamental concept in finance that operating and financial risks are negatively correlated.

Industry Comparisons

Next we examine the relation between the risk metrics for BB and B rated bonds across industry categories for the fiscal year of 2006. To do

TABLE 10.4 Correlations of Financial Metrics

Metric	Rating	Leverage	Z-Score	O-Score	Idiosyncratic Risk
Leverage	29%				
Z-score	27%	61%			
O-score	37%	33%	58%		
Idiosyncratic risk	70%	–26%	3%	39%	
KMV proxy	52%	35%	49%	55%	56%

this, we sort the firms into the Fama and French 12 industry categories. The other (miscellaneous) classification is removed, leaving 11 industry categories. We then examine the median ratio for the five risk metrics, first for BB rated bonds and then for B rated bonds, after sorting the industries by leverage ratios. See Table 10.5.

When examining the table, it is apparent that the median risk metric, no matter which one used, varies dramatically by industry. In fact,

TABLE 10.5 Risk Metrics by Industry Classification

Panel A: Firms with BB Rated Bonds (Sorted by Book Leverage)

Industry	Leverage	Z-Score	O-Score	Idiosyncratic Risk	KMV Proxy
Business equipment	25.0%	−3.48	−1.91	33.65%	0.70%
Manufacturing	25.8%	−3.13	−1.94	40.54%	0.02%
Consumer nondurables	26.0%	−4.10	−1.84	50.00%	0.82%
Consumer durables	27.3%	−2.81	−0.52	79.66%	3.64%
Chemicals	27.5%	−2.84	−1.31	51.01%	0.19%
Wholesale/retail	27.6%	−3.66	−1.66	44.68%	0.32%
Health care	29.7%	−3.50	−1.69	37.36%	1.36%
Finance	30.6%	na	na	128.96%	1.59%
Energy	35.7%	−1.61	−0.46	53.54%	1.14%
Telecommunications	43.2%	−1.64	−0.94	105.36%	0.20%
Utilities	43.4%	−1.31	−1.02	102.25%	0.50%

Panel B: Firms with B Rated Bonds (Sorted by Book Leverage)

Industry	Leverage	Z-Score	O-Score	Idiosyncratic Risk	KMV Proxy
Business equipment	20.1%	−3.75	−2.05	23.93%	0.57%
Finance	23.6%	na	na	86.40%	3.20%
Consumer durables	24.8%	−2.77	−1.86	59.21%	2.76%
Wholesale/retail	26.0%	−3.75	−1.70	44.86%	0.67%
Manufacturing	26.7%	−3.14	−1.57	48.35%	0.22%
Chemicals	27.9%	−3.10	−1.28	48.07%	0.23%
Consumer nondurables	29.1%	−3.30	−1.25	61.66%	0.97%
Energy	30.7%	−2.32	−0.73	52.14%	2.83%
Health care	39.8%	−2.99	−1.14	87.87%	4.70%
Telecommunications	42.4%	−1.54	−0.17	84.46%	0.43%
Utilities	46.3%	−1.39	4.14	188.41%	3.36%

the leverage and idiosyncratic risk ratios are close to two and three times higher, respectively, for the utilities when compared to business equipment. Industries with very little operating risk, utilities and telecommunications, can take on significantly more financial risk and still receive the same bond rating. Given the correlation between the risk metrics, it is not surprising that the relative rankings, if sorted by leverage, lead to generally similar rankings on other metrics.

Risk Metrics by Rating within Industry Classification

It is clear from the prior analysis that any of the risk metrics are highly dependent on the industry analyzed and that using an average risk metric across all firms with the same rating is obviously flawed. Hence, in this section, we further break down bond ratings by industry and provide the median ratios of the five risk metrics for bonds rated BBB through CCC/C for each industry (See Tables 10.6, 10.7, and 10.8 on pages 225–228). This information can then be used to help you understand the risk of an issue. (Some industries do not have a meaningful cross-section of CCC/C firms, and those industries' results are not reported.)

Summary

The historical default and migration studies conducted by S&P, Moody's, and Fitch provide valuable insight into rating trends over time. On the other hand, most empirical evidence would suggest that quantitative market-based models such as KMV do a better job at estimating the probability of default for corporate borrowers. However, investors and lenders should consider a wide variety of credit metrics when assessing credit quality. Furthermore, our analysis shows that all credit metrics must be viewed in the context of the borrower's industry.

TABLE 10.6 Bond Rating and Risk Metrics by Industry (Median Default Measures by Industry for BBB through CCC/C Rated Bonds)

Industry	Rating	Leverage	Z-Score	O-Score	Idiosyncratic Risk	KMV Proxy
Consumer nondurables	BBB	24.0%	−3.64	−2.11	25.0%	0.00%
Consumer nondurables	BB	26.0%	−4.10	−1.84	50.0%	0.82%
Consumer nondurables	B	29.1%	−3.30	−1.25	61.7%	0.97%
Consumer nondurables	CCC/C	28.3%	−4.92	−2.17	78.6%	4.70%
Consumer durables	BBB	19.6%	−3.94	−2.49	18.3%	0.00%
Consumer durables	BB	27.3%	−2.81	−0.52	79.7%	3.64%
Consumer durables	B	24.8%	−2.77	−1.86	59.2%	2.76%
Consumer durables	CCC/C	40.1%	−2.95	0.86	92.5%	8.54%
Manufacturing	BBB	24.5%	−2.82	−1.96	35.9%	0.00%
Manufacturing	BB	25.8%	−3.13	−1.94	40.5%	0.02%
Manufacturing	B	26.7%	−3.14	−1.57	48.4%	0.22%
Manufacturing	CCC/C	30.8%	−2.70	−0.80	72.1%	3.13%
Energy	BBB	22.9%	−2.54	−1.96	31.1%	0.00%
Energy	BB	35.7%	−1.61	−0.46	53.5%	1.14%
Energy	B	30.7%	−2.32	−0.73	52.1%	2.83%
Energy	CCC/C	17.4%	−3.43	−1.17	18.7%	1.95%
Chemicals	BBB	25.3%	−3.36	−1.81	29.6%	0.01%
Chemicals	BB	27.5%	−2.84	−1.31	51.0%	0.19%
Chemicals	B	27.9%	−3.10	−1.28	48.1%	0.23%

(Continued)

TABLE 10.6 *(Continued)*

Industry	Rating	Leverage	Z-Score	O-Score	Idiosyncratic Risk	KMV Proxy
Business equipment	BBB	20.4%	−3.11	−2.34	17.7%	0.01%
Business equipment	BB	25.0%	−3.48	−1.91	33.7%	0.70%
Business equipment	B	20.1%	−3.75	−2.05	23.9%	0.57%
Business equipment	CCC/C	51.4%	−2.55	0.22	142.7%	3.57%
Telecommunications	BBB	46.4%	−1.56	−1.05	151.2%	0.39%
Telecommunications	BB	43.2%	−1.64	−0.94	105.4%	0.20%
Telecommunications	B	42.4%	−1.54	−0.17	84.5%	0.43%
Telecommunications	CCC/C	43.7%	−1.09	0.95	79.9%	11.12%
Utilities	BBB	42.4%	−1.26	−1.34	110.8%	0.02%
Utilities	BB	43.4%	−1.31	−1.02	102.3%	0.50%
Utilities	B	46.3%	−1.39	4.14	188.4%	3.36%
Wholesale/retail	BBB	18.7%	−4.76	−2.02	23.9%	0.01%
Wholesale/retail	BB	27.6%	−3.66	−1.66	44.7%	0.32%
Wholesale/retail	B	26.0%	−3.75	−1.70	44.9%	0.67%
Wholesale/retail	CCC/C	51.4%	−2.96	−0.52	58.6%	1.59%
Health care	BBB	26.9%	−4.24	−2.38	41.2%	0.82%
Health care	BB	29.7%	−3.50	−1.69	37.4%	1.36%
Health care	B	39.8%	−2.99	−1.14	87.9%	4.70%
Finance	BBB	14.2%	na	na	58.3%	0.14%
Finance	BB	30.6%	na	na	129.0%	1.59%
Finance	B	23.6%	na	na	86.4%	3.20%

TABLE 10.7 Risk Metrics by Industry Classification

Panel A: Firms with BB Rated Bonds (Sorted by KMV Proxy)

Industry	Leverage	KMV Proxy
Manufacturing	25.80%	0.02%
Chemicals	27.50%	0.19%
Telecommunications	43.20%	0.20%
Wholesale/retail	27.60%	0.32%
Utilities	43.40%	0.50%
Business equipment	25.00%	0.70%
Consumer nondurables	26.00%	0.82%
Energy	35.70%	1.14%
Health care	29.70%	1.36%
Finance	30.60%	1.59%
Consumer durables	27.30%	3.64%

Panel B: Firms with B Rated Bonds (Sorted by KMV Proxy)

Industry	Leverage	KMV Proxy
Manufacturing	26.70%	0.22%
Chemicals	27.90%	0.23%
Telecommunications	42.40%	0.43%
Business equipment	20.10%	0.57%
Wholesale/retail	26.00%	0.67%
Consumer nondurables	29.10%	0.97%
Consumer durables	24.80%	2.76%
Energy	30.70%	2.83%
Finance	23.60%	3.20%
Utilities	46.30%	3.36%
Health care	39.80%	4.70%

TABLE 10.8 Bond Rating and KMV Proxy by Industry (Median Default Measured by Industry for BBB through CCC/C Rated Bonds)

Industry	Rating	Leverage	KMV Proxy
Consumer nondurables	BBB	24.0%	0.00%
Consumer nondurables	BB	26.0%	0.82%
Consumer nondurables	B	29.1%	0.97%
Consumer nondurables	CCC/C	28.3%	4.70%
Consumer durables	BBB	19.6%	0.00%
Consumer durables	BB	27.3%	3.64%
Consumer durables	B	24.8%	2.76%
Consumer durables	CCC/C	40.1%	8.54%
Manufacturing	BBB	24.5%	0.00%
Manufacturing	BB	25.8%	0.02%
Manufacturing	B	26.7%	0.22%
Manufacturing	CCC/C	30.8%	3.13%
Energy	BBB	22.9%	0.00%
Energy	BB	35.7%	1.14%
Energy	B	30.7%	2.83%
Energy	CCC/C	17.4%	1.95%
Chemicals	BBB	25.3%	0.01%
Chemicals	BB	27.5%	0.19%
Chemicals	B	27.9%	0.23%
Business equipment	BBB	20.4%	0.01%
Business equipment	BB	25.0%	0.70%
Business equipment	B	20.1%	0.57%
Business equipment	CCC/C	51.4%	3.57%
Telecommunications	BBB	46.4%	0.39%
Telecommunications	BB	43.2%	0.20%
Telecommunications	B	42.4%	0.43%
Telecommunications	CCC/C	43.7%	11.12%
Utilities	BBB	42.4%	0.02%
Utilities	BB	43.4%	0.50%
Utilities	B	46.3%	3.36%
Wholesale/retail	BBB	18.7%	0.01%
Wholesale/retail	BB	27.6%	0.32%
Wholesale/retail	B	26.0%	0.67%
Wholesale/retail	CCC/C	51.4%	1.59%
Health care	BBB	26.9%	0.82%
Health care	BB	29.7%	1.36%
Health care	B	39.8%	4.70%
Finance	BBB	14.2%	0.14%
Finance	BB	30.6%	1.59%

11

PRINCIPLES OF MANAGING HIGH-YIELD ASSETS

Mark R. Shenkman

President and Chief Investment Officer,
Shenkman Capital Management, Inc.

The high-yield market is a unique asset class because high-yield securities exhibit the characteristics of both debt instruments and equities. As a hybrid security, the credit cycle influences and magnifies either the debt or the equity features. In bull markets, high-yield securities typically act more like equities, as prices are influenced by the latest corporate developments. Conversely, in a bear market, the debt attributes of the security, such as coupon, maturity, covenants, and ratings, affect prices in the same way as in other fixed-income asset classes.

Managing high-yield assets should be divided into two major components: portfolio optimization strategies and risk controls. Portfolio optimization strategies are the lenses with which to look at and respond to the market conditions and include decision-making procedures, checklists, critical questions, and lastly, a weighting distribution model. Risk controls require developing insightful, comprehensive procedures to identify the four types of risk factors—credit, market, liquidity, and portfolio. Over the long term (and through various economic cycles), those portfolio managers who have avoided defaults and major trading losses typically have outperformed various high-yield benchmarks.

This chapter examines portfolio optimization for managing high-yield portfolios and various risk controls. At the core of both risk controls and portfolio optimization are disciplined procedures and processes that support an unwavering investment style.

Optimizing High-Yield Portfolio Management

In this section, we define the attributes for portfolio optimization and identify the necessary skills to manage high-yield assets, how to put these skills into a decision-making process, how and why to maintain discipline, how to determine if a portfolio manager is meeting his or her client's expectations, and how to think about distributing models in portfolio construction.

Skill Set of Managing a High-Yield Bond Portfolio

The skills necessary to manage high-yield assets require a deep understanding of industry dynamics, knowledge of specific credit fundamentals, and awareness of technical market factors. The diagram in Figure 11.1 identifies these three critical components that must be balanced to arrive at the best investment decision. The most successful portfolio managers have the ability to assimilate all three variables and then focus on the intersection of risk and reward.

The optimal investment should exhibit all three factors: (1) solid credit fundamentals in the form of strong operating metrics with a positive outlook, (2) favorable industry and other macro trends, and (3) positive market factors such as strong trading liquidity and appropriate spread. Too often, portfolio managers get "oversold" on one or two of these factors but ignore or underestimate the third factor. For example, in 2006, when the economy and the high-yield market were

FIGURE 11.1 Three Critical Components in High-Yield Investment Decisions

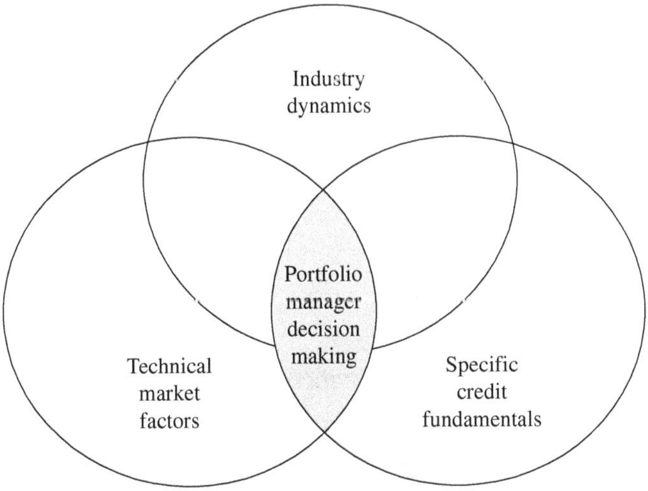

strong, American Axle appeared to many portfolio managers to be an ideal investment. The credit metrics in 2006 were sound with 2.5 times leverage (total debt divided by EBITDA) anticipated to decline to 1.2 times, cash flow expected to grow by 50% in the coming 12 months, and excess cash generation (i.e., after capital expenditures, taxes, and interest payments) of roughly $150 million—all of which happened.

Clearly, two of the three criteria—technical market forces and specific credit fundamentals—were in the best possible position for an investment. However, the automotive industry was severely challenged. When the U.S. automotive industry encountered a major downturn, the Big Three—Ford, GM, and Chrysler—failed to reinvent or reposition themselves to become more efficient and create new appealing products. Instead, these manufacturers mistakenly chose to grow their addiction to SUVs and truck sales. As a major supplier to the Big Three, American Axle's fortunes were directly tied to the business of these three companies.

Consequently, both American Axle's credit metrics and the value of its securities experienced dramatic declines in the periods preceding GM and Chrysler's 2009 bankruptcy filings.

Another problem arises when portfolio managers fail to differentiate between a good company with a bad bond and a bad company with a good bond. In many cases, portfolio managers face the decision to invest in a credit with low leverage, high interest coverage, and a low debt-to-total capitalization ratio, but the bond has weak covenants, has a long maturity, and rarely trades. The opposite situation also occurs when the company has a high degree of leverage, has low interest coverage, but the bond offers significant liquidity, tight covenants, short duration, and a wide spread-to-worst yield. What is the appropriate trade-off?

While it may be difficult to construct an entire portfolio with 100 to 150 credits that possess the optimal intersection of all three factors, the top 20 positions in the portfolio should exhibit a balance of the right industries, the right credit fundamentals, and the right market technicals.

Decision Making for Purchasing High-Yield Bonds

In executing a buy-sell decision, a step-by-step process is required to ensure consistency and disciplined decision making. Often, in the name of expediency or a desire not to miss a particular "hot" opportunity, portfolio managers and traders short-circuit the disciplined process, which can lead to major future losses. Many value-oriented investors believe that price can compensate for risk. However, in the high-yield bond market, this theory has proved inaccurate. Price does not mitigate a bad deal structure, poor macro industry trends, weak credit fundamentals, or sloppy market technicals.

In short, avoiding large losses is not worth any spread, because high-yield bonds represent asymmetrical risk. As such, the upside potential is limited by the call price, but the downside exposure can drop to zero. Moreover, if a bond drops from par to 50, theoretically, it will take ten bonds to advance five points each in order to recoup the 50-point decline in just one credit. Equity portfolios do not have this similar dynamic because one investment can soar by 500%, thereby offsetting the losses in numerous other transactions. The number of bonds, however, that can jump five points or more may be limited. Hence, these concerns require a formalized decision-making process consisting of several steps.

The decision-making process for high-yield bond investments consists of five steps (as shown in Figure 11.2). A checklist of positive and negative attributes should be utilized at each step. If there are more negative than positive factors, the credit should be avoided.

1. *Step 1: Deal structure.* At the foundation of the "decision triangle" is the deal structure, or the way the bond is legally arranged. Details of the covenants, the type of security, the ranking in the capital structure, or any unique features of the issue must be identified, evaluated, and classified. Careful

FIGURE 11.2 Five Steps in High-Yield Investment Decision Making

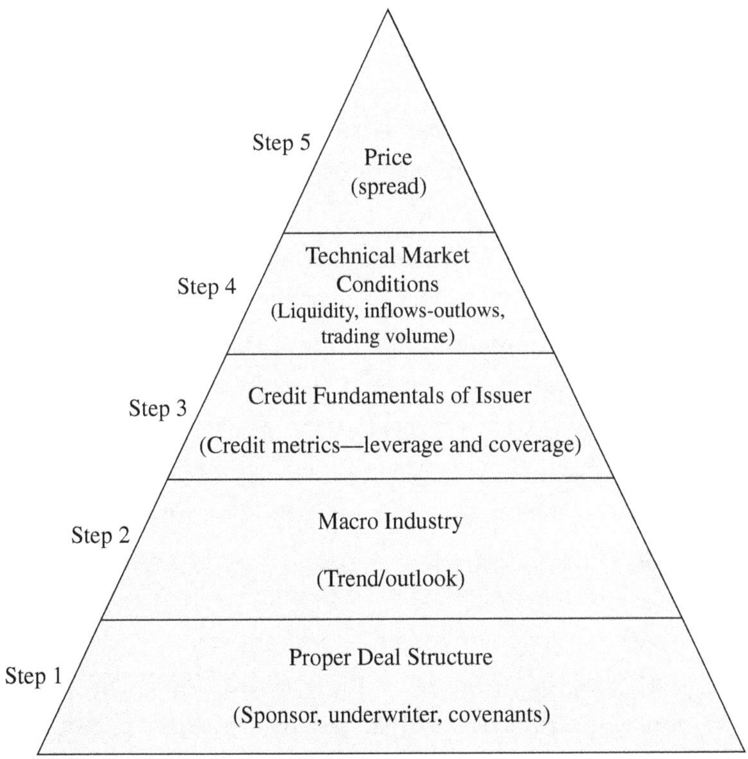

analysis of the covenants and corporate structure is conducted in order to confirm that the bonds have adequate asset protection and a legal claim to interest payments. In addition, the reputation and past track record of sponsors and underwriters should be evaluated during this step. Historically, weak sponsors and/or underwriters are associated with riskier transactions.

2. *Step 2: Macro industry.* The second step in the decision-making process is a thorough review of the industry's characteristics and outlook. Key issues such as growth rate, pricing power, foreign competition, competitive pressures, profitability, event risk, regulatory factors, and market share position must all be incorporated into an industry viewpoint. The credit should then be evaluated against the broader industry metrics. The key macro considerations for portfolio managers are the degree of capital intensiveness, competitiveness, profitability, and growth rates for a given industry. Portfolio managers should overweight the portfolio in industries with the most favorable and sustainable growth and capital characteristics and underweight or avoid industries with challenged prospects. Portfolio managers should always avoid industries (even if they are a key component of a major benchmark index) that are undergoing major structural changes, such as regulatory changes.
3. *Step 3: Credit fundamentals of the issuer.* In the middle of the decision triangle are the specific credit fundamentals of the company. The key aspects to focus on are management experience and qualifications, the degree of leverage in the company, the interest coverage, debt-to-capitalization, operating margins, capital expenditures, amortization schedule, free cash flow, working capital needs, operating trends, revenue growth, and, most important, "cash leakage." Cash that is drained out of the business by dividends to equity sponsors or poorly timed, overpriced acquisitions

with low margins and no apparent growth potential can negatively impact cash flow and the company's ability to make timely interest payments. Cash is always king when a company utilizes leverage! Many times, managements and equity sponsors bleed a company to death (i.e., by diverting cash resources to nonproductive uses). The best high-yield companies consistently pay down debt and de-lever their balance sheets.

4. *Step 4: Technical market.* Even if portfolio managers get the first three steps correct, overlooking or underestimating the market technicals can erode the positive elements of those first three steps. Timing is crucial in protecting the downside of a high-yield investment. Some portfolio managers fail to evaluate liquidity factors, flow of funds into the market, trading volume, dealer capabilities, yield spreads, new issue supply, interest-rate changes, and investors' psychology. All of these factors influence the price volatility of a security and ultimately lead to profitable or unprofitable investments.
5. *Step 5: Price.* At the peak of the decision-making triangle is the last step—price valuation. What a bond is worth is based on the prior four steps. Trade-offs must be made. At some price, every bond should find a potential buyer. The critical question is: Does the spread on a given investment compensate investors for the level of risk (beta) assumed?

Checklist to Reduce Volatility and Defaults in a High-Yield Bond Portfolio

One of the key methodologies leading to portfolio optimization is using risk and volatility checklists on each investment in order to capture the hidden risk factors. Similar to a pilot who is required to perform a checklist before any plane takes off, portfolio managers should engage in a similar rigid review. The following is a list of some key factors that can cause unexpected losses and volatility.

Credit Risk Assessment Checklist

Name of credit	Yes	No
1. Dividend deal	_____	_____
2. Projected down quarter and/or down year	_____	_____
3. High historical default rate industry	_____	_____
4. Rule 144A for life*	_____	_____
5. Toggle or Pay-in-Kind transaction	_____	_____
6. Previously defaulted company	_____	_____
7. Cyclical industry	_____	_____
8. Little or no hard assets	_____	_____
9. Difficult access to management (poor transparency)	_____	_____
10. Management that previously impaired bondholders	_____	_____

*Underwriters perform less due diligence on the issuer for Rule 144A offerings than they would be required to perform for a public offering.

While it is a common practice for portfolio managers to utilize proprietary credit rating systems, prepare comprehensive research reports, and contact suppliers and vendors, it must be done with a disciplined and consistent methodology. The best portfolio managers combine detailed, fundamental, independent analysis with an intimate knowledge of industries and market conditions. The star managers have an *unwavering* style, strategy, process, and risk controls and are never swept up by exciting new market fads, overzealous salespeople, or creative bankers.

Critical Questions for the Client

Under "best practices," high-yield portfolio managers should review the following 10 critical questions with their clients. The answers to these questions will help to set parameters and manage expectations at the outset of the mandate. These questions are:

1. How much volatility is acceptable?
2. What is the risk tolerance of the client?
3. What industry biases, if any, are held by the client?
4. What is the time horizon for the investment?
5. What is the primary investment objective (i.e., income generation, total return, benchmark "hugger," absolute return, or preservation of capital)?
6. How much liquidity is needed given the time horizon of the client? Is the client a tactical or strategic investor?
7. Is the manager's style compatible with the client's objective (risk averse or risk seeker)?
8. How important is it to beat the benchmark?
9. How much credit deterioration is acceptable?
10. Where in the credit cycle is this investment allocation being made?

Based on the answers to these probing questions, various investment styles can be identified, as shown in Table 11.1.

TABLE 11.1 Characteristics of Investment Styles with Varying Qualities of Creditworthiness

<table>
<tr><th>Selection Process</th><th>Baa/BB</th><th>BB</th><th>B1</th><th>B2</th><th>B3</th><th>CCC</th><th>CC, D</th></tr>
<tr><td>Automatic ▶</td><td colspan="2" rowspan="2">Lower yields</td><td colspan="3" rowspan="2">Lack of conviction</td><td colspan="2" rowspan="2">High beta</td></tr>
<tr><td>Rigidly structured ▶</td></tr>
<tr><td>Systematic ▶</td><td colspan="2" rowspan="2">Core plus</td><td colspan="3" rowspan="2">Fundamental analysis</td><td colspan="2" rowspan="2">Poor liquidity</td></tr>
<tr><td>Subjective ▶</td></tr>
<tr><td>Erratic ▶</td><td colspan="2">Focus on technicals</td><td colspan="3">Industry driven</td><td colspan="2">Excessive yield</td></tr>
</table>

One of the biggest mistakes high-yield portfolio managers make is believing they can achieve all goals under various market conditions. It is not feasible to shift from aggressive to conservative and then back to an aggressive style in a short time frame, given the generally poor trading liquidity and the unavailability of many issues in the high yield market.

The formula for successful high-yield portfolio management includes the following:

1. *Defined style:* Portfolio managers' style must be clearly defined, easy to understand, and unwavering in the face of changing markets. The five major styles are:
    a. Absolute return
    b. Total return
    c. Benchmark "huggers"
    d. Income-oriented
    e. Capital preservation
2. *Replicable and enforceable process:* The investment process must be thorough, simple to understand, replicable each day, and formalized. No exceptions to the process should be tolerated and no steps avoided because of market conditions (i.e., as the market is running; hence there is no time to complete the formal process).
3. *Research-driven:* All credits must be thoroughly researched to identify financial and operating risks, and the issuers' ability to meet their debt obligations must be evaluated. Credit research must be independent, and reliance on rating agencies and sell-side analysts should be minimized.
4. *Model portfolio:* Before committing capital, portfolio managers should prepare a model portfolio to measure the composite yield, duration, diversification, and rating composition. Portfolio managers must always prepare a detailed "buy plan" before committing capital in order to avoid impulse buying and to determine real market versus the perceived market conditions.

5. *Hold broker-dealers to high standards:* In the fast-paced world of trading, where millions of dollars are committed every hour, the tendency of some brokers is to highlight only the positives and provide incomplete "color" regarding market conditions. The use of a "penalty box" for brokers who mislead, misrepresent, or shade important facts should be utilized for 1-, 3-, 6-, or 12-month periods based on the seriousness of the infraction. Portfolio managers should refuse to execute trades with a brokerage firm which engages in unethical business practices.
6. *Develop a "critical list":* Portfolio managers should create and maintain a critical list of credits that fail to meet certain prescribed thresholds. For example, the critical list (depending on the style of the manager) could include a company that reports a sharply down quarter, a bond that trades below $80, bonds that have been downgraded by the rating agencies, or companies that fail to report their quarterly results on time.
7. *Build a historical database:* Portfolio managers should keep a detailed database of unique market information and couple it with internal portfolio analysis to validate both strategy and philosophy. For example, portfolio managers should capture and measure performance and default statistics of all deals by private equity sponsor, underwriter, and senior lender. Knowing the past history of management, sponsors, underwriters, lenders, or public versus private placement bonds gives greater insight into the strengths and weaknesses of key players in the leverage finance world. In addition, portfolio managers should never rely on the public rating agencies to confirm creditworthiness. Independent analysis is crucial to a low-default experience. Hence, a credit score system, a liquidity rating scale, a comprehensive financial model, a management evaluation questionnaire, and trading

monitor reports are the foundation of a comprehensive risk monitoring system.

8. *Comprehensive reporting system:* Over the years, there are legends of portfolio managers who have self-destructed because of their excessive risk taking. Daily and weekly feedback is necessary so that managers can make informed decisions based on actual facts rather than seat-of-the-pants intuition. Organized, customized, and detailed reports showing percentages and variance calculations are essential for critical decision making.
9. *The top 10 positions ultimately drive returns:* Portfolio managers must make certain that their top 10 positions generate the best returns. If the top positions are underperforming, it is extremely difficult to achieve superior results. If just one of the top 10 positions should default, a major loss occurs that is often difficult to offset with significant gains. Being aware of and understanding the attribution by position on both a technical and a fundamental basis should significantly and positively affect ultimate performance.
10. *Disciplined sale process:* The ability to execute a sell decision separates an average portfolio manager from an extraordinary one. In high-yield investing, knowing when to sell is more important than knowing what to buy because losses are typically greater than gains due to the call constrained feature inherent in most high-yield bonds. Portfolio managers should utilize "sell triggers" which can limit the downside losses. For example, these sell triggers could include price thresholds, such as bonds which drop below $80, the top two executives of a company leave unexpectedly, a bond that is downgraded in quality, spread-to-worst widens more than 250 basis points, or the company's stock repeatedly hits new lows.

FIGURE 11.3 Distribution Curve of the High-Yield Bond Market

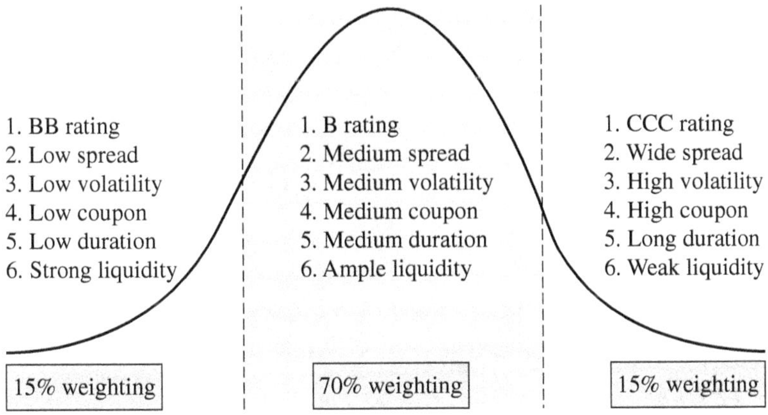

Six Types of Distribution Models

When allocating capital across different fundamental and technical characteristics within the high-yield bond market, a bell-shaped curve is the best way to construct a portfolio. Unlike barbelling, which overweights the extremes to average out to the midpoint, portfolio managers should weight bonds in the middle range of the distribution curve in order to optimize risk-adjusted returns. (See Figure 11.3.)

Risk Controls

In the universe of high-yield bonds, preserving capital and controlling risks are paramount factors in generating superior returns over a full credit and economic cycle. One of the keys to avoiding significant losses is to firmly establish risk control procedures and to develop a formal credit review process that looks at the four risk factors: credit, market, liquidity, and portfolio.

Risk controls are typically talked about but are seldom enforced in many money management organizations. Typically, organizations undertake serious, comprehensive risk controls only *after* a crisis.

However, money managers should carefully measure and monitor the following four types of risks.

Credit Risk

Credit risk involves measuring the ability of a high-yield issuer to meet its debt obligations in a timely manner. A common method for measuring credit risk is the rating assigned by one of the major credit rating agencies. However, the reliability of these ratings should be taken with caution given the past track record of the agencies.

Many high-yield companies share a common characteristic; namely, they have too much indebtedness or they lack sufficient cash flow to cover their interest expense. As a result, the majority of high-yield bonds have substantial risk, but many investors are in denial about the inherent perils of leveraged credit. Classifying this risk by its potential impact instead of its rating can help better control the level of risk taking:

1. *"Landmine" credits:* These credits have a high chance of causing fatal damage to portfolio performance because they have little room for error due to their high leverage, growth requirements, and/or below-average management team. An example of this type of credit would be an issuer with more than 8× leverage and less than 1.5× interest coverage in an issue with limited trading liquidity.
2. *"Firecracker" credits:* These credits have the ability to cause potentially severe damage to performance. These issuers typically have a moderate degree of leverage and coverage but may report disappointing results or show deteriorating trends (e.g., 6× or 7× leverage and 1.5× to 2.0× interest coverage).
3. *"Eggshell" credits:* These credits can cause minimal damage to portfolio returns. Typically, eggshell credits show some signs of fragility, but the credit metrics are strong enough to survive during difficult economic periods (e.g., leverage of less than 5× and interest coverage greater than 2×).

Portfolio managers should calculate and monitor the percentage of their portfolio in each of these three credit risk categories and vary the percentage according to market and economic conditions. Percentages should vary depending on the particular phase of the credit cycle.

Market Risk: Lender/Sponsor/ Underwriter Risks (LSU)

Market risk involves the measurement of a portfolio's exposure to the underpinnings of the high-yield market. One of the methods to measure this risk is by identifying and monitoring the percentage of holdings by the lead underwriter, senior lender, and private equity sponsor. Lead underwriters and senior lenders are important because not all underwriters and lenders are equally committed to the asset class. Some underwriters-brokers enter only when there is a bull market and abandon their efforts when the market declines, leaving the purchaser holding an orphaned bond. Moreover, since broker-dealers possess varying degrees of capital on their trading desks, knowing the liquidity of each credit is critical to understand the ability to execute on a trade idea.

Private equity sponsors, meanwhile, have track records that cannot be ignored. Some sponsors are known for frequently taking major dividends out of their LBO companies, thus leaving the entities more leveraged with no benefit to the debt holders. Other sponsors, however, have a reputation for encouraging their companies to pay down debt or supporting growth initiatives. Overconcentration on any of these factors can jeopardize performance over the long term.

These three identifiable risks—lender, sponsor, and underwriter—must be measured and monitored at all times to determine any overweighting, which is particularly important in a fragile market or poor economic environment. Holdings of 15% or greater in any of these "buckets" can be detrimental to long-term performance.

Portfolio managers should monitor their total percentage of the portfolio assets attributable to each private equity sponsor in order to determine their exposure to the most bondholder-friendly sponsors.

Over time, private equity firms have developed reputations as serial dividend takers, subverting the real intent of covenant terms (i.e., change of control provisions) and developing creative financing techniques (i.e., super holdco structures, Pay-in-Kind or Pay-in-Cash) or issuing more bonds to give themselves maximum flexibility. This flexibility, however, can ultimately damage bondholders' investment opportunities. While the objective of private equity firms is to maximize their investment returns, their "quick return" strategy is often at the expense of senior and subordinated creditors. Ironically, it is these same creditors that typically provide the sponsors with the means to complete new, leveraged transactions. Instead of taking a balanced approach where both equity and bondholders have a "fair deal," some private equity firms take advantage of the dispersed creditor base and utilize "divide and conquer" tactics (such as combined tender and consent offers) to gain the upper hand in their LBO transactions and covenant amendments.

Liquidity Risk

Liquidity risk involves measuring the ability to sell a particular credit on a timely basis. Unlike equities, which often trade on an organized stock exchange or electronically, where buyers and sellers are matched, high-yield bonds trade over the counter, which means investors are dependent on broker-dealers to make a market for the bonds. Also, unlike equities, the majority of high-yield bonds do not trade on any given day. If a particular high-yield bond has poor liquidity, a portfolio manager may be unable to execute his or her buy/sell decisions.

Some of the key elements that help determine liquidity risk are as follows:

1. *Public or private company:* Private companies often possess much less liquidity than public companies because there is either not enough information about the company in the market or the information is not widely dispersed. For example, a potential purchaser of a private bond (e.g., Rule 144A) may only be able to get information about the issuer

by requesting it from the underwriter or the company. New purchasers may be reticent to ask for the information because they may signal to the trading desk their intentions to purchase the bonds, thereby causing the broker-dealer to raise its asking price for the credit. In addition, when intensive, original research is required on a private company, portfolio managers will likely require more time or resources to thoroughly evaluate an unknown credit.

2. *Number of market makers and number of analysts following the issuer:* The fewer professionals on Wall Street who trade or actively "follow" a bond, the less available information there is on a company. Bond issues that have only one market maker and no analyst coverage may be so illiquid that they "trade by appointment" (meaning that a seller has to give an order to a broker-dealer who then tries to sell the bond over a long period of time).
3. *Number of tranches of debt in the capital structure:* The more tranches, or issues, of debt that a company has outstanding increases the probability that more traders and analysts will follow a given credit. In addition, the more tranches of debt outstanding provide more activity in a name because there are paired-trade possibilities, such as shorting senior bonds and going long subordinated bonds if the portfolio manager believes the spread between the two tranches is too wide.
4. *Accessibility of management:* Bonds of companies with inaccessible management typically inhibit trading activity because investors are concerned when they lack sufficient information to give them comfort or conviction, particularly in volatile markets. If a management will not talk when times are good, it is even more likely not to talk when times are bad!
5. *CDX-listed issuer:* The CDX is a widely traded index of 100 credit default swaps (CDSs) that mirrors the broader

high-yield market. The CDX, underlying CDS, and underlying bonds are all linked by the arbitrage that exists if the CDX becomes too cheap compared to the CDS or the actual bonds. Therefore, underlying bonds of CDS in the CDX tend to trade more frequently because investors may be executing arbitrage trades. Moreover, the prices of CDX-listed issues tend to be more volatile because they are more liquid names.

6. *Volume of trading activity according to TRACE:* Broker-dealers are required to report all high-yield bond trades to a self-regulating organization. That organization makes certain trade details of certain high-yield bonds (but not all bonds) publicly available. This system is called TRACE (for Trade Reporting And Compliance Engine). Bonds that have a TRACE history typically have more liquidity because historical patterns and data points are easy to obtain.
7. *Issuer is a major company within its industry:* Bonds of companies that have a real "presence" in their respective industries tend to have more liquidity for two reasons. First, if the underlying company is a major part of its industry, it becomes a proxy for the industry and allows investors to obtain exposure to a sector. Second, high-yield traders typically like to position and trade the biggest names in an industry sector.
8. *Size of issue:* The universe of potential buyers of a bond typically increases with the dollar size of the issue. In turn, the larger pool of potential purchasers increases the ability of a bondholder to sell a particular name.
9. *Ratings of issuer and issue:* Higher-rated names within the high-yield universe tend to trade more frequently because they are perceived as being more stable and have greater demand. CCC rated names require more work and

conviction to purchase, causing traders to be less willing to hold a bond that investors may need more time to analyze.

10. *Crossover name:* Bonds that generate demand from both investment-grade and high-yield buyers, such as utilities, offer greater liquidity. High-yield bonds that are considered crossover companies typically generate a new class of investment-grade purchasers who dip down and buy the high-yield bond tranche from time to time. With a larger universe of such buyers and sellers, liquidity often improves.

Based on these 10 criteria, each credit should be designated as "L1," "L2," or "L3." L1 credits are traded by multiple market makers on a daily basis; L2 names are typically traded by one or more major market maker on a weekly basis; and L3 credits trade sporadically by one market maker (meaning that the issue trades "by appointment only"), which can result in an inability to execute on a timely basis. In many cases, an L3 bond can become an "orphan" credit if the original underwriter no longer covers or makes a market in the credit.

The percentage of the portfolio represented by L1, L2, or L3 liquidity ratings should be calculated and monitored to determine the appropriate weighting in each category.

Portfolio Risk

When examining and constructing a high-yield portfolio, all risk elements should be examined. One methodology is to categorize each bond into "buckets." Unlike credit risk, which focuses on the underlying fundamentals of the company, portfolio risk measures how the bond may perform in the market:

1. *"Termite" holdings:* These bonds represent immediate sell candidates, but the portfolio manager may be unable to sell

the bonds due to poor liquidity. For example, because of changing fundamentals and market technicals, a bond may be given an L3 liquidity and "landmine" designation, but the portfolio manager is unable to sell the credit. Hence, the bond remains in the portfolio month after month, much like a termite in a house.

2. *"Turtle" holdings:* Turtle bonds are classified as long-term holdings and represent companies that historically meet their cash flow projections. For example, an L1, eggshell credit with no market risk should be a core holding and provide a consistent return for the portfolio.
3. *"Pit bull" holdings:* These bonds possess some hidden fundamental risks which rest somewhat underneath the surface of the credit. For example, a bond may be an L1, eggshell designation, but the industry dynamics are in flux and a major decline in cash flow is expected. These pending risks may not yet be reflected in the bond price, but it is just a matter of time before the pit bull bites its holder!

Shorting Risk and Volatility

In recent years, shorting has added greater volatility to the high-yield market as it has become more mainstream as a hedging technique for some aggressive portfolio managers. The growth of single-name CDSs (credit default swaps) and the introduction of new tools such as the CDX index (a basket of underwritten individual CDS names) have allowed shorting to be done with greater volume, as more broker-dealers trade CDS and CDX. Prior to the growth in the CDS/CDX, shorting was a difficult technique because it meant finding and borrowing the actual bond to short. In any event, a high-yield bond can also be expensive because of the high cost of paying the coupon rate plus carrying costs. Hence, the timing of shorting a high yield bond is paramount as the cost of carry can be high.

Summary

For long-term successful investing in the high-yield market, an unwavering investment philosophy is essential. This philosophy should include the following:

1. Focus on risk and what could go wrong by developing risk controls based on the four types of risk: credit, market, liquidity, and portfolio
2. A skill set that understands industry, technicals, and fundamentals
3. A relative value process which is separate from the credit-worthiness analysis
4. Checklists to identify volatility and maintain discipline
5. A defined style and detailed reporting

Being conservative in the high-yield market never goes out of favor! The difference between an optimist and a pessimist is that the latter deals with the facts. If portfolio managers are inherently optimistic, then they should invest in equities where one may be compensated for the volatility and risk. For long-term success in the high-yield market, managers should be pessimists and question conventional wisdom and consensus thinking!

12

THE PITFALLS OF MANAGING HIGH-YIELD ASSETS

Mark R. Shenkman

President and Chief Investment Officer,
Shenkman Capital Management, Inc.

High-yield bonds should be evaluated in the context of the broader fixed-income market, which includes high-grade corporate and government bonds. To most observers, there are similarities across all three asset classes, such as coupon, maturity, and a rating, but the similarities stop there. High-yield bonds possess much more equitylike risk, which is evidenced by their rating nomenclature: speculative. The biggest difference between high-grade bonds and high-yield bonds is that high-yield issuers are directly affected by corporate developments and issuer fundamentals, whereas high-grade bonds are tied more to the yield curve. It takes an experienced eye to know all the subtleties for successful investing in high-yield securities. The major pitfalls in the high-yield market include a lack of discipline, overreliance on ratings, the presence of a herd mentality, the failure to properly assess the risk/reward characteristics of a portfolio, inadequate risk controls, a failure to understand poor market liquidity, improper portfolio diversification, the belief that higher yields compensate for higher credit risks, a tendency to be immobilized by previously high but falling prices until too much deterioration sets in, and tendencies to overvalue high yields and to rely too much on benchmarks.

Lack of Discipline

Because the financial markets and most investors are undisciplined, it is incumbent upon portfolio managers to maintain strict adherence to style, strategy, and philosophy, regardless of market conditions. Fear of loss (underperforming the benchmark) or greed to generate profits propels many portfolio managers to abandon their discipline and chase the market.

Overreliance on Ratings

The public rating agencies have a difficult task in maintaining accurate and timely credit ratings because of a multiplicity of industries and deal structures. As a result, portfolio managers tend to make investment decisions predicated on inaccurate ratings and neglect to rely upon their own independent credit analysis. Internally developed proprietary models are superior because their components are known factors, rather than an "unexplainable black box" developed by the rating agencies.

Additionally, proprietary tools force portfolio managers or credit analysts to do all of their own analytical work, rather than rely on the published ratings of the agencies.

Herd Mentality

Human nature propels many portfolio managers not to be left behind in roaring markets because they do not want to incur a significant tracking error from the various indices. As a result, portfolio managers succumb to market psychology, which influences their decision making. Historically, independent, unconventional, contrary viewpoints typically lead to greater long-term performance.

Failure to Properly Assess the Risk/Reward

In deciding which credits should be part of the portfolio, calculating the potential upside-return versus the potential downside risk is the greatest single miscalculation by portfolio managers. Too often, portfolio managers ignore or downplay the risk factors and overweight the upward returns.

In high-yield securities, the risks are typically greater than the rewards. High-yield bonds are constrained by their call price, which is generally one-half the coupon rate. The downside risk, however, is potentially zero in the event of a default if the bondholders are deeply subordinated in the capital structure. Accordingly, high-yield securities must be properly analyzed, evaluated, and monitored.

Inadequate Risk Controls

By nature, portfolio managers have a strong tendency to be optimistic. Hence, they become reluctant to sell a particular bond before significant price deterioration occurs. Instead of examining the income stream and/or total return potential, portfolio managers must examine all known risk factors which can derail a company's ability to meet its principal and interest payments on time. Risk factors should be identified properly with assigned probability assessments, and then these risks should be compared against alternative investment ideas. A full risk-versus-reward analysis should provide a more complete picture of a given issuer's creditworthiness.

Failure to Understand Poor Market Liquidity

High-yield bonds trade in a dealer market, and hence, the amount of capital committed by a broker-dealer significantly influences trading volume. Over the past several years, dealer capital in the high-yield market has dramatically shrunk because of consolidation on Wall Street and trading losses in the 2007–2008 financial debacles. The implementation of the TRACE system (Trading Reporting and Compliance Engine) has somewhat ameliorated the liquidity problem. With TRACE, broker-dealers must report the size and price of a high-yield trade (excluding Rule 144A transactions) as part of the SEC's effort to improve transparency.

Unfortunately, TRACE information has somewhat diminished broker-dealer profitability, and with lower returns on capital, dealers are less willing to commit their capital for secondary trading. As a result, market liquidity has become more problematic, particularly during turbulent conditions.

When purchasing high-yield bonds, portfolio managers must never assume that they can thereafter timely liquidate a position in order to reposition the portfolio or for fundamental credit reasons. Some high-yield portfolio managers fail to properly assess the liquidity characteristics of a particular credit in the portfolio. Portfolio managers should develop a liquidity classification scale for each credit in the portfolio. Being the first or second seller in a deteriorating credit can at least mitigate significant trading losses.

Improper Diversification

Constructing a portfolio is similar to assembling a jigsaw puzzle. All the components (i.e., position size, rating, industry, yield spread, liquidity) of the portfolio should be properly calibrated and positioned in order to achieve the best diversification objectives.

Most portfolio managers maintain diversification percentages of 2–3% per issuer and 10–20% per industry but fail to utilize additional tests to measure risks. Additional diversification tests should include no more than 20% by underwriter and no more than 20% by senior lender, as well as a limitation on total debt invested in any single issuer across all accounts greater than 20%. One of the most common mistakes portfolio managers make is that they "fall in love" with industries and/or credits and fail to properly diversify their high-yield portfolios.

Higher Yield Rarely Compensates for Credit Risk

Many portfolio managers believe that the higher the current yield is, the more it offsets or compensates for a greater credit risk. In reality, the higher the yield is, the greater the probability of default. The highest-yielding credits should be avoided in a conservative strategy. One of the fundamental principals of high-yield investing is that "yield hogs" almost always get slaughtered!

Immobilized by Price

For many portfolio managers, it takes little courage or emotion to commence an aggressive buy program. However, it takes an exceptional portfolio manager to have the conviction to sell before the "crowd" identifies a deteriorating credit or reads about a faltering industry. One of the hardest lessons for portfolio managers to learn is to sell early and not look back or second-guess their trade decisions.

The window of opportunity to sell in the high-yield market is limited by the lack of depth in the marketplace. The first loss is the easiest to accept. As a credit deteriorates, some portfolio managers become immobilized because they are unable or unwilling to accept defeat and realize a major credit mistake. As a result, many portfolio managers hold a credit too long, even though the company is showing fundamental deterioration. These managers typically sustain even larger losses once a credit files for bankruptcy or restructures.

Avoid Being a Yield Hog

Portfolio managers often feel that they are compensated for the risk when a specific credit has a double-digit yield, either based on the coupon or because it is trading at a deep discount. In fact, the wider the spread over 10-year Treasuries, the greater the inherent risk of default and the more cautious a portfolio manager should be in allocating capital to the riskiest credits (unless the strategy is to invest in distressed or troubled companies). When a credit has a yield-to-worst greater than 1,000 basis points over 10-year Treasuries, it indicates a greater degree of speculative risk. History has shown that credits yielding more than 10 percent over 10-year Treasuries should be classified in the "subjunk" category or stressed status because this entails a higher probability of default.

Mesmerized and Overly Influenced by the Benchmark

Portfolio managers are expected to outperform a designated benchmark in both bull and bear markets. Unfortunately, it is extremely difficult to outperform in both rising and falling markets because it takes totally different types of credits and styles to outperform in a rising or falling market environment.

The high-yield market has never offered sufficient depth and/or liquidity to switch billions of dollars of capital from bull credits to bear credits because dealer capital in the secondary market is insufficient. It is estimated that approximately 70 percent of high-yield names do not trade on any given day, including credits trading "by appointment only." No one can consistently beat a high-yield index in both bull and bear markets because most issues are illiquid. In fact, many names in the various indices are "put away" by long-term institutional investors. Establishing a priority goal of beating a specific benchmark has many fallacies:

1. Benchmarks consist of many financially weak credits.
2. Benchmarks have many default-prone industries.
3. Benchmarks do not have to deal with flow-of-funds considerations.
4. Benchmarks are artificially constructed with no relation to actual ability to execute.
5. Benchmarks are basically flawed and inconsistent in one way or another. For example:
   - There are no issues of less than one year to maturity (BofA/Merrill Lynch High Yield Bond Index).
   - Defaulted securities are removed (BofA/Merrill Lynch High Yield Bond Index).
   - No PIK/toggles are included (BofA/Merrill Lynch High Yield Bond Index).
   - No floating-rate bonds are included (BofA/Merrill Lynch High Yield Bond Index).
   - Only the two largest issues of a particular issuer are represented (Credit Suisse High Yield Index).

As a result, although it is feasible to beat the benchmark with a conservative strategy in a down market, or with an aggressive style in an up market, the combination of aggressive/conservative style outperforming in both bull and bear markets is extremely challenging and flawed. It is a common goal in the money management business to consistently outperform a specified index. However, in reality, for high-yield investors, beating an index in both bull and bear markets means accepting undue risk in many situations.

Summary

Most high-yield issuers have one common characteristic that should never be overlooked. These companies are overleveraged, speculative credits with a somewhat limited margin of safety in the event of a credit crunch or an economic downturn. Since these leveraged companies have less flexibility to withstand adverse developments, they should be considered from a conservative perspective, with the burden of proof of survivability based upon in-depth analysis, uninfluenced by the views of rating agencies, high-pressure salespeople, and/or savvy traders.

Lack of skepticism typically leads to poor investment decisions and increased volatility. Always remember the difference between a salesperson and an investor. A salesperson is paid to sell something you may not want or need, whereas a seasoned portfolio manager is responsible for preserving capital and generating a superior risk-adjusted return.

13

PERFORMANCE ANALYSIS

Frederic R. Bernhard, CFA

Vice President, Business Development,
Shenkman Capital Management, Inc.

Investment management performance analysis, commonly referred to as performance attribution, is the examination of a manager's active investment performance. The objective is to break down the variance between an investment manager's active returns and the passive market's returns into discrete segments that illuminate the investment manager's decision-making process and reveal value-added decisions that made money and those that did not. The study of high-yield bond performance attribution is a relatively new and evolving process that grew in importance as institutional investment consultants and clients began to look for more detailed analysis of exactly why a particular high-yield bond manager under- or overperformed. Unlike stock performance attribution, which has a longer history and can be comparatively straightforward, high-yield bond attribution analysis requires more layers of calculations to take into account external factors such as changes in the yield curve or rating. The complex and developing mathematical process necessary for high-yield bond attribution means that calculating performance attribution is as much an art as it is a science and will remain that way until a standard optimization process is agreed upon.

The basic mechanics of the attribution process, be it for stocks or bonds, entails contrasting a portfolio's overall return to a benchmark by comparing different weights and returns in various smaller trading segments. Analyzing smaller segments of the portfolio is an easier way to dissect isolated decisions of the investment manager. The final analysis will show that performance "success" is overweighting the segments, or sectors, that did well and/or selecting the best-performing securities within sectors. Conversely, attribution can show "failure" in such things as overweighting underperforming sectors and/or selecting weakest-performing names in a sector. Historically, when analyzing equities there has been one key segment, the industry sector, which determines the bulk of the analysis. This could be due to the limited trading segments that correlate to a manager's decisions. In other words, equity investment managers may many times base their weighting stakes on industries and try also to find the best names in each industry. This is not as often done with other segments, such as price-to-earnings (P/E), market capitalization, or total enterprise-to-value multiples.

In the case of high-yield bonds, there are multiple segments that are influential in trading and decision making: industry, rating, duration, and price; each of these affects bond prices and can be considered an attribution segment. For example, a bond investment manager may make large weighting stakes based on rating, duration, industry, and price while simultaneously looking for the best credits in each segment. The challenge is in developing an attribution analysis that best matches up with the bond manager's internal optimization of those four segments.

High-yield bond attribution analysis can be analogous to different sportscasters who have varying ways to analyze the same football game: One focuses on the offensive line to explain why a team (or industry) won, another on the defensive line (or rating), and yet another on the special teams (or duration). So it is too with high-yield bond attribution analysis. It is for this reason—the subjectivity of the manager's optimization across and within these segments—that many professional software packages have shied away from high-yield bond attribution and left that task to the underwriters of the strategy groups at large to execute with optimization models. But even there the process is imperfect, since they utilize self-styled "black boxes," which are a function of their subjective prioritizing of the four segments' output.

This chapter first reviews the two basic methods of attribution: the three-factor and two-factor methods. Second, this chapter demonstrates performance attribution analysis on a sample data set of high-yield bond portfolios. Third, it discusses the challenges and future of attribution analysis itself.

Attribution: The Basic Formulas

Attribution formulas serve to compare weights and returns across a segment between the active portfolio and the passive market, or benchmark index, by producing three explanatory outputs such as asset allocation, security selection, and interaction effect. There are two basic attribution methods that do this: the three-factor and two-factor formulas. The key difference between the two methods is whether the third factor, the interaction effect, is calculated separately or is included as part of the security selection effect.

In order to explain the models, we will use an example to demonstrate how the formulas are applied. In this case the segment we choose to analyze is the portfolio.

The Three-Factor Attribution Model Approach

The three factors include asset allocation, security selection, and interaction effect. The advantage of this model is that the third factor—the interaction effect—is separated out and results in a more pure security selection (or stock or bond picking). The disadvantage is that the added layer of complexity can be time-consuming and the value of the often small interaction effect is often debatable. First we need to provide a basic model of the three-factor approach:

$$\text{Asset allocation } \Sigma\,(W_p - W_i) * (R_i - TR_i)$$
$$+ \text{ security selection } \Sigma\, W_i * (R_p - R_i)$$
$$+ \text{ interaction effect } \Sigma\,(W_p - W_i) * (R_p - R_i)$$

Now we will consider the three factors, one at a time.

Factor 1: Asset Allocation = *$(W_p - W_i) * (R_i - TR_i)$*

Using the data set in Table 13.1, the first task is to assess the portfolio manager's success in allocating assets across industries. In other words, did the portfolio manager move the portfolio's assets into overperforming industries and out of underperforming industries? To do that, you multiply the difference of portfolio and index weights by the difference between industry index return and total portfolio return. The first part of the equation, portfolio weight versus index weight, isolates the magnitude of an over- or underweight decision made by a portfolio

TABLE 13.1 Sample Data for Performance Analysis*†

	Passive Market Benchmark Index			Portfolio		
Sector	**W_i Index Weight**	**R_i Index Return**	**TR_i Return Impact**	**W_p Portfolio Weight**	**R_p Portfolio Return**	**TR_p Return Impact**
Consumer	30%	15%	4.50%	10%	18%	1.80%
Tech	10%	20%	2.00%	30%	25%	7.50%
Services	35%	30%	10.50%	15%	20%	3.00%
Energy	25%	–5%	–1.25%	45%	5%	2.25%
Total			**15.75%**			**14.55%**

*Relative return = 14.55% – 15.75% = –1.20%
†Attribution goal: Decompose the –1.20% of relative performance into investment decisions that the portfolio manager made.

manager. The second component of the equation assesses whether the same industry over- or underperformed the broader market passive benchmark index. Together, multiplying an overweight industry (would be a positive number) by an underperforming industry (would be a negative number) would yield a negative effect based on how the portfolio manager allocated the assets. Note that the portfolio returns are not used here. Passive benchmark returns are used as the measuring stick for purposes of accessing the portfolio manager's skill in choosing the right market industries into which the portfolio's assets were allocated.

The following example uses the energy sector data in Table 13.1 to show how an overweighed sector that underperformed the broader index resulted in a –4.15% effect:

$$(W_p - W_i) * (R_i - TR_i)$$

$$(0.45 - 0.25\ ) * (-0.05 - 0.1575) = -4.15\%$$

The portfolio manager significantly overweighed a sector that underperformed the benchmark as a whole—this decision subtracted 4.15% (or 415 basis points) from his or her relative performance.

Factor 2: Security Selection = $W_i * (R_p - R_i)$

The second task is to assess the portfolio manager's ability to pick the best securities within an industry. The formula for this is the weight of the industry in the index multiplied by the portfolio return for the industry less the index return for the same industry. This formula compares the performance of the actively managed industry to the performance of the passive industry and magnifies the difference by the weight.

The following equation continues the energy sector example:

$$W_i * (R_p - R_i)$$

$$0.25 * [0.05 - (-\ 0.05)] = 2.50\%$$

The portfolio manager picked bonds in the energy sector that had superior performance relative to the benchmark's energy sector bonds—this decision had the effect of adding 2.50% (or 250 basis points) to the portfolio manager's performance relative to the index.

Factor 3: Interaction = $(W_p - W_i) * (R_p - R_i)$

The interaction effect is conceptually difficult to define. Although it does quantify a portion of a variance, it does not directly attribute this variance to an investment decision. Practitioners suggest that it is the portion of excess return resulting from the interaction of the asset allocation and security selection decisions.

A segment's interaction effect equals the weight of the industry in the portfolio minus the weight of the industry in the index multiplied by the difference of the portfolio industry return less the index industry return. In the case of the energy sector, the interaction effect would be calculated as follows:

$$(W_p - W_i) * (R_p - R_i)$$

$$(0.45 - 0.25\ ) * [0.05 - (-0.05)] = 2.00\%$$

The combined impact of the portfolio manager's asset allocation and security selection decisions added 2.00% to the PM's relative performance.

Total Factor Effect

The total factor effect is the total excess value delivered. In the case of the energy sector:

Industry allocation + security selection + interaction = total effect

$$-4.15\% + 2.50\% + 2.00\% = .35\%$$

The portfolio manager's investment decisions as they relate to the energy sector added .35% to his or her overall relative return. By

TABLE 13.2 Factor Effects by Industry Sector

Industry	Factor 1: Asset Allocation	Factor 2: Security Selection	Factor 3: Interaction Effect	TOTAL
Consumer	0.15%	0.90%	−0.60%	**0.45%**
Tech	0.85%	0.50%	1.00%	**2.35%**
Services	−2.85%	−3.50%	2.00%	**−4.35%**
Energy	−4.15%	2.50%	2.00%	**0.35%**
Total	**−6.00%**	**0.40%**	**4.40%**	**−1.20%**

breaking this down we can see the dramatic drag the overweight in energy had on the portfolio.

If the calculations are done for each industry, the analysis looks as shown in Table 13.2.

Challenges with the Three-Factor Approach

The advantage to the three-factor model is that the security selection output (2.50% or 250 basis points for energy) is a more precise analysis of the manager's stock-picking strength because it keeps index weights static and compares the passive benchmark to the active stock picking. However, the challenge with the model is the large interaction effect, which can outweigh security selection, as it has above. Many practitioners have argued that the interaction effect is a spurious correlation to any interaction and should, therefore, be included in security selection. That said, the three-factor model output is preferred.

The Two-Factor Approach

The two-factor approach is based on the theory underlying the three-factor approach but simplifies it by only examining asset allocation and security selection by including the interaction effect as an aspect of

TABLE 13.3 Set-up Formulas for the Two-Factor Approach

The three calculating elements involve the following formulas:

I. Index = $\Sigma(W_i * R_i) = 15.75\%$

II. Allocation = $\Sigma(W_p * R_i) = .1(15) + .3(20) + .15(30) + .45(-5) = 9.75\%$

III. Portfolio return = $\Sigma(W_p * R_p) = .1(18) + .3(36) + .15(20) + .45(5) = 14.55\%$

Factor 1	Asset allocation	II – I (Allocation – Index) 9.75% – 15.75% = –6.0%
Factor 2	Security selection	III – II (Portfolio Return – Allocation) 14.55% – 9.75% = 4.80%
Total factor effect	Asset allocation + Security selection	III – I (Portfolio Return – Index) 4.55% – 15.75% = –1.20%

Market index:	15.75%
Asset Allocation:	-6.00%
Security Selection:	4.80%
Manager Return:	14.55%

security selection. The two-factor model, while less precise, is presented here because of its ease to calculate, which allows for a complete portfolio attribution data set to be generated easily, which in turn becomes the basis for interpreting the output data, which is the same for either method. The two-factor method is described below. There is an interim step to simplify the calculations. Although it involves *three* calculating elements (I, II, III as outlined in Table 13.3), do not be confused; this is still the *two*-factor approach.[1]

Applying Attribution to High-Yield Bonds

High-yield bonds are often considered a hybrid security because they can sometimes trade like a bond and sometimes like a stock. The consequences of this dual nature make applying basic attribution math to high-yield securities unique. Therefore, in addition to the stock attribution, it is necessary to consider investment-grade bond attribution before delving into the attribution mechanics for high-yield bonds.

Investment-grade bonds are highly rated securities (rated at least BBB– or Baa3 by S&P and Moody's, respectively) with low yield and spread over Treasuries. These stronger companies, or credits, typically perform very well, and there is little room for speculation that the company will default. As a result, the bonds primarily move in price based on changes in the underlying economy, for which the U.S. Treasury market is a proxy, and investment-grade bonds move in correlation to maintain a constant spread over the risk-free rate of the Treasury bonds. If the yield on a 10-year T-bond were to increase by 50 basis points (0.50%), then the investment-grade bond with a 10-year maturity would likely move similarly to keep pace with the change in the risk-free rate; this is an example of the concept of duration. Put another way, a bond's duration is its sensitivity to movements in Treasury interest rates. Although high-yield bonds have a low correlation to duration, it is still a factor to consider when doing attribution.

The attribution process for duration is exactly like the industry process analyzed previously; however, instead of having industry sectors to compare weights and returns, the duration analysis uses duration buckets: 0–1, 2–3, 3–4, and so on. Another important side note: High-yield bonds are infrequently affected by changes in broader interest rates, but investment-grade bonds are often directly affected. In fact, duration is perhaps the single largest factor affecting investment-grade bonds. There are attribution models available for investment-grade bond portfolios that segment out duration impact up front. These models break down total return into duration/curve return and excess return. Duration/curve return is further broken down into shifts and twists in the yield curve and is removed from the total return variance, leaving excess return. Using attribution math, this excess return is broken down to allocation and selection against broad sectors such as rating.[2]

High-yield bond attribution includes the industry attribution process from stocks and the duration attribution process from investment-grade bonds. It also has two additional influential segments to consider: ratings and price. Ratings are a correlated bucket with which to assess high-yield bonds because they sometimes move based on rating categories. For example, if managers are looking to increase the credit quality in their portfolio, an easy way to do this is to sell the riskiest CCC securities and buy the safer BB securities. This may happen during times of uncertainty in the economy and may move broad swaths of bonds as a result of this alone.

The other major correlated bucket involves price ranges such as below $80, $80–$90, $90–$100, $100–$110, and $110+. While prices are a function of yield-to-worst for a bond, they may also be a signal of potential default and may complement the rating category. Bonds below $80 are thought of as stressed and signal that difficult times are ahead for a company, and the rating may not yet reflect this. If managers want to reduce the risk in their portfolio, they should reduce the percentage of low-priced bonds.

Table 13.4 demonstrates what a high-yield bond portfolio might look like if its weights and returns were broken down by the four influential trading buckets. We will use this as an example of attribution analysis.

As you can see, each bucket (industry, duration, rating, and price) explains the same portfolio in a different way and arrives at the same return for both the index and the portfolio.

Applying the simpler, two-factor attribution model, the output generates the information contained in Table 13.5.

Interpreting the Data

The output noted on the right-hand side of Table 13.5 shows the attribution of each correlated segment with selection and allocation output. Each section is mutually exclusive, which means that the results at this point are not blended together, so the interpretation is confined to segment-by-segment analysis.

Aggregating the Data

In typical stock attribution work the analysis stops at the industry level of attribution, but for high-yield bonds the attribution process will

TABLE 13.4 High-Yield Bond Portfolio Return Breakdown by Trading Buckets

	Index			Manager		
Industry	**Index Weight**	**Index Return**	**Return Impact**	**Portfolio Weight**	**Portfolio Return**	**Return Impact**
Consumer	30.00%	15.00%	4.50%	10.00%	18.00%	1.80%
Tech	10.00%	20.00%	2.00%	30.00%	25.00%	7.50%
Services	35.00%	30.00%	10.50%	15.00%	20.00%	3.00%
Energy	25.00%	−5.00%	−1.25%	45.00%	5.00%	2.25%
Total	**100.00%**		**15.75%**	**100.00%**		**14.55%**
Duration (Years)	**Index Weight**	**Index Return**	**Return Impact**	**Portfolio Weight**	**Portfolio Return**	**Return Impact**
0–2	10.00%	30.00%	3.00%	84.00%	12.76%	10.72%
2–4	40.00%	25.00%	10.00%	14.00%	25.00%	3.50%
4–6	35.00%	10.00%	3.50%	1.00%	20.00%	0.20%
6+	15.00%	−5.00%	−0.75%	1.00%	13.04%	0.13%
Total	**100.00%**		**15.75%**	**100.00%**		**14.55%**
Rating	**Index Weight**	**Index Return**	**Return Impact**	**Portfolio Weight**	**Portfolio Return**	**Return Impact**
BB	10.00%	20.00%	2.00%	33.33%	8.65%	2.88%
B	60.00%	14.80%	8.88%	33.33%	25.00%	8.33%
CCC	30.00%	16.22%	4.87%	33.33%	10.00%	3.33%
Total	**100.00%**		**15.75%**	**100.00%**		**14.55%**
Price	**Index Weight**	**Index Return**	**Return Impact**	**Portfolio Weight**	**Portfolio Return**	**Return Impact**
Below $80	10.00%	−10.00%	−1.00%	25.00%	8.65%	2.16%
$80–$90	40.00%	15.00%	6.00%	25.00%	25.00%	6.25%
$90–$100	40.00%	20.00%	8.00%	25.00%	6.00%	1.50%
$100+	10.00%	27.50%	2.75%	25.00%	18.55%	4.64%
Total	**100.00%**		**15.75%**	**100.00%**		**14.55%**

TABLE 13.5 High-Yield Bond Portfolio Analysis Using the Two-Factor Attribution Method

Industry	Index I	Allocation II	Portfolio Return III	Allocation II–I	Security Selection III–II	Manager Value III–I
Consumer	4.50%	1.50%	1.80%	−3.00%	0.30%	−2.70%
Tech	2.00%	6.00%	7.50%	4.00%	1.50%	5.50%
Services	10.50%	4.50%	3.00%	−6.00%	−1.50%	−7.50%
Industry	−1.25%	−2.25%	2.25%	−1.00%	4.50%	3.50%
Total	**15.75%**	**9.75%**	**14.55%**	**−6.00%**	**4.80%**	**−1.20%**

Duration (Years)	Index I	Allocation II	Portfolio Return III	Allocation II–I	Security Selection III–II	Manager Value III–I
0–2	3.00%	25.20%	10.72%	22.20%	−14.48%	7.72%
2–4	10.00%	3.50%	3.50%	−6.50%	0.00%	−6.50%
4–6	3.50%	0.10%	0.20%	−3.40%	0.10%	−3.30%
6+	−0.75%	−0.05%	0.13%	0.70%	0.18%	0.88%
Total	**15.75%**	**28.75%**	**14.55%**	**13.00%**	**−14.20%**	**−1.20%**

Rating	Index I	Allocation II	Portfolio Return III	Allocation II–I	Security Selection III–II	Manager Value III–I
BB	2.00%	6.67%	2.88%	4.67%	−3.78%	0.88%
B	8.88%	4.93%	8.33%	−3.95%	3.40%	−0.55%
CCC	4.87%	5.41%	3.33%	0.54%	−2.07%	−1.53%
Total	**15.75%**	**17.01%**	**14.55%**	**1.26%**	**−2.46%**	**−1.20%**

Price	Index I	Allocation II	Portfolio Return III	Allocation II–I	Security Selection III–II	Manager Value III–I
Below $80	−1.00%	−2.50%	2.16%	−1.50%	4.66%	3.16%
$80–$90	6.00%	3.75%	6.25%	−2.25%	2.50%	0.25%
$90–$100	8.00%	5.00%	1.50%	−3.00%	−3.50%	−6.50%
$100+	2.75%	6.88%	4.64%	4.13%	−2.24%	1.89%
Total	15.75%	13.13%	14.55%	−2.63%	1.43%	−1.20%

include analysis of all four factors simultaneously, based on the active management decisions made. Therefore, in order to help prioritize the data analysis, more background is needed in this hypothetical example:

1. Influential Factor: Scenario 1
   Cause: The U.S. economy takes a turn for the worse, and high-yield managers fear a fall in corporate cash flow.
   Effect: High-yield managers seek to raise credit quality and focus their buys and sells on rating. BB bonds do better, while CCC bonds underperform.
2. Influential Factor: Scenario 2
   Cause: U.S, Treasuries rise in price, narrowing the yield, as the U.S. dollar appreciates rapidly over a short period.
   Effect: High-yield managers seek to increase shorter-duration bonds to capture the strength. Shorter-duration bonds outperform as managers buy more short-duration bonds and sell long-duration bonds.
3. Influential Factor: Scenario 3
   Cause: U.S. banks tighten credit standards, which could increase defaults for U.S. corporations.
   Effect: High-yield managers reduce risk by selling low dollar-priced securities. Lower dollar-priced bonds underperform.
4. Influential factor: Scenario 4
   Cause: Technology sector rebounds and performs well.
   Effect: High-yield managers buy technology. Technology outperforms.

In the preceding four scenarios over a one-month period the market moved on four pieces of news in four different ways:

BB bonds outperformed.
Shorter duration bonds outperformed.

Lower dollar bonds outperformed.

Technology bonds outperformed.

One important side note to bring up here: For the purpose of this example, these buckets are discrete and do not overlap. In reality, however, this may not be the case. For example, BB bonds typically are higher in quality and have higher prices, while low-dollar-price bonds typically have long duration, and technology bonds may have long maturities and high coupons causing long duration. As a result, the performance assessment is challenged by the need to decide which analysis to pick to explain performance. Ideally, there should be a multivariate model that integrates all four discrete results by weighting each result with a coefficient, but writing such a model would be subjective or based on historical performance and R-squared. Since a successful industrywide multivariate model is not widely accepted and in use, the analyzer of the information must prioritize and "stitch" together the four discrete results to best fit the decisions made.

One of the main challenges here is that some of the variables are highly correlated (price and rating, for example). The shorter the time horizon under analysis, the easier it is to run attribution since the PM will have a higher chance of making decisions on only one of these factors. The longer the time period, the lower the chance that the PM is making decisions on only one of these factors, thus the more difficult it becomes to run attribution.

Continuing with the same example and hypothetical market environment as previously, the high-yield bond manager made the following investment decisions in the six months leading up to the four scenarios:

1. *Rating:* The manager took no action based on rating.
2. *Duration:* The manager purchased shorter-duration bonds because the manager believed that interest rates would rise.
3. *Lower dollar:* The manager took no action based on dollar price.

4. *Technology:* The manager conducted a comprehensive review and devised a strategy based on each industry.

Based on these actions taken, it is possible to ignore the rating and low dollar analysis and focus on the duration and industry analysis. In addition, if it is known that the manager has analysts who specialize by industry and industry-by-industry analysis is a core focus of their investment strategy, then the focus should be on the industry attribution analysis first. Therefore, the final analysis might look something like the following:

- Overall security selection based on industry added 480 basis points to performance, which means that the manager is good at picking the right companies in each industry.
- Overall industry-by-industry allocation subtracted 600 basis points from performance, meaning partially that the manager's decision to invest more heavily in energy negatively offset the technology overweight.
- The manager's decision to allocate assets from long duration to short duration helped by 1,300 basis points. (Note: The manager's security selection in the duration analysis is not relevant since the manager did not select individual securities within a duration bucket; that was done on the basis of the industry.)

Once the attribution analysis for high-yield bonds moves from interpretation to aggregation, it becomes subjective and lends itself to the following imperfections:

Results across segments are not additive: In the preceding example, the basis points cannot be added across segments. For example the 1,300 basis points that helped on duration allocation cannot be added to the 480 basis points that helped in security selection within industry.

This is because each result is mutually exclusive, and emphasis on the 1,300 basis points over the 480 basis points is, therefore, subjective. There are models that measure multiple factors which are additive. The caveat is that the factors need to be order-dependent (based on the ordering of the employed investment decisions). Top-down attribution is one example of this.[3]

Some of the output is ignored: Depending on the manager's strategy, some of the results will be ignored. For example, security selection by dollar price is not relevant since the investment process in this example does not try to pick the best bond within a basket of credits based on dollar price.

Deciding which result to focus on is subjective: Picking the industry allocation result over the duration allocation result might be easy to determine since the manager in this hypothetical example acknowledges that more of his or her decision was spent on industry over duration, but how much more is hard to ascertain. Was it 20% more, 30% more, or 80% more? An interesting alternative to consider is to blend multiple factors into single ones with the intention of measuring them concurrently. For example, you can combine duration and industry into single factors:

- Energy: 1–3 years
- Energy: 3–5 years
- Energy: 5–10 years
- Energy: >10 years
- Tech: 1–3 years
- Tech: 3–5 years
- Tech: 5–10 years
- Tech: >10 years
- Etc.

Challenges

High-yield bond attribution has four key challenges: The passive market benchmark index is theoretical, the aggregation process is subjective, the results may or may not be relevant, and an industry-standard multivariate model has not been adopted.

1. *The passive market benchmark index is theoretical:* The high-yield index represents a very large cross section of high-yield bonds issued over many years, in varying sizes. To complicate matters further, many bonds are "put away" by long-term institutional accounts, meaning the bonds are held until maturity and do not trade. This illiquidity makes it hard to replicate the market. Also, bond prices in the index change day to day based on market prices submitted by sell-side traders; however, some bonds are not actually traded for months, making real price levels difficult to determine. This can create phantom gains and losses in the index.
2. *The aggregation process is subjective:* As previously mentioned, the aggregation process of interpreted data is a subjective process with no set industrywide standard for compiling multiple segments.
3. *Results may or may not be relevant:* The degree to which high-yield bonds are affected by moves in the Treasury market is up for debate. There are periods in the market when spreads are very tight and changes in Treasuries matter. Conversely, there are moments when high-yield spreads are so wide that moves in Treasuries have no significant impact on high yield.
4. *An industry-standard multivariate model has not been adopted:* Theoretically, creating a customized optimization model that incorporates the results from the mutually exclusive correlated segments based on the manager's individual style is ideal. A multivariate model combines

many attributes into a single formula for the entire portfolio. The output might hypotherically look something like this:

Industry allocation + security selection + rating allocation + duration allocation = output

–40 bps + 50 bps + 15 bps + 20 bps = 45 bps

Bank Loan Attribution

The process for syndicated bank loan attribution is very similar to that for high-yield bonds, except for the duration. Syndicated bank loans are floating-rate contracts that have little duration risk, but the other correlated segments of rating, industry, and price are still applicable. The challenge for bank loan attribution is that there is no universal passive benchmark index that provides daily price movements to compare against.[4]

Conclusion

The attribution process for high-yield bond portfolios is an evolving process because there are multiple correlated segments to consider, each of which is mutually exclusive, and selecting which segment's results takes priority over the others is subjective. The ideal process would involve a multivariate model that statically prioritizes the factors in a way that mirrors a particular manager's decision. This would include a large amount of back testing and interviewing to best fit the variables. If these multivariate models existed, they would be highly customized to each manager and nontransferable. Despite these shortcomings, high-yield bond attribution is very valuable because it provides good insight into a manager's actions, in some cases down to the credit level. High-yield attribution will continue to grow as the asset class matures and as program systems are developed that better fit the analysis to the manager.

14

TRADING IN THE HIGH-YIELD MARKET

Neil M. Yaris

Managing Director, Product Head U.S. High-Yield Trading,
Banc of America Securities LLC

Jason L. Hodes

Senior Vice President, Trading,
Shenkman Capital Management, Inc.

The high-yield market is unique in many ways. It is an over-the-counter (OTC) market in which participants negotiate transactions on an individual basis away from an organized exchange. There exists no industrywide trading platform as compared to Nasdaq or even OTC equities, which can trade on the OTCBB (OTC Bulletin Board). Some might attempt to compare the high-yield market with the U.S. Treasury market, but even though U.S. Treasuries operate in an OTC market, their transparency of quotes and the continuous dissemination of trade prices more resemble the Nasdaq. In addition, the high-yield market has no set hours of operation, and, theoretically, a trade can take place anytime an authorized buyer and seller agree on transaction terms.

The high-yield market is also unique in that its securities are often considered "part bond and part equity." That is, prices and yields are affected by moves in overall market interest rates, temporary buy/sell imbalances (generally referred to as market technicals), and the improving or deteriorating fundamentals of the issuing company.

Institutional investors dominate the high-yield market. The number of trades per day is far fewer as compared to the NYSE, the Nasdaq, or even the high-grade bond market. The size of the trades, however, is generally quite large. Whereas a "round lot" for the Nasdaq market is 100 shares (or $4,000 in the case of a $40 stock), a round lot in the high-yield market is $1 million in the face amount of securities.

Money managers, insurance companies, bond funds, and hedge funds are all active high-yield participants. Individuals desiring exposure to high-yield securities generally purchase them through bond funds or a money manager. This is advisable as it provides a level of diversification and market intelligence individuals would never attain on their own. It is thought that corporate pension departments, represented in the marketplace by money managers and hedge funds, are the largest end buyers in the market. CDOs (collateralized debt obligations) were active participants until recently, but the credit crunch of 2008–2009 and the subsequent unraveling of leverage in the financial system have caused CDOs to lose their cheap cost of capital, which was so crucial to their existence. At the time of this writing, CDOs have disappeared almost entirely from the market. The strategies and objectives of each of these market participants can be quite different.

Different Investors

Investors include the following:

1. *Pension accounts:* Pension accounts are long only, are long-term–oriented, and seek to beat their designated benchmark. They are not compelled to trade based on

changes in ratings or price levels of particular securities. It is thought that they are the largest beneficial owners of high-yield bonds.

2. *Bond funds:* Bond funds look for strong absolute as well as relative performance in relation to their peers. Typically they are long only, but some employ CDS to express negative views.
3. *Insurance companies:* Insurance companies aim to match assets to outstanding liabilities. This is the one group of investors which is loss-constrained. Positions having embedded losses are rarely sold unless the security has little chance of future recovery. Insurance companies are most active in better-quality bonds carrying ratings of BB or higher.
4. *Hedge funds:* Hedge funds are unique because they are the only market participant that can establish both long and short positions. Almost nonexistent from the market 10 years ago, they are significant players today.
5. *CDOs:* Collateralized debt obligations such as CBOs or CLOs (collateralized loan obligations) may have some bond component. CDOs with bond holdings typically operate like a loss-constrained insurance account.

The Primary Market

Because this chapter focuses on high-yield trading, we take just a moment now to discuss the primary market. The primary market refers to the process of raising capital for issuers through the sale of new securities. During this process, capital market professionals work with in-house investment bankers to determine the best options available to their corporate clients. Once the financing is announced to the market, salespeople and traders are often consulted to arrive at the best-priced deal for both the issuer and the purchasing customers, as discussed below.

The Secondary Market

As compared to the primary market in which companies raise capital through the issuance of new securities, the secondary market deals solely with securities that have previously been issued. Trading volume in the secondary market is difficult to calculate. However, most estimates are that between $5 billion and $7 billion of high-yield bonds change hands on an average trading day. This compares to the entire high-yield market, which has nearly $900 billion in outstanding bonds and yearly issuance that often exceeds $180 billion.

The Role of the Sell-Side Trader (Traders Employed by Broker-Dealers)

Although high-yield traders often assist the underwriting team in pricing new issues, for the most part, their responsibilities begin with the "freeing" of a deal. This takes place once all bonds have been allocated to customers and the transition is made from the primary to the secondary market (i.e., the bonds become "free to trade"). Traditionally, sell-side traders provide liquidity for customers in all securities their firm has underwritten. This is the role commonly described as "market making." The best traders not only put buyers and sellers together but also provide customers with trade ideas (offering personal opinions as to which securities are cheap or expensive) and market "color" (giving additional information about the trading pattern of a security which a buyer or seller might find helpful).

In addition to these customer-driven functions, many large trading desks also maintain sizable proprietary positions. These positions can be as large as several billion dollars at any one time. In order for this proprietary business to be successful, traders must work closely with their dedicated research staff to understand each of the companies whose debt they trade. Most traders are responsible for just a handful of sectors—for example, telecommunications, technology, and retailers. As they are assigned just a small portion of the marketplace, it is expected that sell-side traders become resident experts in their securities.

The Role of the Buy-Side Trader (Traders Employed by the Four Largest Market Participants)

The role of buy-side traders is quite different from that of their counterparts on the sell side. First, buy-side traders gather market information that portfolio managers, use to make the most educated decisions possible for their clients. This information often focuses on market technicals (e.g., which bonds have an excessive number of buyers or sellers), as well as credit events and market moving news of which portfolio managers might be unaware.

Second, the buy-side trader is responsible for executing trades once credit committees and portfolio managers have made their buy/sell decisions. At this point, the trader focuses on obtaining the best execution for his or her firm. This is often more art than science.

Consider the following scenario: A portfolio manager of a large mutual fund instructs his trader to purchase $25 million of Hexion 9.75% due X/Y/Z at or around the current market price of $75. His trader makes two phone calls and receives the following information: Dealer A offers $3 million at $75, while dealer B offers $10 million at $76. The trader must now weigh each of these proposals. In many instances involving highly volatile, illiquid securities, purchasing or selling larger sizes at a slight concession to the market price is the best choice. In this particular instance, however, if the trader believes that there are several active sellers of the security, he or she may choose to be patient and purchase the $3 million at the lower price from dealer A while leaving a follow-on order with dealer A to purchase more bonds.

Essential to attaining "best execution" is the ability to acquire information and transact without adversely moving the market. In order to do this, an effective buy-side trader will reveal his or her orders to as few trusted dealers as is necessary. Sell-side traders are sensitive to this dynamic as well and will safeguard this information carefully. Although buy-side traders have more limited capital committing roles than their counterparts on the sell side, they are often responsible for far more sectors of the market (often 12 or more).

Street Brokers

In addition to trades between dealers and customers, many transactions also take place between broker-dealers themselves (e.g., Bank of America, Credit Suisse, J.P. Morgan Chase, or Goldman, Sachs) and are facilitated through interdealer brokers commonly known as "street brokers." Street brokers bring broker-dealers together and are paid a commission for doing so. Street brokers typically do not take positions in securities, provide research, or talk directly to the four groups of customers previously mentioned. They simply facilitate anonymous transactions between broker-dealers.

Liquidity

The need for broker-dealers and street brokers is quite apparent to any high-yield market participant. Both provide speed in execution, accurate price discovery, anonymity for buyers and sellers, and improved market "liquidity" in the marketplace. Although it is customary for dealers to make markets in issues they underwrote, there is no requirement that they do so. In addition, a broker-dealer may choose to provide different amounts of liquidity depending upon his or her opinion about the overall market and current inventory levels, as well as what customer the dealer is dealing with at that particular time. It is unlikely, however, to operate consistently with large institutional accounts unless the dealer offers a reasonable amount of liquidity. So secondary market making by the sell side is certainly viewed by the buy side as mandatory.

Numerous changes to the high-yield market have reduced liquidity dramatically over the past several years. Going back as far as 1996, there were as many at 25 dealers that could be considered "active" in the market on a day to day basis. Most customers put that list closer to seven today, and even that number continues to decrease at a remarkably fast pace. In addition, as customers have grown in size, their security positions have done so correspondingly. Whereas $50 million customer positions may have been unusual several years ago, they are rather commonplace today. Buying and selling positions of this size can be enormously difficult and expensive unless, of course, another large customer can be found to take the other side of the trade. In the absence of this, several smaller trades generally take place over a period of time until the desired sell/buy order is complete. During this process, the buy-side and sell-side traders will discuss how to accomplish the customer's goal at the best possible terms.

Liquidity in any particular bond can also be affected by characteristics inherent in that particular security. Some of the factors that impair a security's liquidity are:

1. Small tranche sizes ($100 million or less)
2. Lesser-known issuers
3. Less active underwriters

It is not uncommon for such factors to cause a security to trade 50–100 basis points cheaper than an otherwise comparable security (e.g., 10.50% or 11% versus 10%). Except for the largest and most active issuers, most bonds have only a handful of active market makers.

The illiquid nature of the high-yield market can translate into extremely large transaction costs for active trading accounts. It is not unusual for round-trip transaction costs to exceed 2% of invested funds. Because of this, it is advisable that buy/sell decisions be made only after thorough examination, as reversing poor decisions can be quite costly.

Like the equity market, the high-yield market is highly credit-intensive (i.e., company fact-specific). Even though it is the research analyst's job to talk to issuing companies directly and advise clients on their prospects, salespeople, traders, and capital markets professionals must also understand the companies whose bonds they sell, trade, and underwrite. To the uninformed, the high-yield market may seem like random numbers flashing on a screen.

Credit Default Swaps

Credit default swaps, commonly referred to as CDSs, have become an important element in the high-yield market. A CDS provides another layer of liquidity in the market because it has often become a substitute for high-yield bonds. For example, if a hedge fund manager wishes to short a high-yield bond but is unable to "get the borrow" or find the bond to sell, he or she could purchase protection in the CDS market instead. If the credit deteriorates as he or she has predicted, the bond price will drop and the CDS price will rise, allowing the hedge fund manager to gain from these credit misfortunes. At times, the CDS market also presents opportunities where the bond price falls considerably but the corresponding CDS does not widen as much (recall that CDS prices and bond prices move in opposite directions). Most broker-dealers have traders that handle both bond and CDS trades in hopes of recognizing and capturing such opportunities.

One of the biggest barriers to understanding any business is its language. Some of the terms and phrases most commonly used in the high-yield business are the following:

1. *Basis point = 1/100 of 1%:* If a security's yield rises from 10% to 10.10%, it would be correct to say that its yield rose by 10 basis points (bps).
2. *Point:* This is not to be confused with "basis point." A one "point" move in a bond refers to a $10 price change. For

example, if Education Management (EDMC) at 10.25% due 6/02/16, moved in price from 99 to 98, it would be said that the bond had moved by one "point."

3. *Hit:* When a trader makes a bid and buys securities, the trader's bid is said to have been "hit."
4. *Lifted:* When a trader makes an offer and sells securities, the trader's offer is said to have been "lifted."
5. *Long:* When a trader or investor owns a security, he or she is said to be "long" that security.
6. *Short:* When a trader or investor sells a security before he or she owns it, hoping to buy it back at a lower price in the future, the investor is said to be "short."
7. *Yield:* Yield is a rate of return that measures the total performance of a bond. In the case of a bond price to maturity, we would use yield to maturity (YTM), which mathematically can be expressed as

$$B = \frac{I_1}{(1+Y)^1} + \frac{I_2}{(1+Y)^2} + \frac{I_n}{(1+Y)^n} + \frac{P}{(1+Y)^n}$$

   where B = current bond price; I = coupon rate of interest; P = par value of bond or call premium; n = number of years until maturity or call; and Y = yield to maturity or yield to call.
8. *Coupon:* The "coupon" is the interest rate an issuer pays on a fixed-rate security. This term is left over from many years ago when, in order to receive a semiannual interest payment, the bondholder was required to cut off the "coupon" stub from the physical bond and send it to the issuer. Today all payments made by issuers are handled electronically.
9. *Quote:* When a trader indicates where he or she believes a bond should be trading without making an actual market, the trader is said to be "quoting" a market. Of course, customers always prefer "live" markets in which they can

transact immediately, but during times of illiquidity, an accurate "quote" may suffice.

10. *Call option:* Many bonds are "callable" before maturity. In these cases, the issuer has the right, but not the obligation, to retire the security before maturity at a stated price. For example, Qwest 7.50%, due 2/15/14, is callable on 2/15/09 at 103.75. The issuer, "Qwest Communications International," has the right to call this bond on or after 2/15/09 at 103.75% of face value (i.e., $1,037.50 for each $1,000).
11. *Put option:* Some bonds are "putable" before maturity. In these cases, the bondholder has the right, but not the obligation, to sell the security back to the issuer prior to maturity at a predetermined price. Hercules 6.75% due 10/15/29, is "putable" on 4/15/14 at 100. The bondholder can sell this bond back to the issuer on or after 4/15/14 for 100% of face value.
12. *Security:* The word "security" is used in two different ways that are entirely unrelated. A "security" can refer to a type of financial instrument (e.g., stocks and bonds are often referred to as "securities" as defined in the Securities and Exchange Act of 1933). In addition, the word "security" can refer to collateral that is pledged to a particular bond or loan. For example CBB, 6.30% due 12/01/28, is said to be a "secured" bond because, in addition to the simple promise of repayment, the issuer has pledged particular assets as collateral to this debt. In the case of a bankruptcy filing, this type of security can become vitally important.
13. *Senior:* One security is said to be "senior" to another if, in the case of a bankruptcy filing, it receives preferential treatment.
14. *Subordinate:* One security is said to be "subordinate" to another if, in the case of a bankruptcy filing, it receives less preferential treatment.

15. *Pari passu:* This Latin term translates to "without partiality." In the bond market it refers to securities that lie at the same level of a company's capital structure and are treated equally in the event of a bankruptcy filing (as opposed to being either senior or subordinate).
16. *Principal:* The face value of a security is often referred to as the "principal." For example, if an investor holds $1 million worth of Alltel at 7.875% due 7/01/32, it could also be said that the investor holds $1 million "principal" amount.
17. *Spread:* This term can have different meanings depending on how it is used. "Spread" is commonly defined as the additional yield offered investors over a benchmark security. When dealing with dollar-denominated fixed-rate bonds, the benchmark would be a U.S. Treasury bond of comparable maturity. In the case of floating-rate securities, as is discussed later, the benchmark would be LIBOR (London interbank offered rate). For example, if Citizens Communications (CZN) at 6.25%, due 1/15/13, trades at a YTM (yield to maturity) of 7% and the corresponding U.S. Treasury bond trades at a 5% YTM, the CZN bond is said to trade at a spread of "200 bp over treasuries." "Spread" can also be used in the context of a bid/offer spread. In this case it means the difference in dollar price between the bid and the offer. If a trader makes a market 96.50–97, he or she is making a 1/2-point bid/offer "spread."
18. *Covenants:* High-yield bonds are generally issued with language intended to protect the investor's principal from decreasing in value. EBITDA and leverage maintenance as well as restricted payments tests are just a few of the more commonly seen covenants.
19. *TRACE (Trade Reporting and Compliance Engine):* This Nasdaq system posts all trades that take place in registered

high-yield securities. This information is available to all market participants with the intended effect of improving market transparency.

Types of Bonds

To understand how to value a bond, let's first understand what a bond is. A bond is simply a stream of cash flows that will be paid by the issuer (the borrower) to the bondholder (the lender). These cash flows can come in all shapes and sizes. Some of the most commonly issued bonds are:

1. *Fixed-rate bonds:* The coupon (interest) the issuer pays is fixed at the time of issuance and will not change over the life of the bond.
2. *Floating-rate bonds:* The coupon (interest) the issuer pays changes every six months depending on the level of LIBOR at that time. The spread the issuer pays "over" LIBOR is fixed at the time of issuance. For example, if LIBOR is 5.30%, an issuer whose securities were issued with a coupon of "L + 200" would pay interest during those six months of 7.30% (5.30% + 200 bps).
3. *Zero coupon bonds:* Issued at a discount to its face value, this security pays no cash interest. At maturity it will pay at face value. If held until maturity, the bond's interest is the difference between the purchase price and its face value.
4. *Payment in kind (PIK):* These bonds pay interest in the form of additional securities rather than in cash. In effect, a PIK bond compounds itself by issuing "baby bonds."
5. *Toggle:* The coupon of this bond can be paid in cash or with additional securities at the issuer's option. For example, if a bond is a 10% "toggle," the issuer can pay $50 in interest semiannually for every $1,000 of bonds or issue $50 worth of additional securities (PIK bonds).

It is important to understand that these are just five of the most popular bonds used by issuers today. By no means are they the only ones. In fact, bonds can be tailored in any way to meet investor and issuer needs.

Market Conventions

A trader is asked to make a market in Level 3 (LVLT) 8.75%, due 2/15/17. His response is "I am 95.50–96 3 × 3." What does this mean? Quite simply, the trader is willing to pay $95.50 for $3 million of LVLT 8.75%, due 2/15/17, while also offering $3 million of the same security at $96. This is an example of "market making" in which a trader has given a customer a price at which a purchase or sale can take place. Notice that even though most bonds are issued in $1,000 denominations, for convenience sake they are still quoted as parts of $100.

As compared to the high-grade market, high-yield bonds, mostly out of convenience, are quoted in dollar prices. If a customer asks a high-grade trader for a market on Comcast 4.95%, due 6/15/16, the trader might respond, "I'm 160–150 5 × 5." The 160–150 represents basis points over the corresponding U.S. Treasury bond. So, if the 10 year Treasury bond yields 5%, the trader is willing to purchase $5 million of Comcast bonds at a yield of 6.60% (5% + 160 bps) or sell them at 6.50% (5% + 150 bps). These yields are then converted into a dollar price for settlement purposes.

The reason for this difference in market conventions is quite logical. High-grade securities are issued by companies of better quality and are less volatile than are high-yield securities. Because of this, their yields and prices generally track movements in the U.S. Treasury market far more closely than do high-yield securities. Thus, it is far easier for a high-grade trader to make "spread" markets rather than "dollar price" markets. High-yield securities are issued by companies of lesser quality and track movements in the U.S. Treasury market less closely. It is easier to quote and trade these types of bonds in dollar prices rather than in spread.

Consider these examples: Sprint, 6.875% due 11/15/28, traded on 8/15/07 at +229 bps over the U.S. Treasury 4.75% due 2/15/37. That translates to having traded at a yield of 7.32% as the 4.75% U.S. Treasury at that time was yielding 5.03% (5.03% + 229 bps = 7.32%). In addition, the dollar price that the Sprint 6.875% traded at was 95.25 (the dollar equivalent of a 7.32% YTM).

On the same day, Saint Acquisition (SWFT), 12.50% due X/Y/Z, traded at 66. That happened to represent a YTM of 20.76% and a spread of UST + 1573 bps (since the corresponding UST 4.75% due 2/15/37, was then yielding 5.03%). Conceptually, this trade could have been quoted in spread over UST, but to do so would have made little sense. After all, even large swings in U.S. Treasury prices are unlikely to have much effect on SWFT's value. SWFT's exceedingly high YTM indicates that the future of this company and its ability to pay its debts in full and on time will be the overriding factors affecting its price. Imagine seeing a red 1959 Cadillac cruising down the street. It would be correct to refer to this car as red, a 1959 model, or a Cadillac. The description you choose to use depends largely on the context of the conversation and the point you are trying to make. This is similar to the conventions in the corporate bond markets.

Comparing and Valuing Different Securities

When determining the value of different securities, market participants go through the same exercise as would a person buying a television set, a house, or any other financial or hard asset. It is best to start with the value of a similar asset whose price or yield is known and then adjust for the differences between the two assets. You might think of this as a "relative value" approach. For example, if a trader is asked to price Citizens Communication (CZN), 6.625%, due 3/15/15, the first comparison might be CZN 6.25%, due 1/15/13. After all, the two bonds are pari passu, noncallable, and only two years apart in maturity. If the

YTM or price of the 2013 bond is known, all that needs to be done is to adjust for the additional two years (2015 minus 2013).

To determine what these two years are worth, one might compare the spread between other securities of different issuers having similar ratings and maturity dates—e.g., Sprint Nextel (S), 6.875% due 10/31/13, and Sprint Nextel (S), 7.375% due 8/01/15. Currently the yield difference between the two Sprint Nextel bonds is 20 bps. By applying this spread to the CZN bonds, where the 6.25% bonds are known to be worth 95.625 (7.25% YTM), we can calculate that the 6.625% bonds should be worth somewhere close to 95.375 (7.45% YTM, or 7.25% + 20 bps). This process becomes far more complex when comparing bonds of different companies and industries. It is important to understand that valuing securities must be thought of as a comparative process. One must assume that market participants are aware of relative value comparisons and will weigh such information accordingly.

Leverage as It Affects Valuation

The trickiest part of valuing a bond is determining the likelihood that its principal and interest will be paid on time and in full. This is the concept of "credit risk," and leverage plays a major part in it. Credit risk is just one of the many risks that influences the price of a bond, but in the high-yield market where companies are frequently highly leveraged, it is often the most important. In thinking about credit risk, some basic definitions must be understood:

1. *EBITDA:* Commonly referred to as "cash flow," EBITDA is the acronym for earnings before interest, taxes, depreciation, and amortization.
2. *Leverage ratio:* Total debt/EBITDA.
3. *Coverage ratio:* EBITDA/interest.
4. *Free cash flow:* EBITDA minus cash interest and capital expenditures.

5. *Enterprise value:* The total value of a company's debt plus its equity market capitalization.

It is essential to understand that no two companies are identical. Depending on their growth prospects, consistency of earnings, quality of management, and many other characteristics, the market may assign a higher or lower valuation to one company versus another.

Consider the following example: Company ABC makes ballpoint pens. In fiscal year 2008, ABC's EBITDA (cash flow) totaled $200 million. Ballpoint pen manufacturing happens to be a slow-growing but steady business, and the market values similar companies at a multiple of 5× EBITDA (5 times cash flow). Given this, ABC's enterprise value would be approximately $1 billion (5 × $200 million). How much of this $1 billion should be attributed to the shareholders? How much of it should be attributed to the bondholders? The answer depends on ABC's current capital structure.

Consider ABC with two different capital structures and varying degrees of leverage—both totaling $1 billion in enterprise value (see Table 14.1.).

As you can see in the table, each of these capital structures has an enterprise value of $1 billion. Capital structure 1 is far less leveraged with a leverage ratio of 1.5× ($300 million of debt divided by $200 million of EBITDA) versus 4.5× for capital structure 2 ($900 million of debt divided by $200 million of EBITDA). Each capital structure is laid out

TABLE 14.1 Capital Structures of ABC

Capital Structure 1	Capital Structure 2
$100 million senior (bank debt)	$400 million senior (bank debt)
$100 million senior bonds	$400 million senior bonds
$100 million senior subordinate bonds	$100 million senior subordinate bonds
Total debt $300 million	Total debt $900 million
$700 million equity	$100 million equity
Enterprise value $1 billion	Enterprise value $1 billion

in order of seniority. In a bankruptcy filing, senior bank debt is entitled to 100% of its claim before senior bonds receive anything, and so on down the line. This may seem trivial in the example we laid out since in each case ABC has an enterprise value that exceeds its outstanding debt.

Consider what might happen, though, if ballpoint pens become unfashionable and in 2010 ABC's EBITDA drops to $125 million dollars. In this case investors would likely view the future growth prospects of ABC quite skeptically and thus, assign an even lower EBITDA multiple than the 5× they had previously. But if we assume, for the moment, that the market still assigns a 5× multiple for this business, ABC would now have an enterprise value of $625 million ($125 million × 5). Creditors of ABC under capital structure 1 would not view this sudden drop in EBITDA favorably, but given that ABC carries only $300 million of debt and the company is now only 2.4× leveraged ($300 million/ $125 million), there would be little reason for panic. Actually, even if EBITDA shrunk to $100 million, ABC would still be only 3× leveraged ($300 million debt and $100 million of EBITDA), and all its debts would likely be worth 100 cents on the dollar.

If ABC was capitalized with leverage as laid out in capital structure 2, this drop in EBITDA could have crippling effects. Assuming again that the enterprise is still worth $625 million (5 × $125 million), the value of the common equity and the subordinate bonds would decrease substantially in the marketplace. In fact, even the senior bonds would trade lower as market participants begin to assess the likelihood that in a restructuring, this class of creditors would be greatly impaired. More specifically, given ABC's $400 million of bank debt, the senior bonds would be left with only $225 million in a bankruptcy filing ($625 million – $400 million bank debt), leaving nothing for the subordinate bonds or equity. This scenario illustrates how leverage can work against a company quickly when its cash flow decreases.

In another scenario, ABC develops a new and innovative pen that becomes wildly popular with teenagers, and EBITDA doubles from its

TABLE 14.2 Examples of Two Capital Structures

Capital Structure 1	Capital Structure 2
$100 million senior (bank debt)	$400 million senior (bank debt)
$100 million senior bonds	$400 million senior bonds
$100 million senior sub bonds	$100 million senior sub bonds
Total debt $300 million	Total debt $900 million
$1.7 billion equity	$1.1 billion equity
Enterprise value $2 billion	Enterprise value $2 billion

2008 level to $400 million. Using the same 5× multiple, ABC would now have an enterprise value of $2 billion ($400 million × 5). Using this information, the two capital structures are presented in Table 14.2.

In each case, all of the debt is completely covered (i.e., worth 100 cents on the dollar), and, as expected, the most dramatic change has taken place in the value of the equity. In fact, the equity of capital structure 1 is now worth $1.7 billion ($2 billion less $300 million of debt) and has increased by 142%. The equity of capital structure 2 is now worth $1.1 billion ($2 billion – $900 million of debt) and has increased by 1,000%. This shows the wonderful advantage of leverage when it works in your favor. Leveraged buyouts have transformed numerous companies that originally looked like capital structure 1 into capital structure 2 over the past several years. The question might be asked, "How much leverage is too much?" Frankly, the amount of leverage a company can comfortably carry depends on many factors.

These are some of the questions one should ask:

1. What EBITDA multiple is this company worth? After all, a company that is 5× leveraged ($5 billion of debt and $1 billion of EBITDA) would be extremely overleveraged if it was in an industry that commanded enterprise values of 4× EBITDA. Its debt level might be quite manageable, however, if it is part of an industry in which companies are valued at 10× EBITDA.

2. Is the company's business very cyclical? That is, can its capital structure withstand a sudden, yet temporary, drop in cash flow?
3. Is cash flow likely to grow rapidly in the near future? For instance, if a company borrows heavily to build a new factory, it may appear overleveraged during the construction process (i.e., it may have increased debt levels but no additional EBITDA to show for it). After the factory is completed, however, it may generate significant cash flow and the company's leverage may again be more reasonable.
4. Is the company's cash flow protected from serious erosion? For instance, does the company have a product that is unique, or might another company come along tomorrow and threaten its existence altogether?

Valuing Different Bonds within a Capital Structure

Just as in comparing two pari passu bonds of different maturities, we can also compare two bonds that lie at different levels of seniority in the same capital structure. Using Company ABC as our example again, in order to determine the appropriate yield difference (spread) between the senior bonds and the senior subordinate bonds, a trader would look at other similar companies with existing bonds that trade in the marketplace. Referring to capital structure 1 again, the senior bonds are 1× leveraged ($200 million of debt through that level and $200 million of EBITDA) while the senior subordinate bonds are 1.5× leveraged ($300 million of debt through that level and the same $200 million of EBITDA).

Let's also assume that ABC's biggest competitor has senior and subordinate bonds that have leverage of 2× and 2.5× (a difference of .5× of leverage) and trade at 7% YTM and 8% YTM, respectively. Given that the leverage difference between the ABC securities is also

.5× EBITDA (1.5× – 1×), it is likely that the spread between the ABC bonds will also be close to 100 bps (8% – 7%).

Hedging and Arbitrage

One way to attempt to reduce risk in the marketplace is with the use of "hedges." The most common practice in hedging occurs when one security is bought and another is "sold short" in order to take advantage of the disparity in value of the two instruments. In a short sale, a trader sells a security his client does not own with the intention of buying it back some time in the future at a lower price. Hedging is employed to reduce certain risks in a portfolio. Another way of thinking about this is that hedging attempts to isolate the aspect or aspects of a security that are thought to be undervalued.

Let's use the following example:

1. Qwest 7.90%, due 8/15/10, is trading at 7.90% YTM.
2. Qwest 7.25%, due 2/15/11, is trading at 8.1% percent YTM.
3. U.S. Treasury 4.50%, due 5/15/10, is trading at 5% YTM.

There are several hedged trades that can be done in this scenario. If a trader believes that Qwest as a company is trading "too cheaply" [i.e., at a spread to U.S. Treasuries (UST) that is too wide], he could buy either of the Qwest issues and sell a similar amount of UST, 4.50% due 5/15/10. In effect, this would isolate the credit of Qwest and take all of the U.S. Treasury risk out of the equation. Another trader might disagree believing that Qwest as a company is fairly valued but that the 7.90% is trading rich versus the 7.25%. This trader buys the 7.25% and sells short the 7.90%, hoping to collapse this trade when the current spread of 20 bps narrows.

High-yield bonds of one company also can be shorted against bonds of another company, or a company's equity can be shorted against its debt. So, as you can see, the numbers of hedged trades that can be thought of is endless. In practice, hedged trades can become cumbersome because the high-yield market is often illiquid. Collapsing hedged trades in a timely and efficient manner can often be difficult.

The Value of News

One of the most fascinating aspects of financial markets is their ability to price in news on a real-time basis. Prices of securities adjust to bad news, as well as good, well before ratings agencies react and quite often before company press releases are issued. For example, a large recall of company ABC's ballpoint pens because of publicized leaking issues will have negative implications for the company's sales and cash flow. Market participants are unlikely to wait for a rating agency to comment on this problem before lowering the prices of its existing securities. By the time a formal announcement from ABC is issued, it may be too late to exit a position in its debt or equity at attractive prices.

Impact of TRACE (Trade Reporting and Compliance Engine)

On January 31, 2001, the Securities and Exchange Commission initiated posttrade transparency in the corporate bond market when it approved rules requiring National Association of Security Dealer (NASD) member firms to compile data on all over-the-counter secondary market transactions in publicly issued corporate bonds. (On July 30, 2007, the NASD changed its name to FINRA, the Financial Industry Regulatory Authority.) For each trade, the dealer is required to identify the bond and to report the date and time of execution, trade size, trade price, yield, and whether the dealer bought or sold in the transaction. Not all the reported information is disseminated to the public. Investors receive bond identification, the date and time of execution, and the price and yield for bonds specified as TRACE-eligible. Investors can access this information on the Securities Industry and

Financial Markets Association (SIFMA) Web site (www.investingin bonds.com) or by subscription through third-party vendors, including Bloomberg and MarketAxess.

Overall, the statistical and anecdotal evidence indicates that the introduction of posttrade transparency in the corporate bond markets has significantly reduced execution costs. While execution costs may have been lowered, in other dimensions the overall trading environment is far more difficult post-TRACE. According to most market participants, the advent of TRACE has reduced riskless commissions per trade by roughly 50% and by far more than that for less liquid securities. At the same time, given that all trades in TRACE-eligible securities must be reported within 15 minutes of execution, the executing dealer has a mere 15-minute "window" to use this information to his or her advantage. Because the trading level of one security has implications for not only that security but also for numerous others, each trade provides an additional data point with which to evaluate and price future transactions.

Clearly, the requirement to share this information in such a broad fashion has made dealers rethink the practice of purchasing customer bonds for their own inventory. Interestingly, to combat the reduced profitability on the "riskless" side of their business, some dealers now dedicate large amounts of capital toward proprietary trading. This trend was not unlike that in many other parts of the financial business where additional risk was taken to offset contracting spreads in riskless businesses.

15

CDS: A PRIMER ON SINGLE-NAME INSTRUMENTS AND STRATEGIES

Sivan Mahadevan

Managing Director,
Morgan Stanley & Company, Inc.

What Is a Credit Default Swap?

A single-name credit default swap is an OTC contract between the seller and the buyer of protection against the risk of default on a set of debt obligations issued by a specified reference entity. A credit default swap (CDS) is essentially an insurance policy that protects the buyer against the loss of principal on a bond in case of a default by the issuer. The protection buyer pays a periodic premium (typically quarterly) over the life of the contract and is, in turn, covered for the period. For issuers with a high likelihood of default, the bulk of the premium is typically paid up front instead of periodically. See Figure 15.1.

Credit Events

A CDS is triggered if, during the term of protection, an event that materially affects the cash flows of the reference debt obligation takes place.

FIGURE 15.1 Settlements in Case of Default

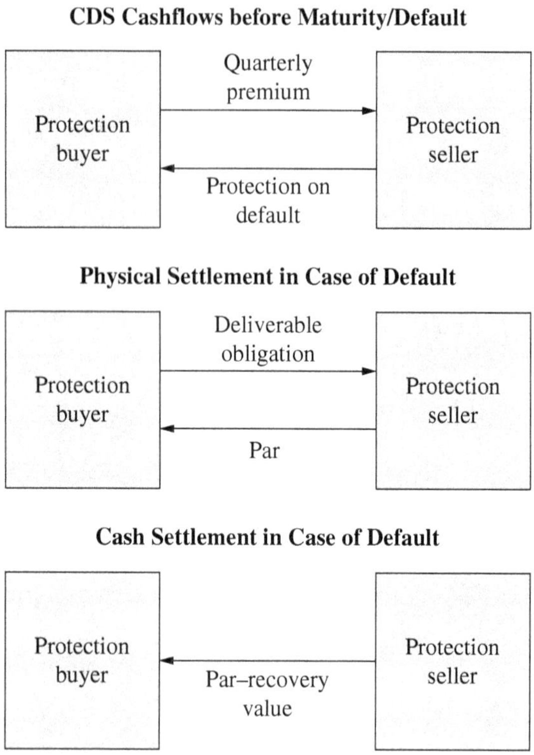

Source: Morgan Stanley

For example, the reference entity files for bankruptcy, is dissolved, or becomes insolvent. Other credit events include failure to pay, obligation acceleration, repudiation, and moratorium.

Restructuring is also considered a credit event for some, but not all, credit default swaps. If the CDS contract covers restructuring (referred to as "R," "mod-R," or "mod-mod-R"), events such as principal/interest rate reduction/deferral and changes in priority ranking, currency, and composition of payment also qualify as credit events. Better matching of requirements of protection seekers and CDS economics has been the primary driver behind the evolution of restructuring. Conseco and Xerox restructuring events played an important role in this evolution.

When a credit event triggers the CDS, the contract is settled and terminated. The settlement can be physical or cash. The protection buyer has a right to deliver any deliverable debt obligation of the reference entity to the protection seller in exchange for par. Deliverable debt obligations include bonds and loans in G7 currencies, and not subordinated to the reference bond, which is mentioned in the trade confirmation. There can be additional maturity restrictions if the triggering credit event is a restructuring. The CDS buyer and the seller can also agree to cash settle the contract at the time of inception or at the time of exercise. In this case, the protection seller pays an amount equal to par less the market value of a deliverable obligation.

The protection buyer receives 100% of par in exchange for the delivered obligation, implying that the difference between par and the ultimate recovery on the delivered obligation represents the protection seller's loss. It is this probability-weighted expected loss that the CDS premium strives to capture.

Reference Entity

A CDS contract specifies the precise name of the legal entity for which it provides default protection. Given the possibility of existence of several legal entities associated with a company, a default by one of them may not be tantamount to a default on the CDS. Therefore, it is important to know the exact name of the legal entity and the seniority of the capital structure covered by the CDS. This point sometimes gets overlooked in relative value trades between bonds and CDSs, where the underlying exposures are closely related but are not legally identical.

The Armstrong default was a case in point, as knowing the appropriate level in the capital structure covered by the CDS turned out to be key in determining which obligations were protected against default. We discuss relative value trading in the Basis section of this chapter.

On a related topic, changes in ownership of the reference entity's bonds or loans can also result in a change in the reference entity

TABLE 15.1 New Reference Entity When Ownership Changes

Ownership of Bonds/Loans	New Reference Entity
One entity assumes more than 75%	Successor
No entity assumes more than 75%, but one or more entities assume 25–75%	Divide the contract equally among such entities
No entity assumes more than 25%	Original legal entity
Ownership of bonds/loans	New reference entity

Source: ISDA

covered by the CDS contract. Table 15.1 summarizes how the new reference entity is determined depending on the level of ownership changes.

If the legal entity does not survive, the CDS contract follows the entity that succeeds to the highest percentage of bonds or loans.[1]

Standardized Payment Dates

Since 2002 the vast majority of CDS contracts have standardized quarterly payment and maturity dates to the 20th of March, June, September, and December. This standardization has several benefits, including convenience in offsetting CDS trades, rolling over of contracts, relative value trading, single name versus the benchmark indexes or tranched index products trading, and so on.

CDS Pricing

The CDS premium reflects the expected cost of providing the protection in a risk-neutral sense. To calculate the CDS premium, one needs to estimate the probability of default and expected loss given default. The fair CDS premium is the one that equates present value of premium payments to the present value of expected losses.

FIGURE 15.2 CDS Cash Flows

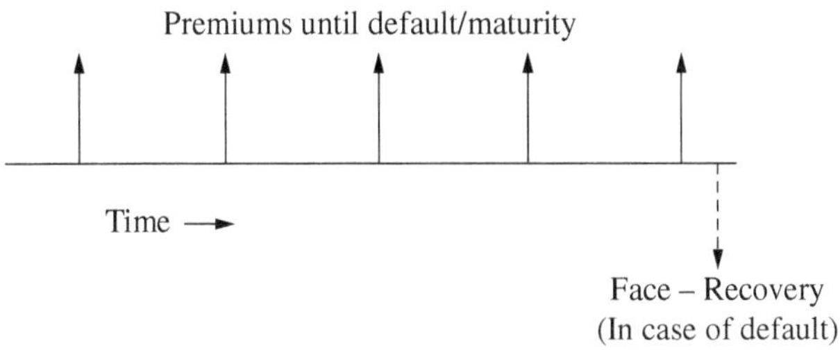

Source: Morgan Stanley

Figure 15.2 shows simplified cash flows of a CDS contract. (In addition, there is typically a payment of accrued premium in case of default.) The following equations summarize the pricing approach:

1. PV of CDS spread = PV of expected default loss.
2. Expected default loss = LGD* probability of default, where LGD stands for the expected loss given default.
3. The LGD equates to the protection notional * (1 – estimated recovery rate).

Let us make some further simplifying assumptions to better understand CDS pricing. First, we assume that we have a CDS spanning only one period, with the premium paid at the end of the period (see Figure 15.3 for other details). We also assume that a default can happen at only the end of the period. In case of default, the protection seller pays for the loss on the bond (i.e., par recovery). Now, we can calculate the implied probability of default from the given CDS spreads, using the logic mentioned earlier and the following equations:

$$s1\cdot(1-p1)=p1\cdot(1-R)$$

$$p1=\frac{s1}{s1+1-R}\approx\frac{s1}{1-R}$$

FIGURE 15.3 Determining Default Probabilities

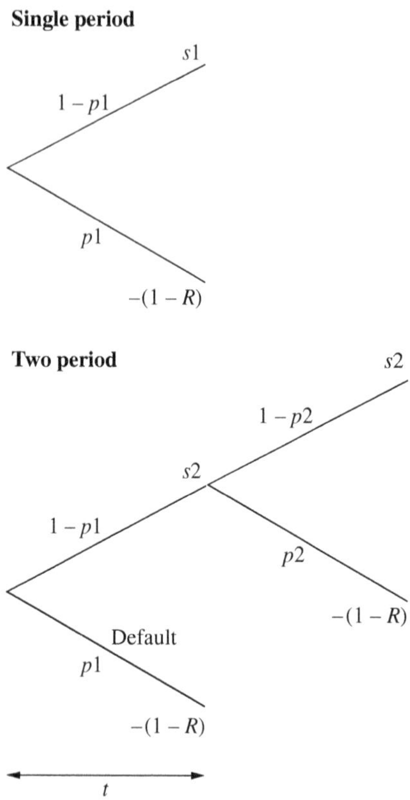

Source: Morgan Stanley

The equations for determining default probabilities are based on the following assumptions:

$s1$ = CDS spread for single-period maturity
$s2$ = CDS spread for two-period maturity
$p1$ = probability of default in the first period
$p2$ = probability of default in the second period
R = recovery rate
t = time period
R = risk-free rate

Now we extend the model to two periods. Similar to one-period calculations, we can equate the present value of the CDS spread to expected losses in the case of default to get the implied probability of default in the second period, as shown in the two-period probability tree. The following equation summarizes this calculation:

$$\underbrace{\frac{s2\cdot(1-p1)}{1+r\cdot t}+\frac{s2\cdot(1-p1)\cdot(1-p2)}{(1+r\cdot t)^2}}_{\text{PV of Spread}}=\underbrace{\frac{(1-R)\cdot p1}{1+r\cdot t}+\frac{(1-R)\cdot(1-p1)\cdot p2}{(1+r\cdot t)^2}}_{\text{PV of Default}}$$

Since we know all the variables other than $p2$, we can calculate it from this equation.

Numerical Illustration

In Table 15.2, we show a numerical example using the discussed approach to calculate default probabilities, given a CDS curve and fixed recovery rate assumptions.

TABLE 15.2 Default Probability–Numerical Examples*

One-year spread	0.50%
Two-year spread	1.00%
Recovery rate	40%
Risk-free rate	2%
P1	0.83%
P2	2.48%
PV default	0.0190
PV premium	0.0190

*Calculation assumes annual premium payment.
Source: Morgan Stanley

Continuous Time Implementations

Since defaults do not have to happen on payment dates and premium frequency does not have to match the time steps in the calculation shown above, most commonly used CDS pricing models consider the default process as a continuous time phenomenon, along with discrete numerical techniques to estimate the present value of defaults and premiums. These models are calibrated to the market CDS curve (typically, to get a piecewise constant default intensity function for a given constant recovery rate).

The CDSW function on Bloomberg gives users an option to pick one of the three available numerical implementations of continuous time models. Further details on the three models are available in Bloomberg help.

By using these models, we can easily calculate a set of risk-neutral default probabilities from an issuer's CDS curve. We can then use them to value other debt obligations—including bonds—and to calculate the mark-to-market value of a CDS struck at a price different from the prevailing market price. Additionally we can use these models to convert a running premium to up front, and vice versa.

Points Up Front

As we mentioned earlier, default swaps on issuers with high default probabilities typically trade on an up-front plus running basis, rather than on a par spread basis (i.e., quarterly premium, no up-front payment). That is, the protection buyer pays a large part of the premium at the inception of the contract and a lower spread quarterly. For example, instead of paying 2,000 bps running, the protection buyer would pay 34% up front and 500 bps running.

Theoretically, the present value of the two premium streams should match when we take default probabilities and timing of cash flows into consideration. However, a higher up-front payment and lower running premium result in better cash flow matching from a hedging perspective, given that the reference entity's bonds would also be trading at a significant discount to par resulting from distress.

Given that the protection buyer stops paying quarterly premiums when a default occurs, the equivalent up-front payment should be lower than the simple present value of the running premium difference (1,500 bps in our example) at risk-free rates.

The first step for converting a par spread to up front is to calculate default probabilities, as explained in the CDS pricing section. Then, using these probabilities, we calculate the present value of the par spread (2,000 bps in our example) by multiplying the spread by the probability of survival at the time of payment and then discounting back using risk-free zero rates. This present value should equal the present value of up-front and running premiums (34% and 500 bps running, in our example), based on the same default probabilities.

A convenient way to do this conversion is to use the CDSW function on Bloomberg. We simply put "Deal Spread" to the running spread and value to the CDS using the par CDS spread. The "Market Value" represents the equivalent up-front payment. We provide additional details on this function in the "Useful Bloomberg Functions" section of this chapter.

Importance of Recovery Rate Assumption

As we discussed earlier, default probabilities and recovery rate are intricately related. That is why the recovery rate assumption can have a significant impact on the mark-to-market of an off-market CDS, and hence there exists the possibility of disagreement between two counterparties on the payment required to close such transactions, even when both parties are using identical models.

The bottom line is that to price a credit default swap, we need to have a view on market-implied recovery rates and default probabilities. However, we cannot directly observe these variables in the marketplace. That said, assuming one of the two is fixed, we can estimate the other using on-the-run CDS pricing. Additionally, since bond spreads also capture default risk, we can use bond data to estimate CDS pricing, if it is not available directly in the marketplace.

Useful Bloomberg Functions

There are a number of functions provided by Bloomberg for finding CDS levels and analyzing values. MSDU <GO> shows Morgan Stanley's daily pricing for various credit derivatives. Another function that facilitates searching for the current market premium levels for protection on an issuer is CDSD <GO>. The screen also allows the user to search for available CDSs for different entities related to the same issuer. Additionally, one can observe the term structure of CDSs in a selected currency and for a selected debt type—senior, subordinated, or other.

WCDS <GO> is another useful screen, where one can scroll down a list of the term structures of CDS by industry sectors.

CDSW <GO> is a default swap calculator, with which we can calculate market value, DV01, cash flows, and other sensitivities of a default swap contract. Potential applications of this tool include calculating delta-neutral hedge ratios, marking-to-market, and converting running premiums to up-front premiums.

The Basis: CDS versus Bond Arbitrage

For most issuers with liquid bonds trading, one can get a good estimate of the market price of the credit risk and hence the trading range for the CDS, if it is not observable directly from the market. This brings us to the subject of basis between an issuer's bonds and credit default swap, given that we can estimate the price of credit risk from both.

In our discussion, we have deliberately compared CDS levels to bond spreads above LIBOR, and not Treasuries. A CDS protection buyer and seller inadvertently takes counterparty risk to the banking system. This risk is captured by the difference between LIBOR and Treasury curves. As such, we tend to treat LIBOR as the risk-free rate throughout our research.

Conceptually, the CDS premium should equate to spread over LIBOR for the issuer's floating-rate note trading at par and represents the compensation for the default risk. While not all issuers have floating-rate debt outstanding, one can interpret this amount by calculating the zero volatility OAS or Z-spread (defined below) on the issuer's fixed-rate bonds, assuming that the bonds are trading at par. If, however, the bonds are trading at a discount or premium, one needs to make some adjustments to determine the default risk premium.

CDS-Bond Basis

The primary objective of the CDS-bond basis is to explore relative value opportunities and technical differences between CDSs and bonds of an issuer. To make the bond cash flows comparable to CDS cash flows, the first step is an asset swap to convert fixed cash flows to floating. (See Figure 15.4.)

FIGURE 15.4 CDS-Bond Basis

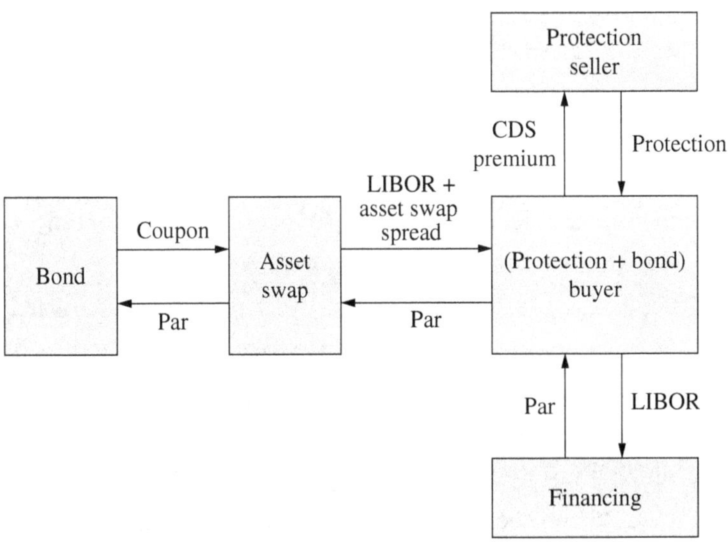

Source: Morgan Stanley

The spread gives us an estimate of a spread over the swap zero curve that matches the present value of the bond's cash flows to its market price. The general price/yield relationship of a credit-risky bond is as follows:

$$P = \sum_{i=1}^{n} \frac{Bond\ Payments}{(1 + Yield_i)^i}$$

We can then decompose the yield into a risk-free component and a spread component: $Yield_i = Risk\text{-}free\ rate_i + spread$. In the case of Z-spread this is: $Yield_i = zeroLIBOR_i + Z\text{-}spread$.

The basis is the difference between the CDS level and a given spread metric, assuming that both instruments have the same maturity and that the bond is trading at par. Typically, this takes the form: *Basis = CDS – Z-spread.*

As shown in Figure 15.4, if an investor buys a par bond and buys protection on the reference entity while financing the transaction at LIBOR, he or she can lock in the basis. If the basis is negative (i.e., CDS premium lower than spread), the investor is getting a positive cash flow during the life of the contract. If the reference entity defaults on the obligation, the investor can simply deliver the bond to the protection seller and receive par, which he or she can use to close out the financing arm of this transaction.

We have made a number of assumptions in the above example, including that the bond is trading at par and that both CDS and the bond have matching maturities. There are other technical effects, such as coupon recovery, accrued interest payments, and transaction costs, which make this argument only an approximate one.

While locking in negative basis is relatively straightforward, an attempt to lock in positive basis may prove frustrating, given difficulties involved in shorting bonds, including trying to short a hard-to-find bond over a long period.

Additionally, if the bond is trading above (or below) par, the credit risk on the CDS and the bond will not be the same; that is, the amount of CDS protection will not be enough (or will be too much) in case of a default. Therefore, we would need to adjust the Z-spread for the principal mismatch. We refer to the difference between a spread metric and CDS as "adjusted basis." Our *Credit Derivatives Insights* weekly publication has been tracking the current and historical Z-spread adjusted basis since December 2002 for various sectors.

Curve Adjustments to the Basis

Having adjusted the basis measure for maturity gaps between the bond and the CDS, as well as for the bond's market price being at a premium/discount to par, we can further sharpen our relative value measure by using the full-term structure of CDS, which is now possible given the increased market liquidity across the curve.

For this adjustment, instead of using a constant CDS premium above the swap zero curve, we can use a spread that varies with the timing of the cash flows, in accordance with the term structure of default swaps. The first step is to determine probabilities of survival for various cash flow dates using the CDS curve. The next step is to calculate present value of cash flows, using survival probabilities for coupon and principal cash flows and default probabilities for the recovery value in case of default. Thus we get a price for the bond that is consistent with the full CDS curve and current interest-rate environment. The following equation summarizes the above calculation:

$$\sum_i \frac{CF_i \cdot (1-p_i) + R \cdot P_i}{(1+r_i)^{t_i}} = \text{Price}$$

where

$$p_i = f(s_i, C), P_i = g(s_i, C)$$

CF_i represents the bond's cash flows (coupon as well as principal), R is the recovery rate assumption, and r_i is the discount rate (bootstrapped from the swap curve). The default probabilities (p_i and P_i) above are determined from the CDS curve (s_i) and the constant C. The factor $(1 - p_i)$ represents the probability of survival up to I, while P_i

represents the incremental probability of default during period *i*. The constant C represents a parallel shift in the CDS curve, and by changing it, we can match the present value of cash flows to the market price. For details on how to calculate default probabilities from spread, refer to the CDS pricing section of this chapter.

Once we have the implied CDS curve from the bond price, we can calculate another measure of basis—this time between the actual default swap and the implied default swap spread. We call this measure the curve-adjusted or fair value basis and have been tracking it in our publications since December 2004.

While the curve-adjusted basis indicates the true relative value taking into account the full CDS curve, the Z-spread basis captures the carry on the basis trade between the bond and the CDS (assuming that the bond is trading at par). When both the carry and the fair value basis measures point in the same direction and the gap is large enough to cover transaction costs, the relative value trade may be compelling, technical factors aside.

Reasons for Nontrivial Basis

There are several reasons for the existence of a basis between bonds and CDSs. We discuss the salient ones here:

1. *Maturity differences:* Maturities of an issuer's CDSs seldom exactly match maturities of its bonds. Consequently, in most cases, one has to interpolate or extrapolate the CDS curve to estimate the default swap premium that is directly comparable to the bond spreads.
2. *Bond price:* In case of a default, the CDS pays the difference between par and recovery rate, implying that the protection would be insufficient for bonds trading at premium and too much for bonds trading at discount.

3. *Difficulty in shorting bonds:* To arbitrage away positive basis, one needs to short the bond (and write protection in the form of a CDS), which is not always easy, especially for an extended period of time.
4. *Bond covenants:* Bonds may have covenants, such as put/call options, tender with make-whole, coupon step-ups, change of control provisions, equity clawbacks, and so on, which would affect their spread. This would distort the basis as CDS assumes a generic reference obligation and, in case of default, a protection buyer would look for a bond with the least attractive covenants for a physical settlement, given the embedded cheapest-to-deliver option.
5. *Restructuring feature:* Restructuring clauses in CDS contracts often create economic differences between taking credit risk in the form of CDSs versus bonds (see the section, "Implications of Restructuring as a Credit Event" for more details). This would also tend to distort the basis.
6. *Technical factors:* Prevailing supply/demand imbalances in the marketplace between bonds and CDS also affect the basis.
7. *Liquidity:* Liquidity may result in temporary misalignments between bonds and CDSs, giving rise to negative or positive basis.
8. *Transaction costs:* To arbitrage the basis, one has to incur transaction costs associated with the bid-ask spread on bonds and CDSs. Thus, arbitrageurs have an incentive to trade only if the basis exceeds this band of transaction costs.
9. *Interest-rate exposure:* In case of a default, the cash flows of a CDS and the bond swapped into floating rate do not match. This is because the interest-rate swap does not disappear with default on the bond. Consequently, we have to incur additional transaction costs and bear the market risk of the interest-rate swap.

Implications of Restructuring as a Credit Event

Earlier we briefly mentioned restructuring as one of the credit events covered by some default swaps. In this section, we further elaborate on this contract feature and analyze its potential implications on CDS pricing. Restructuring of a debt obligation refers to one or more of the following actions:

1. A reduction in interest rate, amount payable, or accrual.
2. A reduction in amount of principal or premium payable.
3. Postponement or deferral of interest or principal payments.
4. Change in ranking.
5. Change in currency to a "nonpermitted" currency.

In order for the above actions to constitute a credit event, such actions must result, directly or indirectly, from a deterioration of the creditworthiness or financial condition of the reference entity.

The evolution of various restructuring options, which we discuss shortly, directly reflects the motivation to improve the matching of economics behind protection selling and bond purchases. Not surprisingly, losses suffered by many protection sellers and buyers during various actual restructuring events were the main driver behind this evolution.

The most vibrant memory that comes to mind in this regard is that of Conseco, which restructured some of its debt. The restructuring did not materially affect the company's bonds with comparable maturities; however, the outcome for the CDS protection seller was significantly worse, highlighting the dramatically different economics for default swaps and bonds. This motivated modified-R changes (see below for details).

The current ISDA agreement offers four types of restructuring options that affect the protection buyer's privileges:

1. *Full restructuring (old-R):* Under this definition, a bond of any maturity is deliverable after a restructuring credit event by the reference entity. There are no limitations on the maturity of deliverable obligations (up to 30 years) and no multiple holder requirements on the restructured obligation (see more details on this point in the mod-R section).
2. *No restructuring (no-R):* This applies to cases of high-yield CDSs in the United States and completely excludes restructuring as a credit event that could trigger the CDS. This feature gives a protection seller significant advantages over a bondholder. We discuss the valuation implications shortly.
3. *Modified restructuring (mod-R):* Modified restructuring has become a market standard in the United States for CDSs on investment-grade credits. Under this application, the most material change is the limitation on the maturity of deliverable obligations. In case of a restructuring credit event, the protection buyer must deliver obligations with a maturity date that is the earlier of (a) 30 months following the restructuring or (b) the latest final maturity date of any restructured bond or loan, but not shorter than the CDS contract. The argument for this limitation on the universe of potentially deliverable bonds is to prevent certain abuses of the restructuring feature. Since longer-maturity bonds are more likely to trade at a significant discount to par due to interest-rate moves even when there are no changes in the creditworthiness of the issuer, this provision limits gains to a protection buyer in cases where restructuring does not have an economic impact on the bond by excluding these obligations from the list of deliverables.

Another important feature of mod-R is related to limitations on debt obligations that can trigger a restructuring credit event. Under mod-R, these obligations have to be held by more than three nonaffiliated holders in order to qualify for a restructuring event. Consequently, for example, a bilateral agreement between a bank and the issuer to extend the maturity of an outstanding loan does not trigger the default swap.

4. *Modified-modified-restructuring (mod-mod-R):* Under this application, which is more popular in Europe than in the United States for both investment grade and high yield, the main difference from mod-R is that the protection buyer can deliver a deliverable obligation with maturity up to 60 months after restructuring (in the case of the restructured bond or loan) and 30 months in the case of all other deliverable obligations. The goal of this improvement over mod-R is to allow for a wider range of deliverables, as in certain cases the 30-month restriction may prove too limiting.

Pricing Implications of Restructuring

To understand the economic implications of these restructuring applications, we assume that we have a fully hedged position combining a deliverable bond and a CDS. Now, if the CDS does not cover restructuring events, our hedge would not work perfectly in case of a restructuring of debt without an eventual default. On the other hand, if the CDS covers restructuring, it would protect us from any losses related to such an event. Furthermore, if the restructured obligation is not the obligation we own, there is a potential gain, even when there is no direct adverse impact on our position. Thus we would be willing pay more for a CDS with restructuring than for a CDS without restructuring.

To get a sense of the magnitude of the impact of restructuring on CDS spreads, let's look at the U.S. high-yield market, where restructuring is more frequent than it is in other markets. About 5% of total high-yield defaults in the United States result in some kind of restructuring (see Figure 15.5), implying a material difference between R and No-R contracts.

FIGURE 15.5 Cause of High-Yield Bond Defaults

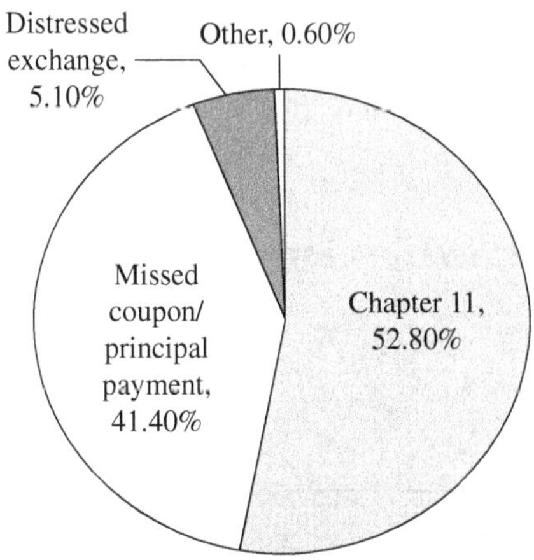

Source: Fitch Ratings

Trading Forward Credit Risk

As liquidity along the curves has developed in default swap markets, curve-based investment strategies have become increasingly popular. Despite increased liquidity and a decent amount of convergence with corporate bonds, default swap curve relationships are by no means mature; in fact, we would argue that the market is still in the infancy stages of thinking about credit term structures. The existence of liquid curves where investors can go long and short to different dates implies that investors can position for "forward" credit risk.

Fortunately, we can borrow quite a bit of math and market experience from the interest-rate world in determining forward credit spreads, but there are also some key differences. Most important, credit instruments are "risky" assets, and as such, any calculation of implied forward rates must take into consideration the probability of default.

We feel that it is important to take a few steps back and begin to discuss forward credit risk from an intuitive perspective. Once this is established, we can begin to explore valuation issues and curve shape expectations and better understand instruments that are built upon forwards, including CDS options and constant-maturity credit default swaps (CMCDS), which we discuss in the next section of this chapter.

What Can We Learn from Interest Rates?

In a nutshell, a forward interest rate is simply the breakeven rate that makes all investments on the curve equally rewarding. If the forwards are realized, an investor should be indifferent about which point to invest in on the curve. As such, forward curves are important inputs into risk-neutral interest-rate derivatives pricing models, which assume, among other things, that there is no relative value among various opportunities, given market pricing. The following equation shows the calculation of a one-year implied forward rate starting at the end of year 1, F_{1-2}, given the one year spot rate S_1 and the two year spot rate S_2: $F_{1-2} = (1 + S_2)^2/(1 + S_1 - 1)$.

What Is Different in Credit?—Implied Forward CDS Premiums

On the surface, the same math and relationships used in interest rates should hold for credit, but a key difference is that credit is "risky." As such, we have to make some adjustments to address the issue that if the reference entity defaults, the protection seller is not entitled to any future premiums and has to pay the difference between par and recovery value. From a set of CDS levels extending up to the end of the intended forward default swap, we can determine the forward spread using the following logic: A long position in a two-year CDS starting now is equivalent to a combination of a long position in a one-year CDS starting now and a long position in a one-year CDS starting one year from now.

The first step toward calculating implied forward rates is to calculate default probabilities for each payment period. To simplify, let us assume that we have two default swap contracts, CDS1 and CDS2, maturing at the end of years 1 and 2, respectively, with annual spread payments. Now we can determine the implied probability of default at the end of year 1 from CDS1, given a recovery rate. Similarly, given the probability of default in year 1 and CDS2 spread level, we can calculate the probability of default in year 2, given that the reference entity does not default in year 1. Thus we can impute default probabilities for each period from a whole credit curve. For more details, refer to the CDS pricing section.

The combination of CDS1 and a forward default swap, which starts at the end of year 1, replicates CDS2. Therefore, by equating the two cash flow streams, we can determine the implied forward default swap level.

The following equations summarize the calculation of forward CDS rates (using the same notation as we used in the CDS pricing section):

$$PV(CDS_t) + PV(FWD_{t-T}) = PV(CDS_T)$$

where

$$PV(CDS_T) = \sum_{t=1}^{T} DF_t \cdot \frac{S_T}{\left(1 + \frac{S_T}{1-R}\right)^t}$$

$$PV(FWD_{i-T}) = \sum_{t=i}^{T} DF_t \cdot \frac{F_{i-T}}{\left(1 + \frac{F_{i-T}}{1-R}\right)^t}$$

The first equation represents replication of a CDS maturity at T with a CDS of term t and a forward-starting CDS that starts at t and ends at T. DF_t represents discount factors and can be calculated using the swap curve.

In Table 15.3, we have assumed the current 5-year spread at 50 bps, while the 10-year spread is 100 bps. This results in an implied forward 5-year CDS five years from now of 188 bps. Now we can compare this figure with our expectations, and if this is too high, we can lock it in by

TABLE 15.3 Forward Trading: A Hypothetical Example

Year	CDS Spread	5-Year Forward CDS
0	0.00%	0.50%
1	0.10%	0.72%
2	0.20%	0.97%
3	0.30%	1.23%
4	0.40%	1.53%
5	0.50%	1.88%
6	0.60%	
7	0.70%	
8	0.80%	
9	0.90%	
10	1.00%	

Source: Morgan Stanley

going long 10-year CDS and short 5-year CDS. On the other hand, if we expect the credit environment to be much worse than implied, we can buy 10-year protection and sell 5-year protection.

Other Developments in CDS

In this section, we discuss newer developments in the CDS market.

Constant Maturity Credit Default Swaps

Much of the development that resulted in today's standard credit default swap contract was driven by definitions of credit events, sparked, in turn, by the many bankruptcies, defaults, and restructurings that the investment-grade market experienced during the past credit cycle. Tight spreads and a lack of differentiation create a natural reach for yield phenomena but also cause concern among those who must be fully invested and don't feel great about the upside potential. Consequently, many market participants are exploring a new variant—constant maturity credit default swaps (CMCDSs).

From an intuitive perspective, CMCDS is an instrument that provides investors with a convenient way to string together a series of forward credit curve trades. We feel that varying risk premiums along the credit curve, combined with the potential for spread regime shifts, can result in impractical forward spreads. One can therefore think of CMCDS as a convenient (and positive carry) means to lean against the forwards. (See Figure 15.6.)

CMCDS Mechanics

A constant maturity credit default swap is a default swap in which the premium is reset (on a quarterly basis) to equal a fixed percentage (called the participation rate) of the then-prevailing premium of a plain-vanilla default swap for a certain term. While this is very much a developing market, a typical CMCDS trade today has a five-year term and references a fresh five-year default swap every quarter during that five-year term. Assuming a 50% participation rate, the seller of CMCDS protection would receive 50% of the prevailing premium on a five-year

FIGURE 15.6 CMCDS Cash Flows

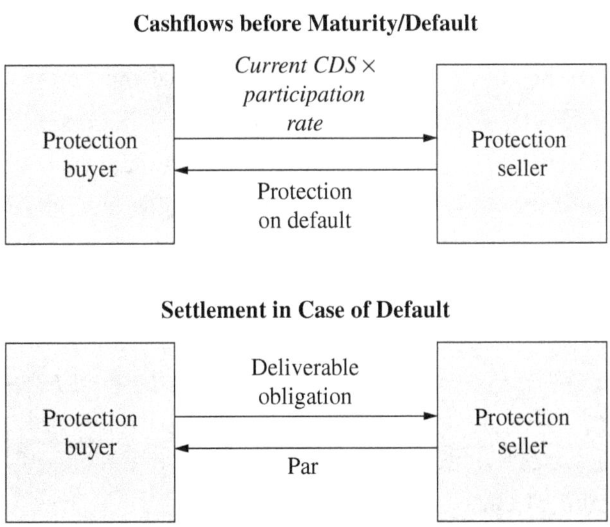

Source: Fitch Ratings

TABLE 15.4 CMCDS–Sample Quarterly Premium Calculation (Notational = $10,000,000.00; Participation Rate = 50%)

Quarter	Five-Year CDS Spread (BP)	CMCDS Spread (BP)	Quarterly Payment ($)
1	100	50	12,500
2	125	62.5	15,625
3	150	75	18,750
4	120	60	15,000
5	100	50	12,500

Source: Morgan Stanley

default swap every quarter, until the CMCDS expires (in five years) or until a credit event occurs (see Table 15.4). Consequently, if spreads widen, the quarterly payment would also increase and the concomitant mark-to-market impact could be significantly lower than a regular default swap. The premium on a five-year default swap is inferred from the market, generally by some type of a fixing process on the reset date by a calculation agent. There can also be a cap on the premium, usually at stressed premium levels.

Participation Rate

Since the protection provided by a CDS and a CMCDS is essentially identical in the case of a default, the pricing of the two instruments should be directly linked as well. Said differently, buyers of protection in either instrument should expect to spend the same amount for the protection at the inception of the contracts. This linkage is enforced through the concept of a participation rate.

We start by using an analogy from the world of interest-rate swaps. The fair fixed rate on a swap is the one that equates the present value of floating leg cash flows to the present value of fixed leg cash flows. Employing the same heuristic, the fair participation rate is the rate that equates the present value of payments of a regular CDS to the present value of CMCDS payments.

The intuition developed from interest-rate forwards can be directly harnessed to understand the participation rate. If the interest-rate curve is flat, then all the implied forward rates would also be flat. Similarly if the CDS curve is flat, the fair participation rate for the CMCDS would be 100%. On the other hand, if the interest-rate curve is upward sloping, then the implied forward rates would be higher than the current short rate. For CMCDSs, if the CDS curve is upward sloping, then the participation rate would be less than 100%. Conversely, if the interest-rate curve is inverted (downward sloping), the implied forward rates would fall below the current short rate. For CMCDSs, the participation rate would be higher than 100% if the CDS curve is inverted.

CMCDS Pricing—Determining the Participation Rate

To determine the expected payments of a CMCDS, we need the implied forward CDS rates, just as we need forward LIBOR rates to calculate the fixed rate in the case of interest-rate swaps. We have already discussed how to calculate the implied forward credit spreads. In the numerical example that follows (Table 15.5), we assume a flat

TABLE 15.5 Implied Forward CDS Rrates–Numerical Example (Discount Rate = 5%, Recovery Rate = 40%)

Year	Discount Factors	CDS Spread	5-Year Forward CDS	CMCDS
0	1.00	0.00%	0.50%	0.20%
1	0.95	0.10%	0.72%	0.29%
2	0.91	0.20%	0.97%	0.39%
3	0.86	0.30%	1.23%	0.50%
4	0.82	0.40%	1.53%	0.62%
5	0.78	0.50%	1.88%	0.76%
6	0.75	0.60%		
7	0.71	0.70%		
8	0.68	0.80%		
9	0.64	0.90%		
10	0.61	1.00%		

Source: Morgan Stanley

zero-coupon curve at 5% annual payment frequency and a participation rate of 40.6%, the calculation of which we show shortly.

Once we have determined the forward CDS rates for each payment period, we can project the cash flows of both a regular CDS and a CMCDS. Now we can compute the participation rate that matches the present value of cash flows of a CMCDS to the present value of cash flows of a regular CDS.

We determine the participation rate, X, using the following relationships:

$$PV(CDS_T) = PV(CMCDS_T)$$

where

$$PV(CDS_T) = \sum_{t=1}^{T} DF_t \cdot \frac{S_T}{\left(1 + \frac{S_T}{1-R}\right)^t}$$

$$PV(CMCDS_T) = \sum_{t=1}^{T} DF_t \cdot \frac{F_t * X}{\left(1 + \frac{S_T}{1-R}\right)^t}$$

The numerical example in Table 15.6 shows the calculation of the participation rate based on the forward CDS rates we just calculated.

TABLE 15.6 Participation Rate Calculation

	Spread PV	
Year	**CDS**	**CMCDS**
1	0.0047	0.0068
2	0.0045	0.0086
3	0.0042	0.0104
4	0.0040	0.0122
5	0.0038	0.0141
Total PV	0.0211	0.0521
Participation rate = 40.6%		

Source: Morgan Stanley

We have overlooked convexity adjustments in our pricing discussion above. Given a fixed participation rate, CMCDS payments change linearly with the benchmark CDS spread, while CDS values have a convex relationship with spread changes. Therefore, we need to make adjustments to reflect the hedging error. Furthermore, our assumption regarding the availability of a full CDS curve with default swaps available for each payment period is rather tenuous, resulting in further basis in our attempts to lock in implied forward CDS rates. These issues imply a wider than usual bid-ask for CMCDS, making some market participants reluctant.

Intuitive Feel

There are effectively two ways one can think of CMCDSs. First, as we mentioned above, a CMCDS is a convenient way to string together a series of forwards. If the curve shape and spread levels implied by forwards are realized over the term, the CMCDS and CDS should have the same return at maturity, and this is the basis for pricing. Thus, a position in CMCDS (versus one in CDS) is a way of expressing the view that the forwards will not be realized. Second, ignoring forwards for the moment, CMCDS is really just a floating-rate instrument, but the credit premium is what actually floats, because there is no interest rate. A floating premium can have more muted mark-to-market volatility than a fixed premium instrument.

Recovery Swaps

In case of a recovery swap, the buyer and the seller agree on a fixed recovery rate; the party committing to take a floating recovery rate receives (or pays) the difference between the predetermined recovery rate and the actual recovery rate in case of a default.

Currently there are two market approaches for recovery swap pricing. First, no premiums are exchanged over the life of the contract, and the payment takes place only if there is default. The second standard uses a combination of a zero-recovery default swap and a vanilla default swap to execute a recovery swap. Given a vanilla default swap pricing, we can easily determine the pricing of the corresponding zero recovery swap by dividing the premium by a factor of (1 – recovery rate). For example, a CDS premium of 100 bps running with 40% recovery translates to 166.7 bps with 0% recovery. From our discussions, it appears that the market is leaning toward the former for pricing recovery swaps.[2]

Cancelable CDS

A cancelable default swap (also known as a callable default swap) is a credit default swap in which the buyer of protection has the right to cancel the protection after a noncall period. The motivation behind cancelable CDSs is an effort to hedge loans or bonds with uncertain maturity, such as prepayable bank loans, convertible/callable bonds, and so on. For example, we can hedge a callable bond by buying cancelable protection, as we can cancel the CDS if the bond is called away. The motivation for the protection seller is the opportunity to make some additional spread to compensate him or her for being short the option. A short cancelable CDS position (long protection) is implicitly bullish on spread, since the cancelable option becomes more valuable as spread declines. In other words, as spreads tighten, the long protection position would have a negative mark-to-market, and the option to cancel this contract would now be in the money.

Spread Options

Spread options provide a convenient way to hedge uncertain credit risk exposure and to position for volatility changes. Options to buy or sell protection on individual credits as well as diversified indexes are now available in the marketplace, albeit liquidity may vary considerably depending on the credit.

Options on default swaps work in a fashion similar to the over-the-counter (OTC) options with a few subtle differences. Upon exercise of an option of CDSs, the option buyer enters a long or short default swap position, depending on the option.

Types of Options

There are two types of options on credit default swaps, as explained below:

1. *Option to buy protection (put/payer):* Upon exercise, the option holder enters into a long protection position on the underlying reference entity.
2. *Option to sell protection (call/receiver):* Upon exercise, the option holder enters into a short protection position on the underlying reference entity.

Option premium is typically quoted on an up-front basis. The strike is typically European in nature; that is, the option can be exercised only on the expiration date. Upon exercise, the two parties enter into a default swap, and the option seller makes an up-front payment reflecting the difference between the strike and the current CDS level, just as one does while entering into an off-market CDS transaction. Options with maturities up to one year are usually available, with the near-term options typically being most liquid. The maturity dates usually coincide with the standard default swap payment dates.

It is noteworthy that single-name spread options typically do not provide protection against default during their life. If a default occurs during this period, the option is simply knocked out. However, spread options on indexes tend to trade without the knock-out feature; that is, they provide protection during the option's life, and the buyer has the right to exercise defaults at expiration.

The default swap option premium depends on the current CDS level, the strike spread, LIBOR interest-rate curve, volatility of spread, and maturity dates of the option and the CDS. The payoff function of an option to buy protection that looks similar to an equity call payoff, while it resembles an equity put option for an option to sell protection.

16

LEVERAGED LOAN CDSs

Vishwanath Tirupattu

Managing Director,
Morgan Stanley & Company, Inc.

Sivan Mahadevan

Managing Director,
Morgan Stanley & Company, Inc.

Much of the innovation in the corporate credit markets over the past decade has been in derivatives (CDSs), structures (CBOs and CLOs), or combinations of both (synthetic structured credit). One major development in the single-name cash markets has been in leveraged loans, which, in their two main forms (bank and institutional loans), have experienced tremendous growth over the past few years. As demand has increased for exposure to secured high-yield credit, there has been an important shift from bank loans to those targeted to institutional investors. As such, the investor base in leveraged loans has grown both directly (specialized funds and traditional high-yield investors) and indirectly (CLOs, which have replaced CBOs as the preferred method of gaining structured exposure to high-yield credit).

Loans used to be seen as arcane, clubby, documentation-intensive bilateral instruments with limited liquidity and secondary trading opportunities. This perception is changing. Syndicated loans have emerged as the dominant way for issuers to tap banks and other institutional capital providers for loans. The adoption of market-flex language—which allowed arrangers to change the pricing and other terms based on investor demand—is often seen[1] as the impetus for transforming the loan markets into the full-fledged capital markets we know them as today. Credit default swaps (CDSs) referencing loans are the latest innovation in this market, which we expect will have a transformational impact on loan markets and, more broadly, on corporate and structured credit markets. While leveraged loan CDSs have much in common with corporate CDSs by virtue of the 2003 ISDA credit derivatives definitions, there are important distinctions as well, both structurally and geographically.

In this chapter, we discuss the unique characteristics of the loan market and highlight differences between bonds and loans to motivate a discussion of CDSs on secured loans contrasted with the established CDS market for unsecured debt.[2] Furthermore, we describe the mechanics and features of the leveraged loan CDS contract (as it looks today) emphasizing the differences between the U.S. and European markets.[3] We also discuss the factors that determine basis relationships between cash and synthetic instruments, as well as between corporate CDSs and leveraged loan CDSs. Finally, we discuss the applications of leveraged loan CDSs from different perspectives. Note that we use the terms "leveraged loan," "secured loan," and even simply "loan" interchangeably in this chapter.

From a derivatives perspective, we want to make it clear up front that plenty of evolution and maturing needs to occur for any standardized leveraged loan CDS contract. We feel that the market is very much in its early stages, which readers will hopefully gather as they go through this book, and we fully expect future credit events and the like to provide teething pains and to help create more mature contracts as the market moves forward.

Why Leveraged Loan CDSs?

The market for secured loans has been booming for the last few years on both sides of the Atlantic (see Figure 16.1). Record-breaking new issuance volumes amid ever-tightening spreads, driven by the explosive growth in CLOs, as well as leveraged finance transactions, have been the hallmark of secured loans business. At the same time, significant changes are afoot that could have profound impacts on this market, with reverberations that could be felt in the broader corporate credit market. These include changes in the regulatory capital regime resulting from Basel II creating new demand for hedging bank loan exposures, changes to rating agency approaches to better distinguish the performance of secured loans from unsecured bonds, and growing institutionalization of the market, particularly in Europe.

The consistent and stable performance of the loan market (to date) has generated a large expansion of investor interest and consequent cash inflows into the loan market. The returns from loan investing as reflected in the S&P LSTA loan index over the last several years

FIGURE 16.1 Global New-Issue Leveraged Loan Volume

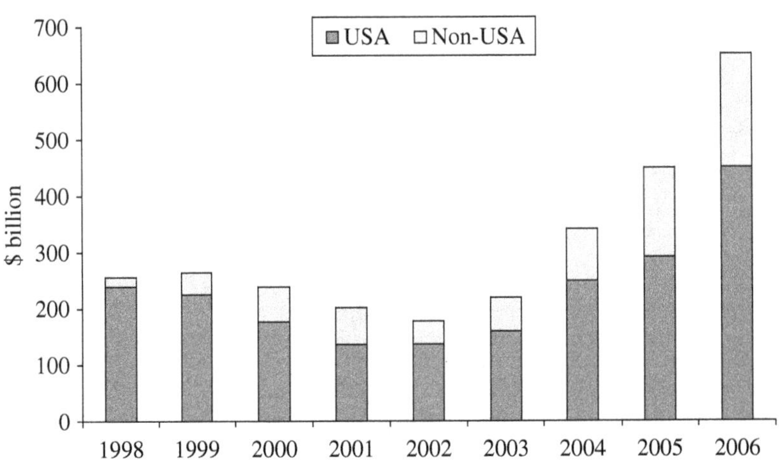

Source: S&P LCD

FIGURE 16.2 Total Return of S&P LSTA Index (1997–2006)

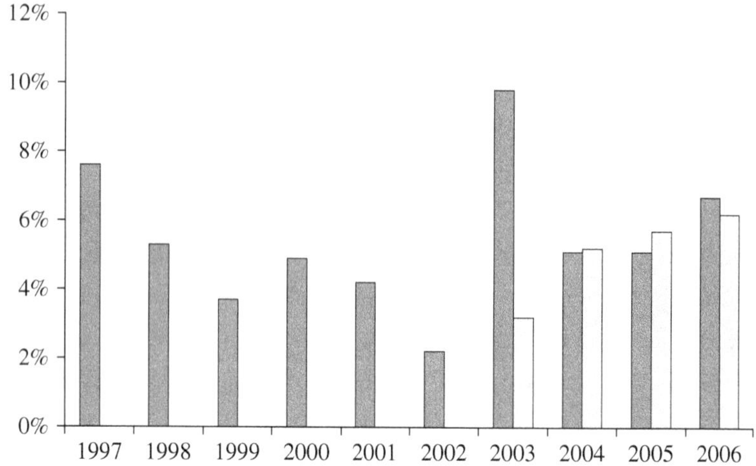

Source: S&P LCD

have been impressive in absolute terms (Figure 16.2). Further, measured on a risk-adjusted basis using Sharpe ratios, loans compare favorably relative to other competing asset classes (see Figure 16.3, based on S&P LCD data).

FIGURE 16.3 Sharpe Ratio: S&P LSTA Index versus Other Asset Classes (1997–2006)

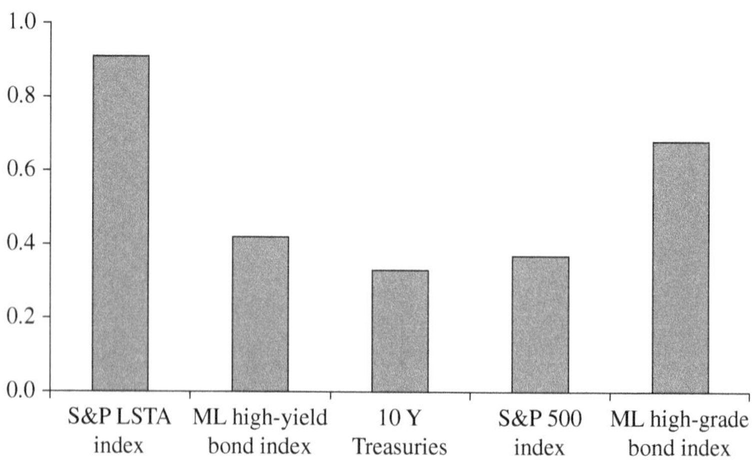

Source: S&P LCD

As the credit cycle appears to be on the cusp of turning, credit investors have demonstrated a shift in sentiment to move higher up in the capital structure by shifting from unsecured bonds to secured loans. This, coupled with the insatiable demand from CLOs, has made access to loans in the cash form a major constraint for investors trying to get long exposures to secured loans as an asset class. However, we caution that recovery value is a zero sum game, so to the degree that secured loans take the place of unsecured bonds in the capital structure, the historically high recoveries of loans are not sustainable.

At the same time, another section of investors is concerned with what is seen as declining credit quality, lack of diversity across CLO portfolios, and exposure to LBOs embedded in the loan market; these investors seek instruments to short the loan market or efficiently hedge their exposures. In addition, commercial and investment banks require instruments that enable them to maintain relationships with issuers while simultaneously managing the capital risks of corporate lending.

Well-constructed, standardized, synthetic instruments can efficiently address these many demands from the long and short sides of this evolving market. Just as the development of CDSs in corporate, emerging market, and, more recently, asset-backed securities has radically transformed the underlying markets, development of a loan CDS contract has the potential to be similarly transformative for the loan sector. Current industrywide efforts to develop a standardized contract for loan CDSs are a natural outgrowth of these evolving dynamics in the marketplace for secured loans, paving the way for innovative methods of transferring risk, implementing hedging strategies, and expanding opportunities for a wide range of market participants.

Unique Characteristics of the Leveraged Loan Market

In this section, we provide an overview of the unique characteristics of the leveraged loan market.

Floating-Rate Instruments

Leveraged loans are typically floating-rate payers with an interest amount equal to a floating-rate index that is periodically reset (usually quarterly) plus a fixed spread (margin). Bonds may have either fixed or floating coupons.

Ratings

Most bonds are rated by at least one rating agency. While it is a lot more common for U.S. loans to be rated as well, European loans frequently do not carry public ratings.

Loan Structure

The majority of loans may be structured as one of two categories—revolving credit facilities and term loans. A revolver is a commitment to make loans to a borrower up to the maturity date of the facility, and a borrower may borrow and repay a revolving credit facility multiple times until the maturity of the facility at the discretion of the borrower. Revolvers are generally unfunded and mainly used by investment-grade borrowers. A term loan is funded at closing, and any repayment results in a permanent reduction in the outstanding amount—that is, no reborrowing. Because of the largely unfunded nature of the revolvers, they are not traded frequently.

There are two principal categories of term loans—amortizing term loans and institutional term loans. An amortizing term loan (TLA) is a fully funded term loan with a specified amortization schedule (usually weighted toward the later years); it is generally syndicated to banks, along with revolvers, as a part of larger syndications. Institutional term loans ("TLBs," "TLCs," "TLDs") are the types of loans that are of most interest to institutional lenders, who generally do not maintain a relationship with the borrowers; these constitute the bulk of the traded loans and, as such, are the category of loans that will be of most interest in the context of loan CDSs. Institutional term loans are secured, rank pari passu with other facilities, and usually have interest margins higher than those of revolvers or TLAs, repaid mostly in a bullet form (scheduled amortization, if any, is minimal and significantly back-ended).

In addition, institutional term loans are longer dated (with maturities of five to seven years) but may be prepaid at any time at par (unless specifically structured with call protections) and used by leveraged borrowers (noninvestment-grade borrowers with debt/EBITDA greater than 2.0×). Multiple tranches with varying maturities can coexist within a facility (TLB, TLC, TLD, and so on, are labeled as such for each maturity). The vast majority of the loan market is composed of institutional loans.

While these structures (especially term loans) have some similarity to corporate bonds by way of differing maturities, their security, amortization, and prepayability features are unique to loans.

Seniority and Security

Loans almost always rank senior to other parts of the debt capital structure. For noninvestment-grade borrowers, they are also secured by all tangible and intangible assets of the borrower in the form of pledges of collateral. In some cases, loans are secured by specific assets. The secured and senior nature of leveraged loans is an extremely important feature that determines the recovery prospects for a loan if there is a default. Historically, the average recovery rates for secured loans have been significantly higher than unsecured debt, as shown in Table 16.1.

In this context, it is useful to discuss another growing type of syndicated leveraged loan—second-lien loans. As implied by their name, claims on second-liens rank behind those of the first-lien loans and, as such, trade at significantly wider premiums than first-lien loans. The recovery potential for second-lien loans is usually lower. The term "designated priority" is used to designate the lien status (whether the loan is first lien or second lien).

TABLE 16.1 Average Recovery Rates for Corporate Debt Obligors (1982–2005)

Loans	
Type of Loan	**Recovery Rate**
Senior secured	70.0%
Senior unsecured	57.6%
Bonds	
Type of Bond	**Recovery Rate**
Senior secured	51.9%
Senior unsecured	36.0%
Senior subordinated	32.4%
Subordinated	31.8%
Junior subordinated	23.9%

Source: Moody's Investors Service, "Default and Recovery Rates of Corporate Bond Issuers, 1920–2005," January 2006

Covenants

A defining feature of leveraged loans, as opposed to bonds, is the significant and onerous set of restrictions on borrowers imposed by covenant protections. While there is a wide gamut of such restrictions specified in loan agreements, in general, the riskier the borrower, the larger the covenant package. Covenants can be affirmative (actions borrowers must take to be compliant with a loan), negative (limitations on the types and amounts of new debt, liens, asset sales, acquisitions, parent/subsidiary guarantees), and financial (enforcing minimum financial performance measures). Financial covenants can include limitations on coverage (minimum cash flow earnings relative to interest and debt service), leverage (maximum level of debt relative to cash flow or earnings), current ratio (minimum ratio of current assets to current liabilities), tangible net worth (minimum levels of tangible assets excluding assets such as goodwill and intellectual assets), and maximum capital expenditure (limiting the purchase of property, plants, and equipment).

The extent of covenant protection is critical in determining the riskiness of the borrower. While bonds, especially noninvestment-grade bonds, also have some form of such covenants, they are not typically as onerous as those with loans. It is worth emphasizing that there is a wide variation in covenant packages across loan agreements. Furthermore, second-lien loans typically have less restrictive covenant packages, and maintenance covenants are set wide of the first-lien loans.

Secondary Trading Conventions

Once a loan transaction is closed upon primary issuance, it can be traded in the secondary market. Such sales can be structured in one of two forms—assignments or participations. The differences between the two forms are mainly in terms of rights, as well as the degree of documentation and consents that need to be sought and obtained. Assignments usually require the consent of the borrower and the agent on a not-to-be-unreasonably-withheld basis; the assignee becomes the direct signatory to the loan and receives interest and principal payments from the administrative agent of the loan agreement. In the event of a borrower default, assignees will have complete rights and access to private information as lenders of record.

Participations do not have the consent requirements of assignments, and a buyer obtaining a loan through participation enters into a separate agreement with an existing lender to take a participating beneficial interest in the lender's position in the loan agreement. The existing lender remains the official holder of the loan and passes on interest and principal payments to the participant buyer. The voting rights of participants may be limited. In practice, varying degrees of voting rights are passed on through participations in the market. Access to syndicate information is different in that it is often indirect and there may be differences in the timing of receipt of information in the event of a default.

Clearly, these trading conventions and differences of rights and responsibilities are not generally as onerous in the context of the secondary trading of bonds. Also, significant differences exist between

European and U.S. conventions in this context. Assignments in Europe can be much more restrictive than those in the United States, requiring the eligible assignees to be financial institutions, sometimes specifying only banks to be eligible. Therefore, institutions such as hedge funds and, in some cases, CLOs may not be deemed eligible assignees and may need to obtain exposure solely through participations. In general, the criterion for eligible assignees in the United States is broader.

Public versus Private Information

Most loan agreements require a borrower to periodically provide information ("syndicate information") to the lenders which is generally not public. Access to such information is transferred when a loan is traded on assignment but not necessarily in participations. Further, traditional "loan-only" institutional investors (CLOs, prime funds) have, for the most part, chosen to remain private and therefore retain access to syndicate information. Clearly, other investors, such as hedge funds, high-yield funds, and other mutual funds, may have exposure to the borrower in other forms as well (bonds, for example), and access to nonpublic information could be problematic. Such investors should create legal or operational "wall-off" infrastructure internally or externally.

We highlight this as an important consideration for market participants. In the early days of (mainly investment-grade) CDS contracts, a common criticism was that banks (which were natural buyers of protection) were privy to private information. In 2002, the Commodity Futures Modernization Act (CFMA) required that CDSs be covered by antifraud measures, which created walls between lenders and hedgers in banking institutions.

Documentation

Loans are documentation-intensive—much more so than bonds. Two separate markets exist within the secondary loan market, each trading with a different set of documentation—one for par loans (still performing and without any financial distress) and another for distressed loans (those already in default, perceived by the market to be on the verge of default, or otherwise considered to be under financial distress). See Table 16.2.

While the buyer's assumption of the seller's rights and obligations is limited to those that result from facts, events, or circumstances arising or occurring on or after the closing date of the loan purchase, the determination of what the seller's obligations and liabilities are requires a significant amount of legal work. This has important implications for the development of a liquid loan CDS contract, and a mechanism has been created to deal with such issues.

TABLE 16.2 High-Yield Bonds versus Leveraged Loans

High-Yield Bonds		**Leveraged Loans**
Interest:	Fixed/floating	Floating.
Spread (margin):	Unchanged	Potential to ratchet.
Seniority:	Senior or subordinated	Senior.
Security:	Unsecured	Secured (first lien or second lien).
Rated?	Yes	Yes in the United States; not usually publicly rated in Europe.
Calls, prepays, and amortization	Calls, protections, and premiums	Usually no call protections for first-lien loans, but there are call protections in second-lien loans. Loans are mainly prepayable (bullets). Some loans amortize (revolvers and TLAs).
Covenants	Incurrence covenants	Maintenance covenants.
Documentation	Limited	Extensive. Credit agreement is the governing documentation. Separate documentation for par and distressed loans for trading.
Funded/unfunded	Funded	Usually funded, but some tranches are not (revolvers).
Secondary trading conventions	TRACE eligible; some exchange trading	Not TRACE eligible; carried out through assignments or participations.

Source: Morgan Stanley

Given the unique characteristics of loans and the differences between European and U.S. market conventions, the development of standardized contracts has evolved to create synthetic instruments that best approximate the credit risk exposure of the loan markets specific to the market conventions of their underlying cash markets. Consequently, two forms of standardized CDS contracts, one for trading in the United States and the other for trading in Europe, have emerged. In the United States, the CDS contract is a lien-specific contract that is generally noncancelable unless there are no secured loans outstanding. In Europe, the CDS contract terminates upon the full repayment of a specific loan. In the next section, we discuss the mechanics of the CDS contract in greater detail.

Leveraged Loan CDS Mechanics

Before delving into loan CDS mechanics, a brief review of CDS concepts in general may be helpful. Recall that a CDS involves protection buyers and sellers and that the CDS protects the buyer against the loss of principal in the underlying asset when a credit event occurs. The protection buyer pays a periodic premium to the protection seller, typically quoted as basis points per annum, until the contract matures or a credit event occurs, whichever is earlier.

The underlying asset is defined as the reference obligation of a specific reference entity which informs the scope of the protection. When a credit event occurs, depending on the settlement mechanism in the CDS contract, the buyer of protection delivers a reference obligation to the seller and receives par in return (physical delivery) or receives the difference between par and the post-credit-event market value of the referenced obligation from the seller (cash settlement). Credit events are specified in the CDS contract; typical credit events are bankruptcy, failure to pay, restructuring, repudiation, and obligation acceleration. The buyer of protection is "short" and the seller of protection is "long" the credit risk of the reference obligation in contrast to the cash market, where a bond/loan buyer is "long" and the seller is "short" the credit risk of the underlying bond/loan.

A few notable differences between being long a leveraged loan in cash form or via CDS are worth mentioning. As long as there are no credit events, sellers of protection do not have voting rights and do not receive the benefits of any margin amendments or fees that the underlying cash loan might receive. Loan CDS mechanics are similar to other CDS mechanics in general, and the terms and provisions in the 2003 ISDA credit derivatives definitions, combined with that document's May 2003 supplement, do form the general framework for loan CDS documentation, with some important modifications discussed in detail below. Table 16.3 summarizes the major differences in CDS between loans and bonds.

Documentation standards have developed on parallel tracks, separately for U.S. and European loan CDSs. To a large extent, these separate tracks are motivated by the dominant loan market participants in each region. Creating a CDS contract that closely resembles the established CDS market for unsecured corporate credit has been an important consideration in the development of the LCDS documentation for the U.S. loan CDS, a market dominated by institutional investors. On the other hand, hedging and achieving regulatory capital relief under Basel II were major considerations in Europe, a loan market still dominated by banks (despite their diminished presence in today's market). In this section, as we discuss the loan CDS mechanics, we highlight the differences between U.S. and European loan CDSs, where applicable.

Syndicated Secured

An important, unique concept fundamental to loan CDS mechanics and documentation is the "syndicated secured" characteristic of a reference/deliverable obligation. It refers to any obligation to pay or repay borrowed money resulting from the funding of an unfunded commitment that arises from a loan agreement and trades as a loan of the designated

TABLE 16.3 How is Loan CDS Different from Bond CDS?

Characteristics	Leveraged Loans	Bonds
Reference entity/reference obligation	Depends upon the tranche/lien	Depends upon the issuer
Credit events	1. Bankruptcy 2. Failure to pay (noncurable default) 3. Restructuring is *not* a credit event in the United States but is a credit event in Europe.	1. Bankruptcy 2. Failure to pay (noncurable default) 3. Restructuring is a credit event for IG and not for high-yield issuers in the United States. Restructuring is a credit event for high yield in Europe.
Cancelability	1. European standard contracts are cancelable if loan prepays. 2. U.S. standard contracts are cancelable only if loans go from secured to unsecured or if no secured loans are outstanding.	Noncancelable
Settlement	Physical delivery. Cash settlement procedures are still evolving.	Cash settlement and physical delivery
Documentation issues	• Par docs and distressed docs • Via assignments or via participations • ISDA standards still evolving	ISDA standard documentation

Source: Morgan Stanley

priority.[4] Note that this is really a trading standard, as opposed to a legal standard, and is meant to reflect the trading practices in the current primary or secondary loan market.

Reference Obligation

The reference obligation is a loan of a designated priority (first-lien loan, second-lien loan, etc.). The CDS confirmation specifies a "relevant secured list," which lists syndicated secured obligations of the designated priority of the reference entity, published and amended from time to time by an appointed secured list publisher.[5] The confirmation provides for new tranches to be added as long as they are obligations arising under a syndicated loan agreement and trade in the secondary markets as a loan of designated priority or higher. The implication of this legalese is that all pari passu tranches/facilities would be deliverable obligations, including tranches and facilities added subsequent to the trade date. As such, this framework facilitates trading loan CDSs on a "class" of assets.

Cancelability

Leveraged loan CDS contracts have the additional characteristic of being cancelable when the underlying loan is paid off. The LCDS contract in North America is effectively a reference entity based contract, while the European LCDS is a reference obligation based contract. What this means is that in the case of North American LCDS, a credit event will be triggered if there is a payment default on any borrowed money of the reference entity (even if only a bond or a second lien defaults and the senior loan does not, there is a credit event triggered). In contrast, the European LCDS contract triggers a credit event only when there is a payment default in the specific reference obligation. The differences in the North American and European rules reflect regional differences in bankruptcy regimes and the relative predominance in Europe of loans in corporate liability structures.[6]

Substitution of Reference Obligation

It is possible that a designated reference obligation is no longer a valid reference obligation. Circumstances that necessitate such a situation include the following: a reference obligation is repaid in whole, or, in a case where it is a revolver, the relevant commitment is terminated and any funded commitment is repaid; the aggregate funded and unfunded commitments under the reference obligation are materially reduced due to redemptions; or the reference obligation may no longer satisfy the syndicated secured characteristic. Under such circumstances, the U.S. loan CDS contracts provide for the substitution of the reference obligation with another reference obligation that satisfies the syndicated secured characteristic, ranks pari passu (or higher in seniority if no pari passu loan exists, at the option of the protection buyer), and preserves the economic equivalent delivery and payment obligations. The calculation agent identifies a candidate reference obligation for substitution in consultation with all the parties involved and notifies all the parties upon which it would be binding unless there is a manifest error. The confirmation provides for a dispute resolution mechanism in this context as well.

Credit Events

The standard credit events for the U.S. contract are bankruptcy and failure to pay. As is the case with the corporate CDS on U.S. high-yield bonds, restructuring is not a credit event. On the other hand, restructuring is a credit event for European loan CDSs, in addition to bankruptcy and failure to pay. The motivation for the intercontinental differences has to do with regulatory relief. European regulators require restructuring to be included as a credit event for banks to obtain regulatory capital relief as protection buyers.

Deliverable Obligations

Any reference obligation that satisfies the syndicated secured characteristic is deliverable in the United States. Deliverable obligations in European loan CDSs are the designated tranche(s) under the reference credit agreement. In addition, for European loan CDSs, deliverable obligations cannot have security diminished as a consequence of restructuring. Successor provisions to determine deliverable obligations per the 2003 ISDA credit derivatives definitions are applicable for U.S. loan CDS contracts and are not applicable for European loan CDS contracts. (For a more complete discussion on succession language provisions, please see Chapter 8).

Borrower/Agent Consent

Loan CDSs, being contracts between buyers and sellers of protection, effectively avoid borrower/agent consent issues and any associated transfer fees in the underlying cash loan market.

Settlement Mechanisms

Physical settlement is the default standard for both U.S. and European loan CDS contracts. Cash settlement remains a somewhat distant goal; the procedures to effectuate settlement in cash form are still evolving. The seller of protection has the cash settlement option if unable to receive physical delivery or unwilling to accept participations. The differences in rights and information access discussed earlier may motivate the reluctance to accept the physical delivery of a loan as participation. It is important to emphasize that the protection seller is not obliged to take physical delivery of loans or participation and both parties have the right to elevate participation to an assignment or novation. The protection buyer must be either the lender of record on the loan or have similar voting rights via a similar CDS or participation agreement in order to transfer voting rights to the protection seller. In the United States, voting rights transfer only in assignments and not via participations, as a default standard. (See Table 16.4.)

Given the documentation-intensive nature of loans and the potential for legacy issues to be carried along the stream as a loan changes hands, efforts toward contract standardization include certain provisions

TABLE 16.4 Comparison of U.S. and European LCDSs

Characteristics	Europe	United States
Reference entity	Any borrower, guarantor, obligor under the reference credit agreement	As shown in confirmation
Reference obligation	Each designated tranche(s) under the reference credit agreement	Loan of designated priority specified in relevant secured list or in the confirmation applied. If there is a relevant secured list, market will act as polling agent, otherwise as calculation agent.
Substitute reference obligation	Does not apply	
Successor provisions	Not applicable	Applicable
Credit events	Bankruptcy Failure to pay Restructuring (mod-mod-R)	Bankruptcy Failure to pay
Termination	When all reference obligations are redeemed, repaid, or otherwise discharged in full	Optional early termination: if no substitute reference obligation can be identified by the calculation agent within 30 business days after a search note becomes effective, either party can terminate the transaction
Physical settlement	Assignment with a participation fallback	Assignment with a participation fallback

Source: Morgan Stanley

to facilitate efficient and expeditious settlement. These provisions take the form of a physical settlement rider and a market standard indemnity.

The former provides detailed guidance to harmonize standards for physical settlement under a CDS with the standard market practices in the secondary loan market. Note that most of the complications we have discussed thus far are not to the result of the CDS contract per se but are really inherent to the underlying loan markets. As such, the credit-specific standard practices evolve for dealing with the many complications that accompany the trading of loans in the secondary market. The physical settlement rider will utilize the closing mechanics and procedures developed by the LSTA, which will be modified as necessary to ensure efficient settlement of CDS contracts. The physical settlement rider confirms the current LSTA practice and effectively provides the order and the manner by which physical settlement of CDS contracts should take place—first by assignment, then by participation if settlement by assignment is not plausible, and then on the basis of partial cash settlement. As such, partial cash settlement is a fallback settlement provision designed to determine cash payment owed by the protection seller to the protection buyer and applies if the protection seller does not take physical delivery of the reference obligation. As it is conceived, it is always at the protection seller's option. The specification of the market standard in this form should help preempt the lengthy negotiations that might otherwise take place.

The market standard indemnity is also conceived to facilitate faster and more efficient settlement through physical delivery following a credit event. As has been the case with corporate bond CDSs, the outstanding CDS exposures are likely to exceed the outstanding amount of deliverable obligations. The potential scramble for physical delivery upon a credit event is further exacerbated given the time and the legal work necessary to review documentation across the upstream chain. The market standard indemnity seeks to protect the seller of protection from documentation deficiencies by requiring the protection buyer to indemnify the protection seller as a result of inconsistencies between the documents used to transfer the secured loan between the parties and the documentation used in the standard market practice applicable at the time of the transfer.

Applications

Just as the introduction of corporate CDSs opened new avenues for the implementation of sophisticated investment and hedging strategies for a wide range of credit investors, we see a similar potential for loan

CDSs. The interest in the use of loan CDSs is likely to be multidimensional—ranging from investors seeking exposure to the loan asset class (including bond investors seeking to move up in the capital structure) and CLO managers seeking diversified collateral, CLO investors and commercial banks in pursuit of efficient hedging and risk management strategies, and hedge funds and other arbitrageurs seeking to exploit potential capital structure arbitrage strategies. We discuss each of the applications from the perspective of each of these classes of investors.[7]

Traditional Single-Name Credit Investors

The consistent and impressive returns and the seniority in capital structure of leveraged loans have drawn a range of new investors as well as facilitated the increased allocations to the asset class of investors with existing exposure. Both of these categories include traditional bond investors such as insurance companies, pension funds, and specialized mutual funds. For these investors, selling protection through loan CDSs offers a much expanded universe of issuers to choose from instead of being reliant on the limited allocations in the new issue market or the relatively limited opportunities in the secondary market. Loan CDSs open up access to private transactions, as well as to issuers that are no longer trading actively in the secondary market. For European loans, sellers of protection will have the ability to sell in USD or EUR or GBP, and so on, regardless of the underlying currency of the loan. It is worth repeating that loan CDSs, being contracts between buyers and sellers of protection, effectively avoid borrower/agent consent issues and any transfer fees.

CLO Managers

For CLO managers and arrangers, loan CDSs offer several advantages. The difficulties associated with collateral sourcing in the cash loan markets and the consequent long ramp-up periods, as well as sector and/or issuer overlap across CLOs, are well known to the CLO market participants. The latter point is a significant limitation on CLO managers' ability to distinguish their performance from each other since dependency on the tight, collateral-scarce cash loan markets constrains their universe of available assets—hence, the similarity across CLO portfolios managed by different managers.[8] Loan CDSs offer a useful expansion of the universe of available issuers and assets, which helps to reduce ramp-up risk and enables managers to distinguish their performance by security and sector selection.

CLO Arrangers/Structurers

In addition to the advantages described above, loan CDSs also enable cash CLOs to have larger synthetic buckets. It is conceivable that both regular issuance of 100% synthetic CLOs as well as hybrid structures that enable exposures to be acquired in cash and/or synthetic form will emerge in the CLO market. Thanks to the unfunded nature of the loan CDS, such structures would have distinct funding cost advantages, the benefits of which will accrue mainly to investors of CLO equity tranches.

CLO Investors

In addition to the advantages loan CDSs bring to CLOs described above, CLO investors may have additional applications as well. Given the sector and issuer overlaps in CLOs, investors holding portfolios of CLO tranches are clearly exposed to overlap risk. Loan CDSs offer them the potential to buy protection and hedge their exposures. The extent and the effectiveness of such hedging depends on investors' risk tolerance, the tranches being held, their sensitivities to changes in loan CDS spreads, and their analytical framework to deduce suitable hedge ratios. Nevertheless, loan CDSs offer investors an instrument for hedging their exposures.

Commercial and Investment Banks

Single-name loan CDSs enable banks to hedge their loan exposures while maintaining their banking relationships by lending in the cash loan market and buying protection using loan CDSs. Basel II provides an effective incentive to banks to hedge their loan exposures. As our colleagues Jackie Ineke and Christine Miyagishima noted in their report ("Leveraged Loans: Suffering Under Basel II," May 9, 2005), banks link risk weightings to credit ratings, which benefits higher-rated assets such as tranched credit and ABSs but works against leveraged loans. But if leveraged loan exposures are hedged by buying protection from a well-rated counterparty, the capital requirements drop significantly, as demonstrated in Table 16.5.[9] For example, minimum capital requirements for a €10 million exposure of a generic double B TLA loan could fall at €0.94 million to just about €0.116 million.

While corporate CDSs do give banks a tool to hedge against such exposure, leveraged loan CDSs give them a more effective hedge that is a better match relative to the risk exposure.

TABLE 16.5 Basel II Impact on Leveraged Loan Risk Weightings

Type of Loan	Rating	Basel II Risk Weighting	Basel II Capital Requirements (mm) without Hedge (for €10 mm Exposure)	Basel II Minimum Capital Requirement with Hedge (mm) (for €10 mm Exposure)
Term loan A	BB	117.53%	€0.940	€0.116
Term loan B	BB	130.33%	€1.043	€0.116
Term loan C	BB	130.33%	€1.043	€0.116
Revolver	BB	117.53%	€0.940	€0.116
Term loan A	B	174.67%	€1.397	€0.116
Term loan B	B	185.56%	€1.484	€0.116
Term loan C	B	185.56%	€1.484	€0.116
Revolver	B	174.67%	€1.397	€0.116

Source: Morgan Stanley

Hedge Funds, Proprietary Trading Desks, and Other Arbitrageurs

Loan CDSs can be thought of as a definitive step toward trading the entire capital structure in synthetic form. With equity derivatives, CDSs on unsecured bonds, and now loan CDSs, opportunities abound for identifying and exploiting potential arbitrage opportunities, the mainstay in the tool kit of hedge funds and other such arbitrageurs.

Basis Relationships

Basis relationships in the context of leveraged loan CDSs (see Table 16.6) can be thought of in many alternative ways, but we would argue that a few key relationships are the most important: the basis between the leveraged loan CDS premium and the spread of the underlying loan, the basis between cancelable (European) and noncancelable (U.S.) leveraged loan CDS premiums, and the basis between CDSs on leveraged loans and CDSs on senior unsecured debt of the issuer. For those of us who have grown up with corporate CDSs, there are useful parallels and lessons to be drawn from that now-mature CDS market.

The Basis between the Leveraged Loan CDS Premium and the Spread of the Underlying Loan

While the nature of risk exposure through selling protection using loan CDSs and buying cash loans is similar, there are several notable differences as well. These differences drive the basis between the cash loan spreads and loan CDS spreads. They include definitional, technical, operational, administrative, financing, and structural differences. In the relatively brief history of the LCDS market thus far, these differences have driven the basis between loan CDS spreads and cash loan spreads to be negative (cash loan spreads are wider than LCDS premiums on the same obligors).

TABLE 16.6 Application of Leveraged Loan CDSs

User	Uses
Traditional single-name investors	• Expanded universe of issuers • Ability to sell protection in different currencies in the European market • Avoid borrower/agent consent issues and transfer fees
CLO managers	• Shorter ramp-up periods • Expanded reference universe decreases sector/issuer overlap • Increased potential to distinguish performance by security and sector selection • Improved funding efficiency
CLO arrangers/structurers	• Shorter ramp-up periods • Improved collateral sourcing thanks to expanded universe • Funding cost advantages will accrue to equity investors • Facilitate use of larger synthetic buckets (up to 100%)
CLO investors	• Hedge CLO exposure and minimize overlap risks • Funding cost advantages will accrue to equity investors • Shorter ramp-up periods • Expanded universe of issuers
Commercial and investment banks	• Hedge loan exposure while maintaining banking relationships • Hedging reduces risk weightings and provides regulatory capital relief under Basel II regime • Proprietary trading opportunities
Hedge funds, prop desks, and other arbitrageurs	• Capital structure arbitrage • Ability to short credit in the loan space • Risk management and minimization of overlap risks • Expanded universe of issuers • Avoid borrower/agent consent issues and transfer fees

Source: Morgan Stanley

Cash loans are prepayable and often are prepaid, in contrast to LCDS contracts that are designed to be noncancelable. The prepayment option that the cash loan investors are "short" is valuable even in today's environment of low implied volatility and is a significant determinant of the basis. In addition, loan holders benefit from being "long" covenants, amendment/fees, and coupon flexes to which LCDS holders do not have access.

On the other hand, besides the obvious funding advantages, getting long risk exposure through LCDS contracts is far less operationally intensive compared to its cash counterpart.

However, these relationships can change, as evidenced in the recent credit cycle downturn. When the spreads are wider, the call option investors are selling might be worth less. LCDSs may widen more than cash loans in such an environment, as the LCDS contract would be the natural instrument to short loan risk.

The Basis between Leveraged Loan CDSs and Senior Unsecured CDSs of the Issuer

The basis between CDS premiums on secured and unsecured parts of the capital structure of the same issuer will be a function of the basis between loans and unsecured debt, which itself is driven by myriad factors, the most important of which we list below:

1. The size of the borrowings at the various levels of seniority (loans, senior secured debt, senior unsecured debt, subordinated debt, etc.) relative to the total borrowings of the company
2. The absolute likelihood of default for the issuer
3. The relative quality of covenants of the loan and senior bond obligations
4. The likelihood of any capital structure changes and relative pricing of the loan and bond portions of a new capital structure in any corporate restructuring

5. Any differentials in maturity profiles between the loans and bonds of the issuer

Conclusion

If it feels like we cover a lot of ground in this chapter, we have our reasons. In our view, the community of investors with significant experience in *both* credit derivatives and leveraged loans is small, and therefore there are experience curves that most need to climb. Furthermore, credit derivatives tied to leveraged loans have unique issues that should result in some interesting tests of contract language over time. We are indeed excited about strategic opportunities in the secured high-yield credit space involving both single-names and CLOs, as well as full capital structure plays. However, we do caution that we are in the early days of a market that will need time (and increased credit risk) to mature.

17

DEBTOR-IN-POSSESSION FINANCING

William F. Maxwell

Rauscher Chair in Financial Investment,
Cox School of Business at SMU

Philip Delbridge

Vice President Credit Risk Management,
Credit Suisse Securities (USA) LLC

Overview of Chapter 11 Financing

The role of the debtor-in-possession (DIP) under the U.S. Bankruptcy Code (the "Code") is to provide short-term financing so that a firm will have an orderly way to work out its finances while in the process of bankruptcy with the goal of maximizing the value of the firm in the Chapter 11 process. DIP financing is an important source of liquidity in Chapter 11 because the Code prevents a firm from making use of prebankruptcy lines of credit during the bankruptcy process. Therefore, firms that have filed for Chapter 11 require alternative financing to meet working capital requirements and other operating expenses. There are two broad financing options to a firm in Chapter 11: (1) cash collateral and (2) DIP financing.

Cash collateral is generally referred to as the cash generated by the firm following a Chapter 11 filing (or cash generated postpetition). The main issue that arises with the use of cash collateral is that the cash generated can come from the sale of inventory secured by a prepetition lien, in which case the lien holder is entitled to the cash generated from the sale of inventory. Typically the firm will offer the lien holder a new lien on postpetition inventory as compensation for the use of cash collateral. However, cash collateral alone is generally not sufficient to finance a firm through the Chapter 11 process. Firms must seek other postpetition financing pending a plan of reorganization[1] (POA).

The Code (under Section 364) addresses special creditor rights to postpetition loans. These loans are usually referred to as DIP financing, and the lender providing such financing can get superior seniority and enhanced security relative to prepetition unsecured creditors that is not available outside the bankruptcy context. Further, commercial terms of POA require DIP loans to be completely paid off before the firm can emerge from Chapter 11.

Although DIP financing has been available since the 1978 Bankruptcy Reform Act, it was not until the wave of bankruptcies in the early 1990s that DIP financing grew in size and importance. The following sections outline the process involved in obtaining DIP financing under the Code, the special characteristics of DIP loans, and some of the economic implications for firms and lenders engaged in DIP financing.

The DIP Financing Process

Although the existing management of a firm filing for Chapter 11 frequently retains control of the business operations and the reorganization process, major decisions (including the decision to obtain DIP financing) require prior approval of the bankruptcy court. The DIP financing approval process usually involves two steps.

In the first step (assuming the debtor already has a lender willing to provide DIP financing), the debtor makes a motion for authorization to obtain credit. This motion is usually filed either simultaneously with the Chapter 11 filing or shortly thereafter.[2]

The court does not commence a final hearing on the motion for at least a 15-day period. However, most motions contain a request for an interim hearing. This hearing authorizes immediate borrowing of a limited amount "only to the extent necessary to avoid immediate and irreparable harm to the estate pending a final hearing."[3] Thus, in most cases, the debtor is able to get a limited amount of DIP funding right away.

In the second step in the process to obtain DIP financing, a permanent or final financing order is entered by the court. This authorizes the borrowing of the full amount of the lender's commitment. This occurs after the court has heard arguments from other creditors who may object to such financing.

DIP financing is governed by Section 364, which has four subsections. Subsections (a) through (d) provide an increasing level of priority and security for the DIP lender. The first form of DIP financing is covered by Section 364(a), financing in the ordinary course of business; it entitles the lender or vendor to administrative expense claims. This form of DIP financing requires no court approval. The purpose of 364(a) DIP financing is to induce vendors (suppliers) to sell on credit to a firm in Chapter 11 so that the firm can maintain working capital requirements.[4] Suppliers often cut off credit to firms prior to bankruptcy to minimize prepetition losses, and they then extend credit following a Chapter 11 filing to gain the benefits of 364(a).

Section 364(b) is similar to Section 364(a), where the court may approve an extension of unsecured credit by a vendor or lender not in the ordinary course of business.[5] Such borrowings could be for a new project or expansion of existing facilities which are in the best interest of the business and capital providers.

In both Section a and b cases, the credit is unsecured, but within the class of unsecured loans it has the first priority along with other administrative claims such as professional fees and costs of administering the estate of the firm. In most cases this level of security is not enough to induce lenders to provide new loans. Financing under Section 364(c) or 364(d) provides better security for new loans, but it also requires prior court approval.

Under Subsection 364(c) the court may authorize DIP credit with a super priority status. Thus, the financing under this subsection enjoys higher seniority as well as enhanced security. Loans under this section may enjoy priority over administrative expenses and a lien on unencumbered assets or a junior lien on encumbered assets or both.

Subsection 364(d) provides the highest level of security for DIP financing because it is secured by a senior or equal lien on the assets that are already subject to a lien. Such a lien is referred to as a *priming lien* and is approved only after stringent conditions are met. These conditions are (1) inability of the debtor to obtain such credit otherwise and (2) adequate protection of the interest of the original holder of the lien; that is, the assets pledged to the existing secured lender have a value in excess of the value of the secured claim.

The majority of DIP financing is under Subsection 364(c) since Section 364(d) financing is very hard to obtain and is a final option for the firm. The firm has to show first that options under Sections 364 (a) to (c) have failed and there are no other alternative forms of financing.

Consider an example with a construction project, such as a hotel, where additional financing is required to complete the project and where completion will lead to a significant increase in the value of the collateral. In this situation the DIP lender may insist on priming the security of the prepetition lender pursuant to 364(d). The prepetition lender must be given notice and adequate protection. The adequate protection provision makes 364(d) financing difficult to obtain because the debtor must show that there will be a sufficient increase in the value of the collateral for the prepetition lender to receive adequate protection. The prepetition lender will also argue that there is no need for the DIP lender to prime its lien if there will be sufficient adequate protection for a lender second in line.

Even though the DIP loans enjoy enhanced security, the DIP lender still faces some risk of loss. The primary source for the repayment of a DIP loan is usually from new credit facilities put in place under a POA. When the borrower emerges from Chapter 11, these new loans take out the DIP loan. The main risk to DIP lenders is that the firm fails to implement a successful POA and is forced to move to Chapter 7 liquidation. DIP lenders might not receive full recovery from any administrative claims or liens granted under Section 364. Further, in the event of liquidation, the DIP lender's super priority status may apply only within the class of unsecured creditors. Also, if the DIP loan is secured by inventory, prepetition lenders and trade creditors can challenge the super priority status of the DIP lender on the inventory claims.

Characteristics of DIP Loans

Chatterjee et al. (2004)[6] conducted a study examining the key characteristics of DIP loans. Some of the key findings of the study are summarized in the following three sections.

DIP Loan Structure

In this section, we provide information on the basic structure of DIP loans.

1. DIP loans typically have a maturity of less than two years and are usually made in the form of revolving lines of credit (RLCs). RLCs can include a letter of credit component and can be accompanied by a term loan.
2. It is rare for a DIP facility to be a stand-alone loan such as a bridge or term loan or for the DIP facility to be in another form of credit such as a standby letter of credit or limited line.[7]

3. The primary purpose of DIP loans is to obtain working capital. The loan purpose of a DIP facility usually restricts the use of funds for working capital needs (more than 63% of DIP facilities restrict the use proceeds for working capital only). About 22% of DIP loans contain a "general corporate use" provision, and 13% of DIP facilities are restricted to operating expenses.

The structure of DIP facilities reduces management's ability to use the proceeds for projects that will not benefit the rehabilitation process of the firm in Chapter 11. The most significant set of restrictions comes from the structure and composition of the loan covenants.

DIP Loan Covenants

The automatic stay provision for Chapter 11 cases eliminates the covenant protections of prepetition lenders. DIP loan covenants effectively reinstate the monitoring provisions of prepetition debt that were suspended by the automatic stay. The DIP facilities can include standard affirmative and negative convents, ensuring that a firm in Chapter 11 maintains usual business requirements, such as financial reporting, and restricts other actions that could harm lenders, such as incurrence of new debt and excessive capital expenditures.

DIP lenders also require the right to inspect books and conduct due diligence of physical inventory. The DIP lender closely monitors cash flows of the firm and the quality of the current assets used as collateral, such as inventory and accounts receivable, in a similar manner to asset-based lenders. This could include close monitoring or even control of accounts receivable or inventory. DIP lenders can also require weekly, monthly, and annual financial reports; consultant and banker's reports; business plans; court motions; applications and financial information filed during reorganization; and material adverse changes.

DIP loans have a greater proportion of negative covenants restricting capital expenditures and disposition of assets compared to similar bank loans and junk bonds. Almost all DIP loans have restrictions on specified operating expenses and operating activities. This compares with only 6% for junk bonds and 67% for bank loans. Further, restrictions on disposition of assets and negative pledges are particularly valuable for the DIP lender since it prevents the firm from diverting or pledging collateral.

DIP Loan Pricing and Fees

DIP financing requires wider interest spreads and greater fees to compensate for higher default risk and monitoring costs. The cost of DIP loans consists of the loan rate and a variety of fees. Generally, there is a commitment and facility (origination and management) fee and an up-front fee expressed as a percentage of the loan.

A DIP loan is typically a floating-rate instrument indexed to the bank's base rate, or LIBOR, or prime rate. Chatterjee et al. (2004) found that the median spread over the T-bill rate is 4.60%. The median commitment and up-front fees are 0.50% and 1.06%, respectively, for DIP loans.

DIP Financing: The Economic Impact

A debate in the law and economics literature centers on the drawbacks and merits of senior and secured financing in general and on DIP financing in particular. One study by Dahiya et al. (2000)[8] examined the merits of DIP financing by distinguishing between firms that obtain DIP financing and firms that don't. The study also examined the turnaround times for firms using DIP financing and the impact of lender relationships.

On the negative side, arguments against secured financing, such as DIP loans, note that such credit provides incentives for managers to undertake risky, possibly negative net present value (NPV) projects (the overinvestment problem). On the positive side, secured financing allows the borrower to undertake positive NPV projects that might be passed up in the absence of senior and secured credit such as DIP financing.

A related question is whether DIP financing prolongs the reorganization process or whether it facilitates a faster conclusion of the bankruptcy legal process. The length of the process can be important because it can affect the eventual outcome (emergence from bankruptcy or liquidation) as well as the value of the firm's assets.

The final outcome and the length of the reorganization process may in turn depend on whether DIP financing is provided by an existing lender or by a lender with no prepetition loans. DIP loans that are provided by prepetition lenders are referred to as "defensive" DIP lending. Loans provided by new lenders are known as "offensive" DIP lending.

Defensive DIP lenders often provide additional funds during Chapter 11 to offset losses incurred on prepetition debt and can reduce some of the complexities surrounding liens and adequate protection for new DIP lenders.[9] Furthermore, the information benefits enjoyed by a lender with prior claims can affect both the likelihood of a firm emerging from Chapter 11 and its time spent in bankruptcy.

An existing (insider) lender would have some prior claims outstanding when it decides to offer DIP financing. An insider lender is also likely to have better private information about its borrower's future prospects compared with a new (outsider) lender, which can lead to faster decision making during the Chapter 11 process.

While many firms receive DIP financing from an existing lender, a significant number obtain it from a lender with whom they have no existing lending relationship. Offensive DIP lenders may provide these funds purely for profit or for strategic reasons if there is a goal of acquiring a large stake in the borrower after bankruptcy.[10]

What Do We Know about DIP Financing?

Studies have found a number of other important characteristics of DIP financing, which are summarized in the following list:

1. DIP lenders seek collateral as a key source of repayment; therefore, they prefer to lend against liquid assets. Research has found that the ability to obtain DIP financing is positively related to the ratio of current assets to total assets and the level of working capital.
2. The information advantage gained by lenders with prior relationships results in insiders lending more frequently to small firms. As prior lenders, they are also more likely to finance prepackaged filings.
3. DIP financing is associated with a higher probability of the firm's emergence from bankruptcy as well as a shorter time in bankruptcy. This is the case for both firms that reorganize and firms that liquidate.
4. The effect of reduced time in bankruptcy for the firm is strengthened when the DIP lender also has a prior lending relationship with the firm.
5. DIP financing is typically not required for prepackaged bankruptcy plans as the Chapter 11 process is too short to require additional financing beyond what has been negotiated in the POA and the borrower continues to have access to its existing credit lines.

Overall, the empirical studies have found that DIP financiers help facilitate a more successful bankruptcy process by identifying firms with positive NPV projects and permitting reduced time in bankruptcy. Thus, the role of DIP financing will play an important role in credit markets as the recent "credit crisis" and slowdown in the U.S. economy will result in a new wave of Chapter 11 filings.

18

DISTRESSED INVESTING

David J. Breazzano

President and Chief Investment Officer,
DDJ Capital Management, LLC

Distressed investing is the investment strategy which, at its core, is buying securities, most often the debt, of companies whose business model has changed substantially for the worse from its initial plan. Distressed investing is not a new investment strategy; it has been in existence as long as there has been debt in the financial markets. What is unique about distressed investing is its scope. Distressed investing spans the fields of finance and law, and it is closely intertwined with bankruptcy law. Hence, it is unique to every country in the same way that bankruptcy laws can vary significantly across countries. In this chapter, we provide an overview of distressed investing in the United States, including the economic and regulatory framework, historical cycle, company distressed stages, and investment strategies and vehicles.

Distressed Investing

Distressed investing is not solely about investing in bankrupt firms. Firms may take a long time to fall into bankruptcy though their end fate may be known well before then. Hence, firms are considered to be distressed based on the price of their risk. There are multiple ways to define distressed investing. Some might define it as targeting debt securities trading at a substantial spread (i.e., 1,000 bps), while others may define the debt securities as trading on a dollar price instead of a yield. Some investors would include equities as well as debt securities in their universe. For our purposes, it is when the target company will need to restructure its balance sheet and/or have a substantial capital infusion in order to meet its obligations in a timely manner and avoid a default.

History of Distressed Investing

Contrary to popular belief, distressed investing has occurred for hundreds, and perhaps thousands, of years, most likely beginning shortly after the very first loan was made. In the United States, a number of our first congressmen and other government officials were distressed investors and perhaps even "insider traders" through trading in the continental currency. Alexander Hamilton convinced Congress that the new country should repay its revolutionary war debts in full, including the full backing of the continental currency. Immediately afterward, a number of congressmen and officials headed to the western frontier to purchase the old continental currency (at a substantial discount) from unsuspecting holders, knowing full well that they would be paid in full by the young government. Though laws have fortunately been enacted to prevent this type of unfair trading now, our country has a long tradition of distressed investing at all levels.

Distressed investors have been very active and successful following the turning points of "boom to bust" in economic cycles because access to capital stops and prevents many weaker companies from refinancing, which steers them toward or near bankruptcy. These turning points stretch back centuries. During the late 1980s and early 1990s, the U.S. economy experienced the implosion of Drexel Burnham Lambert, a savings and loan and commercial banking crisis, and spectacular leveraged buyout (LBO) blow-ups.

There unfortunately is a cyclical pattern to the market. As the capital markets strengthen, credit discipline deteriorates as investors hunt for yield. The early 1990s saw large-scale defaults, followed by a recovery and a gradual deterioration of credit quality. This led to the next credit crunch at the turn of the century, which was caused by the Russian debt crises, followed by the demise of the Long-Term Capital Management (LTCM), and finally the bursting of the telecom and dot.com bubble. (What is interesting is the typical lag between the height of financial crisis and the subsequent peak in bankruptcy, which usually occurs a year or two later.) Once again, this credit crunch allowed investors to acquire distressed securities at significant discounts as the default rate soared into double digits, but the opportunity was of a shorter duration than its decade-earlier predecessor. The double-digit default rate in 2002 soon declined into single digits, immediately returning stability to the capital markets. At that point, the yield spreads contracted to near historic lows and distress opportunities became much fewer. The substantial discounts, consequently, were bid away (or prices rose), and the actual and expected returns declined considerably through the balance of the decade. Heading into 2005 and 2006 as credit risk became less of a concern, credit disciplines of lenders and bond investors began to erode, and deal quality deteriorated. Thus capital markets were once again set up for the next credit crunch. In the summer of 2007, the subprime mortgage market began to implode. Financial firms became suspect, and Bear Stearns was rescued by J.P. Morgan with government assistance. The next credit crunch began.

The financial collapse in 2008 was triggered by a financial market meltdown. The crisis in the financial markets led to a sharp downturn in the real economy. What was unique about the global financial crisis in 2008 was the inaccessiblity of capital markets coupled with (or causing) an economic slowdown. This double hit of slow growth and lack of financing options lead to a spike in bankruptcies. There were excellent distressed investing opportunities in the 2008 and 2009 time frame, like GM and CIT, but the window was short-lived as investors rushed in to purchase distressed credits, like a pared-down GM. This rush of distressed capital spilled over to the high-yield market in the form of more demand, causing one of the largest new-issue calendars in history during 2009. The source of capital provided by the high-yield market has led to much lower levels of bankruptcies than initially predicted.

That being said, it is important to note that distressed investment opportunities can happen away from the traditional bust cycle. Even during a strong economy, companies can get into trouble through poor management, overleveraged balance sheets, operational problems, tough competitive pressures, litigation, and many other factors. While a recession and/or credit crunch leads to increased defaults, some level of corporate defaults exists at all times, thus providing potential opportunities for distressed investors. However, when the default rate spikes into the double digits on a percentage basis, which seems to occur every 7–10 years, distressed investing activity increases dramatically.

Bankruptcy Law

Bankruptcy courts are courts of equity as opposed to courts of law. That is, judges have broad equitable powers and are not obligated to adhere to a strict interpretation of law. For example, leases that state in strict language in their documentation about what happens in a bankruptcy can be voided and restructured by the judge. The uncertainty regarding the judge's decisions means that everything is negotiable and pushes the constituents toward consensus. This is evident from the GM and Chrysler bankruptcies, during which some of the fundamentals of bankruptcy law seemed to be thrown aside.

The uncertainty of outcome is almost written into the bankruptcy code itself as the code is fraught with contradictions. For example, the dual voting procedure is a conundrum. In order to protect larger creditors, a two-thirds vote of the claim amount is required to approve the plan. But in order to protect smaller creditors, the bankruptcy plan also requires 51% of individual creditors (a numeracy vote) for approval. A second contradiction is dual protection. Votes of both large and small creditors have to pass; this is designed to promote compromise and consensus. Another wild card issue is that judges often have limited business backgrounds and cannot be familiar with all aspects of a case. Hence, the constituencies in a bankruptcy proceeding often are uncertain of how the judge may decide an issue, and that uncertainty encourages settlement before the matter gets to the judge.

Bankruptcy Laws and Capital Markets

Bankruptcy laws are integral to the capital markets and the broader economy. Such laws define creditors' and other constituency rights when a borrower is unable to honor its obligations in a timely fashion. Many countries have inadequate or unenforceable bankruptcy laws that have hindered the development of their capital markets. Historically, the alternative to modern bankruptcy laws was debtors' prison. In fact, one of the original American colonies, Georgia, was founded as a debtors' colony, as was the British colony of Australia. A history of debtors settling the United States may have contributed to the inclusion of a bankruptcy law provision in the U.S. Constitution. There was a general belief in American society that debtors should be given a second chance.

While bankruptcy law was important enough to make it into the U.S. Constitution, there have been few significant revisions. The U.S. Bankruptcy Code was substantially rewritten in 1898, 1978, and 2005, but there have been periods when the United States did not have federal bankruptcy laws in effect. The current bankruptcy code has two basic chapters that govern common corporate bankruptcy: Chapter 7 (liquidation) and Chapter 11 (reorganization). There are many other provisions of the bankruptcy code that govern other forms of bankruptcy, but the one we primarily discuss in this chapter is Chapter 11 reorganization, the "second chance."

The bankruptcy process and distressed investors play important roles in finance and the U.S. economy. The bankruptcy process is designed to provide an orderly resolution of a potentially chaotic situation when a company is unable to meet its financial obligations. This process allows all the parties to step back and attempt to negotiate a plan that will maximize the value of a company's assets and thereby recovery to the various constituencies. Other countries' insolvency systems often force liquidation at an inopportune time, frequently causing a substantial erosion of value and creditor recovery. The U.S. system attempts to preserve value and allow for a more rational restructuring of a company's operations, ultimately preserving a number of jobs and allowing a continuation of the business in a more streamlined fashion.

The law constantly evolves to address ever-changing social considerations. For example, in the early 1980s a number of companies, such as Continental Airlines, used the bankruptcy code to abrogate their labor union contracts. Following a major lobbying effort, Congress modified the code to make it much more difficult for companies to break union contracts through the bankruptcy process. Additionally, net operating tax losses were often transferred, or "sold," as part of the reorganization plan; this happened in the Braniff Airline case. Congress subsequently modified the rules regarding the use and transfer of net operating losses (NOLs) in order to make it much more difficult for the transferee to realize value from them. In 2005, Congress modified several aspects of the code to improve landlord and vendor rights as well as limit the time period in which the debtor has the exclusive right to file a plan. This was a result of companies staying in bankruptcy longer than they needed to while different stakeholders vied for control or economic gain.

The summary point is that the law is dynamic, and one should expect that the bankruptcy code frequently will be modified by Congress and/or judicial decisions. In fact we might expect that one day the law will be revamped in its entirety and a comprehensive new law will take its place. However, for the time being, we operate under the existing rules based on a century of buildup, and this chapter touches on a few of the more important basic concepts.

When a company defaults and possibly files for bankruptcy protection, its original lenders often are upset, and such emotions can make the ensuing negotiations difficult. Creditors often believe that management underperformed and perhaps misled the lenders. Managers in turn may feel betrayed by banks or their vendors because they were not given a little latitude to get through what they may consider a short-term liquidity issue. This animosity can impede constructive discussions regarding a reorganization.

The bankruptcy code, if used properly, can preserve and create substantial value for the debtor company and its constituencies by creating a pause so that the business can be objectively reassessed. First of all, if a company defaults, it can become a very chaotic time. Often banks and vendors are making threats in order to get paid, customers are nervous, suppliers are threatening to stop shipment, and so forth. When a bankruptcy petition is filed, all litigation is stayed. The company is allowed to catch its breath and begin to formulate a rational approach to resolving its issues. The judge also has broad powers to help preserve and help create value for the company or estate. For example, uneconomic leases and other contracts can be rejected, and certain leases can be sold or assigned even if the contract restricts such action. Astute distressed investors often aggressively utilize such provisions of the bankruptcy code to get out of bad contracts and sell off money-losing and/or noncore divisions that absorb an inordinate amount of management time and attention. The bankruptcy process is a good way to rationalize a company's operations, allowing it to undertake certain appropriate steps that cannot be accomplished outside such a process.

Bankruptcy: The Basics

First of all, the bankrupt company is called the "debtor" or "debtor-in-possession" because it is in possession of the assets of the estate. A loan made to the debtor after the filing of the bankruptcy petition is called a "debtor-in-possession loan," or DIP loan. Those that are owed money by the debtor are called "creditors."

Generally speaking, creditors are entitled to a recovery based on the "absolute priority rule." This concept states that the most senior creditors are entitled to a full recovery before subordinate or junior creditors are entitled to any recovery. If senior and other creditors have been satisfied in full, any value remaining will go to equity holders.

Unfortunately, determining creditor priorities often can be difficult and nebulous. For example, some creditors may be secured by a first mortgage on certain assets and therefore are entitled to the value of those assets before any other unsecured creditors, even if such unsecured creditors are deemed to be "senior" creditors. If the collateral value is insufficient to cover the mortgage holder, the deficiency amount becomes an unsecured claim associated with the balance of the debtor's assets. In some cases there are not only first mortgages, but second and third mortgages, each with a declining priority in the collateral. Also, there can be different pools of collateral securing different debt obligations. For example, a bank line may be secured by a first lien on working capital, such as inventory and receivables, while a term loan lender may be secured by a first lien on real estate and other physical assets such as factory and equipment. In some instances each of these lenders may take a second lien position behind each other with respect to that collateral.

Another complexity can involve senior versus subordinate lenders and bondholders. Contractual subordination typically is a contract between two classes of lenders whereby the subordinate creditor agrees that any recovery under a plan of reorganization or otherwise will be turned over to the specified senior lender until that senior lender has been paid in full. Other creditors in the same bankruptcy case may not benefit from such subordination provisions, such as trade vendors. Therefore, a senior lender may receive full repayment while a trade vendor may receive a partial recovery, and the contractually subordinated creditor could recover little to nothing in that same case. Consequently, first, second, and third liens; senior creditors; senior subordinated creditors; junior subordinated creditors; other general unsecured claims (such as trade claims and other deficiency claims); preferred stock; and common stock all involved in the same case can cause the outcome under the absolute priority rule to be very difficult to determine.

For example: Assume that a debtor has senior bank debt of $100 million, trade claims of $20 million, and subordinated notes of $200 million, followed by common stock. If the total value of the estate is $160 million, all creditors in the aggregate would receive a 50% recovery on their claims. However, reflecting the subordination of the notes to the bank debt, the banks should receive 100% recovery, the trade keeps its 50%, and the subordinated notes recover only 25%. This occurs by virtue of the notes turning over part of their recovery to the banks until the banks are paid in full. The trade typically is not a beneficiary of the subordination, so the trade creditors maintain their 50% recovery.

One of the fundamentals of bankruptcy laws is that creditors with higher seniority receive a higher recovery rate. This basic notion is now uncertain. With the Chrysler and GM bankruptcies, the unions were able to negotiate significantly higher recovery rates than other more senior claimants. This may be a fundamental reinterpretation of bankruptcy law or may be unique because of the position taken by these firms' most senior lender—the U.S. government—or the bargaining power of the union in these situations.

The bankruptcy code is designed to promote compromise and a consensual resolution by instituting a plan of reorganization. For example in order for a plan to be accepted by an impaired creditor class, it requires two types of votes: (1) approval by two-thirds of the aggregate claim amount of that class and (2) a majority in numbers of creditors voting in that impaired class (unimpaired creditors do not vote). If a plan does not receive the requisite votes from all impaired creditor classes under both of these tests, the judge can "cram down" a plan on nonconsenting (by impaired) junior classes by making certain determinations of fact. Such cram-downs are often difficult, incur considerable legal expense, and create uncertainty, so creditors often seek the approval of junior classes by providing them a modest recovery in order to avoid the cost and uncertainty of a cram-down hearing. Such a demand by junior classes for this recovery is often referred to as "hold-up value."

The two-thirds voting requirement gives a certain amount of power to the holder of one-third or more of an impaired class. Such holdings are often referred to as "blocking positions" because the holder of these claims can vote against, or block, the approval of a reorganization plan. However, a blocking position does not allow the approval of that class because of the numeracy test of 50% of those creditors needing to approve it. So blocking positions can really block only a plan and not force the approval of a plan. Nonetheless, blocking positions often are an important strategic holding because all the constituencies must negotiate with the holder of the blocking position in order to achieve a consensual plan.

Fulcrum Class

The most senior impaired class usually is the key class in a reorganization plan. As a constituency, this is often referred to as the "fulcrum class." For example, if the assets of a bankrupt company are worth $100 million and the company has $50 million of senior secured bank debt and $100 million of subordinated bonds and the balance in common stock, the fulcrum security would be the bonds. This is because the $50 million of bank debt would be repaid in full (or reinstated) from the $100 million in asset value, and the balance of $50 million of value would be allocated to the bonds for 50 cents on the dollar recovery. Therefore, the holders of senior bank debt would not be entitled to vote because they are unimpaired. But approval of the bondholders would be required because this class is impaired. The bonds are the fulcrum class.

The fulcrum class is often sought after by distressed investors in order to gain control of the reorganized company. Of course, challenges exist in accurately identifying the fulcrum class when there are multiple classes of creditors and various pools of collateral and a complex business that make it difficult to determine precisely what the value is and which impaired class ultimately will receive the majority of the postreorganization stock.

Bankruptcy: The Life Cycle

Generally, a bankruptcy follows a typical life cycle. The company files a petition under Chapter 11, obtains a DIP loan, operates as a debtor-in-possession, negotiates a plan of reorganization with its creditors, and files a plan and disclosure statement. The constituencies may challenge various activities of the debtor during the proceedings. Near the end, constituencies may challenge the plan and the adequacy of the disclosure statement. Following a disclosure statement hearing, the judge must approve such a document before it is distributed to all parties eligible to vote on the reorganization. After an appropriate solicitation period, votes are tabulated, and if the adequate number of votes is received, the judge holds a confirmation hearing, approves the plan, and establishes an effective date (at least 10 days later) when the company will emerge from Chapter 11 as a reorganized business.

Prepackaged and Prearranged Bankruptcies

Various parties will attempt to streamline this process in order to reduce the legal and other administrative costs associated with a bankruptcy and the uncertainty and negative impact that bankruptcy could have on the operations of the business. A way to do this is through a prepackaged bankruptcy, often referred to as a "prepack." In such a case, all the parties agree to a plan of reorganization and a disclosure statement prior to the actual filing of the bankruptcy petition. Therefore, the company can be in and out of bankruptcy in as little time as a few months and substantially minimize the business risk and cost of the proceedings. Often prepacks are difficult to achieve, so the next closest thing is a "prearranged bankruptcy" in which most of the constituencies have agreed to the plan of reorganization, but a little more time is needed to finalize all the terms of the plan and the preparation of the disclosure statement. A prearranged bankruptcy will take longer to consummate than a prepack. However, a proper prearranged bankruptcy can reduce the negative publicity associated with bankruptcy and its adverse impact on the debtor's business, as well as reduce much of the administrative costs of the bankruptcy.

If a prepack or prearranged bankruptcy cannot be achieved, the company could face a "free fall" bankruptcy, in which a few or many constituencies are fighting with each other over their respective recoveries and/or priorities within the reorganization. Free falls can become very costly because of the amount of litigation involved and can be very damaging to the underlying business as customers and suppliers become concerned with the viability of the company and its ability to successfully reorganize. Consequently, many distressed investors attempt to achieve a quick reorganization, but this is not always possible.

Chapter 7 Alternative

Up to now the discussion has been from the point of view of Chapter 11, the reorganization. If a plan of reorganization cannot be achieved, the bankrupt company will be forced to liquidate. Corporate liquidations are usually accomplished under Chapter 7 of the bankruptcy code. If a judge determines that a Chapter 11 reorganization cannot be achieved, the judge can convert the case to a Chapter 7 liquidation. Such a conversion can cause a substantial evaporation of recovery value for all parties concerned, and, therefore, most constituencies seek to avoid liquidations. The threat of liquidation is often used by out-of-the-money subordinated classes. This tactic is sometimes referred to as the "nuclear threat" because it is an attempt to achieve some hold-up value in order to gain support.

363 Sales

Assets can be sold fairly efficiently under Chapter 11, thereby avoiding many of the pitfalls of a Chapter 7 proceeding. A common provision used is section 363 of the code, often referred to as a "363 sale" or auction. This is becoming a more frequently used method to quickly move a firm through bankruptcy.

Section 363 essentially allows a judge to hold an auction for an asset or various assets. There are many instances in which a substantial proceed can be earned from a sale and enhance the recoveries of the creditors at large. Typically a 363 auction will have an initial "stalking horse" bidder. Such a bidder will provide a price and then be entitled to a break-up fee if another entity ultimately outbids it in the auction. Secured creditors often can credit bid for their collateral in such an auction. A "credit bid" is where the lender uses all or part of its claim as consideration, instead of cash, to acquire the asset. A credit bid can be attractive if a distressed investor acquired the claim at a substantial discount, thereby allowing the investor to buy the asset in the auction at a lower price than if this investor were to use cash. A significant benefit of a 363 sale is that it removes all claims, thus clearing up the ownership of assets by removing liens and outside claims.

Distressed Investors in the Bankruptcy Process

Distressed investors can perform a valuable function in the restructuring process by purchasing the bank's or other claims and thereby replacing a creditor that may have some historical baggage with a fresh new investor that is more focused on moving forward. Further, distressed investors often have greater flexibility than banks, insurance companies, trade vendors, and/or other original lenders. Distressed investors often can infuse fresh capital. They also are more willing to convert their debt claims into equity, allowing substantial deleveraging of the restructured company. Banks, on the other hand, are more reluctant to "forgive" debt by converting it to equity. This is because of regulatory and often internal policy constraints. Trade vendors typically are more interested in receiving cash as opposed to converting their claims into equity. Consequently, distressed investors provide a new and fresh approach in a restructuring as they have much greater flexibility in designing a more optimal balance sheet and, ultimately, a better plan of reorganization. As we discuss later, certain distressed investors are interested in owning and rehabilitating a target bankrupt company for the creation of long-term value, whereas original lenders often are interested in quickly recovering as much cash as possible in the short run.

The value of distressed investors can be seen over the long term in certain cyclical industries or in the aftermath of unanticipated misfortune, such as an unfavorable litigation outcome. For example, if a company finds itself overleveraged as a result of an unexpected decline in its business or the weak part of a business cycle or because of the unexpected poor performance of a division or acquisition, the presence of distressed investors may allow that company to successfully reorganize, cutting its debt service requirements and surviving to prosper another day. A less tolerant lender may not allow such a company to survive a temporary decline, and, therefore, potential real future value may never materialize. Recently, the very cyclical U.S. steel industry was consolidated as a result of the efforts of distressed investors. Asbestos litigation has forced many otherwise healthy companies into bankruptcy proceedings. Many of these companies were able to successfully emerge without liquidating. This greater risk tolerance on the part of certain investors allows businesses to partially finance their operations with debt, realizing that a temporary downturn or setback might not be fatal. This allows certain businesses to accept more risk in their capital structure in the United States and could provide substantial returns in the future, thus benefiting the overall economy.

Such benefits provided by distressed investors can have a positive impact on the broader economy. They provide companies and industries with a second chance. They facilitate the growth of the debt markets in the United States and have contributed to the growth of more complex and accommodating financial instruments such as the overall growth in the high-yield debt market in the past 30 years. The growth in deferred pay bonds, such as PIK bonds and toggle bonds, allows greater access to capital, fueling more robust capital markets with benefits to the broader economy. If a company's lenders were less tolerant and a default resulted in liquidation, the company might be potentially less willing to incur financial risk, which may hinder the long-term growth of various industries as well as the overall economy. Clearly, accommodating credit markets can create abuses with adverse consequences, but ensuing credit crunches typically last only a year or two, while the intervening bull markets last many more years, creating substantial economic expansion.

Distressed Returns

It must be remembered that the goal of all investors should be to make a fair return for the level of risk accepted. Distressed investing is no exception. Therefore, distressed investors should always focus on maximizing their risk-adjusted returns. Distressed investing is a pure form of deep-value investing. The targeted companies have experienced substantially unfortunate events and a lot of bad news, and their securities are often trading at substantial discounts. If the underlying business has true value, astute distressed investors can acquire a claim to those assets at a substantial discount while similar assets could be acquired if the company was perceived as healthy and was trading on a major stock exchange.

The challenge of bankruptcy investing is seeing past the bad news and recognizing the upside potential that could result if the company is successfully reorganized. For example, if a certain type of manufacturer has an enterprise value of eight times EBITDA trading on the NYSE—but in the same industry a similar company that is experiencing financial duress, or even a default under its bank agreement, may have bank debt that can be purchased at a discount that would allow the investor to create similar assets at four or five times EBITDA—all that would be required would be for the second company to successfully reorganize and then have the market recognize that the two similar companies are trading at a substantial difference and bid up the equity of the reorganized company to perhaps six or seven times EBITDA so that the distressed investor would make a nice return.

The distressed investor must determine if the troubled company's assets are of comparable value to those of the healthy company and that the company can be successfully reorganized. In order to do this, distressed investors must be good at discreetly acquiring claims and valuation analysis and must have a good understanding of and the ability to navigate the bankruptcy process, determining how long the restructuring will take (time value of money is very important), having the skills to sell the securities at the end of the process, and hopefully adding operating value during the process.

Success often requires monitoring target companies long in advance. Deal flow is important and can come from many sources. A common source is the overall high-yield debt market. But many attractive situations can occur in private companies without public debt or equity securities. Bankruptcy attorneys, crisis managers, retail inventory liquidators, and investment bankers all could be good sources of deal flow. The more options a distressed investor has to review, in theory, the greater the potential for strong risk-adjusted returns.

Distressed investors, once they target a situation, will determine what range of terminal value they expect to achieve and how long the reorganization process will take. They will discount those cash flows at the target return requirement. If they can acquire the fulcrum security (or another class that is trading at an appropriate discount) at a price below the calculated net present value, such an investment should be made.

Once the distressed investment is acquired, or even while the position is being built, the distressed investor should endeavor to speed the entire process and attempt to guide it toward the optimal balance sheet and business profile. The investor should aggressively use the bankruptcy code to rationalize the business (i.e., shut down money-losing stores, restaurants, factories, reject uneconomical leases, etc.) such that when the company emerges from reorganization, it will have a more efficient operation and an optimal balance sheet so that the distressed investor can exit at the highest possible price. Clearly such investing is more of an art than a science, so there is no good substitute for experience.

The Investment Vehicles

Many distressed investors operate through investment vehicles that are similar to private equity limited partnerships, allowing for a long-term investment horizon. Others deploy their capital through shorter-term vehicles, such as hedge funds, that have annual or more frequent liquidity options for their partners, thus forcing a shorter-term investment horizon. Consequently, the type of investment vehicle that the distressed investor is managing will have a significant impact on the style of investing the manager should follow.

Matching the type of investment or investment style with the investment vehicle is important. A private equity type of limited partnership matches well with a long-term, illiquid, control distressed approach. A hedge fund type of vehicle with liquidity requirements is better suited to a more liquid trading approach. The introduction of leverage into the investment vehicle, while potentially magnifying gains, clearly also adds risk. In volatile markets that exist during credit crunches, the unforgiving nature of leverage could cause the demise of the distressed investor though margin calls that do not allow the investments to mature, even if the value ultimately would have been attainable given enough time. Market disruptions create both opportunity and challenges for distressed investors.

Not only is it important to match the investment vehicle to the investment approach, but it also is important for the distressed investor to have educated clients. Many distressed investments generate a "J-curve" return pattern. In other words, such investments often trade lower (or are quoted lower with no real trading volume) during the uncertainty (and lack of information) associated with a bankruptcy proceeding. It often is when the company is close to emerging from Chapter 11 that the market recognizes the value and the new reorganization securities trade up. Further, some distressed investors encourage the temporary drop in price so that they can continue to acquire such claims at even more favorable levels. If clients are unfamiliar with the J-curve, they may become disenchanted with the investment or the distressed manager and may withdraw from the fund, thus creating disruption and possible loss of value.

Managing a Distressed Portfolio

A good professional manager will constantly monitor the overall portfolio and balance the winners and (hopefully infrequent) losers. Managers should focus on appropriate diversification, such as by industry and by issuer, so that an unexpected negative event in a particular holding or sector does not have a devastating effect on the overall portfolio. The same basic portfolio management techniques used by more traditional fund mangers should be used by distressed investors. However, because of economic trends, distressed investors often tend to be concentrated in certain sectors (i.e., defaults may be concentrated in auto, airlines, etc.).

Unfortunately, not all investments work out as originally contemplated, so a good trait for distressed investors to have is knowing when to recognize failure and to "cut and run." Also, it is important to stay current with trends in the marketplace as well as regulations, legal rulings, and other changes in the law. Furthermore, it is important not to get caught up in certain broad market trends, because distressed investing at its heart is a form of contrarian investing. As with all forms of investing, discipline is important. One must be careful to avoid the temptation to modify assumptions in order to justify an investment. When distressed investors (or any investors) have spent a substantial amount of time and resources researching an investment target, but the price that the claim can be purchased at has not declined to the targeted level, there can be a temptation to adjust one's assumptions in order to justify paying up to acquire the claim. This temptation must be avoided.

Distressed Targets

The ideal candidate for distressed investing is the ever-prized "good company with a bad balance sheet." The bankruptcy process is ideally suited to deleverage such a company so that the plan of reorganization can deliver a good balance sheet. Unfortunately, good companies that have bad balance sheets often start to develop operational problems that can obfuscate an otherwise strong business. When a company begins to have liquidity issues or has an approaching debt maturity that cannot readily be satisfied, management often will divert cash from operations in order to fund the debt service requirement. Capital expenditures can be cut and trade vendors can be stretched, all in an effort to make the next payments so as to keep the banks at bay. If this company is publicly traded, its stock may trade down significantly, making stock options worthless, and key management may depart to work for healthier competitors or other companies, thereby eroding management talent. All of these factors can cause the company's underlying business to deteriorate to the point where it is difficult to determine if it has a good underlying business. Unfortunately, good companies with bad balance sheets tend to be the exception. Most distressed situations are more problematic.

Companies can get into financial trouble for many reasons. It could be a failed leveraged buyout (LBO) in which the company was overleveraged as a result of such a transaction and could not support its capital structure. It could be a failed roll-up in which the company sought to consolidate its industry by acquiring smaller rivals with the objective of becoming the largest company in its industry, becoming a price leader, and/or realizing operating synergies. Unfortunately, many roll-ups do fail as the acquiring company may inadvertently overpay for its acquisitions, perhaps financing them with too much debt; its acquisitions may have different and conflicting management styles or culture; may have a different and perhaps inaccurate accounting system; and/or may prove to be more problematic in integrating into the consolidation than expected.

Companies can be blindsided by regulatory changes or intense foreign competition. Perhaps the quickest way into default is through poor management. Incompetent management can destroy value very quickly. Some companies also suffer from accounting or other fraud that is difficult to detect. Often such fraud is encouraged by poor underlying operations and management's attempt to hide it. One needs to perform thorough due diligence to make sure that there is not a more severe underlying problem that caused the default. Changing industry conditions or regulations and even poor management can create good distressed investment opportunities if claims can be acquired at an appropriate discount. But such situations require more hands-on involvement than simply fixing the balance sheet.

Distressed investors must analyze all major contracts—are there certain leases that have real value and can be sold; are there certain business locations that are unprofitable and the leases can be rejected; are there noncore divisions that can be shut down or divested? This is all part of the analytical process. Is there an unprofitable business division that obfuscates a good core profitable operation?

Time also is important. If there is litigation or an unreasonable participant in the process, the bankruptcy could drag on for years and substantially reduce any returns. Generally, the time involved to complete a restructuring is substantial—not only does one have to look at the issues and assess the people involved, but one must also view the jurisdiction the case was filed in because certain courts can be viewed as procreditor or prodebtor. Also, certain jurisdictions can at times find themselves inundated with many cases that can clog the court dockets.

Successful distressed investors must be experts at determining the ultimate enterprise value. The value of the underlying business or asset is what typically drives the process. For example, if there is adequate value so that subordinate classes can receive some recovery, then they may be more reasonable and work with other constituencies to complete the restructuring. Alternatively, if they perceive the value to be inadequate, these parties may become disruptive in the overall process—the bankruptcy process involves a substantial cost resulting from fees of attorneys and other professionals, and if the enterprise value of the estate does not support the costs of a prolonged process, it could result in a liquidation, with little recovery to creditors.

Distressed Valuation

There are number of ways to determine the value of an estate, but recognize that doing so is an art and not a science. A good baseline is to determine what a reasonable liquidation value might be. For example, for what value could the business or assets be sold in the short run? This provides a valuation for a worst-case recovery. Distressed investors must also look to determine a longer-term going concern value—in other words, if the business can be improved through the bankruptcy process and more optimal balance sheets can be created, the company may be able to exit bankruptcy, motivate management with new stock options or other equity incentives, catch up on deferred capital expenditures, and secure more favorable vendor terms. Often a business's operations can improve once it exits Chapter 11.

The distressed investor can realize its investment by selling its new securities in either the public or private market or by selling the entire company just as a traditional private equity investor would do. Reorganized companies can be sold to strategic investors, such as competitors, suppliers, or customers looking for vertical or horizontal integrations. Reorganized companies can also complete IPOs so that the parties can exit through the public markets. In addition, there is a provision in the bankruptcy code that allows securities issued pursuant to a plan of reorganization to be publicly traded. Therefore, a restructured company could become public through the bankruptcy process.

The distressed investor should evaluate its various options to maximize the ultimate recovery. At various points in the capital market cycles, financial buyers, such as private equity and LBO funds, are willing to pay more than strategic buyers and the public market are. At other times the public markets or strategic buyers may provide the highest value. The distressed investor should analyze its various exit opportunities (IPO, sale to competitor, LBO) and design a balance sheet and business plan consistent with the optimal exit strategy in order to maximize value. For example, if comparable companies with the highest enterprise value in their industry have capital structures with 50% debt and 50% equity, the reorganization plan should be designed to mirror this. Alternatively, at various points in the market cycles, higher or lower leverage may result in a higher enterprise value. The distressed investor should take advantage of its ability to design the optimal capital structure and clean up certain factors that may impair exit value such as resolving environmental claims, tort litigation, and divestitures of certain unprofitable divisions or units. It is important to use the process to position the company to achieve the highest possible exit value.

These considerations help guide the research and valuation process. Distressed investors employ the valuation techniques used by traditional debt and equity investors. However, certain assumptions need to be made regarding exit valuation, the duration of the process, the administrative costs of the legal proceedings, the amount of cash build (or burn) during the proceeding, and so on. Such valuation analysis and assumptions are dependent on the issues of each particular case—what caused the company's problems, are they solvable and how quickly, who are the other constituencies and what are their agendas, where did the company file its petition, and so on. The world constantly evolves, but there is no substitute for experience.

Two Basic Distressed Investing Approaches

There are two basic approaches to distressed investing: control and passive distressed investing. At one extreme is a passive trading approach in which the distressed investor will generally purchase public securities in a distressed situation at substantial discounts with the goal of selling these securities at a profit when the distressed situation improves (usually as a result of restructuring efforts undertaken by others). Such an investor relies on the efforts of others in the restructuring process such as restructuring professionals, crisis managers, attorneys, bankers, or other more active distressed investors, essentially piggybacking on their efforts. At the other extreme are control distressed investors, seeking to gain control and possibly own the distressed company by acquiring its fulcrum and other securities and then converting them to a control equity position pursuant to the reorganization. There are many distressed investors that fall in between these two approaches, taking advantage of relative value opportunity when various securities and claims may be mispriced during the course of the reorganization process. Sometimes such investors must be prepared to take a more active approach in the reorganization, ranging from serving on creditors' committees and/or gaining a blocking position to influence the restructuring and maybe positioning themselves to take control of the reorganized company.

Certain investors that initially intend to take a relatively passive approach can find themselves forced into a more active role. This relates to the old saying, "A long-term investment is a short-term one that went bad." Last, there are many unintended holders of distressed paper, such as workout people at bond or loan funds and banks that become involved in the process. Since these are unintentional holders, they are excluded from our discussion.

Control Approach

Control distressed investors seek to own the target company by acquiring the fulcrum security and then converting it into equity in order to gain control—perhaps majority and/or total ownership. Some control investors will seek to buy the entire company or division through a section 363 auction or sponsor a plan of reorganization in which they offer cash or new securities to the creditors to fund the plan. Such control investors believe that the distressed market provides a very attractive mechanism to acquire corporate assets relatively inexpensively. The creditors and other constituents in these situations often are not interested in remaining involved with the company over the long term.

An astute distressed investor can benefit from these motivated sellers by gaining control of the underlying assets at a very attractive price. These control investors often have a stable of management talent that can be drawn upon to help stabilize and then grow the business operations once the company is reorganized. This approach is very similar to the objective of traditional private equity firms that acquire companies, often through leveraged transactions, usually through an auction or competitive bidding process. In a distress situation, the valuations typically are lower, but there are the numerous challenges relating to rehabilitating a troubled company.

Such a distressed investor must appropriately value the business, have a plan for rehabilitating its operations, be prepared to make management changes or enhancements, be prepared to infuse additional capital, and be very familiar with the intricacies of the bankruptcy and restructuring processes. A primary challenge is to determine if the business can be stabilized and whether it can be acquired at an appropriate price. Once the control investor has determined that the target company is attractive, it must be able to gain control of such a company through the purchase of an adequate amount of the fulcrum security and/or become the plan sponsor. Building a blocking position is often the key to success. Such investors though must be disciplined and not overpay for the securities or assets and, therefore, must be prepared to walk away if they cannot pay for the acquisitions at appropriate prices.

False starts are a common occurrence for control distressed investors. A false start occurs when such investors seek to acquire a blocking or control position in a target company's securities, but the price moves up to a level that does not provide adequate return potential, or the circumstances change so that they do not justify paying the current market price. Consequently, these investors are not able to build the control position and may either sell the position at hopefully a profit or sit on the position with the expectation that the price may move down to an appropriate level and that the investors can continue to build the position again. If a control position is not feasible, it is considered a false start. Such control investors often will treat this position similarly to the way a more passive, trading-oriented investor would.

Control investors require a longer-term source of capital. Often such investors' funds are organized with longer-term lockups similar to the structure of private equity partnerships. Mismatching the duration of capital to the investment profile can have severe consequences.

Trading Approach

Distressed investors could employ a trading approach that is more passive than the style of control investors. The trading-oriented investor generally seeks to acquire public securities—usually debt but it can be equity—at attractive discounts with the objective of trading out of them at a profit when the target's prospects appear to brighten. Such an approach often is employed by distressed investors with an investor base that requires short-term liquidity, such as hedge funds that may have annual or even more frequent liquidity options for their investors. Many high-yield desks of broker-dealers will use a trading approach in order to maintain acceptable liquidity for their book and to maintain a reasonable level of confidentiality and discretion relating to their investment activities in this area. Sell-side firms risk alienating some of their clients if they take a very active role in certain distressed situations that might be perceived as a conflict with such buy-side customers.

Trading-oriented distressed investors tend to rely on other constituencies in the distressed situation to help realize value. Such constituencies could include control investors, as well as original bank lenders and high-yield investors who may take an active role in restructuring the company. Many trading-oriented investors will embark on varying levels of activity to attempt to influence a restructuring. This could include helping to organize creditor groups, and even official committees, and the retention of legal and financial advisors by such groups and committees to act as a catalyst for the restructuring. Such investors can even sit on creditor committees and sometimes erect a "Chinese wall" (see Chapter 4 for a discussion of Chinese walls) between the individual who sits on the committee and other individuals at the firm who may retain their freedom to trade the debtor's securities because they are not privy to nonpublic information.

The varying degrees of activities employed by trading investors can blur the distinction between them and control-oriented investors, particularly when control investors have a large number of false starts in their portfolios. Also, a trading strategy can morph into a control strategy if the investment unfolds unsatisfactorily and the investor is forced to become more active in order to protect the initial investment. To paraphrase, "A long-term, control investment is a short-term trade that went bad."

Certain investors participate in the distressed marketplace without necessarily having the objective of rehabilitating a target company. Such investors may seek intracapital arbitrage opportunities where they believe securities within the target company's capital structure are mispriced compared to one another. An example is an investor going long on the high-yield bonds of a distressed company and shorting its common stock based on the belief that the common stock is overvalued in relation to the bonds. In such a situation, depending on the hedge ratio (i.e., the number of shares shorted against each bond), the investors believe that the stock will decline more than the bonds will decline once the situation unfolds (or perhaps the bond might even appreciate). In such a situation an investor can profit even if the aggregate enterprise value of the target company declines.

Some investors can just short securities based on their belief that the security or entire capital structure is overvalued in the marketplace. Such investors actually will root for the demise of the target company. Investors may go long on securities in one company and short the securities of a competitor in troubled industries. Often when an industry is in decline, the relative value of securities of two different companies may create arbitrage opportunities. In such instances, the investor might not be interested in the recovery of the industry or the target companies, but is focused on the closing of the gap of misevaluation. Such relative value investors often are organized as hedge funds but could be proprietary capital-of-trading desks as well as other investors.

Other Investment Approaches

There are many other ways to profit from distressed situations. These include making DIP loans at high interest rates, backstopping rights offerings, financing "going out of business" (GOB) sales, and bidding for parts or all of a troubled company's business operations. The inefficiencies that are common in this field create many opportunities.

New strategies constantly appear based on where we are in the credit cycle. For example, a relatively new phrase called "loan-to-own" has surfaced. Such a loan is one made to a troubled company based on the belief of the lender that such a company soon will default on this obligation. Through the default, the investor hopes to gain control of the target company or to profit from an investment in other securities in the capital structure. An example would be a loan made to a company senior to a substantial portion of that company's preexisting debt (i.e., a first or second lien loan to a company that has a substantial amount of unsecured debt behind it). Sometimes these loans are referred to as "rescue financing" because the proceeds provide the company liquidity for a period of time in the hope that this time will allow the company to turn itself around. Proceeds could be used to make interest payments on secured or unsecured debt or to meet an amortization requirement, thereby deferring a potential default into the future. If the company's operations improve in the near term, it could avoid a default entirely. If the company is unable to improve enough over this time period, it may default, but the rescue lender could be adequately covered by its collateral or its priority in the capital structure, and the subordinated creditors would take the hit. Such rescue loans and loans-to-own often are attractively priced, and if properly structured, can afford the lender adequate downside protection in the worst case or give control of the reorganized company to the lender in the best case.

Some firms employ a variety of approaches, including all the above. Their goal is to take advantage of the inefficiencies that frequently exist when companies experience operating or financial difficulties. Strategies and techniques of distressed investors constantly evolve, which makes this a very exciting investment arena.

Conclusion

Bankruptcy and distressed investing play a pivotal role in our capital markets. They are linked closely to the broader high-yield bond and bank loan market because distressed investors provide the means to restructure viable high-yield companies. The level of bankruptcies and therefore of distressed investing is a highly cyclical business that typically lags behind the capital markets. Distressed investing is unique in that it blends an intense knowledge of finance and bankruptcy law. Distressed investing is not an exact science. The bankruptcy law underpinning distressed investing is fraught with conflicting rules. The interpretation of these conflicting rules can also change over time (as with GM and Chrysler). But correspondingly the potential returns can be significant. There are many types of distressed investors that use both active and passive strategies. The key component of a distressed investing strategy is an understanding of basic valuation, knowledge of the bankruptcy law, and a strong understanding of game theory.

GLOSSARY OF KEY TERMS

asset-backed CDO (ABS CDO): Investment vehicle that invests in asset-backed securities. The underlying collateral pool of assets owned by a CDO is funded on the liability side by the issuance of credit-tranched, structured bonds, secured by the collateral pool of assets. The capitalization of a CDO includes one or more tranches of investment-grade debt, below-investment-grade debt, and equity interests. See also *asset-backed security.*

asset-backed security (ABS): Security whose coupon and principal payments originate from a specific pool of assets (mortgages, credit card debt, auto loans, etc.).

collateralized debt obligation (CDO): Investment vehicle that invests in a diversified pool of assets. The underlying collateral pool of assets owned by a CDO is funded on the liability side by the issuance of credit-tranched, structured bonds secured by the collateral pool of assets. The capitalization of a CDO includes one or more tranches of investment-grade debt, below-investment-grade debt, and equity interests.

collateralized loan obligation (CLO): Investment vehicle that invests in a diversified pool of corporate bank loans (the collateral pool of assets). The collateral pool of assets owned by a CLO is funded on the liability side by the issuance of credit-tranched, structured bonds secured by the collateral pool of assets. The capitalization of a CLO includes one or more tranches of investment-grade debt, below-investment-grade debt, and equity interests.

covenant-lite loan: A leveraged loan with no maintenance tests/covenants to protect the lender.

home equity bond ABS (HEQ ABS): Securitization of subprime mortgage loans. Subprime borrowers typically have blemished or no credit histories, have made small down payments for their loans, and use a high percentage of their income to service their debt.

incurrence test: A test that protects the lender by disallowing additional debt from being incurred unless specific covenants are met.

leveraged loan: Sub-investment-grade-rated bank debt. A senior secured obligation between a corporation and its lending institution (CLOs, prime rate/loan mutual funds, banks, etc.). Leveraged loans typically have the highest seniority in a company's capital structure and are contractually paid before subordinated securities in the event of default.

low documentation mortgage loans (low-docs): Mortgages granted in which documented fields in the borrower's profile such as the primary income are not verified by the lender. A common example of this is the stated income loan.

maintenance test: Test that protects the lender by ensuring that covenants must be met on multiple test dates and not only when new debt is issued.

mortgage lender/originator: Mortgage lenders fund mortgages to prospective homeowners. Mortgage lenders are also known as loan originators because they originate loans for securitization into RMBSs.

overcollateralization: Refers to the extent by which collateral principal (assets) exceeds the principal of rated debt (liabilities) and is usually made possible by the issuance of subordinated debt. Rating agencies look to see whether a structure requires payment of senior debt in full before the reduction of junior debt and determine the conditions under which cash flows are diverted from subordinated classes to protect the senior rated bonds.

"piggyback 1st" loans: First-lien mortgages on properties that have a second-lien mortgage which was taken out to facilitate the closing of the first-lien loan.

residential mortgaged-backed security (RMBS): A security whose coupon and principal payments originate from a specific pool of residential mortgages, home-equity loans, and subprime mortgages.

second lien: Leveraged loan with a subordinated claim on assets in the event of a default. This claim comes before unsecured debt holders.

structured finance CDOs (SF CDOs): See *asset-backed CDO.*

subprime mortgage: Mortgage lending to borrowers with credit ratings that do not qualify for market interest rates resulting from increased credit risk.

NOTES

Chapter 3

1. Rousseau, S. (2006), "Enhancing the Accountability of Credit Rating Agencies: The Case for a Disclosure-Based Approach," *McGill Law Journal*, p. 620.
2. Any nonpublic information used to produce a credit rating is kept confidential by the CRAs.
3. Frost, C. A. (2006), "Credit Rating Agencies in Capital Markets: A Review of Research Evidence on Selected Criticisms of the Agencies," working paper series, State University of New York at Buffalo, p. 474.
4. Standard & Poor's (2006), "Corporate Ratings Criteria," p. 13. Annual report.
5. U.S. Securities and Exchange Commission (2003), "Report on the Role and Function of Credit Rating Agencies in the Operation of the Securities Markets," p. 28. SEC report.
6. Standard & Poor's (2006), "Corporate Ratings Criteria," p. 13. Annual report.
7. Estrella, A. (2000), "Credit Ratings and Complementary Sources of Credit Quality Information," Basel Committee on Banking Supervision working papers, p. 1.

8. Basel Committee on Banking Supervision (2006), "International Convergence of Capital Measurement and Capital Standards," p. 19. Report.
9. Frost, C. A. (2006), "Credit Rating Agencies in Capital Markets: A Review of Research Evidence on Selected Criticisms of the Agencies," working paper series, State University of New York at Buffalo, p. 471.
10. "SEC Votes to Adopt Final Rules to Implement the Credit Rating Agency Reform Act of 2006," *Regulatory Register*, vol. 22, issue 6 (2007), p. 1.
11. Standard & Poor's (2006), "Corporate Ratings Criteria," p. 8. Annual report?
12. Moody's Investors Service, Inc. (2008), "Moody's Rating Symbols & Definitions," p. 10. Report.
13. Standard & Poor's (2006), "Corporate Ratings Criteria," p. 15. Annual report.
14. Cantor, R., and C. Mann (2006), "Analyzing the Tradeoff between Ratings Accuracy and Stability," Moody's Investors Service, Inc., Report.
15. Moody's Investors Service, Inc. (2004), "Tracing the Origins of 'Investment Grade,'" p. 5. Report.
16. Standard & Poor's (2008), "Corporate Ratings Criteria," p. 91. Annual report.
17. Standard & Poor's (2007), "Criteria Guidelines for Recovery Ratings on Global Industrials Issuers' Speculative-Grade Debt," p. 1. Annual report.
18. Moody's calculates recovery rates based on postdefault trading pricing. Alternatively, the rates can be calculated based on the ultimate recovery value of debt post–emergence/liquidation following bankruptcy.
19. Altman, E., J. Caouette, and P. Narayanan (1998), *Managing Credit Risk: The Next Great Financial Challenge*, Frontiers in Finance Series, John Wiley & Sons, p. 206.

20. Moody's Investors Service, Inc. (2007), "Moody's Ultimate Recovery Database," p. 10. Report.
21. See S&P fee information at www.standardandpoors.com/usratingsfees.
22. The threshold for S&P is $100 million.
23. Moody's Investors Service, Inc. (1999), "Opening the Black Box: The Rating Committee Process at Moody's," p. 3. Report.
24. Standard & Poor's (2006), "A Closer Look at Industrials Ratings Methodology," p. 3. Report.
25. Standard & Poor's (2006), "Corporate Ratings Criteria," p. 26. Report.
26. Moody's Investors Services, Inc. (2004), "The Analysis of Off Balance Sheet Exposure." Report.
27. S&P does not publish a ratings matrix for each issuer with its research.
28. Standard & Poor's (2008), "Standard & Poor's Revises Its Approach to Rating Speculative-Grade Credits," p. 4. Report.
29. Moody's Investors Service, Inc. (2007), "Rating Triggers in the Asset Management Industry, 2006 Update," p. 1. Report.
30. Moody's Investors Service, Inc. (2002), "Moody's Analysis of U.S. Corporate Rating Triggers Heightens Need for Increased Disclosure," p. 6. Report.
31. Moody's Investors Service, Inc. (2001), "The Unintended Consequences of Rating Triggers," p. 8. Report.

Chapter 9

1. Chan-Lau, J. (2006), "Fundamentals-Based Estimation of Default Probabilities: A Survey," IMF working paper, p. 3.
2. Chacko, G., V. Dessain, H. Motoashi, and A. Sjöman (2006), *Credit Derivatives: A Primer on Credit Risk, Modeling, and Instruments.* Wharton School Publishing, p. 65.
3. Chan-Lau, J. (2006), "Fundamentals-Based Estimation of Default Probabilities: A Survey," IMF working paper, p. 11.

4. Bohn, J., and P. Crosbie (2003), "Modeling Default Risk," Moody's KMV Company, p. 10. Report.
5. Ibid.
6. Altman, E., J. Caouette, and P. Narayanan (1998), *Managing Credit Risk: The Next Great Financial Challenge,* Frontiers in Finance Series, John Wiley & Sons, p. 144.
7. Given the asymmetric returns of lending, creditors should be more concerned about downside risk.
8. Dwyer, D., and I. Korbalev (2007), "Power and Level Validation of Moody's KMV EDF Credit Measures in North America, Europe, and Asia," Moody's KMV Company, p. 6. Report.
9. These opposing forces will not affect the EDF simultaneously.
10. Smith, A. (2007), "SLM News: LBO Blues for Creditors as More Spread Widening Remains Possible," Moody's Investors Services. Report.
11. Bharath, S., and T. Shumway (2004), "Forecasting Default with the KMV-Merton Model." Paper presented at AFA meeting in Boston (2006).
12. Moody's Investor Services (2006), "Ratings Gaps across Models and Their Significance in Ratings Change Analysis," pp. 16–17. Report.
13. The "what if" tool in CreditMonitor will allow an analyst to assess the impact of the acquisition on the EDF at any time. However, EDFs released by KMV will not reflect the change until the release of relevant financial statements.
14. Gupton, G., A. Kocagil, and B. Liu (2007), "Fitch Equity Implied Rating and Probability of Default Model," Fitch Ratings, pp. 1 and 2. Report.
15. Ibid.
16. Berndt, A., R. Douglas, D. Duffie, M. Ferguson, and D. Schranzk (2005), "Measuring Default Risk Premia from Default Swap Rates and EDF," working paper, Graduate School of Business, Stanford University, p. 1.

17. Agrawal, D., N. Arota, and J. Bohn (2004), "Parsimony in Practice: An EDF-Based Model of Credit Spreads." Moody's KMV Company, p. 1. Report.
18. A. Tindlund (2006), "Trading Strategies in the CDS Market." Working-paper, Norwegian University of Science and Technology.
19. "EDF Case Study: Enron" (n.d.), Moody's KMV Company. Brief report.
20. Kealhofer, S., S. Kwok, and W. Weng (1998), "Uses and Abuses of Bond Default Data," KMV Corporation, p. 4. Report.
21. We are not aware of any empirical studies that test the relationship between asset values and stock market performance.
22. Altman, E., and H. Rijken (2004), "How Rating Agencies Achieve Rating Stability," *Journal of Banking & Finance.*, vol. 28, no. 11, pp. 2679–2714.
23. Cantor, R., and C. Mann (2006), "Analyzing the Tradeoff between Ratings Accuracy and Stability," Moody's Investors Service, Inc., p. 2. Report.
24. Löffler, G. (2004), "Ratings versus Market-Based Measures of Default Risk in Portfolio Governance," *Journal of Banking and Finance.*, vol. 28, no. 11, pp. 2715–2746.

Chapter 10

1. Barnhill, T., W. Maxwell, and M. Shenkman (1997), *High Yield Bonds: Market Structure, Valuation, and Portfolio Strategies,* McGraw-Hill, p. 85.
2. Estrella, A. (2000) "Credit Ratings and Complementary Sources of Credit Quality Information." Basel Committee on Banking Supervision working papers, pp. 126–142.
3. Ibid.
4. Dwyer, D., and I. Korbalev (2007), "Power and Level Validation of Moody's KMV EDF Credit Measures in North America, Europe, and Asia," Moody's KMV Company. Report.

5. Dacorogna, M., T. Jung, and G. Oderda (2003), "Credit Risk Models—Do They Deliver Their Promises? A Quantitative Assessment," *Economic Notes.* Paper submitted for publication.
6. Gupton, G., A. Kocagil, and B. Liu (2007), "Fitch Equity Implied Rating and Probability of Default Model," Fitch Ratings. Report.
7. Altman, E. (2002), "Corporate Distress Prediction Models in a Turbulent Economic and Basel II Environment." working paper, Stern School of Business, NYU, p. 10.
8. Altman, E., J. Caouette, and P. Narayanan (1998), *Managing Credit Risk: The Next Great Financial Challenge,* Frontiers in Finance Series, John Wiley & Sons, p. 115.
9. Altman, E. (2002), "Corporate Distress Prediction Models in a Turbulent Economic and Basel II Environment." Working paper, Stern School of Business, New York University.
10. Campbell and Taksler (2003) measured idiosyncratic risk as the standard deviation of excess returns of a stock over market returns.
11. Volatility has a positive impact on the price of a call option.

Chapter 13

1. One of the key shortcomings of the simplified two-factor model can be seen in the different calculations for consumer allocation (Figure 13.2 versus Figure 13.5), where the allocation effect is 0.15% for the three-factor model and –3.00% for the two-factor model. Underweighting a marginally underperforming sector should in theory not produce such a large negative allocation effect. The two-factor model is effectively penalizing the manager for underallocating to a large contributor to the index. Many practitioners prefer the three-factor model. We use the two-factor model in this chapter for the purpose of converting the metathetical concepts into easy-to-generate output data.
2. Lord, T. J. (April 27, 2005), "Leveraging Performance Attribution for Fixed Income Analysis," Bear Stearns Asset Management. Report.

3. Levecq, C., "An Exposure-Based Attribution Model for Balanced Portfolios," *Journal of Performance Measurement.* Paper.
4. As this book was on press, the Credit Suisse Leverage Loan Index was working to potentially provide daily data through a third-party vendor.

Chapter 15

1. Refer to Chapter 8
2. Refer to Chapter 4.

Chapter 16

1. See Standard & Poor's report "A Guide to the Loan Market" (September 2004) for a historical exposition. In other chapters in this book, we draw upon the Standard & Poor's publication to discuss certain features of the loan markets and their terminology.
2. Throughout this book, we refer to the standard CDS on unsecured instruments, such as corporate bonds, as corporate CDSs.
3. See our European colleagues' report, "Leveraged Loan CDS: The Final Piece of the Jigsaw," November 4, 2005, for details on European loans and CDSs.
4. First-lien loans represent the highest priority.
5. The Markit Group is currently designated as the secured list publisher for the loan CDS contracts.
6. In fact, corporate CDSs are terminated prior to maturity without a credit event having occurred only under a rare M&A situation. See Chapter 7 for further details.
7. See "Leveraged Loan CDS: The Final Piece of the Jigsaw," Morgan-Stanley report, November 4, 2005.
8. See "Taking a CLOser Look," November 21, 2005.
9. For these calculations, we assume that the hedge counterparty is at least A-rated. We also note that banks typically hold higher than their minimum required capital.

Chapter 17

1. Epstein, David (2005), *Bankruptcy and Related Law in a Nutshell,* 7th ed., West, p. 415.
2. Over 60 percent of the firms obtain DIP financing within 30 days of filing for Chapter 11.
3. Jacob, M. E. and S. Youdelman of Weil, Gotshal, and Manges LLP (2006), *Reorganizing Failing Businesses: A Comprehensive Review and Analysis of Financial Restructuring and Business Reorganization,* vol. 1, American Bar Association Section of Business Law, pp. 9–24.
4. Epstein, D. (2005), *Bankruptcy and Related Law in a Nutshell,* 7th ed., West, p. 418.
5. Ibid.
6. Chatterjee, S., U. S. Dhillon, and G. G. Ramirez (2004), "Debtor-in-Possession Financing," *Journal of Banking and Finance,* vol. 28, no. 12, pp. 3097–3112.
7. Less than 7% of DIP was found to be stand-alone, and less than 8% was found to be in another form of credit.
8. Dahiya, S., J. Kose, M. Puri, and G. G. Ramirez (2000), "The Dynamics of Debtor-in-Possession Financing: Bankruptcy Resolution and the Role of Prior Lenders," paper presented at AFA meeting in New Orleans (2001), p. 3.
9. Rosenthal, Trent. L. (2005), "Debtor-in-Possession Financing: Opportunities, Risks and Rewards" *The Secured Lender,* May–June 2005, vol. 61, no. 3, p. 10.
10. Ibid., p. 11.

BIBLIOGRAPHY

Most working papers and reports listed here are viewable (in whole, in abstract, or both) or obtainable online in .pdf or other formats.

Chapter 3

Altman, E., J. Caouette, and P. Narayanan (1998), *Managing Credit Risk: The Next Great Financial Challenge*, Frontiers in Finance Series, John Wiley & Sons.

Basel Committee on Banking Supervision (2006), "International Convergence of Capital Measurement and Capital Standards," revised edition. Report.

Cantor, R., and C. Mann (2006), "Analyzing the Tradeoff between Ratings Accuracy and Stability," Moody's Investors Service, Inc. Report.

Estrella, A. (2000), "Credit Ratings and Complementary Sources of Credit Quality Information," Basel Committee on Banking Supervision working papers.

Frost, C. A. (2006), "Credit Rating Agencies in Capital Markets: A Review of Research Evidence on Selected Criticisms of the Agencies," working paper series, State University of New York at Buffalo.

Moody's Investors Services, Inc. (2004), "The Analysis of Off-Balance Sheet Exposure." Report.

Moody's Investors Service, Inc. (2008), "Corporate Default and Recovery Rates, 1920–2007." Report.

Moody's Investors Service, Inc. (2002), "Moody's Analysis of U.S. Corporate Rating Triggers Heightens Need for Increased Disclosure." Report.

Moody's Investors Service, Inc. (2008), "Moody's Rating Symbols & Definitions." Report.

Moody's Investors Service, Inc. (2007), "Moody's Ultimate Recovery Database." Report.

Moody's Investors Service, Inc. (1999), "Opening the Black Box: The Rating Committee Process at Moody's."Report.

Moody's Investors Service, Inc. (2007), "Rating Triggers in the Asset Management Industry 2006 Update." Report.

Moody's Investors Service, Inc. (2004), "Tracing the Origins of 'Investment Grade." Report

Moody's Investors Service, Inc. (2001), "The Unintended Consequences of Rating Triggers." Report.

Rousseau, S. (2006), "Enhancing the Accountability of Credit Rating Agencies: The Case for a Disclosure-Based Approach," *McGill Law Journal*, December 22, 2006.

Standard & Poor's (2006), "A Closer Look at Industrials Ratings Methodology." Report.

Standard & Poor's (2006), "Corporate Ratings Criteria." Report.

Standard & Poor's (2008), "Corporate Ratings Criteria." Report.

Standard & Poor's (2007), "Criteria Guidelines for Recovery Ratings on Global Industrials Issuers' Speculative-Grade Debt." Report.

Standard & Poor's (2002), "Identifying Ratings Triggers and Other Contingent Calls on Liquidity—Part 2." Report.

Standard & Poor's (2007), "Recovery Analytics Update: Enhanced Recovery Scale and Issue Ratings Framework." Report.

Standard & Poor's (2008) "Standard & Poor's Revises Its Approach to Rating Speculative-Grade Credits." Report.

U.S. Securities and Exchange Commission (2003), "Report on the Role and Function of Credit Rating Agencies in the Operation of the Securities Markets." Report.

Chapter 9

Agrawal, D., N. Arota, and J. Bohn (2004), "Parsimony in Practice: An EDF-Based Model of Credit Spreads," Moody's KMV Company. Report.

Altman, E., J. Caouette, and P. Narayanan (1998), *Managing Credit Risk: The Next Great Financial Challenge,* Frontiers in Finance Series, John Wiley & Sons.

Altman, E., and H. Rijken (2004), "How Rating Agencies Achieve Rating Stability," *Journal of Banking & Finance*, vol. 28, no. 11, pp. 2715–2746.

Berndt, A., R. Douglas, D. Duffie, M. Ferguson, and D. Schranzk (2005), "Measuring Default Risk Premia from Default Swap Rates and EDF," working paper, Graduate School of Business, Stanford University.

Bharath, S., and T. Shumway (2004), "Forecasting Default with the KMV-Merton Model," paper presented at AFA meeting in Boston (2006).

Bohn, J., and P. Crosbie (2003), "Modeling Default Risk," Moody's KMV Company. Report.

Cantor, R., and C. Mann (2006), "Analyzing the Tradeoff between Ratings Accuracy and Stability," Moody's Investors Service, Inc. Report.

Chacko, G., V. Dessain, H. Motoashi, and A. Sjöman (2006), *Credit Derivatives: A Primer on Credit Risk, Modeling, and Instruments*, Wharton School Publishing.

Chan-Lau, J. (2006), "Fundamentals-Based Estimation of Default Probabilities: A Survey," IMF working paper.

Dwyer, D., and K. Irina (2007), "Power and Level Validation of Moody's KMV EDF Credit Measures in North America, Europe, and Asia," Moody's KMV Company. Report.

Gupton, G., A. Kocagil, and B. Liu (2007), "Fitch Equity Implied Rating and Probability of Default Model," Fitch Ratings. Report.

Kealhofer, S., S. Kwok, and W. Weng (1998), "Uses and Abuses of Bond Default Data," Moody's KMV Corporation. Paper.

Löffler, G. (2004), "Ratings versus Market-Based Measures of Default Risk in Portfolio Governance," *Journal of Banking and Finance*, vol. 28, no. 11, pp. 2715–2746.

Moody's Investor Services, Inc. (2006), "Ratings Gaps across Models and Their Significance in Ratings Change Analysis." Report.

Smith, A. (2007), "SLM News: LBO Blues for Creditors as More Spread Widening Remains Possible," Moody's Investors Services. Report.

Chapter 10

Altman, E. (2002), "Corporate Distress Prediction Models in a Turbulent Economic and Basel II Environment," working paper, Stern School of Business, NYU.

Altman, E., J. Caouette, and P. Narayanan (1998), *Managing Credit Risk: The Next Great Financial Challenge*, Frontiers in Finance Series, John Wiley & Sons.

Barnhill, T., W. Maxwell, and M. Shenkman (1997), *High Yield Bonds: Market Structure, Valuation, and Portfolio Strategies*, McGraw-Hill.

Bharath, S., and T. Shumway (2008), "Forecasting Default with the Merton Distance to Default Model," *Review of Financial Studies*, vol. 21, no. 3, pp. 1339–1369.

Campbell, J., and G. Taksler (2003), "Equity Volatility and Corporate Bond Yields," *Journal of Finance*, vol. 58, pp. 2321–2349.

Dacorogna, M., T. Jung, and G. Oderda (2003), "Credit Risk Models—Do They Deliver Their Promises? A Quantitative Assessment," *Economic Notes*. Paper submitted for publication.

Dwyer, D., and I. Korbalev (2007), "Power and Level Validation of Moody's KMV EDF Credit Measures in North America, Europe, and Asia," Moody's KMV Company. Report.

Estrella, A. (2000), "Credit Ratings and Complementary Sources of Credit Quality Information," Basel Committee on Banking Supervision working papers.

Gupton, G., A. Kocagil, and B. Liu (2007), "Fitch Equity Implied Rating and Probability of Default Model," Fitch Ratings. Paper.

Moody's Investors Service, Inc. (2008), "Corporate Default and Recovery Rates, 1920–2007." Report.

Ohlson, J. (1980), "Financial Ratios and the Probabilistic Prediction of Bankruptcy," *Journal of Accounting Research*, vol. 18, no. 1, pp. 109–131.

Chapter 17

Chatterjee, S., U. S. Dhillon, and G. G. Ramirez (2004), "Debtor-in-Possession Financing," *Journal of Banking and Finance*, vol. 28, no. 12, pp. 3097–3112.

Dahiya, S., K. John, M. Puri, and G. G. Ramirez (2000), "The Dynamics of Debtor-in-Possession Financing: Bankruptcy Resolution and the Role of Prior Lenders." Paper presented at AFA meeting in New Orleans (2001).

Epstein, D. (2005), *Bankruptcy and Related Law in a Nutshell*, 7th ed., West.

Jacob, M. E., and S. Youdelman, Weil, Gotshal, and Manges LLP (2006), *Reorganizing Failing Businesses: A Comprehensive Review and Analysis of Financial Restructuring and Business Reorganization*, American Bar Association Section of Business Law (publisher), 2 vols., spiral bound, 1,200 pages.

Rosenthal, T. L (2005), "Debtor-in-Possession Financing: Opportunities, Risks and Rewards," *The Secured Lender*, vol. 61, issue 3, May–June 2005.

INDEX

CPSIA information can be obtained
at www.ICGtesting.com
Printed in the USA
LVHW020354100423
743725LV00002B/39